The Shaping of a Behaviorist

THE
Shaping
OF A
Behaviorist

Part Two of an Autobiography

B. F. SKINNER

Alfred A. Knopf   New York

1 9 7 9

This Is a Borzoi Book
Published by Alfred A. Knopf, Inc.

Library of Congress Cataloging in Publication Data
Skinner, Burrhus Frederic [date]
The shaping of a behaviorist.

Continues Particulars of my life.
Includes bibliographical references.
1. Skinner, Burrhus Frederic, 1904–
2. Psychologists—United States—Biography.
I. Skinner, Burrhus Frederic, 1904–
Particulars of life.   II. Title.
BF109.S55A332   1979   150'.19'4340924   [B] 78–20620
ISBN 0–394–50581–6

Permissions acknowledgments appear on page 375.

Manufactured in the United States of America

FIRST EDITION

To Fred S. Keller

The Shaping of a Behaviorist

Harvard University takes little or no interest in the private lives of its graduate students. The policy was affirmed on an issue of moral turpitude shortly before I arrived for graduate study in the fall of 1928. No matter how serious the offense or how lurid the newspaper stories, the University declared itself not responsible; it refused to play a parental role.

I soon found that it was equally unconcerned in lesser matters. There were two small graduate dormitories for men, their halls and rooms, like those I had known at Hamilton College, lined with durable brick, but the only other quarters for graduate students were to be found in a mimeographed list of rooming houses helpfully supplied by the University.

I tried first a pleasant frame house near the Radcliffe quadrangle. This was Law School territory and most of the rooms were taken. I was shown a converted storage closet. It was offered only as a single, while all the other rooms in the house were doubles. The number of people who would be using the bathroom was discouraging.

In a small side street a block from Harvard Square I explored a drab old two-family house with a drab old landlady, who shuffled about in housedress and slippers, wisps of gray hair escaping from scattered pins. She showed me several rooms, moving from one side of the house to the other through a door cut for that purpose. The bathroom problem was eased by a washbowl in each room, but the floors were bare and unpainted, and the only furnishings were an old bed or cot, a table, and a couple of small chairs. (Yes, I could buy an easy chair if I wished.)

On the other side of the Yard, at 366 Harvard Street, I had luck. Mrs. Thomas, the landlady, reminded me a little of my Aunt Alt, and an older man who did some of the heavy work around the house

3

could have been my Uncle Norm. The house looked and smelled clean, and there were carpets in the halls and on the stairs. I could rent a small, well-lighted room on the third floor for $5.50 a week, and there would be no objection to an electric grill to make toast for breakfast or toasted cheese sandwiches for Sunday-night snacks. The bathroom was on the second floor, but, so far as I could tell, I should be sharing it with only three people.

I sent my mother the dimensions of the small bed, and she made a monk's-cloth cover and cushions which gave it the appearance of a sofa. I got a lamp at the Harvard Coop and put up the self-portrait of Cézanne I had bought in the Village and two Michelangelos I had brought back from Rome. On a mantel which no longer had a fire-place beneath it I began to build a library, starting with Bertrand Russell's *Philosophy*, John B. Watson's *Behaviorism*, and I. P. Pav-lov's *Conditioned Reflexes*—the books which had, I thought, prepared me for a career in psychology.

I had not played my saxophone for several years, and because it did not seem like a suitable instrument for a psychologist, I decided to sell it. I had hoped to buy a secondhand piano but my room was too small, and I settled for a portable Victrola. It had a metal case and ran for a reasonable length of time on one winding. The diaphragm was the new "orthophonic" model, but there was no volume control, and when I tried it out in a first-floor room, where I lived while my third-floor room was being painted, I was afraid I would annoy other roomers and put the machine on my bed and stuffed clothes in the opening to muffle the sound. I would be more relaxed on the third floor because my room was on a corner and my only neighbor (pretty but, I soon discovered, with no intellectual interests and closely watched over by a married sister living in the house) had no objec-tion to music at a reasonable hour, and my schedule would send me to bed before an unreasonable one.

My conversion to vegetarianism in the Village had yielded to Italian and French cuisine on my Grand Tour, and I found a small tearoom two blocks away where I could take my meals.

My DAILY SCHEDULE WAS TAXING but not quite as Spartan as I re-membered it when, almost forty years later, I wrote:

4

... at Harvard I entered upon the first strict regimen of my life. I had done what was expected of me in high school and college but had seldom worked hard. Aware that I was far behind in a new field, I now set up a rigorous schedule and maintained it for almost two years. I would rise at six, study until breakfast, go to classes, laboratories, and libraries with no more than fifteen minutes unscheduled during the day, study until exactly nine o'clock at night and go to bed. I saw no movies or plays, seldom went to concerts, had scarcely any dates, and read nothing but psychology and physiology.

I was recalling a pose rather than the life I had actually led. On the boat back from England at the end of the summer, I had met two proper Bostonians, a Dr. and Mrs. Loring. I had told them that I was coming to Harvard and they were kind enough to invite me to dinner. Dr. Loring drove me to their charming old house in Lincoln, where I had my first glimpse of upper-class New England life. After dinner we sat by the fire and I told them about my daily routine. I could see that I was astonishing them as I bore down on my intense dedication to scholarship. Dr. Loring showed some alarm; did I not need relaxation? I assured him I did not.

I wrote in a very different vein to Percy Saunders, the Professor of Chemistry at Hamilton College who was known to his students as Stink. "I'm taking it easy my first semester," I said. "After January I expect to settle down and solve the riddle of the universe. Harvard is fine. A strange and fearful freedom after Ham. Col. or Scranton."

I was not without friends or time to spend with them. Raphael Miller, a few months younger than I, had been a year behind me in Susquehanna High School, but he had gone on to Lafayette College and, undelayed by a two-year interlude as I had been, was now ahead of me in his second year at the Harvard Medical School. On an occasional evening he and I would go into Boston to eat steamed clams at Pieroni's, but I usually saw him on Sunday mornings when I walked over to his room in Vanderbilt Hall, a distance of about four miles. (In the entrance to Vanderbilt I found Pasteur's dictum which Bugsy Morrill had posted in his laboratory at Hamilton: "In the field of observation chance favors only the prepared mind." In Vanderbilt, however, it was in French—a difference between Hamilton and Harvard that I would soon learn to take for granted.)

Even in grade school I had called Raphael "Doc." Not only was his father a doctor; from a very early age he had planned to be one too. At Lafayette a Professor Kunkel had given him a love of biological research, and he had made up his mind to be a medical scientist rather than a practicing physician, though he had not yet chosen his field of specialization. He was interested in tissue culture, but was afraid it might be a trap.

I still looked upon him as a model to be emulated. He was no longer any more religious than I, but he was still the virtuous man. One day when I said that I was angry with myself for being so easily disturbed by the sight of a girl's legs, he surprised me by laughing and confessing that he was not indifferent to that either. But he was engaged to his childhood sweetheart and saw no other women.

A much younger girl whom I had known in Scranton was a freshman at Wellesley, and one Sunday I took her to the Boston Symphony to hear the Beethoven Ninth. I tried to make a second date, but she was off to Dartmouth for the Winter Carnival—a different order of social life and one for which I indeed had no time.

I BEGAN EACH WEEKDAY REGRESSIVELY in a class with undergraduates. I had been admitted with a condition in German, which I could remove most easily by passing the introductory course "with a grade of C or higher." The course was given by Professor A. H. (we pronounced it Ah Ha in the German manner) Herrick, whose deafness was not fully corrected by headphones and a box of amplifying equipment on his desk, a device that occasionally gave out a piercing scream until our gestures caught his attention. The class met at eight in the morning, and at nine each day I renewed myself as a psychologist.

Psychology was one of the last of the sciences to stop calling itself "natural philosophy," and in 1928 I was enrolled in the "Department of Philosophy and Psychology." It was housed in Emerson Hall, a handsome block-shaped ivy-covered brick building in the Harvard Yard. When it was built, President Eliot had chosen (some said slyly) the inscription "What is man that thou are mindful of him?" If you entered the side door, you confronted a large bronze statue of Ralph Waldo Emerson, seated with one foot thrust forward

—possibly, like Moses in the Vatican, to be kissed by devoted followers, though it showed no signs of wear. The front entrance led to a stairway on the wall of which, recalling wistfully the golden age of the department, there hung a large group portrait of Josiah Royce, George Santayana, and William James. (It was rumored that Hugo Münsterberg, the German psychologist whom James had brought to Harvard, was either painted out of that picture or had never been painted in because of his pro-German activities before the Great War.) Psychology had the third floor, together with some fourth-floor attic space useful for small laboratories.

The Director of the Psychological Laboratory, Edwin Garrigues Boring, was on sabbatical leave during my first term. Forty-two and quite unpretentious, he had been brought to Harvard six years before to fill a gaping void in its ranks. Münsterberg had died, and Robert Yerkes had not returned after his work with the Army Alpha Intelligence Tests in the war. The University had brought William McDougall from England to strengthen the department, but a year before I arrived he had moved to the newly founded and richly endowed Duke University.

Boring's scientific aspirations were modest. When he was Director of the Laboratories of Experimental Psychology at Clark University, he called his graduate students together to discuss their futures. One thing an industrious but not particularly creative young person might do, he said, was to write a history of experimental psychology. He soon surprised everyone by undertaking the task himself, finishing it during that fall-term sabbatical. I remember him first in the spring of 1929 as I saw him in the department shop constructing a wooden box to hold the manuscript on its way to his publishers, the Century Company. Though it was the history of only a special kind of experimental psychology, it was a great success.

Boring had been a student of electrical engineering at Cornell when he made the crucial decision to take a course by E. B. Titchener, a British psychologist who was carrying on a tradition that began with the famous Wilhelm Wundt in Leipzig, Germany. Psychology was to be a science of mental life, in which mental elements obeyed mental laws. "Titchener's lectures were magic," Boring later wrote, "so potent that my roommates on each lecture day demanded to be told what had been said." And so he told them, and when I took his courses a quarter of a century later he was still telling us what Titchener had said.

He wanted to build a department like Titchener's, but standing in his way was another senior member of the department who held a different view of the science of psychology. Leonard Troland had come to Harvard in 1916, long before Boring. His specialty was vision, and he had played a part in the invention of Technicolor. Though he attracted graduate students, he was not the kind of man to found a rival school, but he would be a disturbing force in a department established on Titchener's model. A student of Troland's, Eugene McCarthy, was a strong partisan in the intramural conflict, which he tended to exaggerate, and when a year or two later Troland fell from a mountain in California and was killed, Mac "knew" it was suicide; Troland had killed himself because he had not been given a full professorship.

I attended the first meeting of a seminar with Troland. I did not understand much of what he was saying, and during a lull in the discussion I asked him why a pinhole in a piece of cardboard could be used like a lens to look at something close to the eye. He stared at me in utter contempt and then said something I did not immediately understand. The gist of it was that this was an *advanced* course and everyone in it could be assumed to know about artificial pupils! I had revealed myself as a rank amateur and had better get out. I signed up instead for the introductory course he was giving that year, but at the first meeting I found him an incredibly dull lecturer and dropped the course.

One of the younger men in the department was Carroll Pratt, a tall, handsome man with a wonderfully resonant voice. He was extraordinarily diffident. He would invite me to his house for supper or a string quartet as if it were something I might just possibly enjoy if I had absolutely nothing else to do. He was diffident also about psychology, possibly in reaction to Boring's crusading enthusiasm, to which he had been exposed at Clark before he and Boring came to Harvard.

He taught a course called "Experimental Psychology: Quantitative Laboratory" in which the central issue seemed to be how well a person could tell the difference between two stimuli. This was not an earthshaking issue, nor were we encouraged to believe that it was.

The text was by Titchener (who else?), and we used the so-called psychophysical methods—"constant stimuli," "limits," "average error," and so on. The stimuli we judged were pretty crude. Sounds to be compared for loudness were produced by the "fall phonometer," in which a ball at the end of an arm was allowed to swing against a block of wood, the loudness being determined by the length of arc through which the arm fell. Some of the instruments were made of brass ("brass instrument psychology," William James had contemptuously called the whole enterprise), and I liked best a "Stern variator"—a deep-throated whistle blown by the compressed air Boring had had piped into all the rooms. It was the Rolls-Royce of what I had known as a Frisco Whistle when I played in a jazz band. (Boring had tried to improve on the Stern variator by having the department machinist turn a set of steel cylinders, the precise lengths of which were to guarantee precise pitches when the cylinders were struck with hammers like the bars of a xylophone.) When my partner and I would point to some poorly controlled condition or defect in our apparatus, Pratt would say, "That ought not to bother the observer," and we began to use the expression among ourselves as a standing joke.

John Gilbert Beebe-Center was another young member of the Harvard staff. He was one of those who did not need to make their living as teachers but who enjoyed the association with Harvard and were kept on at low ranks until retirement. I envied him because he had been raised in Europe and spoke French and German fluently.

Boring was responsible for most of the graduate research then under way. One student was finishing a thesis on how people judged the weights of little pillboxes filled with lead shot embedded in wax. Another had chosen the question of how well people could estimate the properties of stimuli without comparing them with other stimuli. Another would shortly be seeing how well people could judge the temperature of surfaces on which they placed their fingertips. Boring kept a file of problems like that, available to students intent on making a contribution to knowledge "in partial fulfillment of the requirements for the degree of doctor of philosophy." One of my contemporaries, Dwight Chapman, was an exception. He had just returned from a year in Berlin, where he had been contaminated by Gestalt psychology and had gone so far astray as to be studying the

9

Phi Phenomenon—the "apparent movement" responsible for moving pictures.

I was not entirely untouched by these introspective predilections. The whole field of psychology was new to me and much of it fascinating. I became interested in a problem about which the Gestalt psychologist Wolfgang Köhler had written. If you sound two tones one after the other and ask someone to say whether they have the same pitch, it makes a difference how soon the second tone follows the first. The longer the delay, the higher the second tone sounds, as if the level of the first had slowly dropped. I cooked up a theory to explain this "fall of *niveau*," but I have forgotten what it was. I am not even sure I have the facts right now. Perhaps the second tone sounds lower, or perhaps it is the intensity and not the pitch that changes.

ALL THIS WOULD HAVE BEEN anathema to John B. Watson, and to me, too, in my soberer moments. I was a *behaviorist*, and for me behaviorism was psychology. I had been converted to the behavioristic position by Bertrand Russell. In that wonderful magazine the *Dial*, to which I subscribed in my "literary" days, Russell had reviewed *The Meaning of Meaning* by C. K. Ogden and I. A. Richards. He had referred to Watson and his theories, and at the end he had said, "It will be seen that the above remarks are strongly influenced by Dr. Watson, whose latest book, *Behaviorism*, I consider massively impressive." After reading the review, I bought *Behaviorism* and, a year or so later, Russell's *Philosophy*.

Russell had evidently been interested in behaviorism for some time, because his biographer, Ronald W. Clark, says that he read "behaviorist books" when he was in Brixton Prison as a pacifist in 1917. But Clark says that *Philosophy* was "tapped out at speed for the American market," and very little attention is paid to it by historians of psychology or specialists in Russell's views. Nevertheless, it begins with a careful statement of several epistemological issues raised by behaviorism considerably more sophisticated than anything of Watson's. Early chapters are called "Man in His Environment," "The Process of Learning in Animals and Infants," "Language," "Perception Objectively Regarded," "Memory Objectively Regarded," "Inference as a Habit," and "Knowledge Behavioristically Considered." The middle third of the book is a rehash of Russell's views on the nature of the physical world, and I stopped reading when I reached it. I therefore missed the last third, in which Russell undertakes to disprove the behavioristic part by talking about "man from within."

My first year was not without its bright behavioristic spots. Walter S. Hunter of Clark University drove in from Worcester once a week to give a seminar in animal behavior. He had grown up in Illinois and Texas and had gone to the University of Chicago for graduate work, where he came into contact with the functional school of psychology, as Watson had done. You needed the permission of the instructor to take the seminar, and at the first meeting I handed Hunter a blank permission card. "Well," he said with a dry little laugh, "you'll have to put something on it," and he handed it back to me. I dutifully filled in my name and the title of the course, but I was shaken. I had made a mistake and Hunter had been short with me.

There were about a dozen students in the seminar. Köhler's *Mentality of Apes* was attracting attention, but Hunter sent us to earlier research, mostly by Americans, in the same field. Robert Yerkes had studied "ideational responses" in the great apes, and Hunter himself had written about "symbolic processes." I was assigned a paper about baboons, but the only thing I remember about my report is that I tossed off a reference to their "bright red ischial tuberosities" as if the words were part of my everyday vocabulary.

The seminar dealt with the kind of behavior that seemed to be more than responses to stimuli. Hunter's thesis had been on the "delayed reaction." Let a hungry dog watch you put a bit of food under one of three covers, but make it wait before going after it. How long can it remember which cover the food is under? Undisturbed, it will solve the problem by holding a point, but if it is forced to move about, it will fail. In other words, dogs do not have good "symbolic processes." Apes and children do better.

Hunter was also interested in Watson's studies of how rats learned to run through mazes, and he had designed several mazes in which nothing but the rat's own behavior could serve as a cue. (One day he told us how he had invented one of them. "I sat up one night with a piece of wire and a pair of pliers," he began, and then added, with a wry laugh, as if he were describing another piece of primate behavior, "and that's how I think!") He was a skeptical teacher, clever in tripping you up if you used mentalistic terms or behavioristic terms carelessly. Imitation, for example. Is it imitation when one animal does what another is doing? Well, then, what about a dog chasing a rabbit? Is the dog imitating the rabbit?

Hunter was editor of *Psychological Abstracts* and was looking for people to abstract papers. Abstracting was, he said, a good way of getting one's name before the psychological public. He needed abstracts of articles in foreign languages, and on the strength of my brief sojourn in Italy I rashly volunteered to do some in Italian. As it turned out, psychological Italian was not very difficult, and I did, in fact, abstract several articles. I also undertook to keep an eye on certain German scientific journals in biology and physiology and to send abstracts or at least titles of anything relevant to psychology.

ANOTHER BIT OF behavioristic support came from a graduate student. He was a fellow renegade from literature who had once written book reviews for the *Dial*. His name on the running head, "Charles K. Trueblood," had a noble, if not a regal, look, and now I found the man himself in Emerson Hall studying the behavior of rats in mazes. He had built a maze that could be turned in a horizontal plane. Rats which made perfect runs when it was pointing in one direction made mistakes when it was pointing in another. Were they sensitive to the earth's magnetic field?

The maze was in a room near the west end of the third floor and the rats lived on the fourth floor, reached by a stairway at the east end. I first saw Trueblood, in white coat and sneakers, carrying cages of rats from one end of the hall to the other like a priest carrying the host, moving precisely in the same fashion every day to make sure that spatial stimuli would remain constant. He could not follow precisely the same path to the starting point when the maze was turned, and this, he discovered, was the secret. When the living cage was attached to the maze, so that a rat always started from the same home base, it did not matter how the maze was pointing.

Charles and I began to have lunch together at the Georgian

Cafeteria on Dunster Street. We went early and followed a strict routine. We ritualistically poured the cream into our coffee as soon as it was given to us at the counter because it was then hotter when we drank it at the table. Charles thought of things like that, and I fell into the pattern. He was ten years older than I and was not married, but he occasionally commented on the beauty or sex appeal of someone we knew, like Carroll Pratt's wife, Marjory. He knew American literature much better than I, and he had a marvelous stock of funny stories. We amused ourselves by creating new ones about our acquaintances.

Although Charles was a thorough behaviorist, he was a timid man, not inclined to defend his position in public. A much more important figure, as far as I was concerned, was another graduate student, Fred S. Keller. Thin, slightly stooped, he had a shock of prematurely gray hair and a small black mustache. He spoke with great deference. Rather than challenge or contradict a speaker, he would gently explore what he had said. But he was not easily moved from his own thoughtfully prepared position. He liked funny stories and laughed easily. He was teaching part-time at Tufts College and was seldom around the department that first year, but he came to the colloquiums and took up the behavioristic cause in a quiet but effective way.

The colloquiums were run by that sardonic follower of Troland's, Eugene McCarthy. A perpetually discouraged man, he would drag himself into the colloquium room, a cigarette hanging from one corner of his mouth, drop a heavy glass ashtray on one end of the long table around which we sat, and slide into a chair. He affected a lower-middle-class manner and his speech was uninhibited. We accepted him as a model, and perhaps that is why the colloquiums were so exciting. Pratt and Beebe-Center always attended, and occasionally a new assistant professor, Henry Murray, who had taken over the Psychological Clinic on Plympton Street when its founder, the psychiatrist Morton Prince, had died. They were young, and we argued with them man to man. (The only female graduate student, a Miss Mitchell, said very little.)

A letter I wrote to Murray is perhaps an extreme example of the freedom we enjoyed in our exchanges. He had given a colloquium on his theory of "regnancy," and I saw a chance to demonstrate a bit of

Freudian theorizing. I said there were some things about himself that I felt he ought to know. From his use of the term "regnancy" it was clear that as a child he had been led to believe that it was urine which entered the female during sexual intercourse, and that his unconscious mind was still struggling to separate *p* from pregnancy. (He told me many years later that it was the rudest letter he ever received.)

Early that fall I reported to my parents:

> . . . today I attended a colloquium for psychologists, which is an informal gathering where anyone who wishes to may talk on any pertinent subject. The talk drifted around to a subject I was interested in, and for the rest of the afternoon two or three of the other men and I monopolized the time with a lengthy discussion. I made two or three sharp observations about possible errors in some experiments which seemed to interest the colloquium. Afterward one of their research men came up and introduced himself.

I could scarcely have known what I was talking about. I had had no undergraduate courses in psychology and had been a graduate student for only one month. But one of "the other men" was no doubt Fred Keller, who would have stepped in to save me when I floundered. I am not sure what Fred thought of me at the time, but when the second term began, he asked me to lecture to his class at Tufts.

IT WAS LARGELY BECAUSE OF Fred that I resisted the mentalistic predispositions of the department and remained a behaviorist. Nevertheless, I went on writing notes which were scarcely behavioristic in tone. My ambivalence about literature during that dark year in Scranton was not fully resolved when I became officially a student of psychology. Small "polemics against literature" continued to appear in my notebook, but so did long passages on meaning, with many examples of Proustian recall. I could still write, "The smell of crushed grass and heat remind me of Chautauqua." And I recorded a curious fact about my verbal behavior in a mentalistic way:

> Note the frequent experience of a sudden change of tempo in my thinking or reading. It was more frequent when I was younger. Just

now at the phrase "He found it solitary" the word was broken up into sol-i-ta-ry, each syllable equally accented with a slow hesitating pause between, each syllable subdued beneath a dull humming, giving the effect of interminable lapses, or great gaps in time. Does the unreal time of one's thought suddenly obtrude into the physical time of the eye and produce an effect of relative slowness?

But behavioristic terms—like "stimulus" and "reflex"—were beginning to appear:

Flying from Vienna to Munich in July 1928 I followed the Danube River, at the height of a mile, for some distance. I was not noticing the river especially and did not know its name at the time but after a few minutes we passed directly over it and I looked down, almost vertically, at the surface. There immediately came to my mind the memory of a few pieces of undeveloped photographer's film which I had played with as a child. . . . As soon as I was conscious of the memory, I realized that the color of the river was unusual, and that it was an exact duplicate of the color of the film. . . . I am reasonably sure that the individualizing feature of the color resulted from the reflection of a clear pale blue sky in a stream which seemed from several angles to be, free of reflections, a light muddy color. The important thing was the force with which the memory struck me. It was as if the recollection of the pieces of film was fired into my brain from a blunderbuss. The relation of stimulus to reflex was actually proportionate to the relation of trigger pull and the following shot.

Another episode during the summer led to a more behavioristic note. I had flown from Brussels to Paris at a very low altitude because of bad weather and had observed several bits of animal behavior.

Are they *inherited reflexes?*
Let an airplane fly over a farm yard. Chickens, though it may be the first experience of the sort in their lives, run for cover. A horse, frightened but knowing no direction of escape, runs in circles or stands and kicks. Never before has he, or his ancestors, known enemies of the air; there is no intelligible reaction. Chickens, with what would once have been called an instinctive fear of hawks, react as if the plane were a hawk although it is not.

The organism whose behavior I observed most closely was myself, and I was switching from curious recollections to curious behavior—as a sort of behavioristic Proust. After I had noticed that the morning sun was striking the neckties hung along one side of my dresser and moved them to a closet to prevent fading, I found that I frequently reached for a tie along the side of the dresser. I occasionally found myself doing so several weeks later. Here was a conditioned reflex undergoing extinction.

My verbal behavior supplied many examples:

> The sight of the word Gutta Percha made me repeat to myself, "With love's light wings did I o'er leap these walls." I was startled at this abrupt thought and could discover no connection until I remembered that the word was in reality "o'er perch." I distinctly remember having once quoted the line as "o'er leap." The strangeness of the word may account for my forgetting, as well as for its power of suggestion when the reverse association was called up. The incident, so slight, may be valuable in discovering the process of association. It would be an annoying irregularity in most theories.

MOST OF THESE NOTES were far from behaviorism and they were even farther from physiology, which I thought I should also explore. Pavlov was a physiologist, and if I were to carry on his work I needed to look more closely at his field. Doc subscribed to the *Quarterly Review of Biology,* and from one issue I copied a bit from a paper by William Morton Wheeler: "If in place of arms we had two sets of appendages, one rough and powerful (mandibles), the other delicate, touch-and-chemical-sensitive, we should move through the world like ants . . . and we should probably speak of strawberries as soft, round conical odors, of cigarettes as harder cylindrical odors, table tops as very hard, smooth, oblong odors of a certain quality, etc." In another issue, Curt Richter described cycles in the behavior of rats as they ate, drank, and moved about.

I came closer to physiology in a new branch of the Department of Biology at Harvard. W. J. Crozier had been brought in as its head only three years before. He had done fairly traditional work in biology until bitten by the bug of a new discipline, General Physiology, and now, a true believer, he could not easily control his contempt for those who did not see the light. They included psychologists and medical-school "organ physiologists." His department was tucked away in odd bits of space in the basement of the Museum of Comparative Zoology on Oxford Street. Every square foot was in use, including parts of the hallways, into which visitors invariably found their way when looking for the famous Blashka glass flowers, displayed on an upper floor. The glass flowers were so bitterly cursed by the physiologists that I could scarcely enjoy them when, years later, I went up to see them for myself.

Crozier was ambitious. A new building for biology was on the drawing boards, and he was insisting that physiology should have a large share of the space to itself—its own library, its own shop, and its own storerooms, as well as offices and laboratories. Botany and zoology could take care of themselves. He was building an empire in other ways; instead of bringing in mature scientists with established reputations, he was training a staff of younger men. Among them were two fresh Ph.D.'s from psychology, one of whom, Hudson Hoagland, taught General Physiology 5.

It was exactly the course I was looking for. The text was *Recent Advances in Physiology* by Evans, and it actually discussed the conditioned reflexes of Pavlov! It also reported the work of Rudolph Magnus on the reflexes involved in posture and locomotion. I bought Magnus's *Körperstellung* and struggled with the German as soon as I was able. The illustrations were stereoscopic; you crossed your eyes slightly to bring two pictures together to see the postures and movements induced by various forms of stimulation. Pavlov's reflexes, conditioned and unconditioned, were glandular secretions, but here was physical *movement*, something much closer to what was ordinarily called behavior.

The course also dealt with spinal reflexes. Professor Alexander Forbes in the Medical School was working in that field, and a former Harvard physiologist, John Fulton, had just published a large book called *Muscular Contraction and the Reflex Control of Movement*. I bought Sherrington's *Integrative Action of the Nervous System* and read it with enthusiasm. Written a quarter of a century earlier, it was still the accepted word. When the spinal cord of a cat is severed at the neck (under deep anesthesia), the reflex responses in the resulting "spinal animal" are not obscured by other behavior. For example, a shock to the paw leads to a characteristic flexion of the leg, the properties of which Sherrington studied. The time between the beginning of the shock and the beginning of the flexion is the "latency"; after a strong shock, the leg continues to flex for some time in "after-discharge"; a stimulus will not elicit a second response during a brief "refractory phase"; under repeated elicitation, responses grow weak in "reflex fatigue"; and so on. This, I was sure, was the way to study behavior!

The department encouraged individual research and Hoagland's students were passed about among the staff, who assigned topics. I drew an assistant professor who suggested that I follow up an observation he had made of what might be a conditioned reflex in a frog. The project sounded like Pavlov and I was delighted. I wrote to my parents:

> *It will mean the construction of a great deal of apparatus, very accurate timing devices and recording machines. For one thing, I will have to measure the time which elapses between the time when a frog receives an electric shock and when he jumps. Said time will be measured in thousandths of a second, and I will have to plan a long series of experiments which will run off mechanically, every move being recorded on revolving drums. Every twitch the frog makes (and all the time he is sitting on a plate without any connections at all in order to make conditions as nearly natural as possible) will be recorded. There are great possibilities, all of which came about through the picking up of an observation which I made about polo horses and an accidental experimental result which was made here in the laboratory.*

The "observation" went back to my Greenwich Village days. My friend Stella loved horses, and when she and her husband were stationed in Hawaii, they watched a good deal of polo. Her husband told me about a horse that had been struck on the head by a polo mallet as it turned into a scrimmage to the right. Afterward, it would only go into scrimmages to the left. Could the conditioned reflex in my frog be confined to one eye or possibly one side of the brain?

Unfortunately, I was never to know. I reported to my parents:

> *My experiment turned out much simpler than I expected, for I ended by proving that the observation . . . which was the basis of my*

work was unscientific. It turned out to be, not a case of a conditioned reflex but of lowered threshold. If you know what I mean. The man was somewhat embarrassed and Dr. Hoagland who put me to work on the question was amused. I'll have to try another one now. It may be a question of geotropism in ants or tropisms in Paramecium or other lower forms. I'll explain later after I start.

IT WAS TO BE geotropism in ants. An Assistant in Physiology, T. Cunliffe Barnes, was an eccentric young Canadian who came to his office in wing collar and cravat. He put me to work on the behavior of a large black ant called *Aphaenogaster fulva*. I fastened a sheet of yellow paper to a flat surface inclined at a carefully measured angle. Then, under dim red light, I put a worker ant near the center of the sheet, and as it crawled about, I followed it with a soft pencil, leaving a zigzagging trail. Segments of the trail were fairly straight and the slopes could be measured. When the tilt of the plane was changed, the angle of the paths changed, showing the effect of gravity on the ant's legs as it crawled about. The paths tended to get steeper as the days passed, and we tried to find out why. We made the ant lighter by cutting off its abdomen (it got along nicely for a time without it) or heavier by giving it a pupa to carry in its mandibles.

I learned more about human than formican behavior while we were writing our report. Barnes had a small office in Randall Cottage, a frame building on the site of the present William James Hall. He knew a taxi driver who would bring him a bottle of bootleg whiskey whenever he phoned, and he needed one for his creative labors. He wrote in a large childish hand, and as the sheets of paper piled up on one side and the level in the bottle went down on the other, he grew more and more expansive. He disliked Canadians—"sheepherders," he called them—and, for that matter, all Americans, and he would break into Latin when English seemed too pale to express his contempt. Once, as he talked, he took out his handkerchief and carefully wrapped it around his left fist. Then he said, "Skinner, do you know what we Canadians do when we get drunk? We *break WINDOWS!*" And he thrust his bandaged fist through a small pane of glass in the window beside him. (A friend who had practiced this curious Canadian custom on a store window in Boston had cut himself badly and was suffering from what was then called blood poisoning.) In spite of, or perhaps with the help of, these digressions we finished our paper, and it was received for publication in the *Journal of General Psychology* in June 1929. It was called "The Progressive Increase in the Geotropic Response of the Ant *Aphaenogaster*," and it appeared as a publication from the Laboratory of General Physiology.[1]

MY DAILY LIFE was expanding. I attended some of the lectures and colloquiums announced in the *Harvard Gazette*. I wrote about one of them to Percy Saunders: "I stopped in at a lecture in the Physics Laboratory this afternoon on the physics of music. After two sentences and a mannerism I recognized the speaker as your brother! I asked him afterwards if it were so, and he replied with an emphatic 'Yes!' "

Perhaps that is why I was not suspicious when I received an invitation to a party given by Professor Saunders for new students. There were refreshments, and Professor Saunders spent a lot of time discussing music with one of the students who played the piano beautifully, but it turned out that I had been invited by mistake. The party was for new *physics* students and someone in the Dean's office had evidently found "psych" too close to "phys." I knew none of the other students, and it was a dull evening.

I discovered the monthly concerts given by the Boston Symphony Orchestra in Harvard's Sanders Theatre. You stood in line for half an hour and when the ticket office opened, you paid twenty-five cents for a seat in the balcony directly above the stage; and if you had been near the front of the line and scrambled quickly enough, you could sit in the front row and look straight down on Koussevitzky as he conducted.

I bought new records for my Victrola: César Franck's Symphony in D Minor, Beethoven's Ninth, and Debussy's *L'Après-midi d'un faune*—which Doc thought too dissonant—all somewhat abbreviated for disks turning at 78 rpm. I worried about record wear and used thorn or bamboo needles, which I sharpened with appropriate devices. I worried about fidelity and cut small doughnuts from rubber erasers and pressed them on the bamboo needles in the belief

[1] Full citations of papers mentioned begin on page 371.

that they damped unwanted vibrations. The motor was not too powerful or the turntable very heavy, and a fortissimo would slow the disk
slightly as the needle plowed into a deeply zigzagging groove. In
Beethoven's Ninth some of the *Freude*'s sagged in pitch, as if the
singers were having second thoughts about joy.

I spent a good deal of time with the Pratts. They were musical
and often invited me for an evening of string or piano trios or quartets. Percy Saunders had once played with them. Carroll had done
some experiments on the perception of musical intervals and was
writing a book called *The Meaning of Music*, but he was diffident
about his work and I seldom talked shop with him. Marjory also had
a Ph.D. in psychology but was now raising a family.

I began to enjoy the children, Dana and Anita, and I reported to
my parents that "the baby has suddenly become so fond of me that
she goes around all day asking for 'Phwed' and if I am there she
insists upon my feeding her, dressing her, etc. (chiefly etc.), and
won't let anyone else touch her." I went to see their Christmas tree
and participated in their Easter-egg hunt. When Jean Gros brought
his marionettes to the Brattle Theatre, I took Dana to see them.
Afterward we went backstage to look at them close up, as I had done
when I helped Gros and his co-workers in Scranton two years before.

I did not overlook the chance to try an experiment or two. The
Gestalt psychologists talked a great deal about "closure"—seeing an
incomplete figure as if it were complete, as in not noticing a break in
a briefly glimpsed circle. I made a series of drawings and found to my
delight that instead of ignoring something that was missing, Anita
pointed to where it should be. If I left one picket off a picket fence, or
drew a ring of roses with one missing, she pointed to the gap. Gestalters would doubtless not have been seriously worried.

I WROTE HOME TWICE a week, and a few days after I first neglected to
do so I found a note pinned to the door of my room telling me to call
my mother. My parents had never recovered from the sudden death
of my brother, and I willingly accepted the *corvée* of two letters a
week. Characteristically, my mother saved many of them, and they
show a coyness and a contrived humor which must have embarrassed

my parents in spite of their devotion: "Speaking about finances, I got a big setback the other day when your letter with the comb-cleaner came—two cents overdue."

My laundry case went back and forth as it had done when I was at Hamilton, and my mother not only made things for my room, she bought supplies. Although I was supporting myself on the money I had made on the *Digest of Decisions of the Anthracite Board of Conciliation,* my father was handling my finances and sending me checks as needed. When he mentioned that I might have to pay an income tax, I protested. An income tax was the last thing I thought I had to worry about.

My father had settled into private practice after resigning as counsel for the Hudson Coal Company. He had persuaded a young man from the insurance department of the company to serve as manager of a Workmen's Compensation Office. Many coal companies carried no insurance to cover claims made by employees injured while at work, and these "self insurers" needed counsel when claims were argued. My father, as the author of *Pennsylvania Workmen's Compensation Law,* the only text in the field, was a specialist. He had canvassed his legal friends and had been assured that there would be no violation of professional ethics in organizing such an office, but I am not sure that he did not later hear some criticism or that he himself was ever quite clear about it.

Early in 1929 I replied to something my mother had written about how well the stock market was going: "All your investments sound great. I only hope you are prepared to take the bitter with the sweet. Go ahead and be millionaires if you want to, but *be careful.*" I cannot claim to have predicted the stock-market crash that came later that year, because in November 1928, I had written, "Well, with Hoover and father both presidents, we ought to have prosperity." My father had been elected President of the Kiwanis Club, and nothing better could have happened to him. Though he had always had a few close friends, he had never found it easy to be well liked, and since he was well disposed toward almost everyone, he was continually puzzled and frustrated. He had been invited to join the Kiwanis Club soon after he moved to Scranton and was a loyal member, and now his friends had made him President. "Bill" Skinner (my mother and his Susquehanna friends had always called him "Will") was at last hail-fellow-well-met. As President of the club, he appeared at the annual dinners of the Rotary and Lions Clubs, promoted a new sports stadium and an airport, and was one of a group of community leaders chosen to map the future of the anthracite region. He began to feel like a citizen of Scranton rather than an émigré from Susquehanna.

He also promoted the career of a local singer named Helen Sadowska. Kansas City had sent Marian Talley to the Metropolitan Opera, where she had had a great, if brief, career. Could Scranton not have its place in the sun, too? My father took Miss Sadowska to New York to see Samuel Rothafel, better known as "Roxy." Roxy said that long names were a problem on marquees and that henceforth the girl should be known as Helen Sado. He introduced them to a voice teacher, a "Madame" So-and-So, and arrangements were made for Miss Sado to stay in New York and study for an operatic career. Later Roxy reported to my father that all was going well; Miss Sado had a "magnificent organ." (When this news found its way into the Scranton papers, "organ" was changed to "voice.")

My mother was flourishing in her own way. She had joined the DAR and was still secretary of the Day Nursery. She demonstrated voting machines as a member of the Lackawanna Federation of Women's Clubs and in other ways continued to *serve*.

RAPHAEL MILLER WAS something of a worrier about health. I had reached Cambridge with a boil on my wrist, and he was afraid that faint marks running up my arm meant a streptococcus infection. When I complained that I awoke every morning with a bad "catarrh" —I discovered years later that I was allergic to the feathers in my pillow—he sent me to a homeopathist whom he knew in Boston.

And now he began to worry about himself. He was showing a medical student's syndrome: he developed the symptoms of the diseases he was studying. By midwinter it was heart trouble. He told me about the various signs—something about the shape of his fingernails, the fact that a hot bath raised his pulse inordinately, and so on. He was afraid that I too might have a bad heart because as a child I had had what appeared to be a short bout of rheumatic fever. He began to be severely depressed. He became a vegetarian. He missed classes for two weeks, and his father came up to see him.

One Sunday morning I walked over to the Medical School and found his door locked. A student across the hall said that he had got up that morning convinced that he was critically ill and had gone to a cousin's in West Quincy. I made my way there by unfamiliar public transportation and found Doc in the depths of despair. He had awakened with a swollen ankle and was sure that it was due to an embolism. The swelling had gone down, but it was only a matter of time before another embolus would go to his brain or heart and kill him.

I tried to cheer him up and eventually got him to come to my room. I discovered that he wanted to go home but was afraid he might drop dead on the way, and he did not want to cause trouble. When I offered to go with him, he immediately accepted. We could go to New York by sleeper that night and reach Susquehanna by noon the next day. We went to his room and packed some of his things, and I called my parents and asked them to meet me in Susquehanna. They were to bring Doc's fiancée, Dorothy Glidden, who lived not far from Scranton.

Doc continued to talk as if he had only a short time to live. He was concerned mainly for his father, who had already lost his wife and, many years before, another son, and for Dorothy. Dressing in the sleeper at New York the next morning, he put on a blue shirt because, he said, it made him look ruddier and healthier. In the station in Jersey City, waiting for the Erie train to Susquehanna, we talked for a long time. We had often discussed our careers, and his was now, so he thought, at an end. There were so many things he had wanted to do. He was sure that I would go on to great things, and he wanted me to know that he was glad for me. I had steadfastly refused to agree that he was seriously ill and said, "Don't worry, I'll dedicate a book to you and we'll both be famous." I was joking, but he exclaimed, "Would you?"—smiling for the first time since I had found him at his cousin's.

My parents and Dorothy were waiting for us in Susquehanna, and so was Doc's father. I had not told my parents that we had not phoned Dr. Miller, and Dorothy naturally called him hoping for further details. He had spent the next eighteen hours knowing only that his son was seriously ill and on his way home.

Doc wrote to me every week. In one letter he would speak of improvement.

For one thing the depression is much less—there are times when I go way down but more times when I am quite out of it. I have been walking downtown without too much effort. There are still symptoms but their intensity is less.

Later he would be writing:

I've slumped badly. For the past few days my old weakness has returned and things look black. My chest is beginning to feel quite uncomfortable and that, of course, is bad. . . . It seems quite impossible that things should be as they are, yet it's too true.

But then he came out of it—completely. "In despair," he wrote,

I went to see Dr. Winters of Binghamton, an adept and scholarly man in whom I have great faith. He told me my heart was "sound as a bell and good for fifty years." My blood pressure is nearly normal again. I rode a trolley to his door and slowly, and quite out of breath, climbed the stairs to his office. I went away at a brisk walk and tramped all over Binghamton. It has happened once too often. . . . I have invested in a new pair of hunting boots and used 'em today on a three-mile cross-country hike. Many aspects of religious faith cures, biblical miracles, and so on, have become very comprehensible to me in the light of my late experience.

THE PSYCHOLOGISTS FELT that Crozier was rather too openly wooing their graduate students, and near the end of the fall term he and Hoagland did indeed try to persuade me to change my field. I explained to my parents:

You see the physiology of the nervous system is practically psychology and the facilities of the Department of Physiology are better. They have just received an appropriation of $6 million and are building a new $2 million building next year. Crozier is already widely known and just at present the Department of Physiology is of far more importance here than psychology. Hoagland is especially anxious to have me come over. It would mean, not only that a Ph.D. from Physiology would be a better thing, but that there would be a good chance to line up with a local laboratory under this new endow-

ment fund and get a good position, with nothing to do but my own research. It may be possible to work under the Department of Physiology and still take my degree in Psychology as I planned. I am going to talk it over with the Heads of both departments. Crozier has been very fine to me and seems anxious to help me. He is a big gun in the field and it would be a good chance to line up with an influential man.

Psychology, as I found it at Harvard, had not been all I expected, and I had always liked biology. At Hamilton College Bugsy Morrill's courses in cat anatomy and embryology had been exciting. Botany and zoology were a bore, with their systems of classification, but rather different things were going on in the Museum of Comparative Zoology. Crozier's old mentor, George Herbert Parker, a zoologist, was conducting experiments on the production of carbon dioxide by nerves. (Parker was exempt from Crozier's attack on organ physiologists.) I saw an experiment in which he used the flexible body of a snake in an ingenious way. He had excised a rather long section of nerve, and by bringing the front and back ends of the snake together in a large loop, he could enclose the nerve in a test tube while keeping both ends connected with the snake. Under repeated stimulation the nerve gave off enough carbon dioxide to be detected by the methods then available.

Fortunately I could postpone a decision. I had signed up for a full year's program, including a spring-term course with Crozier, and would not make a change in any event before June. I should then have a clearer picture of both fields.

PSYCHOLOGY WAS NOT without its attractions. I had registered for a course called "The Psychology of the Individual," given for the first time by Assistant Professor Murray. The text was a case history— William Ellery Leonard's *The Locomotive God*. Leonard, a professor at Wisconsin, had written a long sonnet sequence but was better known for a phobia which kept him close to home. (Trueblood told me that the students at Wisconsin called him William *Yellery* Leonard.) His book was an attempt to explain the phobia; as a child he had been frightened by a locomotive which blasted him with steam when he was waiting in a station. Back in Susquehanna I had hung around the Matt Shay, the biggest steam locomotive ever built, and I found the explanation unconvincing. Nor was Murray's Freudian or Jungian analysis scientific enough for my taste. At the end of his first lecture, I went up to him and said, "You are a *literary* psychologist." I was at the peak of my revolt against literature, and it was the worst thing I could say, but Murray's scientific background was embryology, and he had in fact never taken a course in psychology. It was I who had come from literature.

Perhaps this reversal of roles explains why we became great friends and for some reason always found each other amusing. The first paper I wrote for him could have set the pattern. He had asked us for autobiographical examples of two or three psychological principles. One was "ambivalence," and I took my example from my Greenwich Village affair with Stella. I had been alone in the apartment one day rather irked by the relationship. I wanted to break free and decided that I would bring the matter up that evening, but then I went into the bathroom, saw some gauzy black underthings drying over the tub, and changed my mind.

I was not tempted by clinical psychology as a professional field even though certain bits of personal history might have turned me in that direction. At Hamilton I had looked into abnormal psychology in writing a term paper on Hamlet's "antic disposition," and my first attempt at hypnosis—with Stella—had been dramatically successful. In Scranton I had been briefly in love with a girl with whom I had experienced one of those insights which can be so rewarding to the clinician. She had come to me with a strange story about a young man who had been visiting her family. Although she found him attractive, she was puzzled by his behavior, and from some of the things she said I guessed that he might be taking heroin. I had heard that addicts avoided contact with water, and I asked, "Has he taken a bath since he has been staying with you?" It was a direct hit. My friend stared at me in astonishment; the maid had told her mother in some embarrassment that the bath towels in the young man's bathroom were unused. She confronted him with my "evidence" and he confessed. Nevertheless, I was determined to be a *scientific* psychologist!

In the spring term Boring was back from his sabbatical leave, and I gave him his chance to make an introspective psychologist of me. He taught four systematic courses which established the central position of the department. I had missed the first because of his sabbatical, but I took the second, called "Psychological Systems and Theories." Mrs. Boring, herself a Ph.D. in psychology, attended all the lectures and had evidently done so since he began to give them. Possibly with her help, they were carefully planned and punctiliously delivered, but I could not get excited about the material. I remember very little of it, in part because I was excused from the final examination and hence made no effort to pull the course together.

In his daily contact with students Boring was unpredictable. He was a butterball of a man but moved quickly. He laughed a great deal, and it was often hard to see why. Was something he or you had said funny? Or was he nervously covering up a feeling of insecurity? He was full of paternal concern when I developed another boil—this time on the back of my neck—and had to go to Stillman Infirmary; was my resistance low? But on other occasions he could be a harsh disciplinarian.

There were two calculating machines in a room on the third floor of Emerson Hall. The key to the room was kept on a large metal ring in the shop, and one of the few cardinal sins in the department was to leave the door unlocked. One Sunday morning when I was working with a machine, I occasionally ran up to the fourth floor for a minute or two to give some rats small measures of food, and I saw no reason why I should not leave the room open. But once, as I returned, I saw Boring disappearing down the stairway and found myself locked out. He had seen the open door and was taking disciplinary action. My coat with my wallet and keys was in the room, and I could not easily get through the weekend without them. I did not, however, dare to run after him to confess that it was I who had left the door open. Fortunately there is a rather broad ledge running beneath the windows on the third floor of Emerson Hall, and I was able to go out the window of the departmental secretary's office, creep along the ledge, and enter the window of the calculating room, where I retrieved my possessions. The key to the room did not turn up in the shop for several days.

THE PHILOSOPHY I HAD studied at Hamilton College had left me cold, but during that dark year in Scranton I had taken another look, particularly at Bertrand Russell. What had philosophy at Harvard to offer? Were the philosophical colloquiums as exciting as ours? On the day I decided to find out there was plenty of excitement, but the question under discussion was whether an infinite perfect could create a finite imperfect. I knew what Russell would say to that, and I left early and never went back.

The great figure in the department was Alfred North Whitehead. I met him at a joint reception for new students in philosophy and psychology held each year at Professor Hocking's. I received the usual invitation and turned up precisely at the appointed hour, which was rather too early. A little old man with a shiny bald head and deep-set eyes soon arrived and came straight toward me in the friendliest way. He wore a wing collar and ascot tie, stammered slightly, and spoke with an English accent. I sized him up as a clergyman— perhaps an imported preacher in one of the better Boston churches. He asked me where I had gone to college and what philosophy I had studied. I said that my professor had been an Edwardian (meaning a disciple of Jonathan Edwards), and that puzzled him. Was I referring to his age?

He told me that a young psychologist should keep an eye on philosophy, and, remembering Bertrand Russell, I told *him* that it was quite the other way around—we needed a psychological epistemology. Our conversation went on for fifteen or twenty minutes, and the room began to fill up. People crowded around us and eventually began to interrupt and speak to my new friend. A student edging in beside me said that he wanted to get as close as possible to the professor. "Professor who?" I asked. "Professor Whitehead," he said.

On another of those annual occasions, Whitehead himself suffered an embarrassing moment. He had consented to make a few remarks and began by recalling the great days of philosophy and psychology at Harvard when, as he said, there were giants on the earth. "There were James and Royce and Santayana and Boring—" and then, screwing up his face in a paroxysm of disgust, he spat out, "No! Not *Boring!*" There was a howl of laughter, including some, quite genuine, from Boring himself in the front row. It was a cruel and unfair slip. He was disgusted with himself for forgetting a name. He had meant Münsterberg.

Whitehead and a young colleague, Ralph Eaton, offered a

course in the spring term called "Philosophy and the Sciences," and because Whitehead's *Science and the Modern World* was attracting a good deal of attention, I signed up. Each day Whitehead spoke briefly, and Eaton finished the hour. We were asked to write papers, and my first one came back with a C –, not a passing grade for a graduate student. I have forgotten what it was about, but no doubt there were traces of behaviorism in it. Eaton explained to the class how he had graded the papers: "I read each one until I found an idea and then I gave it an A." I saw what was needed and got A's in my other papers. The ideas were to be those we were given in the course.

At times Whitehead stammered badly. I once saw him in the hallway of Emerson greeting a French scholar who had just arrived for a term at Harvard. He was making a series of welcoming remarks, to each of which the Frenchman was replying with a loud "Bon," his head slicing forward in a great arc. He was starting another "Bon," his chin high in the air, when Whitehead blocked. The head came forward in a series of staccato jerks, the word "Bon" frozen on the lips. In class one day I wrote down what Whitehead was going to say whenever he stammered and came up with a curious result. He blocked when he was on the point of mentioning either our grades or his colleague Professor Eaton.

DWIGHT CHAPMAN AND I had signed up for a research course with Hunter in which we planned to investigate "insight" in squirrels. A squirrel might be able to use its hands nearly as well as Köhler's chimpanzees, and we proposed to try some of the experiments reported in *The Mentality of Apes*. We ordered four squirrels from a professional animal supplier.

Before they arrived, I experimented with the squirrels in the Harvard Yard. Several newly planted trees had branches within reach, and I tied pieces of string to them with peanuts dangling at the ends. If a peanut was not too far from the trunk, a squirrel would reach out full length, like a flag in a high wind, its two hind feet gripping the trunk. If it could not reach the peanut that way, it would run up and out the branch and pull up the string, taking in great lengths hand over hand.

The supplier sent four very young squirrels, said to have been found in a tree cut down for timber. One soon died, and when I performed an autopsy, I found its stomach packed tight with dry grain, all digestive juices stanched by capture or transportation. The other three were soon lively enough, and Dwight and I went to work. It was easy enough to get a squirrel to pull in a peanut if an attached string lay within reach, but could it tell which of several crossing strings led to the peanut? We were rank amateurs and, along with everyone else at the time, were leaving too much to the supposed mental processes of the squirrels. We submitted papers and Hunter suggested a joint publication, but "insight" was not a respectable word for a behaviorist, and I refused. Dwight was finishing his thesis (he had tactfully abandoned the Phi Phenomenon and was working on attention) and lost interest. By the end of the spring term, I inherited the squirrels.

I had not been impressed by the ape experiments of Yerkes and Köhler and wrote a short scenario of a demonstration film poking fun at them. A "scientist" in white coat is seen (films were still silent) pointing to the essentials of the experiment—a basket hanging from a high branch of a tree on a long rope, some boxes to be piled by the ape to reach the basket, and a banana. (Russell had already made fun of Köhler for calling a banana "the objective.") The scientist picks up the banana, climbs a ladder against the tree, and reaches for the basket. He slips, grasps the basket, and finds himself swinging from the rope. He begs the ape to pile some boxes under him so that he can get down, but the ape refuses until the scientist throws him the banana.

I WAS CONFIRMED in my choice of psychology as a profession not so much by what I was learning as by the machine shop in Emerson Hall. Every department of psychology had a shop, because researchers made most of their own equipment. An old and valued machinist had recently died and had as yet been replaced only by a framed photograph. Students had the unsupervised run of the shop, and I found it new and exciting. I had never before used anything more complex than a vise, a hand drill, a hand saw, and a coping saw, but the shop had a circular saw, a drill press, a lathe, and even a small milling machine discarded by the Physics Department.

The only buzz saws I had ever seen in use had sliced whole tree trunks at lumber mills or cut large planks in the Erie carpenter shop, and I was startled when I first saw a graduate student start the noisy saw in order to cut a strip of wood no more than half an inch wide. It was not long, however, before I was doing the same thing and, with the help of other graduate students, learning how to tilt the bed of the saw to cut beveled edges, change belts to change the speed of the drill press, and set a cutting tool in the lathe or milling machine at the right angle. All sorts of supplies were available: shelves of brass and iron wood screws and machine screws and nuts in Salisbury cigarette tins (Boring was a chain smoker) and rivets, cotter keys, and small brass and iron pins in tins that once held Cuticura or Resinol ointment (the old machinist had psoriasis). There were boxes of piano wire, with which you could wind springs on the lathe, and shelves of strap and plate brass and steel.

The shop became my center of activity. I had bought a *caffe espresso* brewer and made a tripod to hold it over an alcohol lamp, using strips of brass hammered to an attractive finish, but a remark or two and a few glances among my fellow students alerted me to the fact that the shop and supplies were there only to advance the science of psychology. I was ready to advance it. The ship models I had made in that dark year in Scranton had been digressions for which I was openly criticized; now I had good reason to build things.

One of the first things I made was a silent release box. When you put a rat behind a door at the beginning of a maze and open the door to start the experiment, the noise may disturb the rat; a silent release should be an improvement. I made an aluminum door which rose silently without touching the frame when a small bellows was inflated. I doubt whether it would have made any difference in maze research, but I soon used it in a related experiment where it had some value.

THOUGH I HAD BEEN impressed by Trueblood's careful research, I did not like the maze as a scientific instrument. The animal's behavior was composed of too many different "reflexes" and should be taken apart for analysis. I decided to study the very first part—the way in which the rat first entered a maze. I built a box about two feet square with double walls of Celotex. Inside it against one wall I put a small tunnel-like structure at the top of a flight of steps. (It looked rather like a simplified Parthenon.) I released a rat from my silent release box at the rear of the dark Parthenon, from which it could emerge into the lighted space. I planned to study how it moved forward down the steps and how it pulled back when I made a noise. These were, I thought, reflexes.

I watched the rat through what I hoped was a one-way window and recorded its progress out of, and back into, the tunnel by moving an arm, which in turn moved a pencil back and forth on a strip of paper. The rat would wait in the tunnel for a minute or two after release, then peek out, often glancing suspiciously at my one-way window, and stretch cautiously down the steps. A click (from an old telegraph receiver) would send it back into the tunnel, where it remained for some time. Subsequent clicks were less and less effective, and I hoped to plot a curve showing this process of "adaptation."

As it emerged from the Parthenon, the rat seemed to be torn by competing reflexes. I had seen something of the sort in the squirrels in the Yard. When you toss a nut toward a squirrel, it approaches with a forward-and-backward oscillation. Approach is for a moment "prepotent" (Sherrington's word) over withdrawal but, as the squirrel gets closer, withdrawal becomes prepotent over approach. Once the squirrel has withdrawn, approach then takes over again, and so on.

I wrote some very "scientific" notes about my experiment:

> The bodily metabolism of the animal should be such as to bring it to the door in about half a minute or a minute. Sooner is not desirable. A click should then be given. If the animal does disappear another may follow at a determined interval. [According to Sherrington's process of "summation" two clicks should keep it in the tunnel longer than one.]
>
> If I am investigating change of sign I should deliver the stimulus as soon as positive outward orientation takes place. But the exact moment of this is difficult to ascertain; accidental posture and orientation come in. Some movement forward which is unequivocal is necessary. The appearance of the animal at the door is an early critical moment to choose.

I had no information about that "bodily metabolism," of course, nor was it anything I could change, and a year or so later I would avoid such pseudo-physiologizing, but my observations seemed relevant to summation and adaptation. The only problem was to find a measurable quantity. What could I do with those tracings of forward-and-backward movements?

I WAS SATISFYING REQUIREMENTS with surprising speed. I prepared for, and passed, a statistics examination simply by reading G. Udney Yule's *Introduction to the Theory of Statistics* straight through. I passed the departmental examination in German and could drop Ah Ha's course. (Frank Pattie, a new instructor who graded my paper, said, "You passed your German but you got away with murder!") And I passed my Prelims—if not with murder, at least with mayhem. There were four three-hour examinations designed to guarantee a comprehensive knowledge of psychology, and I was utterly unprepared. I had completed only two courses in psychology, neither of them covering much ground, and I was only halfway through two others. In the examination in Theory, I got a B–, in Experimental Psychology a B and a C, and in History a B–. These were borderline grades, barely offset by an A– in Comparative (where my work with Hunter and Crozier counted).

Nor was I ever to learn much more psychology at Harvard. Because I had passed the Prelims, I did not need to take the finals that spring, and I gave my courses little further attention. From that point on, with only two or three exceptions, I signed up for research courses which did little more than assure the comptroller that I was paying my fees.

I had read some psychology on the side. Early in the fall in the periodical room of Widener Library, I had picked up a copy of the *American Journal of Psychology* and started to read it straight through. I made slow progress. It seemed as if there must be a better way to find out what was going on in the field. Later, for reasons I cannot recall, I bought a copy of Spearman's *Abilities of Man* and spent two or three weeks completely absorbed in it. I learned all about tetrad equations, but that was the extent of my contact with intelligence testing and individual differences. I never learned how to read the "literature" in psychology, and the literature remained largely unread by me.

In my research courses, moreover, I worked entirely without supervision. No one knew what I was doing until I handed in some kind of flimsy report. Possibly the psychologists thought I was being counseled by Crozier and Hoagland, and they may have thought that someone in psychology was keeping an eye on me, but the fact was that I was doing exactly as I pleased.

By April the department had arranged for my appointment as a Thayer Fellow for the following year and clinched my loyalty to psychology by giving me a fairly large room as an office and laboratory. The first inhabitants were the squirrels, and I gave them free rein. From shelves and filing cases they would leap to my shoulder and, with considerably greater effect, to the shoulders of unsuspecting visitors. Unfortunately they soon became destructive, nibbling at my notebook and then at my knuckles and ears, and I had to confine them in a large chicken-wire cage. I added a running wheel, the classic "squirrel cage," in which they took turns during most of the daylight hours.

In the junk room of the laboratory I came across an abandoned electric fan. I set it up facing the running wheel, and connected it to the shaft with a belt. The blades of the fan turned as the squirrels ran, and the faster they ran, the stronger the breeze that blew in their faces. The verisimilitude of the running wheel as an infinitely long pathway was thus strengthened.

My effort to take maze behavior apart and study separate reflexes had left me with data that did not seem to be susceptible to further analysis. Perhaps, I thought, I should go back to the whole maze. Trueblood's work had impressed me, and Tryon had used the maze to study a subject in which I had become interested, the inheritance of behavior. He had produced strains of "bright" and "dull" rats by breeding high and low scorers in a maze. At Crozier's suggestion I planned to take a different line. I would start with inbred strains and find differences in their behavior; then I would crossbreed them and see what happened. I got four strains of rats at the Bussey Institute. Each had been inbred, brother to sister, for sixty-five generations.

They were the descendants of the rats with which William Castle had first demonstrated Mendelian inheritance in mammals. He had worked on coat color, and my rats had beautiful purple or tawny hoods.

As soon as I brought them to my new laboratory, I began to see other reasons for rejecting the maze. Many genetic differences would affect the scores. One strain was so wild that it had to be handled with forceps, but another could be held loosely in the hand. One strain would immediately leap out of a shallow box, in which another would remain indefinitely. I could have built any number of mazes in which one strain would "learn" more quickly than another—and tell me nothing about the inheritance of learning.

I needed some other kind of measurable behavior, and my rats gave me a lead by having babies. In the squirmings of newborn rats I thought I saw the postural reflexes shown in three dimensions in *Körperstellung*. Magnus, like Sherrington, had cut away parts of the nervous system to simplify his reflex systems; perhaps nature had performed a similar operation for me. No part of the young rat's brain was cut away, but parts might still be undeveloped. I decided to repeat some of Magnus's experiments.

I also tried to take advantage of something I had learned in a laboratory course in general physiology, in which I recorded the beating of an excised turtle's heart at different temperatures. Baby rats do not maintain a normal temperature, and I could make them warm- or cold-blooded by warming or cooling the space in which they lived. I might be able to study the temperature coefficients of reflex processes. I built a large Celotex cabinet with a heater and a thermostat. I could look in through a glass window and reach in through sleeves fastened to holes. It was all very scientific but awkward, and I soon gave up temperature coefficients and worked at room temperatures.

I suspended baby rats in belly slings, or with the head and tail also supported, leaving only the legs free to move. I looked for Sherrington's flexion reflex and his "extensor thrust"—a stiffening of the leg when a foot is pushed toward the body. But the movements were too delicate to record mechanically, and I had no camera. I turned to a method rather like Sherrington's in the study of spinal reflexes. I glued a piece of cheesecloth to a thin plate of aluminum about the size of a postcard, which I mounted across two parallel steel wires. The department had hired a new machinist, Ralph Gerbrands, and he made molds for two blocks of cast iron on which the wires were stretched. The plate could move back and forth lengthwise through a short distance as the wires were deflected, and I amplified the movement with a lever that made a tracing on a kymograph.

The Harvard kymograph had been standard equipment in physiological research for decades. A clockwork motor, wound with a crank, turned a six-inch aluminum drum. Speed was controlled by a choice of gears and fan blades. A small blade spun rapidly and the drum turned fast; with a large blade and a different set of gears one revolution took several hours. Glossy white paper was fastened around the drum and held in a kerosene flame until it was black with soot. During an experiment a moving point scratched the soot away and left a sharp white line. The paper was then run through a bath of thin shellac, and hung up to dry. I improved on the system by using sheets of clear gelatin in place of paper; the records could be enlarged by projecting them like lantern slides, and I could make copies with the blueprint paper used by architects.

I would put a baby rat on the aluminum table and pull it gently by the tail. As it pulled against me, the table responded to the tremor of its muscles and a wiggly line appeared on the kymograph. I soon discovered more interesting behavior. When pulled backward, a baby rat suddenly springs forward into the air, possibly sacrificing a bit of the tender skin of its tail. My table and kymograph seemed to report such leaps fairly accurately, and I was overjoyed. Here was the kind of thing I was looking for: the reflex behavior of an intact organism, recorded with a sensitivity close to that of Sherrington's "torsion-wire myograph."

I HAD COME to Harvard not because I was a fully committed convert to psychology, but because I was escaping from an intolerable alternative. The preceding May, from that Bohemian world in Greenwich Village, I had written to Percy Saunders: "I am rather certain (tonight) that I shall have interest enough to do something in this field, although I project myself into the future only for two or three years."

By December I had had a closer look and, caught up in the excitement, I had written:

> *My present condition is excellent. I am working as hard as I have ever worked, but freely—with time and subject matter of my own choosing. I have almost gone over to physiology, which I find fascinating. But my fundamental interests lie in the field of Psychology, and I shall probably continue therein, even, if necessary, by making over the entire field to suit myself.*

Now it was May again and although I had not made over the entire field, I had composed a segment in which I began to be almost unbearably excited. Everything I touched suggested new and promising things to do. I slept well at night, but my days were feverishly active, and I looked for some kind of relaxation.

I wrote home asking to have my leghorn and panama hats sent on, but they led to no social diversions. A friend suggested the L-Street Bathing Beach, a public beach for men only enclosed by two high planked walls and open to the harbor. For ten cents you got a towel and a small triangular piece of cloth with three strings attached —the G-string of the ecdysiast, seldom used. There were handball courts and plenty of sand for sunbathing, and I stretched out and tried to relax, but it was no use. I thought constantly of my rats, designing new pieces of equipment and formulating new questions to be answered. I lost weight and my heart began to skip beats. I went to a doctor for a checkup and learned there was nothing organically wrong.

Doc HAD CONTINUED to write about his progress, and I looked forward to seeing him again in the fall. He had gone to New York to take passage on a boat to the Baltic, where he would work his way into Germany to learn the language before returning to medical school, but he had run short of money and by the first of May had gone to Saranac Lake to work in the Trudeau Sanatorium. He was studying German and pathology. He urged me to join him:

> *My beautiful camp is situated upon a beautiful lake—lower Saranac —in the midst of an almost virgin forest. Here you may bring your*

books and find peace and contentment and real health. . . . Come up and talk Deutsch with me. Bring your animals if you must—the lab has a most complete animal farm.

Near the end of June he wrote:

The lake has been especially inviting on these hot days. I manage a swim nearly every day and this, with wood chopping and general camp duties, serves to keep me from getting too heavy. . . . I believe that I am leading the ideal life at present (for me). Enough regular clinical work to provide a fair income (blood exams, bacteriological work, etc.), and the afternoon in which to do investigation or study. And best of all, life has become once again a very interesting thing!

Early that summer I had moved into a larger room on the second floor at Mrs. Thomas's and had bought a secondhand Mason and Hamlin upright piano. I was playing it one day when I was called to the phone; it was my mother to tell me that Raphael Miller was dead. (I had been playing Scriabin's Prelude in G-flat Major and I have never heard it or played it since then without reliving that moment.) Doc and a friend had gone out at night in a small boat. The motor stalled and as they tried to start it the boat capsized. The friend clung to the boat and was rescued, but Doc set out for shore. His body was not found for several days. According to the coroner's report, he had not drowned, for there was no water in his lungs. Many years later his stepmother told me that his father had attended the autopsy and had reported that Raphael's heart was unusually large. He had undergone a faith cure after all.

Although Doc had always served as a kind of model, I never actually emulated him to any great extent. We had similar backgrounds and were dedicated to similar principles, and when I was with him I behaved as he behaved, but I was not much like him at other times. He was important as a close friend who had faith in what I was doing, as I had faith in him.

ANOTHER FRIEND WOULD PLAY a much more explicit role in my early career. I had learned of the existence of Cuthbert Daniel from his mother, whom I met on the S.S. *Colombo* on my way to Europe. She had told me that her son and his wife, Janet, were in Berlin attending lectures by Hans Reichenbach (possibly without too much profit, because, as Cuthbert later said, "Janet couldn't understand the math and I couldn't understand the German"). I had written to him during the winter. I do not remember what I said, but my letter brought a response that foreshadowed something of our subsequent relationship:

Dear Fred,

First, state assumptions. All right, I assume you are friendly. Have you patience and words enough to tell me what it is all about? I have your letter but it talks around & not about your main idea, doesn't it? Take the "biological concept of mind" for instance. That is a nice arrangement of words & I would like you to tell me about it. A great clarification would be to tell me if it is your expression for your own central idea or do you mean to refer to the same referent as biologists in general when they talk about mind?

Secondly—(but see assumption, da oben) What is this about mathematics? You must know enough to know that I (or, indeed, any other student of it) don't use the word M— to refer to "Introduction to the Calculus" (Osgood? good) any more than I use the word Painting to refer to the Mona Lisa. Their position is about the same, each in its matrix, i.e. well known, well known as wonderful, viewed by millions (fig.) as the embodiment of all ————, viewed ditto ditto as working through deep channels and withal a little mysterious, in short, shit, or, if you are religious, irrelevant to the central problem.

The study of mathematics is the study of logical relations & their symbolic expression. In symbols I include naturally their most important subgroup, words. (I am giving you no esoteric or personal interpretation but a crude summary of what every young man should know.) I hope you don't find parentheses wearing. (I don't know why I use them.)

That is why I like the phrase "the biol. conc. of mind." Query. Do you realize (if you do, fine) how much of a meaning you have already attached to the word mind, as soon as you get to the word concept? I am not saying that a phrase can be pulled apart from left to right, but that "concept of mind" involves an ellipsis of a sort not to be sneezed at by serious people like you & me.

To you again & here I must take no chances on losing you, but must say forehandedly, that I am not saying Huh, if you think

Schumann lousy, let's see you write a better quintet. The question is this, if you are studying Calculus (which should be taught in High School with typewriting & good manners), then you haven't got very far into Whitehead. I refer to the 3 books. (Concept of Nature, Principles of Nat. Knowledge, principally The Principle of Relativity) & not to Science and the M.W. – Religion and – – –, or Symbolism, where I feel as you do, that White—— is slipping & therefore misleading.

Ninthly and lastly, although the feat of sawing off one's own little branch has been done, and indeed often, I have never seen salutary results follow, nor even a theory as to how they could, but downing Math. looks excessively like it to me, & your philosophy will be a new one if it doesn't use words, sentences & logical relations in general, i.e. Math.

I have never been able to classify myself metaphysically, probably because the word came to me too late in life for me to use it easily. Regards to you anyway, & write when you've time or feel pedagogical.

Daniel

In the margin he wrote: "The careless scholarship of a German beer garden is another good phrase, do you do it often?" The "Daniel" was significant. His mother had called him "Buddy" and his second letter was signed "B" but from then on we both used "Cuthbert."

And now he and Janet had come to Cambridge so that he could work with P. W. Bridgman in the Department of Physics. I saw him first when I came back to my room one day after taking a bath. He was standing before my shelf of books eating an apple he had taken from a bowl on the table. My library had grown and included things like *Space, Time and Deity* by S. Alexander, and *Chance, Love and Logic* by C. S. Peirce (recommended by Crozier for the chapter called "Man's Glassy Essence").

"Well, you have all the right books," he said. But he told me that I should add Bridgman's *The Logic of Modern Physics*, and I promptly bought a copy.

THE INTERNATIONAL CONGRESS of Physiology met at the Harvard Medical School in August 1929, and Ivan Petrovitch Pavlov gave the principal address! I had met Hallowell Davis, in the Department of Physiology at the Medical School, and he arranged for me to serve as a volunteer at the congress. One of my tasks was to operate a slide projector, which I did competently except for a biochemist whose slides showed little more than the letters C, O, and H arranged in various hexagonal patterns. There are four ways of putting a glass slide in a projector in all of which O and H, and in two of which C, appear unchanged. I got one of the slides right side up and facing the right way only on the fifth trial, when I was applauded.

I took a group of visitors around Boston, of which I myself as yet knew very little, and wrote my parents a highly exaggerated report of my linguistic competence:

> *I talked some in French, German & Italian. However the rule of foreign languages is—speak in your own tongue unless asked to do otherwise. It is an insult to a German, for example, to speak to him in German, because that implies that he does not understand English. A Frenchman and a German will converse by speaking each his own tongue. The proper conduct therefore on the bus ride was to speak very clear slow English using as many words resembling the German or French as possible. The foreigners on the other hand used either their own languages (which I understood well enough) or bad English (which was hard to get). Some of them mixed them up, which was worse still. Occasionally if someone did not understand, I used his language. In that case I was usually understood. It is a very complicated business, as you can see.*

I also served as the personal guide of a German physiologist who wanted to see the new Fatigue Laboratory of L. J. Henderson at the Harvard Business School. He spoke almost no English, but as we watched some subjects exhausting themselves on treadmills and stationary bicycles, I saw him composing a little speech. Very carefully he brought it out: "You-haf-manny-metodes-uff-fatik," he said, and smiled brightly. By pointing to some leaflets he had been given, he managed to let me know that he wanted to spend the rest of the day at the Museum of Fine Arts, and there I left him.

I heard Pavlov's presidential address (in German) but did not try to shake his hand. I did get his autograph. A photographer was taking orders for a portrait and had asked Pavlov to write his name on a slip of paper so that his signature could appear on each print. I offered to buy a copy if I could have the slip of paper when the photographer was through with it, and he sent it to me.

Vivisection was a problem at the congress. There was an active antivivisection society in Boston, and the Harvard Medical School was particularly careful not to offend, but some European physiologists were breaking all the rules in setting up their demonstrations. One group planned to bring an unanesthetized dog's kidney to the surface where its functions could be observed, and I saw Madame Lapicque, the wife and colleague of a famous French physiologist, in whose theory of "chronaxie" I would become interested, slowly peel the skin off a live, unanesthetized frog. These were the "scoundrels" whom George Bernard Shaw had attacked but who, in the minor case of Pavlov, had been defended by H. G. Wells in that passage which confirmed my decision to become a psychologist.

I WAS IMPRESSED by scientists speaking other languages and I decided to do something about my linguistic shortcomings. I could read French with reasonable fluency, but I did not speak it well because I had never recovered from the self-instruction with which I began. I had barely passed my German examination, and so I wrote to the Stechert company in New York about subscriptions to German periodicals. They gave me a quotation on *Tageblatt* and suggested *Die Woche*, but I decided to submit to an even more thorough exposure. Magnus's *Körperstellung* was a kind of bridge between Sherrington and Pavlov. Sherrington had published in English, of course, and Pavlov had been translated, and in a missionary effort to complete the picture of a science of behavior for English readers I wrote to the German publisher asking if I could translate Magnus. I told Crozier and Hallowell Davis, and they wrote letters supporting my request and testifying, rashly, to my competence.

The publisher replied that the proper move was to find an American publisher, who would make the appropriate arrangements. I tried three without success, and since the book runs to more than 700 large pages, I was saved from what would have been an exhausting task. (I was probably also saved from some embarrassing mistakes. A graduate student in the department before my time had translated a

German text in which he reported some experiments by Hühner. The appearance of that distinguished scientist in the psychological literature was caught just before publication. The experiments were indeed "*bei Hühner*"—that is, "on chickens.")

I signed up for a research course that summer with Carroll Pratt. He did not know what I was doing and I submitted no report. He gave me an A. When the fall term began, I went to Boring with a bill for rat food and other summer supplies. It was for $35, and he was rather startled, for I had not been authorized to spend any money. He was not unduly disturbed, however, because other arrangements for animal psychology were being made. Early in the spring he had stopped by the door of my laboratory, sniffed, exclaimed, "Nasty rats!" and hurried on. The philosophers on the lower floors were behaving in much the same fashion. The problem had arisen with the expansion of animal psychology, and plans were under way to clear the air. New quarters, primarily for the study of animal behavior, were being set up in Boylston Hall, on the south side of the Yard.

The space was not quite ready, and since my office in Emerson had been assigned to someone else, I moved my rats to another room. I had a much larger colony than I had started with, and when I moved it out of my office there were several new litters. A kind of mass infanticide followed: I found all the baby rats dead with a pair of small wounds at the nape of each neck. Rats sometimes eat their young, presumably because of dietary deficiencies, but these were killed in the emotional excitement of a strange location. Their mothers had picked them up in the usual manner but a little too roughly. I regretted the loss, but I was impressed by the fact that all the rats had behaved in precisely the same way.

THAT FALL I SIGNED UP for one course each with Crozier and Boring. The laboratory course in General Physiology in which I recorded the beating of an excised turtle's heart (and also followed the growth of seedlings dipping into various chemical solutions) was pretty irrelevant to my interests, though I was impressed by the "science." Crozier's own course was right along my line. It was called "The Analysis of Conduct." Crozier used "conduct" because Watson and the psychologists had sullied "behavior." The course sampled many of the activities of the department, including the work of Arrhenius on the effects of temperature on biological processes, but it emphasized Crozier's own work on tropisms.

Crozier acknowledged his debt to Jacques Loeb, whose *Comparative Physiology of the Brain and Comparative Psychology* Bugsy Morrill had shown me at Hamilton. Like Loeb, Crozier was fascinated by any demonstration of lawfulness in animal behavior. Shine a bright light on one side of an insect, and in a dim light it will then crawl in circles. Put a very young rat on a sloping surface and, like my worker ants, it will crawl up along a diagonal path at an angle which depends upon the slope of the surface.

Crozier once told me how Loeb was converted to physiology. He was visiting the laboratory of a biologist and noted that some plants growing in an aquarium were all turned toward the light. He pointed this out to his host and commented on how neatly it demonstrated heliotropism in plants. "But those are not plants," said his host, "they are animals!" Crozier easily reproduced Loeb's excitement: forced movement in *animals*!

It was said of Loeb that, in his concern for the organism as a whole, he "resented the nervous system," and Crozier did, too. He dismissed the nervous system as one of the "organs" studied in the Medical School. General Physiology dealt with overall quantitative laws. It was a methodology rather than a subject matter, and almost any data would serve if studied with the right methods. It was not terribly important at what angle a young rat climbed up an inclined plane, but the chance of finding a functional relation between the two angles was exciting. It did not really matter that a lizard or an insect "played possum" after being disturbed, but the length of time it displayed this "tonic immobility" varied with its temperature, and Arrhenius's equation could be applied. An emphasis on method suited me, for I had my subject matter and was looking for ways of dealing with it.

I did not take warmly to tropisms, however. I remembered Loeb's book and the tank with slanting rays of light in which organisms said to "seek the light" all found themselves in the dark. I remembered the earthworm that wove itself into a screen as the screen was flipped over again and again. But the stimulating environment I cared about could seldom be described as a field of force or behavior simply as orientation or movement. Nor could I abandon Pavlov, Magnus, and Sherrington quite so cavalierly. Nevertheless, I began to think of reflexes as behavior rather than, with Pavlov, as "the activity of the cerebral cortex" or, with Sherrington, as "the integrative action of the nervous system."

For Crozier's course I wrote a paper criticizing an article called "Mode of Inheritance of Reaction Time and Degrees of Learning in Mice." It was a bad experiment, but it did not deserve my scathing denunciation. The author, a Miss Vicari, had used 900 mice divided among four strains. Each mouse was to learn to find its way through a simple maze by turning either right or left at two choice points. How often it went through without a mistake, how often it did so consecutively, and how often it went through before making a correct run were said to show "degree of learning." I pointed out, among other things, that correct choices were fewer than would be expected from chance. The time elapsing between the mouse's release and its entrance into the food box at the end of the maze was called the "reaction time," and I attacked that measure. I alluded scornfully to the fact that in an earlier design of the maze the animals "curled up in the corner and went to sleep." I contended that any differences between strains could be "attributed to so many incidental factors showing genetic differences that we scarcely need to discuss the matter further." Nevertheless, I discussed it further. The different strains might be disturbed to different degrees by being put into the maze. One strain had defective balance and was also deaf, and another was "either blind or nearly so." Was any part of the result relevant to the inheritance of reaction time or learning?

Crozier, alas, thought the paper should be published and sent it off to the *Journal of General Psychology*, of which he was an associate editor. Again I was said to be affiliated with the Laboratory of General Physiology. Crozier was proud of the number of papers issuing from his department, but I was soon far from proud of my ill-tempered piece.

I had signed both my papers "B. F. Skinner." I had been named B. Frederic, and even at an early age I struggled with that ostracized initial. A poem I published at the age of ten was signed "B. F. Skinner" and so was a letter from camp to my parents a few years later. At Hamilton College John Hutchens picked up "Burrhus" from a class list, and my passport demanded "Burrhus F." I told Fred Keller about a poem published in the college paper about Hutch and me in which I appeared as Sir Burrhus de Beerus, and Fred was amused and began to call me Burrhus, although everyone else called me Fred.

I noticed that among the names appearing in the *Harvard Gazette* the preachers in the University Church usually used all their names: Willard Learoyd Sperry, Harry Emerson Fosdick, Henry Bradford Washburn. In the Humanities and Fine Arts, it was often a given name and an initial. But physicists, chemists, biologists, and mathematicians tended to use initials only, and I was eager to be of their company. I would sign myself "B. F. Skinner." (Many years later, when I was being introduced to audiences in Britain, I noted the ingenious ways in which chairmen avoided calling me "B. F.," a common alternative to the vulgar "bloody fool.")

THOUGH I REMEMBER NOTHING about it, the course I had taken with Boring during the spring term on "Psychological Systems and Theories" may have been interesting, but his course that fall on "Perception" was simply painful. I am sure Boring himself eventually looked back on his vassalage to Titchener with a good deal of pain, too. He spent *three* full lectures on the Müller-Lyer illusion, describing in detail the work of the ten people (one of them Marjory Bates Pratt) who had tried to find out why one line looks longer than another if the branches at the tips flare out rather than fold back. I sat and listened—and listened, too, for the clock in the Catholic church. It struck the quarter hours in the Westminster pattern, and about halfway through the term something went wrong. Each four-tone phrase lost its initial note and ended with the initial note of the phrase to follow.

The worst of it was that I should have to take the final examination. I had been excused from my finals in the spring because I had passed my Prelims, but the exemption no longer held. How could I give back the stuff I had been hearing? I had taken notes (there was nothing else to do), but I could not imagine studying them, let alone memorizing them. Instead, I composed twenty mnemonic sentences, representing the twenty topics covered in the course, with the names of the psychologists who had worked on them. I went into the final examination armed with these sentences. A few days later Boring saw me in the hall, asked me to wait a moment, and went back into his office. He came out with a list of grades, "And lo, Ben Adhem's name led all the rest." To my parents I reported: "Only one other A given. It really was not a fair mark as I did not care much about the course and don't even now know much about the subject. I can't help getting A's even when I don't know anything."

I WAS NOW SEEING much more of Fred Keller. He had given up his teaching at Tufts and was spending all his time in the department. Although he and I would soon be exiled to Boylston Hall, we did not intend to let that relax the behavioristic pressure in Emerson. I wrote to my parents that I would be talking before the psychological colloquium on "A Stimulus-Response Phenomenology."

> *I am looked upon as the leader of a certain school of psychological theories and this will be a broadside, as it were, into the camp of the enemy in announcing our position for the year. There are two or three "camps" among the faculty and the graduate students, according to the special system of the science which each follows. The behaviorists, whom I represent, have acquired a good deal of strength this year because of the new laboratory and this talk will be the first platform we have announced. The thing is all friendly, of course, but hotly argued.*

Shortly afterward I sent a further bulletin:

> *Well, my talk was a great success. It lasted for an hour and a quarter and the discussion afterwards equally long. The place was in an uproar afterwards, everybody trying to talk—which was exactly what I had hoped for. It means that many of the new men, coming here this year, will come over to our "party," giving us more moral and physical support—by working on matters related to our doctrines rather than to those of the other parties. Keller is the name of the man who is my colleague in our party. (He has a twin bicycle with mine.) He is to talk next week, and between us we expect to sew matters up.*

I was not above seizing an opportunity to maintain good relations: I wrote that "the editor of the *Saturday Review of Literature* [which I used to take in Scranton] wants me to write a review of a book which will be out a little later by Boring, head of the Department here at Harvard." It was his *History of Experimental Psychology* and I had written to ask if I might review it. The editor, Henry Seidel Canby, had said that I might if I had no personal ties with the author. I explained to my parents: "I am going to write the review mainly to help Boring out on selling the book. It will help me in the Department's political situation also." I wrote the 800 words Canby specified and showed them to Boring, who, I told my parents, "said that it was a better review than he himself could write and that he would be honored to have it appear. So much for keeping in with the — head of the department." I sent it off but I believe it was never published.

THAT FALL I AUDITED a course in the history of science. It was taught by L. J. Henderson, a biochemist who had done pioneering work on the blood and had founded the Fatigue Laboratory at the Harvard Business School. (He told me later that he had given it that name because almost any conceivable subject could be studied under the name of fatigue.) His lectures were witty, urbane, often brilliant. He was a Francophile, and there were rumors of a French mistress, but it was hard to imagine him in love. He was given to less admirable emotions but kept them pretty much under control. He once used the word "damn" in commenting on something of Aristotle's and then spent several minutes explaining why he had allowed himself to be carried away.

He suffered from ulcers, and several years before, when he was recovering from an attack in a Paris hospital, his friend William Morton Wheeler had given him a copy of Pareto's *Traité de sociologie générale*, a book that was to dominate him for the rest of his life. I bought a copy soon after I began to audit his course, but Pareto was not a behaviorist, and I was not quite sure what to do with him.

I took the history of science seriously. I bought the extant volumes of Sarton's great *Introduction to the History of Science*, joined the History of Science Society, and bought all available back issues of *Isis*, the journal of the society. (I also planned to observe the history of science as it unfolded and, following Francis Bacon a little too closely, to take all knowledge to be my province. The following year the famous astronomer William de Sitter gave the Lowell Lectures in Boston on "The Development of Our Insights into the Structure of the Universe," and I braved the rigors of public transportation to hear the whole series.)

EVENTUALLY THE MOVE to Boylston Hall was made. The building had been a museum of comparative anatomy, a physics laboratory, an herbarium, and a mineralogical museum. (The famous "New Jersey mastodon" first appeared there, the bones improperly assembled.) The Chemistry Department had used it last, before moving into a new building on Oxford Street. The best space now went to the Yenching Institute, and animal psychology got the top floor, reached by climbing two long flights of stairs, past an unused second floor containing the debris of storage and display cabinets.

I had a large office looking out on the Yard. Across the hall a "soundproof" room would soon be built within a larger room, and beyond it were large animal quarters with one chicken-wire enclosure for cats and another for my squirrels. The shop was much smaller than in Emerson and suitable only for woodwork or crude metalwork, but it was all I needed.

The Boylston laboratory was in the hands of Morgan ("Kelly") Upton, who had taken his degree in the department a year before but was moving toward General Physiology. He had an office and a laboratory in Boylston, and somehow he got grants from funding agencies for the study of "central nervous integration," but I seldom saw him doing any work. When in the building, he spent most of his time making furniture, using some of the seasoned panels and doors to be found in the debris left by chemistry on the second floor. Some of the tools in the shop, such as a planing saw, seemed to have been purchased with cabinetmaking in mind. I learned from Kelly how to rub down a shellacked surface with pumice and linseed oil to get a pleasant if not very durable finish. Fred and I, together with a younger graduate student named Stavsky, had Boylston Hall pretty much to ourselves.

I wrote to my parents to say that I was "uncovering so many new things that it will be some time before I can systematize them for publication. . . . This doesn't mean that I have set the world on fire yet, but my results so far are above the average." (The stock market was crashing and I added, "I saw an awful quotation for Prudential this a.m. which I hope was a misprint. If it is way down, how about buying some to bring down my average?") My problem was not that I had too many data but that I did not know what to do with them. A systematic treatise on the posture and locomotion of baby rats—a miniature *Körperstellung*—did not appeal to me. The vibrating platform had given me precise records of the "behavior of an organism as a whole," however, and I thought I could use something like it with an adult rat. It would be an improvement over those tracings of movements in and out of the Parthenon.

I mounted a ten-foot strip of light spruce on tightly stretched steel wires. It moved forward and back as the spring of the wires permitted, and the movement was amplified by a lever, which again traced a line on smoked gelatin. (Eventually I planned to use a beam of light writing on a moving photographic film.) A tunnel of galvanized iron above the strip converted it into a kind of covered bridge.

From my soundless starting box I released a hungry rat at one end of the strip and induced it to run to the other end by giving it food. My kymograph recorded the pressures exerted on the strip, and when the rat was halfway along I sounded a click (its loudness carefully calibrated, of course!) and recorded the way in which it came to a stop. It was again the principle of Sherrington's torsion-wire myograph applied to a freely moving organism rather than a muscle or leg. I planned to measure changes in behavior as a rat slowly got used to the click; perhaps I could even get it to stop in response to a conditioned stimulus.

In an application for a Harvard fellowship, I supplied tracings which I said showed the backward thrusts of the four legs of the rat as it ran down the strip, noting that it had a leading foot which "delivered a good share of the energy." I included a curve showing a strong deviation in the opposite direction as the rat came to a sudden stop, and also a set of hypothetical curves to show the possibility of following "adaptation" as the rat grew used to the click. It was not a bad project but the instrumentation was faulty. I reported that the natural frequency of the substrate was not above forty per second, which was only "slightly above the top frequency of the steps of a rat in running." Moreover, the strip bounced slightly, and the effects of irrelevant vertical movements were not entirely eliminated when I replaced the supporting wires with vertical glass plates.

I got something out of the experiment because it led me to watch a rat and try to account for its behavior. I appealed to adaptation, summation, and particularly "prepotency," the triumph of one reflex over another, which, I thought, might explain some of the sudden changes that Köhler and others had attributed to a mysterious "insight." I wrote a note analyzing an example.

> A rat runs down a dark runway and finds food in a well-lighted food box at the end. He seizes some food in his mouth, returns to the dark runway, and eats it. He comes again to the food box, takes food, and returns. On the third trip, a door is closed behind him. . . . He noses at the door, runs swiftly about the food box, tries many times at the door. After a little time, he makes a final examination of the door, then turns quickly and goes to the food dish where he sits quietly and eats.
>
> In what way can we explain the sudden change from "attending to the door," "trying to get out," etc. to the "decision" to eat in the open lighted space. The immediate anthropomorphic guess is that the rat concludes that he is actually caught, cannot get back into the tunnel, and must make the best of it and eat here. [Another] so-called objective explanation . . . equally false is that the sudden change is one of the characteristics of "insight."

A long account then followed in which I discussed shifting "adaptations" and "prepotencies" in conflicting reflexes, ending:

> When the door is interposed, the reflex orientation to adapted territory is interrupted resulting in intensification of the negative-to-the-food-box behavior. The freedom reflex [Pavlov's term] thus resulting will persist as long as the condition of the animal determines. If the food box has been partially adapted to, it will wear off quickly. If not, it must continue until adaptation or some other reflex supervenes. . . . As the food box adapts out, the orientation toward the dark tunnel weakens, and as a result the door is no longer a stimulus for the freedom activity.

This was pretty tortured stuff, and it was clear that the experiment was not getting anywhere. What was wrong? I seemed to be behaving as scientists behaved, and my laboratory smelled scientific because the kymograph records hanging up to dry gave off a strong odor of denatured alcohol. Moreover, the tracings on my records looked like the white-on-black records I had seen in articles on muscular contraction. But what was I to do with them? Pavlov could quantify his results by counting drops of saliva. How was I to convert those wiggly lines into significant magnitudes?

ONE EVENING I FOUND Cynthia Ann Miller, the great love of my sophomore year at Hamilton, waiting in line for a Boston Symphony concert at Sanders Theatre. She had graduated from Radcliffe and had stayed on in Cambridge. It was a friendly encounter but not encouraging, and I made no effort to see her again. I had not met anyone in Cambridge who interested me in a romantic way. For one thing I had been busy catching up after a late start in psychology. For another it was not easy to meet women. It would be many years before Harvard scheduled social functions worthy of the name of mixer.

I was also diffident about personal contacts. When I noticed an attractive graduate student in biology—attractive in part, no doubt, because she looked as my mother must have looked when I was a child—I could not walk up to her and introduce myself. Instead, for a consideration of five dollars, I asked a young woman whom I had met through Fred Keller to make her acquaintance and introduce me. I was soon reporting to my parents: "The girl's name is Grace DeRoo which is as close to Grace Burrhus as I could get. She is very interesting but I have not taken her out yet." My letters became unbearably coy:

> Grace and I had dinner together last night and when I got home I forgot to write. Also we are having dinner together tonight so I must hurry. I had intended to write Sunday but Grace and I had dinner together, so then I thought I would write Sunday night but we had supper together, too. All I can tell you now is that she is a wonderful girl. . . . We disagree on nothing except the theory of nervous conduc-

tion and the right amount of olive oil in salad dressing. We are almost exactly alike. We even have only one tooth missing apiece, and it's the same tooth (lower right first molar). We haven't done anything rash yet as we are both a little bit suspicious of such a sudden start. So far as I am concerned it is going to last, however. Right now I have known her only 193 hours and ten minutes, so it's a bit soon to pop the question.

I went to Scranton for Christmas, and when I came back, I had dinner with Grace and her parents. We went dining and dancing at the Statler. Then we spent a weekend with one of Grace's friends and her family in Peekskill and things began to go wrong. The friend's mother was French and I asked her to read to us in French. Grace did not speak French and told me later that she felt I was deliberately cutting her out. It was no doubt thoughtless of me, but nothing more. Nevertheless I was soon reporting to my parents:

Had lunch with Grace yesterday. We have decided not to get married. While we have a great deal in common there are certain incompatibilities of temperament which we are both afraid of. We are much too much alike to get along together when we are with each other for any length of time. So it's all off. Nevertheless we are still good friends and I see as much of her as ever.

There were no other women in my life that year. An attractive young wife who lived on the other side of Mrs. Thomas's duplex had a lovely voice, and I bought some of the kinds of things she liked to sing—some songs of Rachmaninoff's—and played her accompaniments. But she was not interested in sex—not even, she told me, with her husband. When Mrs. Thomas's young granddaughter, visiting for a few days, told me she had seen me kissing a girl in my room, I could honestly say that it wasn't so. A young artist living on the first floor whose hair was also reddish-brown must have been the guilty party.

THE PROBLEM OF QUANTIFYING my data was solved by an accident. It was my practice to sit at one end of the straightaway near the kymograph and food box. After each run I got up and carried the rat back to the other end. Doing this was not only a chore, it probably disturbed the rat. It would be better if the rat started from the food box, and so I added a back alley along which it could return to the far end of the straightaway. "The disappearance of food," I wrote in my notebook, "would be the stimulus to begin a run."

Unfortunately, the rat did not always begin at once. Instead, as I noted, "it may explore the food box, sniff, gnaw at the corners, or stand motionless with its nose in the air. The beginning of a new run may be delayed five to ten minutes. . . ." I began to measure the delays and plot them on squared paper. I knew very little about making graphs, and to represent time on both axes I measured off horizontal distances and erected squares on them. The curious thing was that adjacent squares were rather alike in size. I wrote a note:

> If the start of the run is determined by fortuitous stimulation, we should expect these delays to be scattered in chance order. If on the other hand we are dealing with a varying threshold (i.e. with the interplay of two reflexes) we might expect some order in the distribution of delays. As a matter of fact this order is found.

I speculated at length about that "interplay between two reflexes." "We must first regard the food box situation as an adequate stimulus for a run. . . . Our next step is to discover some reflex antagonistic to the running which can conceivably be evoked by the food box." I thought I could spot two, but "whereas throughout the course of an hours experimentation the running reflex (being 'reinforced') persists, the [antagonistic behavior] *adapts out*." The delays should get shorter, but in fact they got longer. "Another factor must be taken into account. The presence of an autocoid affects the above distribution by weakening the food reflex and strengthening [the antagonistic behavior]." "Autocoid" was a bit of gratuitous physiologizing; there was a current theory of hunger in which the inclination to eat was attributed to a hormone.

Whatever the explanation, a systematic change in delay was the kind of thing I was looking for. I had failed to quantify those wiggly lines, but I could measure a delay in starting a run with a stopwatch.

If I no longer cared about a sudden stop in response to a click, I could dispense with that ten-foot straightaway. Something much simpler would do, and I saw a chance to save more labor. The back alley had greatly simplified my life, and if I now made the apparatus entirely automatic, I should not even need to be present during an experiment.

I built a narrow rectangular track about three feet long, and mounted it like a seesaw; it tilted slightly as the rat ran from one end to the other. I made a food dispenser by drilling a ring of holes in a disk of wood. Pieces of food were put in the holes, and each time the rat ran around the track, the tilt turned the disk and dropped a piece into a cup. I needed food that could be easily dispensed, and I found that rats liked pearl barley, readily available. The tilt of the track also made a mark on a kymograph, the time between runs appearing as the distance between two marks. I began to see a regular pattern. At first a hungry rat worked fast, starting on another run immediately after finishing a piece of barley, but as it became satiated, the times between runs grew longer and the marks farther apart.

I still had to measure the distances between the marks and plot them on a graph, but an accidental feature of the apparatus suggested a better (and still easier!) way. I had found the wooden disk of which I made the dispenser in a room full of discarded apparatus. It so happened that a short spindle, like the hub of a wheel, was attached to one side, and I had left it in place. It occurred to me that if I wound a thread around the spindle, it would unwind slowly as the disk turned and could be made to lower a marker on the kymograph drum. The marker would record a *curve* rather than a row of marks. When the rat was working rapidly, the thread would be payed out rapidly and the line would be rather steep, but as the rat slowed down, the curve would grow flatter. From the slope I could estimate the speed at which the rat was working at any moment. By having the thread unwind rather than wind I had got my curve upside down according to standard practice, but that was easily corrected, and before long I was getting what are now standard cumulative records.

IN THE SPRING TERM the course in the history of science was taught by George Sarton, the great man in the field. He was not only a better scholar than Henderson, he had a more human touch. He had just published a small book called *The History of Science and the New Humanism,* and I bought a copy. It was dedicated to "those strange twins May and Isis." May was Sarton's daughter, born the year in which he founded the journal *Isis*, and I dreamed of meeting her. I later saw her in a production of *The Cherry Orchard* as the understudy of Eva Le Gallienne, and many years later gave her a bit of verse that came to me one morning just as I was waking up:

> Between the Is (is)
> And the May be
> > Falls the shadow of Unsartonty

In the preface to his *Introduction* Sarton wrote:

> The saints of today are not necessarily more saintly than those of a thousand years ago; our artists are not necessarily greater than those of early Greece; they are more likely to be inferior; and of course, our men of science are not necessarily more intelligent than those of old; yet one thing is certain, their knowledge is at once more extensive and more accurate. *The acquisition and systematization of positive knowledge is the only human activity which is truly cumulative and progressive.* Our civilization is essentially different from earlier ones, because our knowledge of the world and of ourselves is deeper, more precise, and more certain, because we have gradually learned to disentangle the forces of nature, and because we have contrived, by strict obedience to their laws, to capture them and to divert them to the gratification of our needs.

Sarton was convinced that the world was also moving cumulatively in the direction of a better moral order, and to make his point he described the public torture of the demented Damiens, whose misfortune it had been to attack the King of France with a pocket knife. Sarton gave us all the gruesome details: the platform in the public square, the huge crowd, the royal family with their children on a balcony, window space sold at a high premium, and then the stages of the torture, the man's hand plunged into a bowl of burning sulfur, time taken to allow him to recover when he fainted, and at last his limbs attached to four horses and torn from his body. "Gentlemen," Sarton said, "we have made progress." (Hitler would become Chancellor of Germany a year and a half later.)

I took Cuthbert to hear Sarton. "What a pleasure," he said

afterward, "to hear someone who knows what he is talking about." When Sarton finished on the last day of the term, we began to applaud. He picked up his books and papers and left the room and the building, and I saw him through the window beginning to go up the steps of Widener Library before we stopped clapping. We were telling each other how great he was.

Henderson and Sarton agreed that seldom if ever in the history of science does a creative idea burst upon the world fully formed. Great scientific discoveries grow step by step. Even in the life of the individual scientist, it is only after a long and often painful history that a point is finally clinched. I wrote a note about my own field:

> No new idea can be fully accepted at once, nor can it even be born at once. The crux of Harvey's discovery lay in demonstrating that all of the blood passed from the right to the left ventricle by way of the lungs and not through the septum. This was a difficult thing to discover because the macroscopic anatomy pointed to something else. Harvey's revision of the older notion, however, was preceded by the view of Servetus and Columbus that *some* of the blood passed in this way. When this idea had been tolerated for a necessary length of time, the further idea that all the blood so passed was possible.
>
> Similarly, it would no doubt be impossible to arrive at the belief that all behavior is reflex, if a preparatory step (that some behavior is reflex) had not long ago been taken.

The slow growth of a scientific doctrine was reassuring for two reasons: I could more easily imagine being a successful scientist if great ideas were not needed, and, since early steps in a discovery were simpler, they were easier to interpret as reflex behavior, traceable to circumstances in the life of the discoverer rather than to some mysterious, creative process in the mind.

IF THE ONLY IMPORTANT THING was the rate at which a rat got pieces of food, I could dispense with the tilting runway. The rat could simply open the door of a bin. I should still want a cumulative record, however, and some other way would have to be found to mark the kymograph. Ralph Gerbrands helped me build a recorder in which a ratchet on a shaft wound up the thread to the marker. A contact on the door of the food bin operated an electromagnet that turned the rachet one notch whenever a piece of food was removed.

If my rats were to get all their food in the apparatus, I could no longer go on using pearl barley. In a book on the breeding and care of the white rat I found a formula for a balanced diet: wheat, corn, flax seed, and bone meal, with a bit of salt, cooked in a double boiler. The mixture would have to be converted into pellets of uniform size, and I consulted a druggist, who showed me his pill machine. You laid a rope of a stiff paste across a fluted brass plate and put a similar plate over it, face down. As you rolled the top plate back and forth, the material was converted into small spheres. This was such a beautiful device that I remembered it many years later as the one I had used and actually published an account of using it, but when Ralph made one, the brass warped slightly when milled. I made a substitute of razor blades, which, when rolled over a rope of the mixture, scored it lightly so that, when dried, it could be broken into cylindrical pieces. The kind of grease gun used to lubricate bearings on automobiles extruded suitable ropes of the mixture and speeded production.

I built a food bin with an electric contact on the door and installed it in a double-walled box, with a similar bin for water alongside. I deprived a rat of food for twenty-four hours and then let it get its daily ration from the bin. The pellets were hard and took some time to eat, and a session lasted as long as two hours. With the behavior thus reduced to opening a door, I began to get more orderly results. The rat ate rapidly at first but then more and more slowly as time passed. The cumulative curves were smooth.

I showed some of them to Cuthbert Daniel, and he told me how to test them to see what kind of function I had turned up. When plotted on logarithmic paper, my records became straight lines. By the end of March I was writing to my parents:

> The greatest birthday present I got was some remarkable results from the data of my experiment. Crozier is quite worked up about it. It is a complicated business and deep in mathematics. In a word, I have demonstrated that the rate in which a rat eats food, over a period of two hours, is a square function of the time. In other words, what heretofore was supposed to be "free" behavior on the part of the rat is now shown to be just as much subject to natural laws as, for example, the rate of his pulse.

Crozier was indeed worked up. Orderly processes in the organism as a whole composed the field of General Physiology, and I had turned up a reproducible example. He was soon to give a talk at Rutgers and took a slide or two of my records with him, and later I reported to my parents that "what Crozier said about me at Rutgers stirred up a lot of comment." I also reported that he was sending me notes almost every day about things to be done, and that he wanted a couple of articles before summer.

I wrote a paper about the experiment and called it "On the Conditions of Elicitation of Certain Eating Reflexes." The title hinted at my theoretical position (I was studying *reflexes in the organism as a whole*), and my first sentence left no doubt: "The behavior of an intact organism differs from the reflex activity of a 'preparation' chiefly in the number of its independent variables." I presented records from two rats with superimposed curves for a power function and five records for each rat plotted on logarithmic coordinates. Boring and Crozier agreed that the paper should be published, and Crozier gave it to G. H. Parker, who sent it to the *Proceedings of the National Academy of Sciences*. It was received there in April and published in June. (I had given my university connection as "Psychological Laboratory, Boylston Hall, Harvard University," but the editor wrote to say that they did not publish addresses and would leave out "Boylston Hall." I replied that Boylston Hall was a special branch of the department—vastly exceeding my authority or the facts —and the address stayed in.)

I was still interested in general issues, and when Crozier asked me to talk to the General Physiology Colloquium, I did not talk about my experiments but about "Summation and Facilitation." I reported to my parents that the talk "was a great success, as only half of the people knew what I was talking about. The half that knew thought it was good."

With the psychologists I discussed the experiments—and I did so in an expansive way. Fred and I were riding our behavioristic hobby-horses at a reckless speed, and the Psychological Colloquium was still exciting. (It was also still uninhibited. A new student had arrived from the University of Kansas where he had studied with a Gestalt psychologist named Wheeler. He gave a paper which lasted an hour and a quarter, during which he must have used the words "structure," "function," "part," and "whole" at least a hundred times. Afterward, as the discussion grew to a close, I said that it had occurred to me that the function of a part without respect to a whole was masturbation. Boring jumped up. "Oh, if you're going to get dirty, I'm going home!" he said, and he laughed and left, as we all did with relief. When Boring saw me that evening at the annual reception at Professor Hocking's, he said "Skinner, your verbal threshold is very low.")

Troland had been scheduled to give a colloquium but had fallen ill, and Mac had asked me, on very short notice, to take his place. Troland's title was "The Location of the Will in the Brain," and I decided to keep it, except that I should ask what could possibly be located in a brain by way of a will. At the beginning of an experimental session, a rat eats rather rapidly, but, as the rate falls off, there are pauses between pellets of the order of a minute or two, during which the rat moves rather aimlessly about the box. A moment arrives when it "decides to eat another pellet and wills to do so," but why is it just the right moment to continue a smooth curve? Evidently the will is not free, and if it is not, is it necessary to talk about it at all? Magnus had discussed the postural reflexes which prepare a cat to pounce on a mouse: "The only thing the cat has to do is to decide: to jump or not to jump." In my experiment the only thing the rat had to do was to decide: to eat or not to eat. But the decision was made *for* the rat, and presumably for the cat, by some orderly physiological change.

ALTHOUGH THE CURVES I recorded were surprisingly smooth, they had occasional blemishes. Sometimes a rat would stop eating for as much as fifteen minutes. But when it began again, it ate at a higher rate and eventually got as many pellets as if it had not stopped. This recovery after a long delay was another process worth studying. Behind the door of the bin I put a small bellows which I could inflate to lock the door at some point during an experimental session. The rat would stop eating, of course, but as soon as it discovered that the door could be opened again, it began to eat at a higher rate, which it maintained until it was back on schedule.

I was studying "eating behavior," but I was not happy about "eating" as an adjective. "Ingestive" implied digestion and took in too much territory. I turned to the remnant of my Greek education at

Hamilton College and in my report to the psychological colloquium I suggested "phagous." Boring wrote me afterward: "I wish we could avoid *eating behavior*. It is potentially humorous." He supported "phagous" and was not disturbed by my fear that it would be easily confused with "vagus." I continued to use "eating."

I WAS STUDYING what Pavlov would call unconditioned reflexes, or at best the physiological process of ingestion, but I was interested in learning. Running around that tilting rectangular track was learned, but, like behavior in a maze, it was composed of too many "reflexes." Pushing open the door of a bin was also learned, but it was not a sample of behavior that would be easy to study. I needed a simpler response.

I bent a heavy wire into a square U and mounted it like a lever so that the crosspiece moved up and down. A spring held it up, but a rat could easily press it down. In doing so, it lowered a needle into a cup of mercury, closing a circuit to a food dispenser and a cumulative recorder. The conditioned response I proposed to study was "pressing the lever."

I needed a different kind of dispenser and made several models. One was a disk with a ring of holes around the edge turned by an electromagnet. Another was a vertical glass tube just large enough to take the pellets, with an escapement at the bottom. I installed one of the latter, together with a lever, in a double-walled box of Celotex. I found that when I added the response to the lever to the usual "eating reflexes," the shape of the ingestion curve did not change.

THE ANNOUNCEMENT OF A BOOK called *Reflex Action* by Franklin Fearing caught my attention, and I bought a copy. I was curious to see what the author was doing in my field. It was obvious at once that he did not share my enthusiasm, for the first page contained a quotation from C. J. Herrick to the effect that ". . . attention should be especially directed to the futility of attempting to derive intelligence and the higher mental faculties in general from reflexes, habits, or any other form of fixed or determinate behavior. . . . The nervous system is more than an aggregate of reflex arcs and life is more than reactions to stimuli." And the book concluded with the author's own opinion that "although we must proceed with the greatest caution, at least we may take hope that the sterility of faith that mind and behavior can be envisaged by number and measure has been exposed."

This was anathema, and I wrote a vitriolic review accusing Fearing of prejudice. He had cited the work of Sherrington, Magnus, and Pavlov as the "most important in determining the direction of theory and research in this century," but he had added Herrick and Child. "If the reader," I wrote, "is a little surprised to find the names of Herrick and Child grouped with those of Sherrington, Pavlov, and Magnus in this particular connection, he will be no less so in discovering that Dr. Fearing himself apparently does not regard the work of Child as worthy of a single word of description and refers to Herrick only in connection with anti-mechanist theory and other nonexperimental matters." I attacked the author's scholarship: "Unfortunately there is a curious garbling of the quotation from Descartes." I had been looking into the history of the reflex in Sir Michael Foster's *History of Physiology* and had gone to a first source by reading Descartes' *Traité de l'homme*. Fearing had used without acknowledgment some passages from Foster's translation of Descartes and had rejected others in favor of his own "less felicitous and again inexact" translation.

I was less splenetic in discussing the central issues. Fearing had attacked the "myth of the knee jerk as a simple spinal reflex," but I pointed out that Sherrington had repeatedly testified to the conceptual nature of the simple reflex, and that Fearing himself had quoted Watson to the effect that "the reflex arc is only a convenient abstraction in both physiology and behavior."

According to Fearing, a reflex was involuntary, unlearned, predictable, and uniform, and not conditioned by consciousness. In addition the term was "reserved for those neural arcs which did not involve the so-called higher or cortical centers." I pointed out that since four of these conditions excluded parts of the field of behavior, it was no wonder that the reflex seemed to be inadequate as an explanation. "The surviving condition of the definition is that of predictability and uniformity," and that, I contended, was really the point. A reflex was an observed "correlation" of stimulus and response.

I took the review to Crozier, who toned down a phrase or two (I suspect that he inserted "in this particular connection" after my comment on the contributions of Child and Herrick) and added his name as co-author because the paper needed more authority than my criticism of Miss Vicari. It was automatically published in the *Journal of General Psychology.*

"ON THE STRENGTH OF a nibble on my saxophone," as I wrote to my parents, I had bought that bicycle of which Fred had a twin, and when spring came we began to explore the countryside. My hay fever grew worse and Marjory Pratt suggested that I might be free of it on Monhegan, an island off the coast of Maine. I took the Bangor night boat to Rockland, a taxi to Thomaston, and the mailboat down the Georges River and out to the island. I stayed at the Island Inn, a large wooden structure overlooking the harbor. It was early in the season and there were only a few guests. With two of them, I talked shop. Warner Fyte, a philosopher from Princeton, had a house on the island, and he and his wife took their meals at the inn. A German philosopher came for a brief stay. He felt that I was simply restating Kant and urged me to soften the "ch" in *Mach.* My hay fever was no better, though another guest, a young woman osteopath, treated it by pressing very hard on the bridge of my nose.

A young man, Bob Reid, struck up an acquaintance one day as I was sitting on the wharf. He and his wife, Edie, were spending the summer on the island, and a Smith College classmate of his wife's was staying with them. The four of us spent a good deal of time together. We did some rather dangerous climbing on the eastern side, going halfway down the face of Whitehead, a precipitous headland, without benefit of rope or other equipment, heavy surf striking the rocks below.

I spent another part of the summer at the Marine Biological Laboratories at Woods Hole. Early that spring Crozier had driven me down to look the place over, and I had written to my family:

Crozier can get me a table in the laboratory for nothing (otherwise costing $75) and board will be cheap. I will be working on lobsters! Lobsters (and crabs) have a peculiar kind of nerve in their *claws. There is nothing like it in higher animals. It offers a chance to investigate a special condition (inhibition) which has been bothering physiologists for a long time.*

There was indeed something special about lobsters. Stimulating a certain nerve caused the claw to open or close depending upon the strength of the current. Unfortunately, the condition was still bothering physiologists when I returned to Cambridge.

Later in the summer I went home for two weeks and saw my old friend Dr. Fulton. (He had come to Boston in the fall of 1928 to be made a Fellow of the American College of Surgeons, and Doc and I had attended the wholly uninteresting event in Symphony Hall.) I told him about my research on eating and said that someone had noticed that a baby taking milk from a bottle would suck faster when the bottle was restored after a delay. He said there was a baby in the hospital under his care that I could use to check the point if I wished. I rigged up a clamp to hold a bottle straight above the head of the baby as it lay on its back and recorded how fast it drank by noting when the air space reached the graduations on the side of the bottle. In applying for a National Research Council Fellowship that fall I said, "I have obtained essentially the same curve from a 9-month-old baby," but "essentially the same" was a bit generous. It was obvious that the baby could suck much more efficiently when there was more air in the bottle, and I did not have time to construct a nipple and tube leading to an open dish from which the ease of flow would not change.

The journey from Cambridge to Scranton was time-consuming and unpleasant, but I dutifully went home two or three times a year. Letters were also a burden I continued to accept. I sent my parents all available tidbits about my success—what people said about my talks and the acceptance and publication of my papers. I do not remember any explicit commendation in return; I was left to assume that my parents were proud of me. Nevertheless I had to protect myself against their tendency to boast. When I first reported that I would have a paper published, I added, "Now don't rush down to the newspapers with this. A silly 'hometown' article might hurt me considerably if it happened to be picked up by the clipping bureaus and sent back to either Harvard or the Journal."

My mother and father understood very little of what I was doing, and I made almost no effort to explain. When, to fill out a page, I described my experiments, my mother would respond wistfully, "What is there to be accomplished if you succeed in them?" Once when I was home my father rather timidly asked, "Could you describe your work in simple terms—what you are getting at?" From his manner I thought he was going to ask me to speak to the Kiwanis Club, and I replied that, no, I could not. He said nothing more; but later I surmised, and still later was quite sure, that he simply wanted me to explain my work to *him*.

FRANKLIN FEARING'S BOOK led me to look further into the history of the reflex. It could be said to have begun with an accident. In the Royal Gardens in Paris and Versailles there were automata which simulated living things. Descartes described one of them in the *Traité de l'homme*. If one approached a bathing Diana, she would retreat among rose bushes, and if one tried to follow her, a Neptune would come forward threatening with his trident. The figures were moved by hydraulic pistons when plates in the paths were stepped on. (In Widener Library I found a treatise on the subject by an engineer of the period, Isaac de Caus.) The effect was entertaining because the figures responded to the world around them and therefore seemed alive, but Descartes was more than entertained. It occurred to him that nerves and muscles in the body might work in the same way, and he developed what was essentially a theory of reflex action.

I discovered that the Boston Medical Library, then on the Fenway, had a wonderful collection of original texts. It was often nearly deserted, and the librarian gave me a good deal of help. I began to treat the reflex on the model of Ernst Mach's *Science of Mechanics*, to which Henderson had drawn my attention. In Mach and in Henri Poincaré's *Science et méthode* I found early versions of what was beginning to be called operationism. The philosophers of the Vienna Circle, not yet dispersed by Hitler, were taking a rather similar line and calling it logical positivism, and Russell, who had introduced me to behaviorism, had been influenced by another, if renegade, Viennese, Ludwig Wittgenstein. Somewhere Russell had said that the term "reflex" in physiology had the same status as the term "force" in physics, and I knew what that meant because I had discussed P. W. Bridgman's *Logic of Modern Physics* with Cuthbert Daniel, who was working with Bridgman.

I began to write a long paper called "The Concept of the Reflex in the Description of Behavior." I reviewed the experimental work on reflexes from the middle of the seventeenth century down through Magnus and Pavlov. I argued, as I had done in reviewing Fearing's book, that the central fact was simply "the observed correlation of the activity of an effector (i.e., a response) with the observed forces affecting a receptor (i.e., a stimulus)."

> The negative characteristics . . . which describe the reflex as involuntary, unlearned, unconscious, or restricted to special neural paths have proceeded from unscientific presuppositions concerning the behavior of organisms. When Marshall Hall decapitated his famous newt, he pointed quite correctly to the reflex activity of the parts of the headless body, to the observed fact that movement followed, inevitably, the administration of specific stimuli. But his assumption that he had imprisoned in the head of the newt the source of another kind of movement was irrelevant and unsupported. The fact before him was a demonstrable necessity in the movement of the headless body; his failure to observe similar necessities in the movement of the intact organism was the accident of his time and of his capabilities.
>
> Tentatively, then, we may define a reflex as an observed correlation of stimulus and response. When we say, for example, that Robert Whytt discovered the pupillary reflex, we do not mean that he discovered either the contraction of the iris or the impingement of light upon the retina, but rather that he first stated the necessary relationship between these two events. So far as behavior is concerned, the pupillary reflex is nothing more than this relationship.

I was not sure of the scientific status of a "correlation" or, as I might better have said, a functional relation. Stimuli and responses had many different physical dimensions and could not be quantified in any very consistent way. I found some help in J. W. Mellor's *Higher Mathematics for Students of Chemistry and Physics,* a book Crozier had strongly recommended:

> Although the pressure of the aqueous vapour in any vessel containing water and steam is a function of the temperature, the actual *form* of

the expression or function showing this relation is not known. . . . The concept thus remains even though it is impossible to assign any rule for calculating the value of a function. In such cases the corresponding value of each variable can only be determined by actual observation and measurement.

Cuthbert, too, thought I was on solid ground: I could speak of a functional relation without specifying quantities.

My paper was in part an attack on mentalistic explanations of behavior. In the nineteenth century, for example, there were those who defended the "soul" of the spinal cord, the "*Rückenmarkseele*." It was also an attack on the misuse of physiology. The reflex arc was an anatomical structure, and early research was largely a matter of locating pathways by cutting away parts of the organism. Sherrington had done more than that by looking at relations between times of occurrence and magnitudes of stimulus and response, but he had called them the properties of the synapse, the point of contact between nerve cells. I argued that he had never seen a synapse in action and that the properties could be defined operationally by referring to behavior and environment without mentioning the nervous system.

I rejected Sherrington's physiology not because, like Jacques Loeb, I "resented the nervous system," but because I wanted a science of *behavior*. Early workers had "divided the behavior of an organism into parts by the expedient method of dividing the organism," but it was now time to trace the relation of the behavior of the *intact* organism to the environment. Some features (I called them laws) of a reflex involved "strength." If a weak stimulus could elicit a response, and if the response was vigorous and followed quickly, the reflex was called strong. If a strong stimulus was needed and only a feeble response followed, and then tardily, the reflex was called weak. Other "laws" involved changes in strength. For example, when a strong reflex was repeatedly elicited, it grew weak—in "reflex fatigue."

I argued that other changes in the behavior of the intact organism could be formulated in the same way:

Conditioning, "emotion," and "drive," so far as they concern behavior, are essentially [to be regarded] as changes in reflex strength,

68

and their quantitative investigation may be expected to lead to the determination of laws describing the course of such changes. . . . It is difficult to discover any aspect of the behavior of organisms that may not be described with a law of one or the other of these forms.

I had, of course, an experiment up my sleeve as an example. Orderly changes in reflex strength were what I had been studying in my work on rate of eating, with or without the "precurrent" reflex of pressing the lever. The only trouble was that rate of responding—my measure of strength—was not on Sherrington's list. In a true reflex, rate was no measure at all; it was determined by the rate of stimulation. In my experiments, however, it was a sensitive—indeed, a crucial—measure, a fact made especially clear by my use of a cumulative record, in which I could see at a glance how rate changed from moment to moment. Rate was also particularly appropriate in the analysis of behavior because it could be said to represent the probability that an organism would behave in a given way at a given time.

FRED AND CONNIE KELLER lived in an apartment at 2 Arlington Street. It had been built when families had live-in maids, and in a basement opening out on a rear court there were six or eight small bedrooms with two or three baths. They had been unused for years, but because of the Depression the management was preparing them for rental. Fred tipped me off and I got one of the first. They were unfurnished and there would be no services, but they were cheap, and I could save money even though I should have to buy a cot, a mattress, and a work table and chair. I made a small bookshelf in the Boylston Hall shop and kept my new fourteenth edition of the *Encyclopaedia Britannica* in the wooden box in which it came. I could park my bicycle in the basement. (Fred's had been stolen when he left it unlocked near Boylston Hall.)

I thought I deserved an easy chair, and the Italian proprietors of a nearby upholstery shop persuaded me to let them make one. They drove me to a factory where I chose a frame, which they would upholster with my choice of fabric. On the way back we were stopped by a burly Irishman who was directing traffic. My driver had started to cross an intersection without waiting for a sign, and he got a ticket.

As we started to drive on, it was discovered that no one had got the policeman's number, which was needed if the ticket was to be fixed. Would I please go over and note the number of the officer's badge? Since I did not approve of fixing tickets and had never conquered my fear of policemen, I demurred. But my companions were eloquent. It was *terribly* important! I surrendered and timidly approached the officer, who was back in his box directing traffic. I improvised something about my friends not being too familiar with the rules. "Then they'd better not be driving a car!" he shouted. I gave up and started to walk away, my mission unaccomplished, but he called after me, with a sneer, "Did you get the number?" That was too much, and I turned back and said, "No. What is it?" Whereupon he told me. The chair was comfortable enough, but it elicited unpleasant autonomic responses for weeks.

Another of those refurbished rooms on Arlington Street went to Marian Stevens, who had been a student of Fred's at Jackson College (associated with Tufts as Radcliffe was with Harvard) and was now enrolled for a master's degree in psychology at Radcliffe. Her family had lived in Needham for generations, and she spoke with a pure New England accent. (I still pronounced "aunt" like "ant," said "Hole-y-oke" for "Hol-yoke," and had not yet put the z-sound in "Quincy.") She was friendly, and we were soon doing some research together in Boylston Hall.

I WAS CONVINCED that the concept of the reflex embraced the whole field of psychology. I proposed to divide behavior into reflexes, devise measures of their strength, and then search the fields of conditioning, drive, and emotion for the variables of which that strength was a function. I thought it was a suitable project for a Ph.D. thesis, and when I ran into Beebe-Center one day I told him what I proposed to do. He stared at me for a moment and then said, "Who do you think you are? Helmholtz?" (In another field he would have said, "Einstein?") He insisted that I had more than I needed for a thesis and should submit one at once.

I was not sure. Hallowell Davis had said, "You must remember that you will be known for a number of years for what you are doing now," and the project I had in mind was the kind of thing I hoped to be known for. It was not the *Nova Principia Orbis Terrarum* I had begun to write in high school, but it was on the same scale. Nevertheless, Beebe-Center was probably right; I should get my degree. I could complete a larger work later.

Beebe-Center thought my paper on the concept of the reflex, with some examples from my research on ingestion, should be enough, and I soon found myself in possession of a thesis most of which I had not known I was writing. I had not, however, dashed it off. The paper was the first serious work I had done since I had abandoned literature, and I had not abandoned my old concern for style. Now that I had, or so I thought, something to say, I began to look hard again at expository writing. I gave myself instructions:

> Avoid qualifying words, phrases and clauses, especially those with a diminutive effect: Somewhat, rather, slight, almost a, little, but a ——, mere, a bit (adv.).
>
> Avoid gratuitous concessions especially if attempted to gain credit. See Bergson.
>
> Avoid colloquial idioms. It was an old fetish.
>
> Avoid superlatives. "Best described." "Great change."
>
> Use more pronouns, giving the reader credit for greater sustaining power.
>
> Words and phrases to avoid: all kinds of, all sorts of, a good deal, a great deal, thus, indeed, a considerable distance, some (as a word alone or in combination), somewhat, something, etc., shall we say, let us say, etc.
>
> Use metaphors only when the thought demands them and never for effect.
>
> Avoid exclamation points. They grow cold.

My intentions were good but a few touches of fine writing are still to be found in the paper. "A circumstance of its development," "in despite of the historical usage," "in point of satisfaction," "in respect of," and "according as" were not my standard usage.

The second part of my thesis was on hunger as a drive. I worked backward from the peristalsis of the alimentary tract to swallowing, chewing, seizing food that touched the lips (the reflex nature of which Magnus had shown in a "thalamic" rabbit), and the approach to food, the last step "raising the basic problem of variability." How can we call picking up and eating a piece of food reflex if it does not always happen when food is available? The answer, I thought, lay in accounting for the variability. If the change in strength is orderly, we may "assert the necessity of the reflex relationship," as Sherrington asserted it in spite of such a change as reflex fatigue.

ON ALL THESES SUBMITTED to the department "in partial fulfillment of the requirements for the degree of doctor of philosophy" Boring had the last word—and usually a great many words before that. He was said to have insisted upon so many revisions in some theses that his name should have appeared as co-author. He was a punctilious stylist. (Years later, when I had joined the department, I would often see him leave the luncheon table and return carrying *Webster's New International Dictionary* to settle a point.) He was also committed to a logic and a scientific method that were quite rigorous.

I could expect that the first part of my thesis would run into trouble. More than half of it was historical, and Boring was now the established historian of psychology. Another part was theory, and that was also his field. His report fulfilled my expectations. He had nothing to say about my style: "Only rarely (less than half a dozen times) did I pause over stylistic, quasi-grammatical matters, and I let them all pass without notation, too trivial and too much a matter of opinion for argument" (though later, when I defended the thesis against his criticism, he turned my style against me: "You seem to me to suffer from your versatility and glibness, and this characteristic combined with your most excellent English style tends to make fallacies very subtle"). But as to my central argument, he felt that I was misusing history:

> You are making an argument for keeping the word *reflex* and giving it a new, broader, and relatively strange meaning. No one would guess this to be your goal as you start in, and you yourself may not think of it in that way. Perhaps I needed the introductory paragraph, which you did not furnish, but the impression grew upon me that you were being a little disingenuous, that you were making a controversial argument under the guise of a factual description—as Titchener used to do.

Two single-spaced pages later:

> I fear that you may be distorting history. (This is also my criticism of Titchener. His method was to make a fine show of consulting all the authorities—modern generally, not ancient—killing off those that did not suit him, and then seeming to find just what he always had been wanting. Thus he would get what he wanted with the responsibility put on others.)

And one page later:

> You have given a very broad, strange, almost bizarre meaning to the word *reflex*. You have taken it away from the constrained anatomical reflex-arc meaning, and you have equated it to the concept of the psychological fact-as-relational-correlation which already has terms for itself. What is the use? To wrench the word from its well-entrenched meaning, you need more than a paper; you need propaganda and a school. And if you succeeded you would have merely an equivalent for Gestalt with a special epistemology back of it. Skinner's school of reflexes then would have a history like Köhler's school of Gestalt, and at the end I'd be saying of you as I say of Köhler, "It's only a matter of terminology, there is nothing new."

Then followed an outline of what Boring thought I should say, below which I immediately penciled "Jamais de la vie!!!"

I submitted the thesis again essentially unchanged, with a note containing a couplet from Thomas Hood's "Bridge of Sighs":

> Owning her weakness, her evil behaviour,
> And leaving with meekness her sins to her Saviour.

Boring again advised a complete revision and sent an outline. I should leave out history altogether and—as an afterthought—

> I should think you would have to go on to discuss such things as:
> Consciousness vs. response.
> Correlation vs. cause; and thus the problem of continuity, thus anatomical continuity.
> Advantages and disadvantages of entity vs. construct in the reflex, in the synapse.

Relation of reflex to habituations; cf. reaction experiment, artificial reflex,

Phenomena that have been called instinct

And probably half a dozen other things that have not yet occurred to me because I have not been writing the paper.

Yours,

EGB

When I stuck to my guns, he gave up and wrote to say that he
had asked the chairman of the department to appoint a committee,
adding, "I have especially asked to be left off since I have already
expressed myself so positively about it to you." The chairman appointed Pratt, Troland, and Crozier. I hired a professional typist and
took a final draft, simply as a box full of loose pages, to Carroll Pratt.
He tactfully suggested that it would be nice if I bought a binder at the
Coop, and I did so.

The committee approved the thesis and two examinations were
scheduled. The first would cover "Fundamental Concepts," "Animal
Behavior," and "Psychology and the Nervous System," and my ex-
aminers would be Boring, Crozier, and Upton, respectively. Boring
on Fundamental Concepts was the one I feared. I wrote to Percy
Saunders:

*I am coming up for my degree this month. There may be a good deal
of trouble about it, as I have taken a very active part in opposing the
department on several systematic issues. Either way, the outcome is
going to be interesting. . . . I have spent a very busy and profitable two
years and a half. Good experimental results and some exhilarating
theorizing. . . . As ever (but infinitely more happy). . . .*

Fred

I was nevertheless uneasy. I reread Boring's *History* and a book
or two in the Titchenerian tradition. Gordon Allport had joined the
department and would no doubt attend the examinations. What
would *he* ask me? And when Mac took me aside and said he had
heard that the department was out to get me because I had gone over
to Crozier, I put out a peace feeler. An operational analysis of psychological terms was needed, and it seemed to me that it called for
little more than a rather mechanical application of a few principles.

Could I not serve psychology better by performing such an analysis than by preparing myself for a doctoral examination? I took the question to Beebe-Center. Would the department excuse me from anything more than the most perfunctory examination if I prepared an operational analysis of half a dozen key terms from subjective psychology? Beebe-Center was so astonished by my proposal that I did not wait for his answer.

As the day of the examination approached I spent a good deal of time in my room on Arlington Street. I played and replayed a record of Marlene Dietrich singing two songs from *Der Blaue Engel*, a movie I had seen at the Fine Arts Theatre in Boston, and in the bathtub one day I was alarmed when I could not tell whether water dripping on my toe was hot or cold.

As it turned out, the examinations were plain sailing. I struggled through Fundamental Concepts with Boring, and Crozier and Upton gave me no trouble. I was embarrassed only once. Allport asked me, "What are some of the objections to behaviorism?" and I could not think of a single one. In my second examination, in defense of my thesis, Crozier was there again and the atmosphere was warm and helpful. The degree was officially granted at the June commencement but it never occurred to me to attend, and I was eventually asked to drop by the Dean's office to pick up my sheepskin.

The theoretical half of my thesis was published that year as "The Concept of the Reflex in the Description of Behavior." (All my early papers were published quickly. Clark University supported several journals, and Carl Murchison, the editor, accepted almost anything submitted by a long list of associates, among whom Crozier was one of the more active.) I sent a reprint to my parents with a letter explaining that "soul" (as in the soul of the spinal cord) was an older synonym of "mind."

Having passed my examinations I was no longer a graduate student, but I had been given a Walker Fellowship for the whole year and it was now only January. Fortunately no one objected to my continuing to receive payments or to go on working in Boylston Hall. I was hoping to get support for a postdoctoral year. The psychologists would recommend me for a Sheldon Fellowship, but the stipend ($1500) had to be spent abroad. I wanted to go on with my research, and Crozier had urged me to apply for a fellowship from the

National Research Council. I would not hear the result for some time, and Boring wrote:

> This matter of the Sheldon needs to be cleared up at once. . . . The department feels that it ought to ask you to say now whether you would accept the Sheldon if the N.R.C. fails in February. Can you answer this question immediately? . . . I am not of course asking for a literal promise, but merely for a prediction made in gentlemanly good faith.

The National Research Council fellowship came through, and Harvard appointed me Research Fellow in General Physiology for the year.

I WAS STILL SEEING the Daniels, and an evening with them was not always "deep in mathematics." At Carroll and Marjory Pratt's there were still music and fun with the children. I had even ventured to suggest playing four hands with Marjory, though as a pianist she, like Carroll, was out of my class. She told me later that it was the most onerous demand I ever made upon her.

I was also seeing more of Hal and Pauline Davis. I borrowed a small camera from the department and took some movies of their children. For Christmas presents I used the woodworking facilities in Boylston Hall to make two puppets. They were Pinocchios, about two feet tall, of shellacked pine, fully jointed. They could be manipulated in realistic ways with standard controls. A Pinocchio could bend over, pick up a balloon, toss it in the air, and kick it. (Before taking them to the children, I tried them on another species. In the animal room about a dozen cats were living in a large space enclosed by chicken wire. The wire ran all the way to the ceiling, which was at least fifteen feet high. When I came into the room with the two Pinocchios walking beside me, all the cats scrambled up the chicken wire to the very top. I doubt that they would have done so if I had come in with two small children, and I have often wondered just what feature of the phylogeny of cats I had hit upon.)

I saw a good deal of Fred outside the laboratory. We usually had lunch together at a small restaurant just off Massachusetts Avenue and occasionally dined together at the Athens-Olympia in Boston, where, in those Prohibition days, one could buy a coffee-cupful of red wine for a dollar. At 2 Arlington Street we made our own beer and, in an experimental spirit, added different, carefully measured quantities of sugar to the bottles before capping and labeling them.

We played (and sang!) those Marlene Dietrich songs and listened to a set of instructional French records that I had picked up (*Bonjour, Mme. Gobinet, comme il y a longtemps que je ne vous ai pas vue!*).

One day we cycled to Providence, Rhode Island—a distance of about fifty miles—to visit the Department of Psychology at Brown University. On the way back the next day we were growing rather tired when Fred rode off a rough edge of the road and nearly fell under a passing car. We were badly frightened and professionally interested to find that we were revitalized by the adrenaline we secreted.

I HAD GIVEN MY SQUIRRELS a squirrel cage in return for locking them up in their small prison, and when I moved them into more space in Boylston Hall the cage went along. From that article by Curt Richter in the *Quarterly Review of Biology* I had learned that spontaneous activity was a serious subject. Given free access to a wheel, Richter's rats, like my squirrels, went for a number of runs each day. Since they also ate several times a day when given free access to food, I decided to see whether spontaneous activity gave a satiation curve.

I did not like the standard laboratory running wheel. It was rather heavy, and when a rat stopped running, it swung back and forth like a pendulum. The wheel was also so small that the rat ran downhill with one pair of legs and uphill with the other. I built a much larger but lighter wheel, of aluminum screen on aluminum hoops with bicycle spokes. When a bit of friction was applied to a brake drum, the rat ran on an almost flat surface and could stop without swinging. By changing the friction, I could change the slight grade at which it ran. Revolutions of the wheel wound up a thread to a cumulative recorder.

A rat that was free to run at any time ran intermittently, as Richter had reported, and, as I could now add, at a constant speed. When I fed it only once a day and it became used to the schedule, it ran for several hours just before feeding time and, except for a brief warm-up, also at a constant speed. But when I let it run only once a day, as I had let it eat in my earlier experiment, the cumulative curve showed a rather similar decline in rate. Spontaneous running seemed to obey the same law as eating. In a paper reporting my results I made it clear that I was still interested only in behavior: "We need not go beyond a quantitative description . . . of strength as a function of some such independent variable as time," and I added, "The identification of a 'physiological correlate,' which varies in the same way, may yield supplementary information but it is not essential to the solution, so far as the description of behavior is concerned."

It was a natural step to make food contingent upon running, and I did so with Marian Stevens's help. A pellet of food fell into a dish alongside the wheel whenever the rat ran sixty feet. The rat was active from dusk to dawn, running about a mile at a time with rest periods of twenty or thirty minutes. We slowly increased the distance required for each pellet, until the rat was putting out more energy than it got from the food. It lost weight but continued to run, in shorter bursts, at a lower overall rate and during the day as well as at night.

A year or two later I also recorded some satiation curves for drinking. A drop of water fell onto an inverted watch crystal whenever a lever was pressed. Some of the curves looked like those for eating and running; the rat started at a high rate and gradually slowed down. At times, however, it pressed at a fairly steady rate until satiated and then stopped.

OTHER EXPERIMENTS WERE under way in Boylston Hall that year. Kelly Upton was using a conditioned reflex to see how exposure to a very loud tone of a given pitch damaged the ear. In some unused attic space he put several guinea pigs near a loudspeaker which emitted an earsplitting tone twenty-four hours a day. A window was left open to freshen the air, and people living across Massachusetts Avenue complained of damage not to their ears but to their peace of mind.

A student of Harry Murray's, Dave Wheeler, was studying crime and punishment. A male rat was allowed to approach a female in heat and at the very moment of copulation a trap door was sprung and both rats fell into ice water. It was customary for a professor to explain to the faculty the doctoral work he was sponsoring, and when Murray reported this experiment, Kittredge, the snowy-bearded Professor of English Literature, rose and protested: "But gentlemen, that's no *crime!*"

I did a rather casual experiment with the so-called double-alternation maze. It has the plan of two adjacent city blocks. A rat runs down the street between them, takes two turns around the left-hand block and then two around the right, and is rewarded. It tends to turn too soon to the right, presumably because a right turn is rewarded in the end. The usual pattern is one turn to the left and three to the right. On the assumption that a rat might need a great many trials, I built a maze which automatically reinforced the correct pattern. The rat got all its food by operating it around the clock. It remained very active but never learned the correct pattern.

Fred had chosen the double-alternation maze for his doctoral dissertation, and he had a better idea. He would use a very long maze, in which the rat would have run very different distances when it made the crucial choice between turning right or left. One of the abandoned storerooms on the second floor of Boylston Hall was big enough for a maze thirty feet long.

It was a risky experiment for a doctoral thesis. To avoid contaminating one trial with stimulation from another, Fred thought it best to have only one trial a day; the experiment would therefore take a long time. Discovering that rats could *not* learn such a maze would not be a great contribution to knowledge, and there would be no time to do anything else for a degree that spring.

Eventually Fred's rats began to make successful runs. An occasional success could be due to chance, but three successful runs in a row might be taken to show mastery. As more successful runs were made, we both grew tense. Fred would take a rat down the long flight of stairs to the second floor and enter his improvised laboratory, while I sat on the top stair and waited. A few minutes later he would come out, look up at me, and either nod or shake his head. When a rat had made two successful runs in a row, the tension on the third day was almost unbearable, because a bad run would mean starting again on another string. There were many disconsolate shakes of the head, but the day came when Fred emerged from his laboratory, looked up the stairs, and nodded with a broad smile. Three successful runs in a row!

His other rats eventually solved the problem, too. He would get his degree and would soon be off to teach at Colgate.

THAT SPRING BORING CANCELED the last meeting of his course and gave a lecture to answer the behaviorists. Fred and I were only graduate students, but we had kept our position steadily at the center of attention in Emerson Hall. Possibly we had done so not only because our cause was just, but because we worked well together. There was a complementary difference in our styles. Fred was a cautious thinker, skeptical of his own ideas as well as of those of others. He spoke quietly, often hesitantly. I once heard him describe my very different style in this way: "Burrhus says a thing in its most extreme form and takes some of it back if he has to."

There were many things about behaviorism that I would never take back. Thanks to Fred I was now so much the complete behaviorist that I was shocked when people I admired used mentalistic terms. When Percy Saunders came to Cambridge, I brought him to Boylston Hall. Watching one of my squirrels running in the squirrel cage, he chuckled and said, "He likes that," and I was shaken. Once I was talking with Hallowell Davis about the Burma Shave roadside advertisements, humorous verses painted on a series of five or six small signs spaced far enough apart to be easily read. We agreed that they could be a dangerous distraction. "They hold the attention too long," said Hal, to my dismay. "Attention" was too close to the psychology of Titchener and Boring.

I had trouble with my own speech, catching myself as I started to say "mind" or "think," like an atheist who finds himself saying "Thank God." I began a note: "A man smoking does not feel his desire to smoke until . . ." and then crossed out "feel" and put in "mention," though it was not what I had started to say. It took me a long time to realize that in using the vernacular I was no more a traitor to my science than the astronomer who comments on a beautiful sunset knowing full well that the sun does not "set."

BECAUSE THE RUNNING-WHEEL experiment and my unsuccessful solution of the double-alternation problem were not time-consuming,

I devoted much of that term to theoretical issues. I read further in the literature of the reflex. I discovered the library of the Museum of Comparative Zoology and went systematically through a number of journals, such as the *Journal of Physiology*, in search of relevant material, making notes on three-by-five-inch cards. My thesis had by no means covered all the terms needing operational definitions. "Inhibition" was one, and "facilitation," a reciprocal term, another. They were used with several different meanings. What were the actual facts, and could they be described in other ways? "Prepotency" seemed to refer pretty directly to an observed effect.

If I had never heard of Pavlov, Magnus, or Sherrington, I should have seen that my basic fact was the *rate* at which an organism engaged in a particular kind of behavior, but because of my exposure to reflex theory I wanted rate to be a measure of reflex strength. When late in the spring I wrote a paper expanding the second part of my thesis, I called it "Drive and Reflex Strength" and kept as close to Sherrington as possible. "The strength of a reflex," I said, "is given by the value of its threshold, the ratio of the values of its stimulus and response, the duration of its latency, the amount of its after-discharge, and so on." I probably did not mean to include rate under "and so on," and I tried to make a case for it as a joint product of the other measures. If one response could be regarded as the stimulus for another, then how quickly the other followed should depend upon its threshold and latency, as well as upon the after-discharge and refractory phase of the former response. But the *lever* was the stimulus, not the preceding response. I also appealed to an undefined something that "facilitated a response or enabled it to override 'inhibiting influences.'"

Fortunately, my commitment to operationism saved the main point of the paper: An organism was not *driven* by hunger or thirst. A drive was not a force. I would stick with my observations, as Bridgman had done with the concept of force in physics. "The problem of hunger presents itself . . . as a variation in the strength of certain reflexes, a variation which ordinarily appears haphazard." It could be solved by finding some condition (a "third variable" in the terminology of my thesis) of which the variation was a function. In my experiment, how fast an animal ate depended upon how long it had been eating.

The fact that "drive" seemed to refer to a thing was a verbal accident. The concept had no experimental usefulness. "That there are physiological conditions correlated with all aspects of behavior no one will be likely to question," and the present result no doubt had physiological significance, but no physiological cause of the variation in strength had been demonstrated. Significantly, I added: "The same criticism may, of course, be applied to the concept of reflex strength, if that term is taken beyond the simple operational definition that we have given it."

That summer I wrote a second paper in which I reported that rats produce a similar curve when pressing a lever to get pellets. Again, though I talked about rate, I said that "a given rate is determined by the refractory phase of the reflex initiating the behavior."

SOMEONE HAD TOLD ME that no one suffered from hay fever in Franconia, New Hampshire, and early that summer I spent two weeks there in a small inn. The season had not yet opened and I was the only guest. The proprietor's wife, afraid that I might complain of loneliness, fed me too much. A great fire was laid for me every evening in the lounge. An old square piano was badly out of tune. I have never been able to memorize music, but there were two or three popular songs on the piano which in desperation I played again and again, as I might touch a sore tooth.

I busied myself in miscellaneous ways. The proprietor had put in a small golf course, the greens of which needed watering. A small stream ran through the course, and I designed a waterwheel that could have sent a trickle of water to each green during the night. I did not bring it to the proprietor's attention. A son in his early teens was unhappy, and his mother asked me, as a psychologist, what I would suggest. Her husband owned a lumber mill not far from the inn, and remembering my early years, I suggested that they give the boy the material needed to build a small shack. She was afraid her husband would find my proposal extravagant.

One day I walked back and forth between two telephone poles, at different speeds but in natural strides, and timed myself and counted steps. I worked out a theory of the leg as a pendulum. On another day the proprietor drove me to the foot of Mt. Lafayette, where he would return for me in a few hours. I climbed and scrambled to the top in what I later found was nearly record time.

I had brought only two books with me, and I read them slowly and with fascination. One was Edward F. Dakin's *Mrs. Eddy, the Biography of a Virginal Mind.* It was something of an exposé, and of a religious figure at that, but I found myself on the side of that lonely, courageous, and eventually triumphant old woman. The other was Emile Meyerson's *Identity and Reality*, and sitting alone before that roaring fire on chilly evenings, I read it and wrote in the margins. I did not try to follow Meyerson's efforts to "graft identity onto reality," but I found phrases, sentences, and paragraphs that were reassuring and useful, not only in supporting a science of behavior but also in showing "the reflex nature of scientific activity." Nature was orderly. Science was, as Poincaré put it, a rule of action that succeeds. "Where our ancestors saw only miracles, eluding prevision, we observe more and more the effect of exact laws."

Science had stopped assigning mental causes to physical events, and Meyerson cited as an example of the older principle the sentence "It is strange to suppose that a body leaves its position without seeking another." Unfortunately, he himself made the same mistake in speaking of behavior: "The dog to whom I throw a piece of meat knows how to catch it in the air; this is because he knows in advance the trajectory that this body will describe in falling. It appears, without doubt, to him no less than to us, as a way of behaving, peculiar to the object thrown under certain circumstances—that is, as a law. Goethe has said: 'In the beginning there was action.' " Action (behavior) yes, but was it meaningful to say that the dog catches the meat because he knows about its trajectory if our only information about his knowledge is the fact that he catches it? Was not the behavior of catching it the very thing we meant by "knowing"?

When I returned from that lonely vigil, I found that Edward C. Tolman was teaching summer school at Harvard. The class was small and he handled it like a seminar. I went to all the meetings as if I were registered and talked for more than a fair share of the time. Two of his former students, Merle Elliott and Howard Gilhousen, had recently become instructors at Harvard, and we all spent a lot of time together. Tolman's *Purposive Behavior in Animals and Men* was in press, but he made no use of it in the course, nor did we talk about it outside. The same could not be said for my thesis, which was also in press, for we argued at length about reflexes and drives. (Kurt Koffka, the Gestalt psychologist, was also teaching that summer, but I caught only one glimpse of him, confronting his class with a fierce hypnotic stare.)

That summer a professor at the Law School wrote to "Messrs. Skinner" in Scranton, asking where he could get a copy of my *Digest of Decisions of the Anthracite Board of Conciliation*. Less than four years had passed since I had fought off sleep while writing it.

John and Katherine Hutchens were vacationing at Provincetown and I spent a few days with them. We got sunburned on the almost deserted beaches, and a young Portuguese fisherman took us out in a sailboat on a very rough sea. I suggested to Hutch that we write a play about Mary Baker Eddy, ending with her dramatic confrontation with the press after the *New York World* had claimed that a friend was taking her place on her daily drive and that she herself was seriously ill or dead.

THAT FALL, with Fred gone, I gave up my converted maid's room in the basement of 2 Arlington Street. My fellowship made me reasonably affluent, and I rented a one-room Murphy-bed apartment at 85 Prescott Street and hired a cleaning woman to come in once a week. I bought kitchenware and dishes and began to get my evening meals, wrapping vegetables in sheets of "Patapar" so that two or more could be boiled in one pot without mixing flavors. I moved beyond home-brewed beer and began to buy casks of wine-grape juice from California. (Instructions were supplied in the form of warnings. "Caution: If allowed to stand in warm place for about a month and skimmed occasionally may become alcoholic.")

The apartment paid a psychological dividend. For some time I had been interested in "paradoxical color." I had made a Benham's top—a white disk with black arcs which, when spun, showed faintly colored bands. I had also made a box to demonstrate binocular color fusion; you looked through a reddish glass with one eye and a greenish one with the other and you could see a white surface as white. The bathroom floor in my apartment was made of hexagonal white tiles, and one day I discovered that in a dim light they appeared faintly colored. I could not pin down the color of any one tile but the colors were certainly there—a purplish red, a yellow, and a blue-green.

I made a plate to demonstrate the effect. Since it was hard to draw hexagons, I settled for closely packed white disks with black areas between them. I tried the plate on Selig Hecht, a friend of Crozier's, who was a specialist in the chemistry of vision. We had studied his work on the response to light of the siphon of the clam. I met him one day in a fairly dark hallway in the biology building and showed him my disks. He looked at them for rather a long time, until I began to worry, but finally he exclaimed, "Oh, there they are!"

I thought I had a plausible explanation. There are three or more elements in the retina which respond to different wavelengths of light, and white light is seen as white because it excites a particular mixture. At low illuminations, only a few of the elements are excited by one tile and the mixture needed for white cannot be composed. The actual mixture should take the color of the dominant element. (Why the whole tile should take on the color given by the elements distributed over it, I could not say.)

I published a note and sent a reprint to Don Purdy, a former student of Troland's. He wrote, "Your discovery of the funny colors was anticipated, I am told, by one R. M. Ogden at Cornell, but he never published anything about it, and now will probably be annoyed."

THE NEW BIOLOGY BUILDING was five stories high and shaped like a shallow U, with a small Divinity School dormitory in its lap. A frieze of animals was carved into its brick walls and two great bronze rhinoceroses guarded the main entrance. The building was not without its imperfections. The contractor had failed to put a waterproofing layer in the walls, and for a year the building rang with the rat-a-tat-tat of air hammers drilling out the mortar between the bricks so that waterproofing could be added. The cinderblocks with which the hallways were lined erupted, and every morning a few cone-shaped fragments were swept up from the floors.

None of this dampened the excitement of a department that had escaped from the basement of the Museum of Comparative Zoology into vast reaches of space. I was a mere Research Fellow but I was given an office on the second floor and a special suite of rooms two floors underground which were practically soundproof. A few months later in applying for a renewal of my NRC Fellowship I described my laboratory:

> I have constructed four identical sets of apparatus, each of which consists of the following: (1) a small sound-proofed box built of felt and "Arborite," containing (2) a problem box; (3) an automatic release cage; (4) a food magazine; (5) a circuit breaker which automatically eliminates superfluous contacts made at the problem box; and (6) a rate recorder. The four sets are assembled in a double compartment sound-proofed room. Suitable ventilation has been arranged for the room and boxes.

The rate recorder included a gang of four drums driven by a Telechron motor—one of Ralph's more beautiful pieces of equipment, much more reliable than the old kymographs.

The circuit breaker was a version of one I had used to hold the circuit open until the door to the bin of food had been closed for at least a second (when, presumably, the rat was eating). Kelly Upton had suggested that a wire dipping into a cup of mercury would have the same effect, and the drawing in my first report on lever pressing shows one in place. I continued to use the circuit breaker as an additional safeguard "to avoid superfluous contacts due to the inexpertness of the rat's manipulation of the lever." No doubt there was an effect on my early results. I did not record or reinforce a response if it followed another within a second or two. The effect could not have been great in experiments on ingestion or pressing a lever when every response was reinforced, but some of the more rapid responses in extinction may not have been recorded.

The new model had an effect on my health. When the rat pressed the lever, a small horizontal disk began to rotate and a wire rose from a mercury cup, breaking the circuit from the lever. When the disk returned to its home position a second or two later, it forced the wire back into the mercury. Kelly had seen such contacts on metronomes used to produce rhythmic pulses, the mercury not seriously interfering with the movement of the arm. They were safe because the current was weak, but in my apparatus a small wisp of vapor rose from the cup every time the circuit broke, and in some of my experiments four rats were pressing levers at a fairly high rate.

While running an experiment I sat within two feet of this possibly lethal device, and it was not long before my hair began to fall out. At Woods Hole I had joined a consumers' organization, and one of its publications recommended hexylresorcinol for falling hair. I bought some and gave it a scientific test. Every morning I massaged my scalp over the washbowl and carefully counted the number of hairs that had grown weak enough during the night to break off. I plotted a curve and found to my dismay that the hexylresorcinol was having no effect. On the contrary, the loss was increasing at an alarming rate.

I went to a dermatologist. He immediately asked whether I was in chemistry, but I did not think to tell him about the mercury cups. He prescribed a rather complex lotion to be applied to my hair whenever I washed it. Curiously enough it contained bichloride of mercury. My hair continued to fall out until I changed my apparatus for other reasons.

IN MY EXPERIMENTS on rate of eating I had added pressing a lever as a new "initial reflex," but I had not paid much attention to how my rats learned to press it. My main interest was conditioning, however, and I now tackled it head on. I would apply the techniques I had developed for the study of eating to a much more important process. I was recapitulating Pavlov's history, for he had also studied ingestion before moving on to conditioned reflexes.

My experimental arrangement was not unlike the famous problem box of Edward L. Thorndike. In a series of lectures at Harvard in the spring of 1896 the British philosopher and biologist C. Lloyd Morgan had reported how a dog unlatched a gate to escape from an enclosure and how a young chicken pecked at a spot to tip over a wall of its cage. Thorndike is said to have attended the lectures. In any case, he began to study similar behavior. He put a cat in a slatted box from which it could escape by turning a latch. He found that it escaped more and more quickly as unsuccessful behavior dropped out. By plotting the times taken to escape in a series of trials, he constructed a "learning curve." He called the principle the "Law of

Effect." He spoke of the "stamping in" of successful behavior, but his curves were produced by the "stamping out" of unsuccessful, and psychologists began to call the process "trial and *error* learning."

I had arrived at my "repeating problem box" (I used the term for the lever and dispenser only, rather than for the whole apparatus) by a different route, and it led to a different result. I had learned from Pavlov how important it was to control conditions, and I made every effort to avoid disturbing my rat. I put it in the Arborite box for several hours so that it became accustomed to its new environment, and I operated the food dispenser until it was no longer disturbed by the noise and would eat as soon as a pellet dropped. In order to give it time to recover from being handled, I put it first into the "automatic release cage" mentioned in that application and quietly released it long after the box had been closed. I did all this while the lever was resting in its lowest position and could not be moved. When at last the rat found it in a slightly higher position and pressed it, the delivery of food was for the first time contingent on the response.

Because of these careful preparations, two of the four rats in my first experiment began to respond at a high rate as soon as a first response was followed by the delivery of food. In a paper on the experiment I reported that *"the greater part of the change with which we are concerned takes place practically instantaneously upon the first occurrence of the [response→food sequence]."* True, a third rat reached a high rate only after a second response and the fourth only after a fifth, but these were not serious exceptions. I had not been able to eliminate the possibly disturbing effect of the first movement of the lever, and it was also conceivable that some depressions were incidental to other behavior (for example, the lever might be struck by the rat's heavy tail as it explored the ceiling of the box). In carefully controlling my conditions I had eliminated almost all the unsuccessful behavior in Thorndike's "learning curve" *before conditioning took place*. There was nothing to be "stamped out." The successful response did not merely survive; it was conspicuously strengthened. So was the successful response in Thorndike's experiment, but the evidence was not to be found in his "learning curve."

The speed with which the behavior changed was surprising. Pavlov's "all-time record holder" was said to have needed seven reinforcements before making a conditioned response, and Pavlovian conditioning had been criticized as too slow to explain most learning in daily life. My rats learned to press the lever in one trial, and no learning could be faster than that. (I noted, with a touch of regret, that because the change was so quick I could not record a learning curve. But "it should not be difficult," I said, "with some suitable change in conditions, to retard the process.")

My protocols show some of the difficulties of working with a new procedure and a new apparatus. I lost a record when "pointer did not write." Friction in the slider carrying the marker produced "a wavy effect in the record." A rat that mysteriously left food uneaten "probably got food from neighboring [living] cage or was ill." These were problems to be solved, of course, but they did not raise any question about my results when things went well. I had apparently found a process of conditioning that was different from Pavlov's and much more like most learning in daily life.

I was soon writing to Fred that I had a new theory of conditioning. He had not yet looked too closely at my research, and in his first letter from Colgate early in October he wrote:

> The only thing that bothered me about your very welcome and newsy letter was that talk about a brand new theory of learning. In about a week's time I'm going to work on the conditioned reflex with my seventy-odd students in Social [Psychology] and I had just about concluded that the whole story could be told with the w.k. [well-known?] principle without benefit of clergy, etc. I had concluded also that maze-behavior was maze-behavior and, like the lily, nothing more. Now I'm going to look over the situation again while I await the rough draft of your notion; so please get busy—I don't want to turn "culture" and "culture patterns" into conditioned reflexes unless I do it advisedly.

I replied:

> About the new theory of learning. Don't worry. The principle of conditioning is still good with me. This is simply an interpretation of the learning curve. It has at least two novel points: (1) It assumes, though not necessarily, that the act of conditioning, given one invariable response and one invariable stimulus, may take place completely with only one occasion. In other words the learning curve is not a

conditioning curve. This item is good fun because it leaves the insight boys with their mouths open. (2) It takes account of the fact, harped upon by Lashley, the Gestalters et al, that upon two successive occasions the stimulus presented by a problem box, let's say, varies considerably. One time the rat sees it with his left eye, another with his right, etc. All of this, ladieees and gents, for one dime.

And in an early abstract reporting my experiment I kept as close as possible to the Pavlovian formula: "The records indicate that a reflex may be fully conditioned after only one occasion upon which the conditioned and unconditioned stimuli appear approximately simultaneously." I meant, of course, the lever "eliciting" the response and the food that was delivered.

The following spring, when I described my experiment in a colloquium, Boring wrote to say he thought my report was "very interesting and very important." He went on:

> *I am just finishing up a little book that has a half-chapter that seemed to me to have a theory of learning that was very much like what you presented Wednesday. My first fear was that you might think I went home and wrote it after listening to you, but my second thought is that you will repudiate the whole thing when it is published, because its terminology is steeped in sin (from your point of view), because it couches its ideas with reference to the central nervous system, because it gets where it gets by inference from Lashley's results.*

LITERATURE HAD BEEN the great love of my high school and college years, but when I risked a year after college to test myself as a writer and failed, I turned rather bitterly against it. The pages of my copy of the last volume of Proust's *À la Recherche du temps perdu*, which I had picked up in Algiers before coming to Harvard, remained uncut beyond page 96. I had, however, not actually burned that bridge. When my mother wrote to ask if she could throw away my magazines, I said no. I still wanted my old issues of the *Dial*, Ezra Pound's *Exiles*, and Samuel Roth's *Two Worlds Monthly*, which had begun to pirate Joyce's *Ulysses*. And now after three years as a philistine psychologist, I began again to read fiction and poetry and to go to the theatre.

Among other plays, I saw a Theatre Guild production of *The Brothers Karamazov*, with Edward G. Robinson playing Smerdyakov, and Shaw's *Apple Cart*. Shaw had just published his *Adventures of the Black Girl in Her Search for God*, in which he poked fun at Pavlov. Possibly he had read the article in which H. G. Wells posed an ethical question: If Shaw were drowning on one side of a pier and Pavlov on the other, and you had only one life preserver, to which would you throw it? Wells's decision to throw it to Pavlov had confirmed my decision to abandon literature for behavioral science. The movies had also come to life as "talkies," and I saw Chaplin in *City Lights*, with its hesitant use of sound, and René Clair's *À Nous la liberté*.

In the fall of 1931 Olivia Saunders and her Bryn Mawr classmate Mary Louise White came to Cambridge and took an apartment in an old frame house at 52 Brattle Street, next to the house in which Longfellow's village blacksmith was said to have lived. Via was the younger daughter of Percy and Louise Saunders, whom I had taken to my Junior Prom. Mary Lou was the daughter of a prominent Philadelphia lawyer whom I had heard my father mention. They were figures out of my past and seeing them again hastened my return to literature.

It also sustained my interest in music. I had sold the old Mason and Hamlin upright when I left Mrs. Thomas's, but I had missed it and had bought a red five-octave mini-piano for my laboratory in Boylston Hall. It had not seemed quite the right thing for the new Biology Building and there had been no room for it on Prescott Street, so I had sold that, too. But Via and Mary Lou had a piano, and Via played at about my level. I went to Theodore Schirmer's vast loft of music in Boston and bought four-hand transcriptions, and we batted out symphonies by Haydn and Mozart with gusto. At Via's Uncle Fred's I also heard string quartets.

Through Via and Mary Lou I met James Agee, a senior at Harvard and editor of the *Advocate*, the student magazine that had published his work since his freshman year. Jim was in love with words. As he talked he used his hands to mold his sentences, as if speaking were a plastic art. He also loved music, and he and I spent many evenings with Via and Mary Lou in their apartment listening to Jim's records. The room was sparsely furnished and we often stretched out on the floor in the dark as we listened.

Though Jim and I talked about literature, I seldom mentioned my literary past, and my letter from Robert Frost remained in my files. We had similar tastes and I liked Jim's work. A year or two later he put me on the long list of dedicatees in his first book, *Permit Me Voyage* (between Einstein and Walker Evans, whose photographs appeared later in Jim's *Let Us Now Praise Famous Men*).

Jim also sang, and that year the Boston Symphony did the Bach B Minor Mass with the Harvard and Radcliffe choruses. Louise Saunders came to Boston for the occasion. Jim must have got us into a rehearsal, because I remember Koussevitzky reaching over and patting Matzenauer on the head when she finished an aria, and he would never have done that at a performance. But we heard the Sunday-afternoon performance, too, and Jim, Via, Louise, Mary Lou, and I dined afterward at a Chinese restaurant half a block from Symphony Hall.

At Via's and Mary Lou's I also met I. A. Richards, with whom I argued language and literature at length. He had produced something like a science of literary criticism, though it was not wholly behavioristic. I had read Russell's review of *The Meaning of Meaning*, which Ivor had written with C. K. Ogden, and I now bought a copy. We also talked about Ogden's new international language, Basic English, and Ivor gave me one or two of the little volumes written in Basic which were then appearing. He also gave me a volume of *Psyche*, a journal edited by Ogden, which contained Ivor's review of Stern's *Meaning and Change of Meaning*.

BEFORE PUBLISHING MY EXPERIMENT on conditioning, I gave up the attempt to use Pavlov's formula. I distinguished between two types of conditioned reflex. In Type I, as in Pavlov's experiment, a new reflex is formed. The dog salivates in response to a tone, for example. In Type II, as in my experiment, two reflexes "are chained together . . . and . . . remain in that relation" (the lever is pressed and the pellet is eaten). But I moved with caution. In both types, I said, the important thing is simply the strengthening of "a quantitative relationship of a stimulus and a response."

Pavlov was struggling with the same problem at just that time. In November 1931, two Polish physiologists, Konorski and Miller, had gone to Leningrad to persuade him to change his theory. They had done some experiments in which a hungry dog flexed its leg "to produce food," but they had taken explicit steps to bring out the successful response: they had either shocked the dog's foot or flexed its leg by hand. Pavlov discussed the topic in his Wednesday seminar on April 20, 1932: "Something more has to be introduced into the doctrine of higher nervous activity, something that identifies it with the phenomena of mental life. . . . J. M. Konorski and S. Miller have extended the use of conditioned motor reflexes, making them conditioned stimuli for either attractive or noxious substances according to different patterns of the experimental procedure." I knew nothing about what was happening in Leningrad, but I should not have been much impressed by that way of stating the issue.

IN DECEMBER, Boring gave an address at the annual meeting of the American Association for the Advancement of Science. He picked up the theme of his counterattack on behaviorism and asserted that "psychology needs to save for its use both consciousness and the nervous system, and it must have both if it is to survive." So much for Fred's and my attack on consciousness and my dismissal of the nervous system in the definition of the reflex.

And so much, too, for Boring's own earlier views. His four systematic courses had really been Titchener's, and Titchener, as Boring now said, "left the nervous system and the stimulus ruthlessly in the outer darkness of physiology." Behaviorism was a "very natural" reaction, but it went too far. "Theoretically, you can answer for animals, by tests of discrimination or by observation of conditioned reflexes [as Fred and I had tirelessly insisted] any of the questions about sensory or perceptual capacities that have been answered for human beings by the use of the introspective method," but the procedure "is terribly laborious and no added precision is gained for the added pains."

When the address was published in *Science* in January 1932, under the title "The Physiology of Consciousness," I wrote to Fred: "Have you seen Boring's article in *Science*? It's scandalous. Probably the most astonishing misunderstanding of behaviorism yet attained, even by Boring. 'Without consciousness, behaviorism has nothing left but the nervous system.' That sort of thing. Well, here's *to* him, the stupid son-of-a-bitch." (Fred had his own violent opinions of some of our contemporaries, and they were not softened by his current heavy teaching load. A postscript in one of his letters read: "Knight Dunlap is a goddam fool; Woodworth is a simple ass; Boring is blind in some respects, but a credit to the science as a historian; Pillsbury is in Woodworth's class; you and I have the significant dope, but our old friend J. G. B-C is a better organizer than either of us! Incidentally, I still think that Crozier is somewhat of a smart aleck.")

Boring developed the theme of his address in a book called *The Physical Dimensions of Consciousness,* which I used for years as an instrument of self-management. Whenever I found myself losing interest in the work at hand or even simply feeling tired, a few pages of Boring's book had the effect of a dozen cups of coffee.

What infuriated me was his refusal to recognize the possibility of a science of behavior. He had escaped from mentalism by going into the nervous system. "Introspection," he said, "is a method for the observation of certain events in the brain." Psychology was like any other science; psychologists observed "mental objects such as sensations just as others observed molecules." With one point Fred and I agreed: Behaviorism "owed its ism to consciousness." It had "preserved itself as psychology and as something that is not physiology . . . by persistently attempting to solve the problems that originated as introspective problems of the psychology of consciousness." That *was* a mistake. Watson and the others had spent too much time on a behavioristic explanation of mental life. The subject matter at issue was *behavior.*

IN JANUARY 1932 I submitted a report to the National Research Council on my first half-year as a Fellow and described my plans for further work on this new type of conditioning. What would be the effect of a short delay between pressing the lever and the delivery of food? Would I get the same result with a response that was a much more or a much less common part of the rat's behavior than pressing a lever? What about the level of drive and the kind of food used in the experiment? (But I was interested in "hunger and appetite wholly as aspects of behavior.")

Pavlov had studied a process that was in a sense the reverse of conditioning and took place more slowly. He called it "extinction." In my early notes I sometimes called it "adaptation," because it resembled the slow disappearance of the unconditioned response to a click. My first extinction curve turned up by accident. A rat was pressing the lever in an experiment on satiation when the pellet dispenser jammed. I was not there at the time, and when I returned I found a beautiful curve. The rat had gone on pressing although no pellets were received, at first more rapidly than usual since no time was lost in eating, but then more and more slowly as time wore on. Some oscillation between high and low rates made the cumulative record wavelike.

The change was more orderly than the extinction of a salivary reflex in Pavlov's setting, and I was terribly excited. It was a Friday afternoon and there was no one in the laboratory whom I could tell. All that weekend I crossed streets with particular care and avoided all unnecessary risks to protect my discovery from loss through my death.

In my new laboratory I collected more extinction curves, all with roughly the same wavelike form—the rats pressing rapidly at first but then more and more slowly until they stopped. It appeared that extinction was simply a reversal of conditioning; the reflex had been strengthened when the response was followed by food, and it grew weak when no food was forthcoming. Here was another difference between my result and Thorndike's. What could Thorndike say if the latch no longer opened the door of the problem box? Would the cat simply eliminate one more error and do nothing, or would the old errors return, and if so, why? Thorndike apparently never asked the question or tried the experiment.

I now had four processes—deprivation, satiation, conditioning, and extinction—under some kind of experimental control. In each case the rate of pressing a lever changed when I changed some feature of the environment. From the strength of the reflex alone one could not tell what had been done. In my first paper on conditioning I pointed out that "so far as the response to the lever is concerned, it is impossible to distinguish between a conditioned non-hungry rat and a hungry unconditioned rat. The response is simply lacking in both cases. Between these two extremes, moreover, it is impossible to tell from a single observation whether a given state of the reflex (an observed strength) is to be attributed to a degree of hunger or to a degree of conditioning." But if one pellet brought a response to full strength, "degree of conditioning" had no meaning. "Degree of extinction" was more to the point.

There was something more to an extinction curve than a drop in rate; it contained a number of responses. Conditioning not only increased the rate, it built up a store of responses which would later appear without further reinforcement. I began to speak of "resistance to extinction" and eventually of a "reflex reserve" exhausted in extinction. I thought at first that the reserve must reach some limiting size when the rat "knew" that pressing the lever produced food, and I tried to discover it by conditioning all responses for several days and then extinguishing. But when I reconditioned again for several days and got a second curve, and then a third and a fourth, extinction occurred more and more rapidly. (It would be some time before I knew why.)

I turned instead to the resistance to extinction generated when a single response was followed by a pellet of food. A few weeks earlier the very possibility of measuring the effect of one pellet would have seemed remote, but I was gaining confidence. I tried first a new way of adapting the rat to the apparatus: I simply let it eat its daily ration there for several days. Part of the time the lever was in place and could be pressed down, although no food followed. I recorded the rate of responding, or what Fred would later call the "operant level," and I noted that I might run into trouble: "If the response has already been made and the stimulus been adapted to, one could almost speak of extinction having taken place before the conditioning was set up. The rat had many times pressed the lever and not obtained food. This might work against the result of a single response → food."

If there was any extinction prior to conditioning, my experiment succeeded in spite of it, because when I discharged three pellets after a single response, an extinction curve immediately followed. It was wavelike and contained almost fifty responses. The rat not only began to press fast, it emitted a stock of responses. I did the experiment again using water instead of food. When a thirsty rat had been adapted to the box and to the sound of the water dispenser, a single measure of water following a response led immediately to an extinction curve.

(When I published my results on resistance to extinction I spoke for the first time of *reinforcing* a response rather than conditioning it. "Reinforce" was, of course, Pavlov's term—or rather his translator's —and it was an improvement. Where conditioning was properly a change taking place in the rat, reinforcement was the sequence of events in the environment that brought about the change. Moreover, reinforcement emphasized strengthening.)

I PLANNED AN EXPERIMENT to get a better measure of the effect of a single reinforcement. In one group of rats I would reinforce only one response before extinguishing, in another group I would reinforce the first three responses, in still another the first five, and so on. I could then, I thought, "determine the effect of 1 [reinforcement] exactly by extrapolating from 3, 5, and 7." Fortunately, the experiment was not done, because I could not, at the time, have made any sense of the results. I described a different procedure in a letter to Fred:

> I'm trying to find out how much extinction corresponds to a given amount of conditioning, and am doing the following. Rats are put in at 9:00 a.m.—no food in magazines—response to lever is extinguished. Then at 9:15 I put one pellet in each mag. Rat gets this (noise of dropping pellet facilitates a response) and then extinguishes the amount of reconditioning set up by this one "rewarded" response. At 9:30 same thing is done again. This is repeated day after day. Very soon a sudden inhibition begins to appear, taking bites out of the [extinction] curves. A clean break followed by a make up . . . Now, when the total curve for 8 or 10 days is pretty well flattened off it is possible to get an average no. of pushes per 15 minute interval. These are due to the single pellet reconditioning.

The experiment was not entirely due to theoretical considerations. I had found myself on a Friday afternoon with only a few pellets on hand and did not want to spend part of the weekend making more. If I reinforced only an occasional response, my supply would last for many days.

The sound of the pellet dropping into the tube was an unwanted complication, and I dealt with it by filling the dispenser with pellets and disconnecting the circuit to the escapement. I could then reinforce a single response without previously stimulating the rat simply by closing the circuit until a response was made. I began a series of experiments with four rats in which pressing was reinforced once every three, six, nine, and twelve minutes respectively. I reported the result at a meeting of the American Psychological Association in September 1932 at Cornell University.

I had been elected an associate member more than a year before, but this was my first appearance, and I suffered the fate of all newcomers: my paper was scheduled at the very end of the last day, when many members were on their way home. As I had done at Hamilton College in those compulsory courses in public speaking, I rehearsed the paper aloud in my room, going over it again and again until I could somehow feel the next sentence coming up as I spoke and could dispense with my notes.

My published abstract read in part:

> The reflex is alternately reconditioned and extinguished by allowing the response to be followed by the delivery of food only at set intervals. The separate curves for extinction then fuse, and the reflex assumes a constant strength, which is maintained without significant modification for as many as thirty experimental hours. The value of the strength assumed is a function of the interval at which the reflex is reconditioned. At the higher rates of elicitation, i.e., with shorter intervals, the delivery of the food eventually comes to inhibit the reflex for part of the succeeding interval, but a compensatory effect leaves the total number of responses per interval unchanged.

I did not know it, but Pavlov was experimenting with a kind of periodic reconditioning at the same time and also using the concept of inhibition, as well as excitation, to explain his results, although they were very different from mine. One of his dogs formed a conditioned response to a visual stimulus "in spite of the fact that it was reinforced only every fourth time it occurred," but not every dog did so. The trouble was that "while the light is being repeated three times without reinforcement, extinction of the conditioned response is occurring; on the fourth reinforced trial, however, a conflict occurs, an acute clash between the inhibition formed during the extinction trials and the food excitation." The dogs that could not cope with intermittent reinforcement lacked "mobility"—a term Pavlov used to refer to "the ease with which the animal can shift from excitatory to inhibitory processes and back."

At times I called my new procedure "repetitive extinction" rather than "periodic reconditioning." I also spoke of "conditioning to an interval of time," but I was not sure that I could call an interval of time a stimulus. "Time is involved in all stimuli," I wrote in a note, "but *something* must be *acting in* time."

I seemed to get a certain number of responses in extinction in return for every response I conditioned, but this "extinction ratio" was considerably less than the 50:1 I had observed when I reinforced only one response. I was not worried, however. An unusually large extinction curve followed periodic reconditioning; perhaps it contained an accumulation of unused responses.

I was not immediately aware of the significance of these results. Up to that time the study of learning had been concerned almost exclusively with acquisition and forgetting, but I had stumbled onto the *maintenance of behavior in strength*. My rats acquired the response of pressing the lever with almost embarrassing speed. Thereafter I was looking at the conditions under which its strength was sustained.

FRED WAS NOT HAPPY in his new job. He wrote that he missed the contacts around Harvard—"no matter how I neglected them when I was there. Our president (ex-Baptist preacher) resents cigarette smoking and atheism, and this holds for many of the big guns on the faculty. One is truly watched like a hawk for signs of radicalism or free thinking, and beer drinking—well—beer drinking is beer drinking and all that that means. I've not been to chapel, although expected there, and I smoke when I damn please—without feeling guilty. Connie likewise. I don't know what will happen to us."

I missed Fred too, but my colleagues in biology were more stimulating than Fred's at Colgate. Crozier called me into his office almost every day to show me new graphs or equations which had

turned up in the work he and Gregory Pincus were doing on geotropism in rats. He gave me reprints, including several of Pavlov's,
and one by Rachevsky, a physicist, on similarities between memory
and the physical process of hysteresis. He sent out my papers with
others from his department, and I received some in return. Alfred
Korzybski sent me carbon copies of some pages from an article about
Science and Sanity. He also sent a flyer announcing the International
Non-Aristotelian Library, listing more than sixty volumes, of which
only one, by Korzybski himself, seems to have been published.

Crozier never tried to bring me closer to his own field, nor did
he ever take credit for anything I did. When I took him the manuscript of my first paper as a member of his department, he saw the
standard acknowledgment at the bottom of the first page ("The author wishes to thank Professor W. J. Crozier for his support and
advice. . . ."). He picked up a blue pencil and struck it out. "We do
not exact tribute," he said.

I made friends with a young Chinese plant physiologist, Pei Sung
Tang. His father was a professor at Peking University, and two of
China's greatest poets had inscribed poems, in blue silk scrolls, celebrating his departure for America. We played Ping-Pong and often
dined together at a Chinese restaurant in Boston. The day of the juke
box had not yet dawned, but the restaurant had a mechanical piano
and *violin*; the strings of the violin, occasionally tuned by a service
man with a bad ear, were activated by small revolving disks. Pei Sung
ordered authentic Chinese dishes and made sure that they were properly prepared. They were not always to my taste; I preferred to have
the taste of fish masked. I cooked a standard American dinner for him
in my apartment.

When I got to know him better, I found that he was married and
had a beautiful baby boy. His wife, Violet, cooked Chinese meals,
and through her I learned how to shop for roast pork, bean curd,
dragon's eyes, and other delicacies in Boston's Chinatown. Rather
suddenly she became blind, and when Pei Sung returned to Wuhan
University in 1933, he left her and the baby in the charge of an older
woman. He asked me to look in on them from time to time, adding, "I
just want to say one thing. I don't believe in witches but my wife
does." I went to see Violet and the baby once or twice and looked in

vain for signs of sorcery. I soon found the apartment vacant and had no way of tracing them.

I went to all the physiological colloquiums. One was a serious evaluation of the evidence for a mitogenetic ray, which *Webster's New International* defines as "an ultraviolet ray said to be given off by a physiologically active cell and to stimulate mitotic activity of cells." The speaker criticized the experiments rather sharply but was not willing to dismiss them as worthless. The mitogenetic ray was the kind of mysterious force that turns up from time to time in any science, though seldom as often as in psychology. A year or two before I came to Harvard, William McDougall, Boring, and Hudson Hoagland took part in an investigation of the famous Boston medium Marjorie.

I knew almost nothing about many of the subjects discussed at the colloquiums and began another program of catching up. I audited a course in biochemistry which went into Debye's work on the structure of molecules—in far too much detail. And I bought and read with complete absorption Hugh Taylor's two-volume text in physical chemistry. I liked the concept of a system, in Willard Gibb's sense, and soon found it helpful in thinking about the behavior of an organism as a whole.

I also continued to see a good deal of Hal and Pauline Davis and their children, and I went to an occasional lecture in the Department of Physiology at the Medical School. The great nerve physiologist Adrian spoke there in the fall of 1931. He was introduced by Professor Alexander Forbes, who had worked with him at Cambridge. Forbes said he had always admired the graceful way in which Adrian could admit that he was wrong, and in his response Adrian explained that it was because he had had a great deal of practice. I thought it was terribly witty and wondered if they had cooked it up beforehand.

My mother was still worrying about her health, and she came to Boston to be examined at the Lahey Clinic. She stayed in a hotel near the clinic and, of course, I spent some time with her. She had once told me, giggling, that she thought my father was jealous of her attentions to me, and when she went back to Scranton there seemed to be no doubt of it. She started to tell him all about her trip but when she said, "Frederic gave me all the attention I could have asked for," he stopped her and would not hear any more of the story.

IN MY THESIS I had assumed that "every movement of an organism was in response to a stimulus," and I was not alone in making that assumption. In 1931 E. B. Holt, whose *Freudian Wish* I admired, published *Animal Drive and the Learning Process*, and in it he insisted that "in the last analysis all the activities of an organism, including the highest mental achievements, are reflexes." But I was beginning to have my doubts. The stimulation arising from the lever did not seem to "elicit" pressing as a shock elicited flexion or a bell the flow of saliva. The stimuli did not start and stop; I could not turn them on or off; I could not *see* them act. I had no way of knowing whether the same stimuli were acting upon different occasions. In my letter to Fred clarifying my new theory I had specified "one invariable response and one invariable stimulus," but where could they be found?

Some experiments were in order. If my rats were working in total darkness, I could add the visual stimulation from the lever simply by turning on a light. My first plan was to assess its importance by reinforcing the behavior with a light on and then extinguishing it in the dark. Partway through extinction I would turn the light on again. Fortunately, I did not try the experiment, because if I had done so, the rats would have responded faster when the light came on and, at the time, I should have found that hard to explain. Instead, I used the light in a simpler experiment suggested by the "facilitative effect" of the noise made when a pellet dropped into the empty dispenser. That noise was much more like the stimuli of Sherrington and Pavlov because I could control it; I knew when it acted.

Into each box I put a small light, which I turned on at the beginning of a new session of periodic reconditioning. I reinforced the first response and then turned the light off. The rat continued to respond in the dark as it had done before. After five minutes I turned the light on again, reinforced another response, and turned it off. I continued in this way throughout the session, reinforcing a response periodically with the light on and allowing all other responses to go unreinforced in the dark. (I maintained these contingencies simultaneously for four rats by hand, watching a clock and throwing switches as the intervals expired.)

The result was clear enough. The rats gradually stopped pressing the lever in the dark, as if I had stopped reinforcing altogether, but pressed within a few seconds whenever the light came on. They could be said to be discriminating between two stimuli, light-on and light-off, by responding to one and not to the other. The light was a *discriminative*, rather than an eliciting, stimulus. I represented it as S^D, with S^Δ for a stimulus present when a response was not reinforced, using the Greek letter to represent the absence of the property represented by the Roman, as G. Udney Yule had done in his book on statistics.

I reported these results also at Cornell, and another part of my abstract read:

> In establishing a discrimination an extra stimulus is introduced at each reconditioning but is omitted during the intervening periods of extinction. The response to the lever-plus-extra-stimulus then remains fully conditioned, while the response to the lever alone is extinguished. The curve given experimentally for this change has the properties of the normal curve for extinction. . . . The concepts of conditioning and extinction thus afford an adequate description of a discrimination of this type.

In other words, I had found no separate process of discrimination.

A year or two later I published support for that view by showing how a discrimination could be abolished. When a rat was responding immediately in the light but only sporadically in the dark, I could either extinguish the response to the light (I then got a smooth extinction curve, very much like the curves when all previous responses had been reinforced) or I could omit the light and return to simple periodic reconditioning (when the rat gradually accelerated to the old periodic rate). I discussed these new data in the fall of 1933 when Hudson Hoagland, who had become Chairman of the Department of Biology at Clark University, asked me to give a colloquium. My title was "Further Properties of Discrimination."

I planned another experiment on discrimination, but it never got beyond a notebook entry: "The Pavlovian generalization of a discrimination to other reflexes could be tried by getting ⅕ [periodic reconditioning every five minutes] on eating and drinking (alternate days) then establishing a discrimination to one and seeing what effect the 'signal' has upon the ⅕ rate in the other." I added, significantly: "Note the use of the ⅕ rate to make up for inability to use the size of response in reflexes of Type II." The extent of flexion of a dog's leg would do for Sherrington and quantity of saliva for Pavlov, but when it came to pressing a lever, I would use rate.

I began to use the rat's performance under periodic reconditioning as a standard against which I could observe other effects. I had heard that people who worked with X-rays often "felt nervous," and I decided to see whether heavy doses of X-radiation would disrupt the performance under periodic reconditioning. I got a fairly powerful X-ray tube and set it up rather carelessly in the spare room in which Pei Sung and I had played Ping-Pong. I had no way of measuring exactly how much of a daily dose I was giving my rats (or myself, lurking in a far corner of the room), but it was presumably fairly large. I found no difference in the "grain" of my rats' records or in their rate of responding.

My CONTENTION that discrimination was simply a kind of extinction left something out of account. For one thing, the process never seemed complete. As I wrote in my notebook: "If no signal is given, the response eventually comes through." ("Eventually" was the right word because the unexplained responses came near the ends of the dark intervals.) I suspected a "time interval effect," but it was more likely that reinforcing in the light slightly strengthened responding in the dark—an effect I called "induction," borrowing the term from Sherrington.

I found better evidence of induction (though in the opposite direction) in a later experiment in which I sought the answer to a troublesome question: would discrimination resemble extinction if responses in the dark had never been reinforced? I adapted a rat to the apparatus and food dispenser with the light on, and at the beginning of a new session I reinforced a single response. Then I turned the light off. The box was now dark for the first time and, perhaps for that reason, the rat made no other responses for five minutes. When I turned the light on again, it responded. Again I reinforced the response and turned the light off for five minutes. I continued in this way throughout the session. Responses were made and reinforced in the light, but little or no responding occurred in the dark. There was no extinction because there was nothing to be extinguished. The rat had learned the discrimination "without making any errors."

Not only were no responses reinforced in the dark, there was evidently no induction from reinforcement in the light. But there was clear evidence of induction in the other direction: the response in the light remained very weak. In my earlier experiments the rats pressed the lever within four or five seconds after the light came on, but in this experiment the average delay was twenty seconds, and one rat averaged forty. Two out of eight rats eventually stopped responding altogether.

Light-on and light-off were, of course, very different stimuli, and in that respect my experiments were not orthodox. The orthodox question was whether an organism could see something—say, a very faint light or the difference between two colors or patterns. I was not interested in capacity but in the role played by the stimulus. It was becoming clear that the light did not *elicit* the response in the sense in which a tap on the patellar tendon elicits a kick of the leg, nor was the lever simply a collection of sights, smells, and touches having that effect. Of course, the lever stimulated the rat before a response was made and reinforced, but its effect was upon the probability that pressing would occur. As in my treatment of drive, I was breaking away from the traditional view of a stimulus as a goad. (The two concepts were combined by psychologists who included drive in a "total stimulus situation.") The temporal order of stimulus and response suggested causal action, but it was not the action of a force.

MY SOCIAL LIFE was restricted by the routine to which I had committed myself. It was best for my rats, and hence in the long run for me, if an experiment was conducted at the same time every day. Lower organisms are not Sabbatarians, and I could not take a weekend off without upsetting my experiments. When spring came, however, I took a break and went back to Franconia. To celebrate my return to literature I read nothing but novels, among them *Oliver Twist* and

The Ordeal of Richard Feverel. Near the end of my stay I received a telegram from Cuthbert. He and Janet had been in Spain for a year. He had sent me Emile Meyerson's *Du Cheminement de la pensée*, bound in the only durable cloth he could find—a horsehair material used by tailors to stiffen the lapels in men's suits. Now they were back and looking for a place to live. The Cooper-Frost-Austin House on Linnaean Street was available but it was too big. Would I share it with them? It was said to have been built in 1657, and permission to build it had indeed been granted in December of that year. Among its features, according to Cuthbert's wire, was a "tie-up for six horses." Mary Louise White added further details in a letter: "It is the broth of a house you have waiting for you though! Horses? You've got room for a race track, and a primeval forest and lilac bushes, and an old 1800 dog house and a sign in front that invites all the Daughters of Antiquities to step right in."

I could have a living room with a walk-in fireplace on the first floor and a bedroom with a smaller fireplace and a tiny bath on the second, reached by a shared stairway. Cuthbert would take care of the furnace (though it was I who rigged an alarm clock to open the damper early in the morning). I could use the kitchen when it was free, but I gave up cooking my evening meal and in fact made very little use of the kitchen, which was beyond a dining room used by the Daniels. There was much more space than I had had on Prescott Street, and I picked up some additional pieces of secondhand furniture, giving no thought to the visitors who were allowed to view the house every Thursday afternoon. A Kilim rug and a bamboo chaise longue would have seemed strange to anyone expecting Early American, but no one ever called when I was there. I bought still another secondhand piano (one dealt freely in used pianos in those days because lofts over the music stores in Boston were full of them for $25 or $30 each) and half a cord of firewood (it was the chestnut that had been killed by the blight in the late 'teens and was now dry-rotted and almost uninflammable).

Some evidence of my housekeeping, with an indication of expanding personal relations, is preserved in a letter from a new friend which I found one day upon returning from a holiday. (The Daniels were away and Janet's brother, Robert Goldwater, was staying in their part of the house.)

If you look on the mantle in your bedroom, beside the right hand
blue bottle among the mouse shit you will find a seashell. It was in my
pocket and I left it for you on Friday.

That being the kind of fool I am it never occurred to me that you
wouldn't be there. I let myself in the back way and it was very sunny
and funny and dead and I was scared to death. I didn't drink your
wine or read your letters, but I looked at things and touched them and
looked in your closets and into the suitcase of dirty clothes under the
bed [my fiber laundry case which was still going back and forth
between Cambridge and Scranton], and I will always remember the
cork floating in the bottle and the litter on the desk and the box of Old
Golds on the piano stool, and the hard pieces of camphor on your
bureau. I cut my nails with your manicure scissors.

And I lay for a long time on your dirty sheets and thought, He
might come back, and knew damned well that it would be Robert who
would come back. And at last I got up and went home.

Mice were one of my lesser problems. A topcoat I had carelessly
thrown across the chaise longue one evening lost part of a pocket
before morning. I had left a few peanuts in the pocket and a rat had
got at them from the wrong end. The Daniels and their friends
thought it was hilarious retribution for what I had done to rats.

IN APPLYING FOR REAPPOINTMENT as a National Research Council
Fellow I said I wanted to work part-time in the Department of Physiology at the Medical School. I would study reflexes in partially
dissected animals "in order to make a clearer analysis of my observations of the behavior of intact organisms." I would do so with Professors Davis and Forbes.

Alexander Forbes, an old Bostonian, lived on a large family estate
in Milton. He had grown deaf at an early age and fiddled a great deal
with a hearing aid. His gray hair was cut short and brushed forward.
Perhaps because he so often misunderstood what people said, to their
amusement, he joked a great deal and had a stock of amusing stories,
slightly scatological *obscene* in the medical tradition. He was never on time for
appointments, and a joke about him heard around the department
was that if he had been born fifteen minutes earlier, he would have
been on time all his life.

He had worked at Cambridge University with some of the pioneers in the physiology of the nervous system—Keith Lucas, killed in the war, and later Adrian. He himself was studying reflex activity, and his laboratory owed much to Sherrington. There I saw for the first time the torsion-wire myograph, in which a muscle of the leg of a cat is attached to a lever, the movement of which is recorded photographically as the muscle contracts. John Fulton had used the myograph in the research reported in his heavy volume *Muscular Contraction and the Reflex Control of Movement*, and some of us were enjoying a bit of *Schadenfreude* over the "angle" artifact. When a muscle contracted and relaxed, a sharp break appeared in the record as relaxation began. Fulton had made a great deal of it in his theory, but it had been found to be due to friction in the torsion-wire bearing.

Professor Forbes suggested that I take up a project abandoned by a medical student who had moved on toward his degree. I was to develop a reversible spinal block. Sherrington had studied reflexes by cutting the spinal cord of a cat near the neck, so that the limbs were not moved by the higher centers in the brain. It might be possible to get the same effect by cooling a section of the cord until it no longer conducted nerve impulses; the normal function could then be restored by raising the temperature. It would be hard to do this in an intact animal, but it might be done in a decerebrate preparation.

With the help of another Research Fellow, Elizabeth Lambert, I set about learning to use the Sherrington guillotine. A cat was deeply anesthetized and connected to an air pump for artificial respiration. The forepart of the head above the jaw was then cut away with a guillotinelike blow slicing down through the skull. We followed a curious local practice and mashed up the part of the brain we removed, so that it would not "suffer" when the anesthesia and shock of the operation wore off. (One day Lambert and I were working on a cat when a member of the Boston Society for the Prevention of Cruelty to Animals made a surprise visit. He came through the laboratory with Professor Cannon. The decerebration had been finished and our cat was covered by a towel under a heat lamp, the respiration pump working. The cat's tail, uncovered, hung lightly over the edge of the table. As the visitor watched us, some irritation set off a "pseudo-affective reflex," and the tail flicked. "He seems to be enjoying it," said the visitor, as he and Professor Cannon moved on.)

From a piece of copper tubing I made a jacket that could be placed against the spinal cord and cooled with ice water. The cord was exposed by cutting away the bony spinal column. I had seen much the same operation during that dark year in Scranton when my friend Dr. Fulton was trying to interest me in medicine. A broken back was a common accident in coal mines because poorly supported roof would fall on the men, and it was often necessary to expose the spinal cord to assess the damage. In a letter to Percy Saunders I described an operation, adding some rather morbid reflections:

> I put on white gown and cap—stand beside an operating table and watch my friend the doctor operate on a broken back. Ether—a breathing body under a white cover—a square hole in the white showing iodine painted skin. A long slow cut—a rolling out of blood—vertebrae exposed, chewed off with forceps—pieces of ivory-like bone crunched out—three inches of spinal cord exposed—mangled cord. Here is an ounce or less of tissue—crushed—meaning a life of complete paralysis—or, better, death. My friend the doctor stops to tell a story about a chiropractor. "A chiropractor could have fixed this one all right!" The flesh is sewed up—No hope.

There was no hope for our experiment either. There were too many problems we could not solve, and Professor Forbes tactfully suggested that we change to a different project for the balance of my year.

THERE WAS NO ONE to take care of my rats while I was at the Medical School, and in any case taking care of an expanding colony was becoming more of a chore. The animal quarters were on the top floor of the Biology Building and my laboratory was two floors underground, a long way away. It occurred to me that rats might take care of themselves if given the chance. I bought a lot of covered tin cans about the size of shoeboxes and cut openings in the ends to be used as doors. I mounted them like separate apartments along an elevated path and put the whole thing in a small screened enclosure, together with food and water and a supply of nesting material. I released about two dozen rats and waited for them to move into their individual quarters. It was a complete failure. Instead of making nests for themselves, they crowded together in two or three of the apartments, leaving the nesting material untouched. I went back to standard wire cages with water bottles and food baskets.

I needed some other means of caring for the rats in my experiments. It was standard practice to maintain a given level of hunger by feeding a rat a daily ration shortly after it was "run" in an experiment. If the rat was not run, it was given its ration at about the same time. I could not do this if I was at the Medical School, but I thought I could solve the problem in another way.

My rats seemed to respond faster under periodic reconditioning when they were hungrier. If I used large pellets and let them get all their food by pressing a lever around the clock, and if I made the amount they ate proportional to how fast they pressed, they should remain at an almost constant hunger. Whenever they got slightly hungrier they would press faster, get more food, and grow less hungry, and whenever they got slightly less hungry they would respond more slowly, eat less, and grow hungrier. I visualized a machine with a dial that I could set to make available, at any time of day or night, a rat in a given state of deprivation.

To make the amount of food ingested correspond to the rate of pressing, I tried a new schedule of reinforcement. If pressing produced a pellet once every five minutes and if the rat pressed on the average twenty-five times during that time, I could not see that it would make any difference if I simply reinforced every twenty-fifth response. The rat would still get a pellet every five minutes. But if it pressed faster it would get pellets oftener, and if it pressed more slowly it would get them less often, and that was what I wanted.

I tested the scheme first in my regular apparatus. I reinforced a response every five minutes for a few hours and calculated the number of responses for each reinforcement. Then I began to reinforce whenever the rat completed that number. During the first one-hour session one rat maintained a stable rate, slightly higher than on the preceding day, but on the next day it began to accelerate and reached a high rate before the end of the hour. Other rats behaved in the same way.

I had overlooked an important fact. If a rat responded at a steady rate, like the ticking of a grandfather's clock, there would indeed be no difference between reinforcing every so many minutes and every so many responses. But responses tend to be grouped. When a reinforcement is set up by a clock, as in periodic reconditioning, the reinforced response is likely to occur after a pause rather than between grouped responses, since the clock is more likely to close the circuit during a pause. But when a reinforcement is set up by a counter, all responses are equally likely to be reinforced, and since there are more responses in groups than at the beginnings of groups, reinforcements occur more often when the rat is pressing rapidly. Under periodic reconditioning, reinforcements tend to occur when the rate is relatively low; under what I would later call a fixed-ratio schedule, reinforcements occur when the rate is relatively high. A fixed-ratio schedule produces rapid responding.

My scheme for the control of deprivation would not work, and I turned to a mechanical solution. I put my experimental rats in two large cages where they could nibble at dog biscuits held in wire baskets. Most of the time a shield covered the baskets, but a motor uncovered them for an hour or so at the right time each day.

I ENJOYED MY CO-TENANCY with the Daniels. Cuthbert had abandoned his plans for a musical career and had sold the parlor organ on which he played a number of Bach fugues flawlessly. He was still interested in music, however, and he and I explored the shops on Charles and Beacon Streets in Boston in search of keyboard instruments. We found a number of early-nineteenth-century pianos in fairly good working order at quite reasonable prices (and at quite reasonable profits too, as we discovered when one dealer left us alone in a large storeroom; on each price tag the cost to the dealer was encoded in letters, and we were able to break the code). Early pianos did not give out a very pleasant sound, and there were no harpsichords or clavichords for sale. We solved the problem in another way. I had met a pianomaker named Julius Wahl. He had worked for the Chickering Company, and when the company moved away from Boston, he had opened a repair shop for musical instruments in Wellesley. Marian Stevens and I used to go to his house, a small Swiss chalet beside a lake, for Sunday afternoon kaffeeklatsches. Mrs. Wahl served coffee and cakes, Wahl played the zither, and we sang endless verses of "Schnitzelbank."

Wahl had built himself a clavichord patterned after one by Dolmetsch, the English instrumentmaker who had worked briefly with the Chickering Company in Boston. He had not been able to get the proper strings and was using piano wire, but, even so, the instrument had a lovely tone and a delightfully yielding touch. I asked him how much he could make one for, and he estimated that, in a lot of ten, it would be $250. I found five or six friends who were interested, but in the end he made only two, for Cuthbert and me, at $300 each.

He started work in the spring of 1933, and when I saw mine under construction, I wrote my name on the frame where it would be covered by the sounding board (to be added by a violinmaker named Hans Bubert). Cuthbert told me triumphantly that he had asked Wahl to sign *his* name. The pattern for the keys, bridge, and pins was taken from Dolmetsch, and the Dolmetsch Company supplied the brass strings. Wahl copied my case from one in the Boston Museum of Fine Arts made in Dresden in 1759. Cuthbert chose a simpler design.

The Daniels had something of a salon. Interesting friends came to dinner, among them John Brooks Wheelwright and Sherry Mangan, minor poets, and a novelist, Victoria Lincoln, who was writing a roman à clef, *February Hill,* with a clef that fitted so well that she left the state after the book was published. I was frequently asked to come in after dinner and often talked literature with Sherry. Cuthbert supported my position, which was scarcely a traditional one, and later Sherry would be writing in a review in *Poetry*: "In its eventual importance, perhaps the most fruitful literary criticism now being done is that of Frederick [*sic*] Skinner, who in the Harvard laboratories humorlessly and behavioristically breeds and conditions his actuary rats."

The Daniels were much impressed by Freud and his confreres, and if I ever took psychoanalysis seriously, it was because of them. I was always skeptical, and so were others. Sherry once wrote to me:

Rank still rankles with me; and I am filling my coast-defense howitzer with broken doorknobs and rusty syllogisms for a blast at him. . . .

But perhaps I shall merely make a monkey of myself. In any case, it will force me to go through the whole Vienna Dream Book school, lest I be thrown out of court for not crossing my peas and dotting my culs; and in that matter I shall beg your advice.

Emigrés from Germany came to the Daniels' and made me all too aware of the little interest I had taken in public affairs. My father's speeches on behalf of the Republican Party had not impressed me, and the liberal course in political science at Hamilton College in which we subscribed to the *New Republic* had left no permanent mark. During my first years at Harvard I read no newspapers or magazines, and my only glimpses of public life were from the newsreels and one or two Russian films, about the joys of labor, seen in an art theatre in Boston. I did not register or vote. Roosevelt slipped into office almost unobserved by me.

At the Daniels' I began to hear stories of the things that were happening in Germany, but I was not clear about the issues. I was against Hitler and assumed that I should be for Stalin. One day when I was filling my pipe with Edgeworth tobacco I said to Cuthbert that I had read that Stalin smoked Edgeworth. I expected him to be pleased that I was *au courant* with international affairs, but he gave me one of his more withering stares.

Certain aspects of public life could not be avoided. A soldier in uniform occasionally appeared in the streets, and veterans were to be seen in newsreels dropping bags of water from hotel windows at their annual conventions. Nor could one be unaware of Boston politics. The mellifluous Mayor Curley was a favorite of newsreel cameramen, and everyone told stories about him and his machine. The Catholic Church was always visible. I saw newsreels of Cardinal O'Connell laying cornerstones and of lesser figures blessing the fishing fleet at Gloucester. The Cardinal appeared regularly at the State House "in the name of decency" to support bills opposing birth control and vivisection, with Walter Cannon from the Medical School on the other side. The Boston papers carried a good deal of Catholic news, and I did not see them often enough not to be startled by an occasional sports headline: IMMACULATE CONCEPTION TROUNCES SAINT MARY. I hated it all and could not have said why. When I passed a church I often speculated on how it could be converted into a behavioral laboratory.

IT IS HARD TO LIVE in New England without becoming a New Englander. If I read any paper, it was the *Boston Evening Transcript*, whose readers, said T. S. Eliot, "sway in the wind like a field of ripe corn." Every day I passed that statue of Ralph Waldo Emerson on the first floor of Emerson Hall, and when some friends drove me to Concord, I visited Emerson's study, preserved by an antiquarian society. (In a room upstairs there was a caned frame said to have been used as a bed by Thoreau.) I visited the Alcott House and drove past Hawthorne's, recalling the paper on *The Scarlet Letter* for which Chubby Ristine gave me an HH, Hamilton's version of A.

Then I discovered Walden Pond, and I began to go there to swim, either with friends who had a car or on my bicycle. We did not swim where a beach house was later built but in the cove near the site of Thoreau's hut. The bottom of the pond was muddy, and I recalled Thoreau's fluvial walks.

IN DECEMBER 1932 I reported to the National Research Council that I had corroborated my finding that "the conditioning of a simple reflex may be essentially complete with only one elicitation," and that I had also discovered a "better indication of the amount of conditioning"—the extinction that followed the reinforcement of one response. But I said I had been spending most of my time on the process of discrimination and had shown that it was similar to extinction. I had also been studying spontaneous activity and was classifying "a large amount of extraneous material with a view to later more direct investigation."

My experiments had indeed gone well. I was getting data from a single rat that were more orderly and reproducible than the averages of large groups in mazes and discrimination boxes, and a few principles seemed to be covering a lot of ground. Now, midway through the second year of my fellowship, I began to look to the future. In a rather expansive mood I drew up plans for the second thirty years of my life:

November 17, 1932
PLAN OF THE CAMPAIGN FOR THE YEARS 30–60

1. *Experimental description of behavior.* Continue along present lines. Properties of conditioning, extinction, drives, emotions, etc. No surrender to the physiology of the central nervous system. Publish.
2. *Behaviorism vs. Psychology.* Support behavioristic methodology throughout. Operational definitions of all psychological concepts. Don't publish much.
3. *Theories of Knowledge* (scientific only). Definitions of concepts in terms of behavior. A descriptive science of what happens when people think. Relate to experimental work. Include a theory of meaning. Publish late.
4. *Theories of Knowledge* (non-scientific). Literary criticism. Behavioristic theory of creation. Publish very late if at all.

These are in the order of their importance, although 2 and 3 are about equal. By far the greater bulk of time should go on 1.

Plan for the years 60—(?)
(These are beyond my present control.)

The second and third projects had their roots in Russell's discussion of Watson. Behaviorism and epistemology were closely related. Behaviorism was a theory of knowledge, and knowing and thinking were forms of behavior. I had written "Don't publish much" and "Publish late," but I was already at work on something called *A Sketch for an Epistemology*. There are evidences of what it was to be about in several places.

I became a charter subscriber to two new journals concerned with scientific method, *Erkenntnis*, published in Germany, and, a year or two later, *Philosophy of Science*, published in America. Causality was a common theme, and I thought it was clearly a behavioral one. I wrote notes about observations not unlike those which the Belgian psychologist Michotte would later publish in his book on the perception of causality. For example, I described what happened when "a straw is drawn across a shallow vessel of water upon which are floating many small bits of material": "The surface film is disturbed and the small bits move in various ways without a very obvious plan. But an object which moves contrary to the expected way is instantly noticed and perhaps considered alive. We evidently learn matters of

1 1 5

complicated movement very easily and are shocked at an illogical movement."

Life as a cause intrigued me because it was close to Mind. In the Sistine Chapel I had seen Michelangelo's "Creation of Adam," in which Adam's and God's fingers make a kind of spark gap across which Life and Mind will jump as Adam becomes a live, sentient, rational creature. I used the tinted photograph I had brought back from Rome in a colloquium on behaviorism in Emerson Hall.

I witnessed an appeal to a psychological cause when I bought some jumping beans for Dana Pratt at Daddy and Jack's Joke Shop in Boston and converted a few of them into turtles by pasting them on small squares of paper, with the corners bent down as legs. On a glass plate the turtles moved about when the beans "jumped," and when Dana saw one move toward another just as the other moved away, he said that the second turtle was "scared."

In my *Sketch* I projected a "description of the activity of science wholly in terms of the behavior of scientists . . . Examine some of Whitehead's statements about *what science did* and get at them in terms of the behavior not of Science but of scientists."

In my thesis I had proposed an operational definition of a reflex, drawing upon Bridgman, Mach, and Poincaré. It was the Mach of *The Science of Mechanics,* not of *The Analysis of Sensations*—the Mach who had influenced Einstein by asserting, as Einstein's biographer, Ronald W. Clark, puts it, "that Newtonian laws would have to be re-written in more comprehensible terms, substituting in the law of inertia, for example, 'relation to the fixed stars' for 'relation to absolute space.' " I was talking about something less global or universal, but still important: substituting statements about behavior for statements about mental processes.

I had attacked the field briefly in that skirmish with Emile Meyerson in Franconia, and another book I now read in the same spirit was C. I. Lewis's *Mind and the World Order.* Marjory Pratt had said that Lewis, whom I occasionally saw in Emerson Hall, had had a great success with it, and I was challenged—particularly when I bought a copy and found Lewis acknowledging the help of his "friend and colleague, Professor E. G. Boring." I planned to write "a running marginal account, either stating a position in behavioristic terms or making some comment on the importance to behavioristic theory." I grew tired after six chapters, but a transcription of my marginal notes runs to twelve pages. Here are some samples:

> What is the organism doing when we say it is thinking?
>
> Behavioristic equivalent of "sense datum" is sensory stimulation [but this] has nothing to do with an immediate given, and in no way capitulates to a dichotomized mind.
>
> "Instinct" and "will" are describable simply as changes in the response to a given stimulus. They are not things which cause changes.
>
> Variation in strength is what is meant by "interest."
>
> Language, in the broader sense, is thought. "We understand each other" means only that we use language in the same way. That is all that is verifiable. There is no necessity for the assumption of common (subjective) meanings.

Of the *Sketch* itself some fifty pages survive. I described methodological behaviorism:

> It is . . . possible to be a behaviorist and recognize the existence of conscious events. . . . We may set up a distinction between a public and a private world, the first a communicable one in which all terms refer finally to the act of communication between persons (i.e. to behavior) and the latter forever reserved from scientific treatment. If psychology is to be a science (i.e. a public science) its concepts must be defined as if they did not refer to a private world. . . .

But I preferred the position of *radical behaviorism*, in which the existence of subjective entities is denied. I proposed to regard subjective terms "as verbal constructs, as grammatical traps into which the human race in the development of language has fallen." I was not concerned with the nature of the stuff of which mind was composed: "The behavioristic argument is not that of the naive materialist who asserts that 'thought is a property of matter in motion,' nor is it the assertion of the identity of thought or conscious states with material [brain] states. (Cf. Boring.)" I thought it was a mistake to speak of knowledge of a *thing* possessed by a *mind*. "Try the operational method of knowledge. What can the human mind *do* peculiarly well?"

> Traditional psychology has for historical reasons fixed upon a rather remote part of the field of behavior. . . . In approaching the study of, say, human behavior, one of the *last* things we would do is study those fine discriminations which comprise the subjects of "Vision" and "Audition." . . . It is easy to understand the lack of sympathy of end-organ specialists with behaviorism. . . . But end-organ study is going over to physiologists anyway. . . . To the practicing behaviorist whose interests are determined by the logical development of his science the typical questions of experimental psychology are of no pressing importance.

I proposed to cover not only *how* scientists worked but *why*: "A theory of knowledge should include a theory of motivation to supply a complete description of the phenomena. Not only how do men think? but under what circumstances? . . . Have we really any *conviction* of the lawfulness of nature (as Meyerson says)? What is the operational definition of conviction?"

The old problem of possessing knowledge about knowledge could be solved: "You cannot talk about talking without talking, but you can say something about talking that refers inclusively to your present act. There is, of course, no ultimate question of whether what you say is *right*."

A science of behavior supplied a new set of concepts to deal with psychological subject matters. It was not merely "a new vocabulary for old things. The astrologist [sic] could have accused the astronomer of that, and the alchemist the chemist. It was a vocabulary which worked better. It produced order instead of disorder, simplicity instead of piling confusion upon confusion (see Ptolemy)." I listed a few terms for which alternatives might be found: "wanting, looking for, willing, deciding, reasoning, frustration, anxiety, and freedom of action."

In his laboratory practices as well as in less experimental undertakings, the experimental psychologist deals extensively with verbal behavior:

> . . . either the verbal statements made by what is technically called the "observer" or nonverbal behavior in response to situations which include words, i.e. the "instructions" given by the experimenter. We are naturally interested in what is done with the use of language in the

treatment of these data. The psychologist . . . does not confine himself to words simply as behavior but deals extensively with their referents —in particular such so-called subjective referents as sensations, meanings, strivings, emotions, and so on. He goes beyond his immediate observations by including in his experimental results the meanings that these words have *for him* and in this way he arrives at what he takes to be the real subject matter of his science.

Behaviorism certainly went through a phase when kymograph readings were preferred to verbal reports, not because of their usual greater clarity and definiteness, but because they were "objective" and "scientific." But as we have already seen there is no reason at all for a behaviorist to avoid what is usually called introspection except on grounds of reliability.

My *Sketch* appeared in its proper guise in July 1933 when I wrote to Fred from Monhegan, "I am working on a book (publication not certain) on Behaviorism. A restatement of the central argument . . . It seems to me now to be hot stuff throughout. I work on it for long periods with no apparent fatigue. It will make everybody mad, I'm afraid, if it gets published." I had no doubt of its importance and I considered getting a fireproof filing case for my notes when I returned to Cambridge.

WHEN WE ABANDONED our efforts to block the spinal cord reversibly, Elizabeth Lambert and I chose an experiment on chronaxie of subordination. The French physiologist Lapicque had proposed that nerve impulses find their way through the central nervous system not so much by following pathways as by seeking matching "chronaxies." He claimed that the higher centers in the brain changed the chronaxies of the nerves coming off the spinal cord and that this explained some of the properties of spinal reflexes. (It was to test this theory that Forbes wanted a reversible spinal block.) But Lambert and I, working on frogs and decerebrate cats, found little or no change when a nerve in the leg was separated from the higher centers. I never fully understood what we were doing, and our paper was written primarily by Lambert and Forbes.

If I got anything out of my Medical School experience, it was not from the work I did so inexpertly but from contact with the kind of physiology that was said to be relevant to my field. Professor Forbes was as close as I could get to the history of nerve and reflex physiology, and a lesser man in the field, Philip Bard, gave a colloquium on "the stepping reflex" that confirmed my decision to avoid "botanizing reflexes." Hallowell Davis began working in the field of hearing shortly after Wever and Bray had discovered that the frequency of a tone played into the ear of a cat could be picked up in the electrical changes in the nerve going to the brain, and he was soon looking at "brain-waves." Walter Cannon, the gentle head of the Department of Physiology, was well known for his *Bodily Changes in Fear, Hunger, Pain and Rage* and for a theory of emotion which differed from the more famous theories of James and Lange. He lived in Cambridge, and I passed his house on my way to the Biological Laboratories. His friend Pavlov had stayed there, and Cannon told amusing stories about him.

I liked these people and I could discuss their fields more sensibly for having worked in them, but I found nothing that would be particularly helpful in the analysis of behavior. On the contrary, a limitation was becoming clear. From spinal reflexes to bodily changes in hunger and emotion physiologists talked about responses to stimuli; magnitude of response was their measure. They were not interested in the consequences of behavior or their effect on the probability that an organism would behave in a given way at a given time.

When spring came, I sought help in a very different place. I read John Maynard Keynes's *Treatise on Probability*. It was an enjoyable intellectual exercise but had little bearing on the probability that a rat would press a lever.

WHILE DRAWING UP THAT PLAN for a thirty-year campaign, I faced a problem nearer at hand. I needed a job. Third-year appointments to an NRC Fellowship were granted "only in very exceptional cases," and the Depression was at its worst. I wrote to Hunter and he replied, "I shall be only too glad to keep my eyes and ears open for you this spring, but as you know, this will probably be the worst year on record for placing new men." He advised me to write to Yerkes at Yale asking him about "the possibility of working in his Institute for enough pay to keep you alive and asking him, if nothing is available there, to keep you in mind if any position comes up for which one of his own men is not available. You may tell him that I suggested that you write him. I should also write to any psychologists about the country whom you know and inquire about possible openings. These are hard times, and such letters will not be misunderstood, I think." He also suggested that I register with teachers' agencies and "if you are willing to work in Mental Hospitals, I suggest that you write to Carney Landis and also to David Shakow, the latter here at Worcester State Hospital. [Frederick] Wells might have some little job at the Boston Psychopathic which would keep you from starvation."

Carmichael at Brown wrote to say that he was "certainly very sorry to hear of the bad judgment of Harvard University . . . [but] I am afraid that I must reply that for next year our books are closed."

Tolman at California wrote: "I wish like the devil that we had a place for you here but there are to be no new appointments, promotions, or such. And we shall have some seven young PhDs, past and present, of our own looking for jobs and not being able to get them. It certainly is a devil of a situation and it behooves all you young intelligentsia to get busy on the economic revolution. I mean this . . . I will keep you in mind and I will pray."

Suddenly, in early March, I learned that I was being considered for a particularly plush fellowship. A. Lawrence Lowell, President of Harvard, and L. J. Henderson, a biochemist, were unhappy about the Ph.D. program in American universities. They felt that it did little to promote original thinking. When Whitehead came to Harvard, he joined them in discussing the problem. Whitehead had been a Trinity Prize Fellow at Cambridge University, and it was not long before the Trinity Prize Fellows (and the Fondation Thiers in Paris, with which both Henderson and Lowell were familiar) suggested a solution. In 1926 Henderson and Whitehead, together with John Livingston Lowes and Charles Curtis, a member of the governing board of Harvard University, submitted a report to Lowell that began by citing a curious fact: "One-half of the British Nobel Prize winners, one-fifth of the civil members of the Order of Merit, and four of the five Foulerton Research Professors of the Royal Society have been fellows of Trinity College, Cambridge. At present every officer of the Royal Society is a Trinity man."

Certainly this was not chance, but how could it be explained? Trinity's high reputation no doubt attracted superior students, and since candidates competed for the fellowships, there was a competitive spirit that was "unhappily almost absent in America." But the most important point seemed to be that the Fellows were chosen when young (six out of seven when they were no more than twenty-seven years old). They were chosen, therefore, for their promise rather than their achievements and at a time when they were presumably at the peak of their creative powers. They were given a chance to exercise those powers for a period of six years, free from care, under pleasant living conditions, in the company of other scholars, and with full support for their research.

On the model of the Trinity Prize Fellowships a plan was drawn up for a Society of Fellows at Harvard. Lowell tried to find support but no foundation would take it on. He tried the matching-gift maneuver: if a foundation would put up a million, he would find another (presumably his own money). Finally, when he announced his retirement as President, Henderson and Whitehead pressed him to let the Society of Fellows be his last achievement, and he gave all the necessary money himself—"though it took nearly all I had," as he later said.

Henderson, Whitehead, Lowes, and Charles Curtis were to be Senior Fellows, with the Dean of the Faculty of Arts and Sciences (Kenneth Murdock) and the President, *ex officio*. When Conant became President, Lowell was prevailed upon to become a Senior Fellow himself, his only remaining connection with the University. There would eventually be twenty-four Junior Fellows, but during the first year only six. They would live in the houses, or outside the university if married, and would be given a generous stipend and support for their work.

Hallowell Davis and Crozier proposed me, separately, for a Junior Fellowship, and on March 18 I received a letter from President Lowell: "The Senior Fellows of the Society of Fellows are to have a meeting to consider candidates at my house, 17 Quincy Street, on Monday evening, March 20th, and I write to ask if you can meet them there at 9:00."

The house was in the Harvard Yard. (Lowell had built it at his own expense after moving the old presidential house across Quincy

Street.) A maid met me at the door and showed me into the living room, which was full of heavily stuffed late-Victorian furniture, with pictures in huge gold frames and many knickknacks on the tables. I sat and waited, hearing voices in the distance, where another candidate was presumably being examined. Eventually Mr. Lowell came in, bowing cordially with his characteristic stoop, and took me to the other room. In a large semicircle before a fire sat Henderson, Whitehead, John Livingston Lowes (whose "Road to Xanadu" I had heard hotly discussed at Bread Loaf, Vermont, years before), Charles Curtis, and Kenneth Murdock. It was a pretty frightening jury, but Henderson recognized me as a faithful auditor of his course in the history of science, and the discussion was friendly and helpful. We got onto behaviorism, and Whitehead quizzed me closely. I took some sort of monistic line; I could not say what the world was made of, but I was sure it was of one stuff. "I want all my eggs in one basket," I said. It was a dangerous line. Henderson was interested in scientific method (he had made a novel use of the nomogram in his book on the blood), and I talked with him about Mach, Poincaré, and Bridgman.

New appointees were to be no more than twenty-four years old. After three years they might be reappointed for another term. If I were appointed, it would be as if for a second term, but even so, the limiting age would be twenty-eight at the time of appointment. The day on which I was examined by the committee was my twenty-ninth birthday. Nevertheless, three weeks later I received another letter.

> I write to inform you that you have been selected by the Senior Fellows as a Junior Prize Fellow for the next three years.
> Congratulating you upon your choice, I am
> yours very sincerely,
> A. Lawrence Lowell

I was not only rescued from disaster, I found myself with what was at the time the most generous support a young scholar could ask for. I soon received a letter from Dr. Ronald Ferry, Master of John Winthrop House: "I am writing to ask if you won't come to live in Winthrop House where we have a room reserved for you and where, of course, you will be able to take your meals in accordance with the usual arrangements." I wrote to Henderson, as Chairman of the Society, asking if I might move into Winthrop House as early as July 1 and was told that I might. I had also asked whether I could spend some money during the summer to improve my apparatus, since I should then get on with my work in the fall more quickly. Henderson consulted Lowell and it was agreed that I might spend $200.

I declined a lesser honor that spring when I was invited to join a Greek-letter fraternity. The invitation said that the society "embraces no features of secrecy. The motto is an epitome of its ideals and aims:—'Companions in zealous research.'" The writer no doubt meant to dissociate the organization from Greek-letter college fraternities, but his references to secrecy and mottoes renewed unpleasant memories of Hamilton College, and I wrote to say that I did not "wish to accept the election at the present time." Unfortunately, it was the prestigious and useful Sigma Xi Society, an organization of scientists, and when I returned to Harvard fifteen years later, my refusal had not been forgotten.

My parents were overjoyed at my election to the Society of Fellows and bought me a Ford runabout with a rumble seat. It was my first car, and it made some substantial changes in my life. I suspect that my parents had a particular change in mind: I was twenty-nine and should be getting married. A car would broaden my exposure to eligible women.

I behaved as they had no doubt predicted by looking up a senior at Wellesley named Martha Young. I had met her on Monhegan, where she was visiting the younger sister of Edie Reid. She invited me to a garden party given by the President of Wellesley for the senior class. I drove out early and found that she had a problem: she had no hat to match the dress she wanted to wear at the party. In a store window in Wellesley she pointed to the kind of hat she needed, and I said I thought I could make one. She bought a yard of crisp white material while I was buying wire and a tube of Duco cement. We drove out of town and parked, and I made the hat, which was a great success.

Hawthorne said of Thoreau that he made his friends feel guilty, and as soon as I got a car I saw what he meant. I could now drive to Walden Pond to enjoy a bit of life in the woods, but Thoreau had said that he could walk from the pond to Cambridge before his neighbor could earn enough money to buy a ticket on the railroad. That was no longer true, perhaps, but I felt guilty, and I bought a copy of *Walden* to take the curse off the car. I am usually prompt, and promptness, as Oscar Wilde said, is the thief of time. I saved a good deal of otherwise stolen time by reading bits of *Walden* at random.

A tutor at Harvard whom I knew had a brother who was an aspiring portrait artist. He hoped to do Whitehead, but he would begin with lesser lights. Shortly after my election to the Society my friend suggested that his brother do my portrait. The price was modest, and I thought my father and mother would be pleased. I sat for him for many hours, and the portrait passed through a reasonably acceptable stage. In the end the likeness was questionable, but I sent it home. My parents wrote to say that it looked as if I were just spitting out a cherry pit, and one day they broke it up to start a fire in the fireplace.

Via Saunders had gone back to Clinton (and would shortly marry Jim Agee) and Mary Lou had moved into an exclusive boardinghouse on Louisburg Square in Boston, where I occasionally saw her. Roosevelt had brought Prohibition to an end, and we were beginning to discover something better than spiked beer, cheap red wine, or bathtub gin. One evening Mary Lou brought out a square brown bottle and poured me my first glass of Cointreau. Later, as we were leaving the house for the evening, a temporary boarder, thought by some to be S. S. Van Dine incognito, met us in the hall and urged us to see Mae West in *She Done Him Wrong*.

Mary Lou and I drove to Clinton for a weekend with the Saunderses. There would be no string quartets, because Ivor Richards was there and he did not like music. He had recently had his fortieth birthday and was rather depressed, but we discussed behaviorism at length. Even where he agreed with me, he felt he could not use behavioristic terms with the people for whom he wrote. I argued that it was fatal to use anything else.

On July 1 I moved into F-35 Winthrop House. I had a large living room with a fireplace, a combined bedroom and study, and a bath. I brought with me a few of my more comfortable and serviceable pieces of furniture and a new radio shaped like a Gothic arch. My clavichord would be finished before the fall term began; it would be an ideal instrument for a dormitory because it could not be heard in the next room.

I WENT BACK to Monhegan, by car rather than the Bangor night boat, following the old U.S. Route 1 through dozens of small towns on Maine's heavily indented coast. On Monhegan in 1929 I had discovered a small inn called the Trailing Yew, run by Josephine Davis, a young member of an island family. Room and board were about $2.50 a day, the food was excellent, and the guests dressed informally. Spruce and alder had not yet taken over the island, and the view from the porch, especially in the evening, was magnificent.

I soon met Marianne Chase. Her family had been one of the first to come to Monhegan (by sailboat) for the summer. She had spent her summers there as a child and knew the island people well. She liked to swim, and although the water was bitter cold I swam with her and thought I liked it too. She knew all the old paths, which we followed even though many had become almost impassable. She knew where to find the Geodetic Survey marker on the highest point and where, exactly at sunset, one could see Mt. Washington a hundred miles away. She knew where the wild strawberries and raspberries were most abundant and where, precisely at low tide, one might reach the pool, at the base of the headland called Whitehead, where beautiful sea anemones grew. Joe Davis often put up lunches for us, and we spent whole days on the far side of the island, rock climbing or just watching the surf. Near Burnthead we once worked a great boulder free and watched and heard it plunge thundering into the sea below. The Trailing Yew was named for an evergreen ground cover, and at night we lay on beds of it and studied the brilliant stars.

We decided to try making pottery, and on a trip to Cambridge I bought seventy-five pounds of potter's clay and brought it back to the island, together with the turntable from an old phonograph. Behind their cottage Marianne's father had a small shop where I converted the turntable into a potter's wheel, arranging two large stones on a crosspiece as a kind of flywheel. One of us kept the wheel spinning while the other worked the clay. We lacked professional advice and never made anything worthwhile.

I drove back to Cambridge early in September but Marianne

stayed on—alone after her family left. I checked the Winthrop House office for mail a dozen times a day, but there were not many letters and they told me little more than that life on the island was becoming rigorous. The walls of the cottage were thin, and a fireplace and small kerosene heater could not keep it warm. The water supply had been turned off because the pipes lay on the surface of the rocky island and had to be emptied before there was any danger of freezing. A pail of water brought from a neighbor's well would have a crust of ice to be broken in the morning. The winds grew stronger. "Stormy Weather" was a popular song at the time, and it began to mean Marianne to me in more ways than one. Thinking of her was painful, but as I became caught up in my new life the pain was eased and I simply stopped thinking of her. I stopped writing, too, and so did she, and that was the end of the affair.

WHEN THE FALL TERM OPENED, I was not yet quite affluent. I wrote to my parents:

> *I have not yet been paid but expect to be tomorrow. Most of that will go for necessary expenses so I shall have another fairly lean month. $50 to clavichord, $24 for season symphony tickets, $5–$10 to have moth holes rewoven in the suit I got last winter in Scranton. [I had been attacked by moths as well as rats in that house on Linnaean Street.] I want to get curtains fairly soon and a new rug or two and a wall hanging. If you have any small (or large) oriental rugs you are not using send them along.*

Life in Winthrop House was luxurious. There were waitresses in the dining room and a charming hostess, and we chose our meals from printed menus. The food was excellent and rich. A cartoon in the *Lampoon* showed a Harvard student eating at a cafeteria in the Square, saying to a puzzled friend, "Do you think I want lamb all the time?" After dinner I joined tutors and instructors for coffee before a fire in the Senior Common Room. I had money for apparatus and books, and a car. Could anyone ask for more?

My self-satisfaction was shattered by a story in the *Boston American*. The founding of the Society of Fellows had attracted a good deal of attention, and a reporter was sent to interview the three

Junior Fellows who were in Cambridge before the fall term opened. He saw me in my laboratory, and a photographer took pictures of me there and as I walked to work. He interviewed the others in their new quarters. He probed for unusual things about our ways of life and teased out absurd acknowledgments of how important we thought it was to be a Junior Fellow. Our pictures were spread across the page and the headline read: *Three Members of Harvard's Newly Created Super Brain Clique Pose for Camera.* A picture of me sitting by my apparatus was titled: BOY FROM COAL REGION IS SUPER SCHOLAR. Frederick Watkins was shown at his piano playing "a tune of joy at his election."

Nothing could have been further from the character of the Society, and I lay awake all night tossing in agonies of shame. What would Henderson think? Or Lowell? I had once seen Lowell in cap and gown returning to his house after commencement, paying no attention whatsoever to the photographers who were trying to get pictures of him. Nothing was ever said to us about our indiscretion, even when, the following spring, the reporter dug up his notes and sold an article to the *New York Times* in which he said that Harvard had taken a look at us and had pronounced us "regular fellows." The *Harvard Crimson* reprinted the article under the heading "Funny Fellows."

EARLY IN SEPTEMBER I received a letter from Henderson: "The Society will meet on Monday evening, September 25th at half past six o'clock. . . . The rooms of the Society are in Eliot House, Entry M. It has been agreed that we shall not dress."

Eliot House had been built before the Society was founded, but two handsome rooms had been included in its plan without explanation, and now their use was revealed. We met for our first dinner on Monday evening, September 25, 1935. I wrote a glowing account to my parents:

> It was possibly the greatest evening in my life. We have a Common Room like a very rich club room and a dining room for our exclusive use. Beautifully decorated with fine portraits, etc. We sat down thirteen at dinner. On the table were thirteen solid silver candlesticks with a name engraved on each, as placecards. I will get my

candlestick when I leave the Society. Henderson, chairman of the society, sat at one end, with Pres. Lowell on his right. Pres. Conant (see American magazine) sat at the other end and I at his right. Murdock, the dean of the Graduate School and the man we all thought would be president of Harvard [he was, or soon became, Dean of the Faculty of Arts and Sciences, not the Graduate School] sat on my right. We had possibly the best dinner I have ever eaten. Sherry and bitters before, imported Dutch beer with, and cognac and other liqueurs afterward. [Prohibition was not repealed until December. I suspect that Charlie Curtis was responsible for the anticipatory supplies.]

We all signed the record of the Society. I signed first of the junior fellows. The record is a beautifully bound book that will eventually contain God knows how many great names. Lowell copied into it a sort of creed for the members of the society.

The conversation was wonderful and we were at talk [table?] more than three hours. Very genial atmosphere and very brilliant. The other junior fellows are fine although I haven't got to know them well yet. I am keeping a sort of diary of the stories told at the meetings and of the principle [sic] conversations. It is all very wonderful and I was genuinely thrilled.

The "diary" had only one entry, with some examples of that wonderful conversation:

Our being thirteen led to stories of superstition. Whitehead told about a woman who dreamed of the number 3 on 3 successive nights and became very rich because, she said, she multiplied $3 \times 3 \times 3$ and arrived at 28 and put all her money on 28 and won.

Lowell told of a man (I think he said his father) who [met a farmer who] contended that more chickens would be hatched from a setting if there were an odd number of eggs. "For example," said the [farmer], "you will probably get more chicks from 13 than from 12 eggs." "What about 14?" Lowell's father asked. "Oh," said the farmer, "that's more eggs!"

Someone suggested that we occasionally have a paper read for the sake of revealing our professional interests and to start discussions. Henderson said that a Frenchman had told him that this custom, which is very common in England and America, is incomprehensible to a Frenchman, who would find it intolerable. Whitehead countered by saying that a French Society, or Dining Club, was on the other hand always making dictionaries. He said [that a friend] had once insisted upon his visiting a French Philosophical Club and when they arrived, sure enough there they were, making a dictionary. They were busy defining *causation*.

I mentioned Richards to Murdock who was much interested to hear he was in these parts and passed it on to Lowes, across the table. Lowes was in Cambridge the year Richards was here and had met him only for a moment. Murdock suggested to the company that we ask Richards to dine with us. This was generally approved but on second thought it appeared that our first guest should be the master of Eliot House. This will probably rule Richards out as he will leave too soon to be asked two weeks hence. [Garrett] Birkhoff, who has been at Cambridge the past year, says Richards is the most discussed and the most popular figure there. [In my letter to my parents I had said, "Richards came in to Cambridge with his wife. They spent yesterday morning in the lab and we had an interesting and profitable discussion. He is much interested in my book on Epistemology and Behaviorism which by the way is coming along well. I get up at 6:30 and work on it for 1 and ½ hours before breakfast every day."]

Conant talked mostly about the necessity of a classical education in science, using [William] Arnold as an example of a deformed mind. He also detailed a personal report from Friedrich [?] about German Universities, which was very pitiful. The tradition of the German Universities is apparently at an unbelievably abrupt end, and is being too thoroughly demolished to recover for many decades. I was much depressed and looked with trembling upon the gay and distinguished party in which the story was told.

The creed I mentioned was not a credo but an injunction:

You have been selected as a member of this Society for your personal prospect of serious achievement in your chosen field, and your promise of notable contribution to knowledge and thought. That promise you must redeem with your whole intellectual and moral force.

You will practice the virtues, and avoid the snares, of the scholar. You will be courteous to your elders who have explored to the point from which you may advance; and helpful to your juniors who will progress farther by reason of your labors. Your aim will be knowledge and wisdom, not the reflected glamour of fame. You will not accept credit that is due to another, or harbor jealousy of an explorer who is more fortunate.

You will seek not a near, but a distant, objective, and you will not be satisfied with what you may have done. All that you may achieve or discover you will regard as a fragment of a larger pattern, which from his separate approach every true scholar is striving to descry.

To these things, in joining the Society of Fellows, you dedicate yourself.

Somehow I disliked Conant. I had heard some anti-Conant gossip—that when the Harvard Corporation was considering candidates for president, he had killed the chances of Mr. Lowell's favorite, Kenneth Murdock, and that he himself had wanted the job because his work on chlorophyll had reached a dead end—but I was also bothered by his manner that evening. He had been abroad all summer preparing for his first year as President of Harvard by visiting the English universities, and he seemed quite sure that he knew precisely what a university should be. When we talked about Bill Arnold, a friend of mine in General Physiology, he seemed equally sure of precisely what a scientist should be.

I did not know until he died many years later how much I liked Henderson. Though best known for his work on the chemistry of the blood, he had written a remarkable book called *The Fitness of the Environment* in which he argued that life as we know it is highly favored by the earth's environment. The prevalence of carbon in the atmosphere and the extraordinary capacity of the carbon atom to form complex molecules was one example. The fact that water contracts as it cools but begins to expand just before it freezes was another, because it meant that lakes and rivers froze from the top down. Freezing from the bottom up would have made early forms of life difficult if not impossible in cold climates.

Henderson could be rude ("Skinner," he once said, "that is the stupidest remark I have ever heard you make"), but the only things that enraged him were matters of intellect. Beneath his bluster, he was quite gentle. One evening when another Junior Fellow, Willard Van Orman Quine, and I refused to be silenced by his autocratic manner and went after him, he melted immediately. He was a staunch Francophile. I thought of the rumor that he had had a French mistress when he once expressed the absolute absurdity of something someone had done by commenting, "You could as well expect an old man to be in love." When, a year or two later, a younger Junior Fellow, Henry Guerlac, told me that he was going to resign from the Society because he was no longer interested in biochemistry and wanted to be a historian, we went together to see Henderson. "We didn't elect you as a biochemist," he said. "We elected you as a man." And Henry remained a Junior Fellow and became a historian.

Henderson was not a man to whom one spoke with any great freedom. Nevertheless, on one occasion when Van Quine and I were talking with him, I risked calling his attention to a possible spoonerism in Constance Garnett's translation of Dostoevski in which she called something an "artless farce." Henderson laughed appreciatively, but I was glad to have Van's later assurance that I had taken a step toward a more relaxed relation between the Junior and Senior Fellows.

Henderson looked like Edward VII, and someone contributed a portrait of Edward that hung for some time in the rooms of the Society. It was appropriate because Henderson had a curious sense of humor about himself. Even at his most pompous (except when angry) he seemed aware that he was reading a possibly amusing script. He sometimes seemed to boast of his mistakes. He once showed me one of his early papers, in German as I remember it, in which he described the condition of the blood that was soon to be called acidosis. In it he said that a corresponding alkalosis was unlikely. It was, he said angrily, a stupid thing to say. When his famous book on the blood was published, he opened his first copy, looked at a diagram, and saw immediately that the blood was going the wrong way. He had seen the diagram scores of times in manuscript and proof; the thing that intrigued him was that the mistake had jumped out at him as soon as it could not be remedied. And once, when we were talking about *The Fitness of the Environment*, he said, "My colleagues have forgiven me for writing it."

He was also strangely persuasive. One evening he began to talk about P.G. Wodehouse. A master of prose style—did we not agree? Who in the present century could equal him? Harry Levin, then a Junior Fellow, mentioned Joyce, and a few other names were muttered. Henderson suggested that we put it to a vote. A piece of paper was passed around the table, and each of us wrote down the name of his candidate and folded it out of sight before passing it on. When the votes were tallied it appeared that, in the opinion of the assembled company, the greatest master of prose in the twentieth century was P. G. Wodehouse.

Mr. Lowell had had a long and successful career as President of Harvard. His predecessor, Mr. Eliot, had been something of a nuisance, dropping in to offer advice about what should be done with the university. When Lowell retired, he made the break complete. Some months after our first meeting I saw him go up to Conant, put his hand on his shoulder, and say, "Well, how are things going?" He was an amusing conversationalist. He once spent the better part of an hour analyzing the strategies of David and Goliath. David, the smaller man, naturally chose a weapon that could be used at a distance. We all thought that he had made a mistake in the Sacco and Vanzetti case, and I once heard him refer to it as "that affair of Sacco . . . Sacco . . . and the other fellow."

John Livingston Lowes had made his reputation by tracing the literary origins of Coleridge's "Ancient Mariner" and "Kubla Khan" and was trying to do the same for something else of Coleridge's. He occasionally asked us if we knew where Coleridge might have read a particular phrase, though it was most unlikely that we could have done so. When there was a pause in the conversation at dinner, he would pull out his watch and say, "I'm testing a well-known theory" —namely, that pauses occur at twenty minutes before or after the hour. He made a purely mechanical effort to be interested in our work. If we mentioned a book or paper he had not read, he would carefully write its name on a slip of paper and put it in his pocket. There was never any sign that he looked at the slips again.

One evening Edwin Arlington Robinson came to dinner. He and Henderson had grown up in Gardiner, Maine, and they knew Laura Richards, whose sentimental *Captain January* had moved me as a boy. I sat next to Robinson and plied him with questions about his work habits. He answered in monosyllables.

Charles Curtis was a lawyer and alone among the Senior Fellows we talked with him man to man, not only because he lacked the frightening distinction of the other Senior Fellows, but because he stammered rather badly, disguising his blocks as lapses of memory, saying "What's its name? What's its name? What's its name?" as rapidly as possible. He was interested in everyone and everything, and it was a great loss when, in my third year, he was asked to resign from the governing board of the University. He had divorced his Bostonian wife and married a well-known writer. Such a thing was simply not done among those who held responsible positions at Harvard at the time. The Junior Fellows gave him a first edition of Hobbes's *Leviathan* and sent President Conant a strong letter expressing their regret at his departure.

EARLY IN THE SPRING of 1933 the *Atlantic Monthly* had received a manuscript called *The Autobiography of Alice B. Toklas*. It came to the desk of Mary Louise White, who was then on the editorial board. She had not read much of it before she recognized the hand of Gertrude Stein, and her suspicions were confirmed by the last paragraph: "About six weeks ago Gertrude Stein said, it does not look to me as if you are ever going to write that autobiography. You know what I am going to do. I am going to write it for you. I am going to write it as simply as Defoe did the autobiography of Robinson Crusoe. And she has and this is it."

Mary Lou was the only one to enjoy the joke, for when the *Atlantic* published selections, they were from "*The Autobiography of Alice B. Toklas* by Gertrude Stein." Marianne and I had read two or three issues of the *Atlantic* that summer, and I was curious about the following passage:

> She was one of a group of Harvard men and Radcliffe women and they all lived very closely and very interestingly together. One of them, a young philosopher and mathematician who was doing research work in psychology, left a definite mark on her life. She and he together worked out a series of experiments in automatic writing under the direction of Münsterberg. The result of her own experiments, which Gertrude Stein wrote down and which was printed in the *Harvard Psychological Review*, was the first writing of hers ever to be printed. It is very interesting to read because the method of writing to be afterwards developed in *Three Lives* and *The Making of Americans* already shows itself.

That fall I looked up the article. It was by Leon M. Solomons and Gertrude Stein and was called "Normal Motor Automatism." It purported to show to what extent the elements of a second personality could be found in a normal human being. The authors tried to split their own personalities in an artificial way, particularly through automatic writing. They began by writing while reading a book, but they reported that spontaneous automatic writing became quite easy after a little practice: "We had now gained so much control over our habits of attention that distraction by reading was almost unnecessary. Miss Stein found it sufficient distraction often to simply read what her arm wrote, but following three or four words behind her pencil." The examples she gave were very much like the material she later published in *Tender Buttons*.

I called on Mary Louise White one evening (she had moved to an apartment on Beacon Hill) and told her about the paper. Would the *Atlantic* be interested in an article arguing that *Tender Buttons* was essentially automatic writing? She thought it would, and I went to work.

There were problems. I admired *Three Lives*, in spite of its strong preoccupation with the present participle, but what could I say about *Tender Buttons*? In my article I called it "the stream of consciousness of a woman without a past," but there was a very different current view—namely, that it was the first literary version of what was happening in the visual arts. Gertrude Stein was the Picasso of literature. I also had to deal delicately with the statement in the *Autobiography* that "Gertrude Stein never had subconscious reactions, nor was she a successful subject for automatic writing." I suggested that when she began to write *Tender Buttons*, she had forgotten her research.

I called the article "Gertrude Stein and Automatic Writing" and gave it to Mary Lou. She passed it on to Ellery Sedgwick, the editor of the *Atlantic*, and he wrote to say that he liked it. It was, he said, a "small classic of the dissecting-table." (John Hutchens, who saw the article in Paris, was evidently in extrasensory contact with Sedgwick, for he wrote to say that I should have called it "A Stein on the Table.") Sedgwick added that "the curious volume of interest which has followed the Stein serial in the Atlantic gives us a chance to gain just the hearing we want." He had only one suggestion: "The hook should be barbed with the right title. Yours gives the case away, and also suggests a certain dullness wholly absent in what follows. I want to call the paper 'Has Gertrude Stein a Secret?' and let it go at that."

It appeared in the January 1934 issue. The mountain of the Society of Fellows had labored and brought forth a mouse. But it was a lively mouse and attracted a good deal of attention. An editorial in the *New York Times* called it "acute and urbane" but defended Gertrude Stein. A. E. Housman had said that "Take, oh, take those lips away" was "nonsense but . . . ravishing poetry," and the *Times* agreed. "Is Mr. Skinner deaf to music and obdurate to magic?" (My father sent a telegram to make sure I saw the editorial.)

Three months later Conrad Aiken, writing in the *New Republic*, not only agreed with me but went much further. "For nearly twenty years," he said, "we have been sedulously taught, by the high brow critics, the literary left wingers and all the masters of the subtlest schools, that in Miss Stein's work we were witnessing a bold and intricate and revolutionary and always *consciously* radical experiment in style, of which the results were to be of incalculable importance for English literature." My article, he said, "makes of the whole thing a very cruel joke."

Sherwood Anderson, writing in the *American Spectator*, defended Miss Stein: "All good writing is, in a sense, automatic. It is and it isn't. When I am really writing, not doing as I am doing now, thinking the words out as I go, making an argument, but am really writing, it is always half automatic," and in the *New York Herald Tribune* Lewis Gannett agreed with Anderson.

According to a reporter in the *Boston Sunday Herald*, Gertrude Stein "dismissed recent efforts of scientists to explain her work" by saying "Popcock!" but that was not what she wrote to Ellery Sedgwick:

> *Thanks so very much for your good wishes and for the* Atlantic *with the Skinner article about my writing. No it is not so automatic as he thinks. If there is anything secret it is the other way too. I think I achieve by xtra consciousness xcess but then what is the use of my telling him that, he being a psychologist and I having been one. Besides when he is not too serious he is a pretty good one.*

Stella, the model I had known in Greenwich Village, saw my article and dropped me a note, and when I was next in New York I had cocktails with her at the Plaza, just across the street from Bergdorf Goodman, where she worked. She was still beautiful.

DURING MY FIRST YEAR as a Junior Fellow I met Nedda, who had come to Harvard for graduate study. She was younger than I by four or five years, but we liked each other immediately and after a date or two we made love. She had an apartment where we spent a good deal of time. She cooked delicious meals, and I took her to the Boston Symphony and the theatre (we saw O'Neill's *Days Without End*). I fell very much in love with her, but I did not see much of her friends or have much in common with them. After two or three months it was clear that I was not really a part of her intellectual or social life. One evening I took her out to dinner and she told me that we should break it off. She had been more or less engaged to a young man who was chronically ill, and she was going back to him.

It was a reasonable decision, but it hit me very hard. As we walked back to her apartment from the subway, I found myself moving very slowly. It was not a pose; I simply could not move faster. For a week I was in almost physical pain, and one day I bent a wire in the shape of an N, heated it in a Bunsen burner, and branded my left arm. The brand remained clear for years. My mother saw it once when I was changing my shirt and said, "Where'd you get the N?" I said, "It was an accident. I burned myself," and she wisely let it go at that.

PROBABLY BECAUSE OF the success of my article, Mr. Sedgwick asked me to Sunday-night dinner at his home on Beacon Hill. "Informal" the invitation said, and I was lucky enough to ask Mary Lou White what that meant. She said I should wear my tuxedo. I arrived precisely on time and found among other guests Katherine Mayo, whose *Mother India* was then a best seller.

The dinner was beautifully served. The gentlemen stayed at table for cigars and brandy after the ladies withdrew. We rejoined them to hear Mr. Sedgwick tell (and to see no sign from Mrs. Sedgwick that he was retelling) fascinating stories about his editorship, such as how Opel Whitely—who claimed to be the daughter of the Dauphin of France—had brought him her diary, torn to pieces by a jealous sister, and how they had reassembled it during a weekend in the Sedgwick attic. Of Miss Mayo I wrote in my notebook: "Brilliant dialogue between us on free will." She was all for intentional design but I defended chance; if César Franck had only said an extra word or two to his wife as he left his house, he would not have been run down and killed by that hansom cab, and we might now have more than one Franck symphony. We also talked about the inheritance of acquired characters but I remember only that she thought some behavior, such as the sheepdog's, must be innate. My note concluded, "She was friendly, warm, but upset about me. Said God would take care of me."

Mr. Sedgwick was soon writing to ask if I might not have something else for the *Atlantic*, but there was nothing at the time. "I've been working," I replied, "on a very technical study of the use of words, and have been reading, at the same time, Empson's *Seven Types of Ambiguity*. With this I am tremendously impressed, and it may be that by the end of the year I shall have distilled off something of a nontechnical nature on the use of words or meanings, and I shall want to talk with you about it, if that is the case."

I was drifting back toward literature, but I was still suppressing my own small part in it. When Robert Frost came to dinner at the Society, Van Quine and I talked with him for a long time. "Science is only a kind of metaphor," he said, and we more or less agreed. But I did not remind him that we had met, or that he had sent me a letter that had derailed me for a year or two after college.

The letter was, however, moving toward publication. I had planned to take Nedda with me to Brown University, where I was scheduled to give a colloquium and dine with Professor Carmichael and his wife. Instead I took a friend of hers, Caroline Ford, a senior at Radcliffe, whose father was Professor of Social Ethics at Harvard and whose mother was very much a Cantabrigian. Caroline's honors thesis, a study of Robert Frost, was to be published, and I gave her a photostat of my letter. She sent it to a friend in the Amherst College Library. Lawrance Thompson, who many years later would publish a collection of Frost's letters, saw it there and made a copy.

Caroline played the piano and we began to work on Max Reger's four-hand transcriptions of the Brandenburg Concertos.

ALTHOUGH PRESSING A LEVER was a fairly simple bit of behavior, it was not one reflex. At best you would have to say that the lever and the surrounding apparatus evoked pressing, the sound of the food dispenser then evoked approach to the food tray, and the touch and smell of food evoked picking up and eating (a step, I noted, "capable of further analysis"). Obviously I was dealing with a chain of reflexes, which I decided to take apart. I would break the chain at different points and extinguish the segments.

The results were beautiful. When I disconnected the food dispenser so that pressing the lever was not followed by the sound, the first link in the chain disappeared in an extinction curve. When I reconnected the dispenser but left it empty, so that the rat heard the dispenser and went to the food tray but found no pellets, the second link was restored (but not reinforced) and I got another, larger curve. If I began the experiment with both links—leaving the dispenser connected but empty—extinction occurred, but when I disconnected the dispenser, there was no renewed responding. I got the same result after periodic reconditioning, except that the extinction curves were smoother.

AT THE ANNUAL MEETING of the American Association for the Advancement of Science in December 1933, Professor Walter Miles gave several paper-and-pencil tests to those who were curious about their personalities. I took them, and a month or two later learned that I had better judgment than 95 percent of the others in the group, was more extroverted than 57 percent, and was more readily annoyed than 65 percent. I do not remember what I judged or called annoying. Other evidences of my personality, closer to daily life, were less reassuring. A young woman who typed manuscripts for me said that I had a reputation for conceit—that, indeed, someone had told her he wanted to meet me for that very reason, as if I were an unusual specimen. I was shaken. Conceit had been my father's problem, and my mother's countercontrolling measures had reached me as well.

Was I not weathering my appointment to the Society? Was my faith in the importance of my research too obvious?

Or was I really afraid that I would fail? I was associating every week with half a dozen older men of proven brilliance and with five men of my own age chosen because they would presumably be brilliant. If I referred too often to my achievements, such as they were, was I perhaps simply trying to keep in the race? In a note written at the time, I seemed to be preparing an alibi for failure. It was called "Why No Great Science of Behavior?" and it began: "When compared with the Galileos, Newtons, and so on of other sciences, psychologists are a second-rate lot." But we should say, rather, that "the men who have turned to psychological subjects have done second-rate jobs." This could mean either that "only second-rate men try this field or that men never appear as first-rate in this field." The first alternative is "not flattering to great men—they were not deliberate cowards, choosing the easy fields. . . ."

The foolishness of psychology is not due to the foolishness of psychologists but to a subject matter that makes fools of everyone. . . . The question is "Why has an unsuccessful job been done in psychology?" It is no explanation to say that psychologists are below the caliber of other scientists. It cannot be said that the subject matter is unimportant or escapes notice. It cannot be said that a Galileo or a Newton never asked himself questions about psychology. . . . The field is a devilish one.

I was also showing medical symptoms. The complete absorption in my work that drove me to the L-Street Beach had long since moderated and my heart was no longer skipping beats, but I began to have indigestion for two or three weeks at a time. Even the blandest food disagreed with me. (If I had ulcers, they left no scars.) It was the kind of symptom that was beginning to be called psychosomatic, a term which, as a behaviorist, I deplored.

I was taking reasonably good care of myself. I often played squash with a young tutor in economics named Dan Smith, who lived in the suite above mine. We were also movie devotees, and twice a week we ate our dinners quickly and raced to the University Theatre in Harvard Square before the price of admission went up at seven o'clock. Music remained a pleasant distraction, which I did not always take too seriously. At the piano in the Winthrop House Common Room, with Henry Guerlac on the violin, I played von Suppe's *Poet and Peasant Overture* for a performance of *Lady Audley's Secret*. I memorized with difficulty. I spent all one Thanksgiving Day mastering the C Major Prelude from the first book of the *Well-Tempered Clavier*. I could play only a few bars of it a month later.

I was often bothered by "tunes that ran through my head," and I discovered a behavioral remedy. If I simply switched to a theme that I liked, such as the Andante from Mozart's Sonata No. 19, it displaced the tune that was bothering me and in turn soon vanished. I also toyed with visual stimuli. Just after waking I would lie on my side, close my eyes, and imagine the desk beside my bed, bright in the morning light. Often I could not tell whether my eyes were open or closed.

An old phobia persisted. Beebe-Center once suggested that we drive to his home in Swampscott and cook ourselves a good dinner. His wife was away on business (she had inherited a spice company), and we should have the place to ourselves. We bought steak, two bottles of wine, and some onions (I had offered to make an onion soup)—and I followed him in my own car so that I could return afterward. He lived in a large rambling frame house with a wide porch, separated from the beach by a street that had regrettably become a highway. We prepared an excellent meal. One bottle of wine was French and the other American, and we wrapped them in paper before opening them. Then we tasted them and agreed that one was better than the other. It was the French.

That was pleasant enough, but on the way back, driving at a moderate speed, I crossed an intersection and heard a police whistle. I drew to a stop, caught in one of the speed traps then widely used by small communities as a source of revenue. My name and address were taken; a summons would be mailed.

When I told Beebe-Center the next day and said that I was canceling a trip because I was afraid the summons might arrive when I was away, he pooh-poohed the whole thing and proposed that we go to the Cambridge Police Station in Harvard Square and fix the ticket.

I refused and when I received my summons I dutifully drove to the town courthouse, appeared in court, and paid my fine.

My distinction between two types of conditioning was becoming clearer, and in 1935 I published a more detailed account called "Two Types of Conditioned Reflex and a Pseudo Type." I confused matters by renumbering the types, and in a later paper I abandoned numbers in favor of "Type S" for the Pavlovian case, where the reinforcer is paired with a stimulus, and "Type R" for the case in which it is made contingent upon a response.

Two years later a symposium was held at the annual meeting of the American Psychological Association at Dartmouth College. The main paper was by Elmer Culler, who was treating the flexion of a dog's leg pretty much as Pavlov had treated salivation. I was a discussant, and part of my notes read as follows: There are two types of conditioning—"one in which the reinforcing stimulus is correlated with another stimulus (Pavlov's type or Type S) and another in which it is correlated with a response, yielding a law similar to Thorndike's Law of Effect (Type R)." Culler's example involved both, "since cessation of such a stimulus as a shock [to the dog's paw] may act as a . . . reinforcement in Type R. . . . No similar condition prevails in Pavlov's salivary experiments." I considered a possibly comparable case:

> Let a mild continuous shock cease when the organism makes some arbitrary response *not elicited by the shock* (e.g. if the shock is to the tail, let the response be lifting the right foreleg). Then through conditioning of Type R the dog comes to lift its leg as soon as the shock begins in order to stop the shock. If a bell precedes the shock, the organism will come to lift its leg because such a response is not followed by a shock. In Dr. Culler's example conditioning of this type is combined with Type S.

What I called a pseudo-reflex was a relation between a response and a discriminative stimulus. When I turned on the light and the rat pressed the lever, the light seemed to "elicit" the response, but the temporal sequence was misleading. Because the light had been present when a response was reinforced, it now made it more probable that a response would be made again. The pseudo-reflex, I told Fred, "may seem like a quibble to the old boys who talk about 'habits' but is, I believe, an important distinction."

I was obviously abandoning a stimulus-response psychology. The pseudo-reflex was the entering wedge of a new formulation according to which the greater part of the behavior of an organism was under the control of stimuli which were effective only because they were correlated with reinforcing consequences. The control they exerted was more subtle than "elicitation" and capable of modulation over a much wider range.

A discriminative stimulus seemed less powerful than an eliciting one, but the stimulus in stimulus-response psychology had long since succumbed to theoretical fudging. In order to support the principle of "no response without a stimulus" (as Leonard Carmichael once put it to me), various internal states had been included in a "total stimulating situation." But such a situation could not be identified for purposes of prediction or produced for purposes of control. The discriminative stimulus, on the other hand, could not only be manipulated for experimental purposes, it could often be plausibly identified in field observations.

ALTHOUGH MY SCHEDULE and my absorption in my work were still social handicaps, I was not entirely without friends. I could not always make a date for Saturday night by calling as late as 5:30 in the afternoon. But through Van Quine I met Pietro Pezzati, a portrait artist, and his sister, Maria, who had recently lost her husband in a boating accident. Maria and I went painting together. She thought my sketch of a tree in a pasture was very English.

I went to a cocktail party at which a baritone from the Longy School was to sing. When his accompanist did not turn up, I was pressed into sightreading accompaniments for him. Afterward, I said I envied him because I could not sing. He said, "Your speaking voice is good—how do you know you can't sing?" I said, "I can't even carry a tune." At his suggestion, I dropped into his studio a day or two later and sang "Ah" up and down the scale as he played supportive chords on the piano. He said he could not tell whether I would be a tenor or a baritone, but that I could certainly sing if I wanted to take lessons. I could not very well practice in Winthrop House, but I could have used my soundproof room. Nevertheless, the possibility that some visitor might find me singing "Ah" in my laboratory was too strong a deterrent.

That spring Mary Louise White and I drove to Clinton again to spend a few days with the Saunderses. Theodore Spencer was there and we played four hands, as we had done in Cambridge on his full-length concert grand. Mrs. Winthrop Chanler came, bearing an enormous bouquet of geranium leaves, arranged in small clusters, each with its distinctive odor, to be enjoyed as a work of art with one's nose. Mrs. Chanler loved Italy, and she suggested to Ted and me that we read Dante aloud with her. We took turns and I was so intent on pronouncing the Italian correctly that I lost the thread of the poem and ended my turn with a phrase dangling.

I HAD ADJUSTED to life without Nedda, but one day she called and asked if she could see me. She came to my office and handed me a letter from her family physician. It read, "I am sorry to tell you that you are pregnant." I said, "Is this *me*?" "I have not been with anyone else," she said. Would I pay for an abortion? I said I would, but would she not marry me, have the baby, and let me keep it after a quick divorce? She said she could not, for reasons she could not tell me.

A friend who had had an abortion in New York gave me the name of an apparently reliable doctor. I phoned him and he set a date. Nedda was to turn up at his office without having had breakfast. The fee would be $300. It was before the day of antibiotics, and infection was a danger, and I wanted her to have an extra $100 so that she could spend a day or two in a hotel watching her temperature. If she began to run a fever, she was to throw herself on the mercy of a gynecologist.

I went in some embarrassment to a loan company in Boston. Could I borrow $400? I said I could pay it back very soon, but the manager laughed and said there was no hurry; they preferred to have their money out on loan. The terms seemed high, and I consulted Dan Smith. He lent me part of the money himself and Cuthbert lent me the rest. Nedda went to New York with her fiancé and had the abortion, and they were soon married.

Cuthbert had said, "Aren't you proud to be the father of a three-centimeter embryo?" but I learned later that any pride I might have felt would have been unwarranted. A third man, very handsome but irresponsible, had been interested in Nedda, and after breaking up with me she had one date with him. They had not used contraceptives, and when she told him she was pregnant, he refused to do anything about it. He was irresponsible in another way and told the story to a young woman who later passed it on to me. It explained a great deal. I had always used contraceptives, and there had been no failures. And now I knew why she could not marry me: she could not have let me keep a child that was not mine. I loved Nedda and should have given her the money if I had known the truth. To Fred I wrote: "Fell badly in love this mid-winter—got in a bad jam—out again safely but subdued. Present status—perennial bachelor."

ALTHOUGH I HAD IDENTIFIED deprivation and satiation as the operations which defined a drive, I continued to speak rather carelessly of drives as things. When I said that one could strengthen a reflex by increasing the hunger drive, I meant simply depriving the organism of food. There appeared to be such an operation associated with every reinforcing consequence and hence a very large number of drives. When I said so at a psychological colloquium, Boring wrote:

> It appeared last Wednesday that the freedom of the reflex from physiology lets it go all sorts of places where the old reflex could not go. Not only may you have a sugar-reflex as distinguished from a salt-reflex but you have a stuffed-olive reflex as different from an anchovy-reflex. This seems to me something like the difficulty that Behaviorism got into. At first a stimulus would be something like radiant energy of a given frequency. Later it turned out that a grandmother might be a different stimulus from an aunt. I conclude that we are both still,
>
> As ever,
> E.G.B.

In my reply I spoke only of the problem of the stimulus:

We observe a very large number of stimuli to which ingestive responses exist. . . . But this is only a fact of nature and must be faced. No amount of theorizing . . . will do away with it. The mere collection of reflexes (the botanizing of reflexes) is to me futile and uninteresting. The point I have tried to make during these past two or three years is that the important business in psychology (behaviorism, for me) is to examine the properties of typical reflexes, selected on the basis of their convenience, and especially to examine those phenomena (called drive, learning, etc.) which I have shown to be expressible as changes in the state of such a reflex, i.e. as changes in reflex strength. Thus I am not at all in sympathy with the lack of rigor that permits a grandmother to be a stimulus, although I must confess that I am still trying to define the proper systematic use of such a term, especially where the intact organism is in question.

In March 1934 I gave a colloquium at Brown University on "Studies in the Definition of Stimulus and Response," and I developed the same issues in a paper submitted that summer called "The Generic Nature of the Concepts of Stimulus and Response," the only part of my *Sketch for an Epistemology* to be published. I wrote to Fred that it was "a very important subject" and that I had "several ulterior experimental motives in arriving at the conclusions I do."

In reassuring Fred about my theory of learning, I said that "on two successive occasions the stimulus . . . varies considerably. One time the rat sees [the lever] with his left eye, another with his right eye, etc." Something of the same sort could be said about the response. Although a rat presses a lever in a fairly stereotyped fashion, all instances are not exactly alike. By "stimulus" and "response" we can mean only classes of events. That is what I meant by their "generic nature."

The point of my paper was that, although we naturally simplify the behavior we study, as reflex physiologists did by surgical means and as I did by controlling the conditions in my "problem box," complete reproducibility was not essential. Orderly changes emerged in spite of minor differences in stimuli and in topography of response. Although all instances of pressing a lever are not alike, most of them apparently make the same contribution to an extinction ratio or a reflex reserve. We can work with certain defining properties of stimulus and response rather than with exact specifications and justify the practice by the orderliness of the processes we then observe, or by the smoothness of our curves. We thus respect and use the "natural lines of fracture along which behavior and environment actually break."

I CONTINUED TO BE interested in how many presses a rat paid back in return for each press reinforced. Some exploratory experiments had shown that the number was smaller if the rat ate a bit of food before the session began, and at the annual meeting of the American Psychological Association at Columbia University in September 1934, I reported that the decline in rate was proportional to the amount fed.

It was my second appearance at a meeting, and I faced a problem that would become acute as the years passed. Only a few people knew about my procedure, and I had to begin by explaining many small details. Since my time was limited, I talked fast, and the chairman of the session, Harvey Carr, out of the distant past, obviously found my performance amusing.

Later I outlined an experiment to test another effect of a change in hunger—or, as I wrote in my notebook, the "Nc/Ne ratio as f (hunger)." Four rats were to be "overconditioned"—that is, periodically reconditioned for some time—and extinction curves then taken for many days. Two of the rats would be fed, say, three grams of food just before each session. I predicted that although they would press more slowly, they would press the same number of times (unless, as I noted, changes due to "forgetting" would have to be taken into account).

In a paper that winter I reported extinction curves obtained after continuous reinforcement which showed the predicted effect, at least up to six grams of food fed before the session. Less hungry rats eventually made as many responses as hungry ones, although the latter made them sooner. When I reduced the hunger by prefeeding only on the first of four days of extinction, however, I was disappointed to find that the responses which were not emitted on that day had not all been recovered by the end of the fourth. I sent Fred some theoretical curves and a comment: "Note that failure to get compensation means that reconditioning effect depends upon hunger."

When visiting my family in Scranton, I had once whiled away the time by making a hydraulic model of conditioning and extinction.

A "reflex reserve" of water in a large can dripped into a smaller can. The latter was delicately balanced and tipped and dumped its contents when a given level was reached. Each dumping represented a response. As the reserve in the large can was exhausted (as in extinction), the smaller can filled more slowly, and responses became less frequent. I could now ask whether a change in "drive" changed the quantity in the large can, the rate of dripping, or the quantity that caused the small can to dump.

PAVLOV HAD CALLED extinction a kind of inhibition, but I saw no reason to talk about a suppressing force. Conditioning strengthened behavior; extinction weakened it. But Pavlov seemed to have some supporting evidence, because during extinction an incidental stimulus sometimes produced extra salivation, as if the reflex had been "disinhibited." When Clark Hull visited my laboratory in March 1932, he suggested that I introduce an extraneous stimulus when an extinction curve was in progress. If disinhibition were real, the rat should respond faster and a bump should appear in the cumulative record. Pavlov would be supported, and my theory of extinction would be in trouble.

I began the experiment with a weak stimulus, as Hull had suggested, and got no bump. I tried increasingly stronger stimuli to no effect. Finally I opened the box, tossed the rat in the air, replaced it, and closed the box. The extinction curve recovered and continued on its course. I wrote to Fred: "I have tested my extinction curves for *disinhibition* and don't get any—as I was sure I would not—Hull to the contrary!" To Hull I reported my failure and asked for comment on a paper I planned to submit for publication. He replied: "In spite of your negative results, I am not convinced that there may not be something there. . . . I myself have obtained some results which, while not absolutely negative, were certainly inconclusive. . . . Mr. Miller, a graduate student here, as well as Dr. Spence, using rats in a maze, obtained certain results a year or two ago which looked rather markedly positive."

Hull had come to see me after attending a meeting of the Society of Experimental Psychologists at Harvard. I reported the meeting to Fred in another connection:

A couple of months ago Boring ate some very bitter humble pie. There was a meeting of the Exp Psych here in Emerson. All the local younger men were invited except Cinderella Burrhus. Some of the Yale group asked for me. Boring, much confused, said I wasn't there. They said they'd like to see me. Got in touch with me late in the afternoon. I turned up in old clothes at tea at Emerson Hall, had my coat taken by one person, hat by another (not quite—as I didn't have a hat). Boring took me by the arm and presented me to the crowd— saying "Well, we've finally located Skinner!" Big moment, old man. You should have been there to share it. We can at least delight in a sort of posthumous victory. The truth is marching on. (Applause)

In the same letter I wrote: "B.-C & Pratt have practically come over to Behaviorism. Latest behaviorist: Carnap, the logician. B.C. and Pratt are seriously concerned. As I have had Carnap on my list for 3 years I again have the jump on them."

ALFRED NORTH WHITEHEAD attended the Monday-evening dinners of the Society regularly and was always eager to talk with the Junior Fellows. Unfortunately it was seldom very profitable. He was seventy-two years old when the Society first met and he tended to fall back on well-tested anecdotes. One evening, however, he and I were sitting together after the port had gone around and everyone else had left the table. Years later I told the story in this way:

We dropped into a discussion of behaviorism, which was then still very much an "ism," and of which I was a zealous devotee. Here was an opportunity which I could not overlook to strike a blow for the cause, and I began to set forth the principal arguments of behaviorism with enthusiasm. Professor Whitehead was equally in earnest—not in defending his own position, but in trying to understand what I was saying and (I suppose) to discover how I could possibly bring myself to say it. Eventually we took the following stand. He agreed that science might be successful in accounting for human behavior provided one made an exception of *verbal* behavior. Here, he insisted, something else must be at work. He brought the discussion to a close with a friendly challenge: "Let me see you," he said, "account for my behavior as I sit here saying, 'No black scorpion is falling upon this table.' "

The next morning I drew up the outline of a book on verbal behavior. My qualifications were limited. At college I had majored in English Language and Literature and minored in Romance Languages. I had published an article on Gertrude Stein and had discussed language and literature with Ivor Richards and Jim Agee and at Cuthbert and Janet Daniel's (I had not yet seen Sherry Mangan's testimonial). But I knew nothing about linguistics, and there was not very much, apart from the structures of specific languages, that seemed relevant at the time. Otto Jespersen and Edward Sapir were among the important figures, but both were mentalistic. A metaphor like "thought riding on the crests of speech" enraged me.

When I told Fred that I was writing a book on language from a behavioristic standpoint, I explained:

> *Somebody ought to do it—and it seems to be up to me. But what a field! Almost all the professional linguists are all wet psychologically and anxious to avoid psychological questions. Of course that can't be done. And the psychologists feel almost the same way. Watson: "The field is too wide to permit any but the simplest treatment here." DeLaguna: "Space does not permit—" etc. etc. Bloomfield, the best linguist in the field today, has come around from Wundt in his first edition (1915) to behaviorism in his last (1932) period. But his account of what is happening when words are used is laughable. [Bloomfield had acquired behavioristic leanings at Ohio State University, where A.P. Weiss, an early social behaviorist, was carrying on the tradition of George Herbert Mead and the functional school of psychology centered at Chicago. His text, Language, contained a simple analysis of verbal behavior in which Jill asks Jack to get her an apple, but it was oversimplified, and not much was made of it in the rest of the book.] I've done no end of dull reading on the subject and now have about ten chapters outlined which seem to me adequate. I feel hopeless about convincing the linguists;—but language is part of behavior—a damned important part—, and as behaviorists we've got to tackle it sometime. What I'm doing is applying the concepts I've worked out experimentally to this nonexperimental (but empirical) field. Although it's damned hard going, I've had quite gratifying results so far. I write so slowly that I hesitate to predict when I'll have a decent draft finished.*

In my room in Winthrop House I fastened some large sheets of cardboard together with key rings and began to formulate what I was calling verbal behavior. (I was not sure that "verbal" was the right adjective, and I searched my Greek dictionary for alternatives. Should I say "phrasal?" or "phatic"?) Exercising the Baconian side of my scientific behavior I began to classify "verbal reflexes." I took instances of behavior from my reading or from overheard speech, identified what seemed to be the stimulus, the response, and the reinforcing consequence in each case, and entered them in an awkward and constantly changing classificatory scheme. One instance might be composed of a verbal stimulus and a nonverbal response, another of a nonverbal stimulus and a verbal response, still another of a verbal stimulus and a verbal response. Grammar and syntax, especially the "moods" said to represent the speaker's "intentions," found their place. Verbal slips, spoonerisms, puns, and witty remarks were all relevant.

(I collected a good example one evening when I called on the wife of a young instructor whom I had recently met. He had gone abroad to do some scholarly work and upon his return had confessed that he had spent the summer with a young woman whom he had met on the way over. His wife was much more deeply disturbed than he had expected, and for the moment they were living apart. She played the piano as well, or badly, as I, and she asked me over to play four hands. It was a very rainy evening when I called, and, as she met me at the door, she said, "What a night for seamen—*sailors!*")

For a time the material seemed too much for me (possibly Whitehead was right), but eventually bits began to fall into place. Van Quine offered support, and so did a student of Ivor Richards, Eric Trist, who was spending a year with Sapir at Yale. He came to see me at Winthrop House (where I kept all my verbal material to avoid contaminating my laboratory), and we spent a day or two together going over my analysis.

When I told Henderson that I was writing a book on verbal behavior, he warned me that it might take five years, and during the summer he sent me a postcard from Italy: "A motto for your book— 'Car le mot, c'est le verbe, et le verbe, c'est Dieu'—Victor Hugo."

* * *

ON MONHEGAN I HAD MET a talented cellist, Bettie Zabriskie, and when another summer came, I was bold enough to invite myself to visit her in Omaha. I drove out to that strange land of the Midwest, stopping to visit the World's Fair in Chicago. Sally Rand was fan-dancing on the Midway, but I remember only a more exciting per-formance, demonstrating the perfection of a commercial product, in which a ball bearing emerged from a hole, fell about two feet, struck a steel plate, bounced in a beautiful arc, struck a second plate, and bounced back into another hole.

Bettie was a much better musician than I, but she was kind enough to let me accompany her on some of the simpler cello pieces, and we had fun with the pipe organ in a large church where her mother played. Although it was a week of record heat, I enjoyed my visit and must have outstayed my welcome.

IN THE EARLY THIRTIES my father and mother had found the summer place they were looking for. The Belmont Hotel in West Harwich on Cape Cod was a large, rambling, gray-and-white wooden structure with wide porches looking out over the ocean. There was a golf course nearby and a putting green in front of the hotel. Luncheon could be enjoyed at a beach house, though my parents did not swim or sun-bathe. A friendly headwaiter presided over the dining room, and the cuisine was excellent. My mother could play bridge and my father find friends for a game of golf at almost any time. The drive from Scranton in the Packard was not taxing, and they often spent as much as a month at West Harwich, where I went to see them for a few days each year. Once I took Marian Stevens with me.

Though my father and mother were not social climbers (for one thing they had never acquired the necessary skills), they liked being with the right people, and one summer they were taken up by a couple from Boston who must have seemed all they could have hoped for. Mrs. de Grote, a charming woman, paid particular attention to me and offered to "do anything she could for me in Boston," without explaining what she meant. Mr. de Grote was in the insurance busi-ness, and he arranged for my father to play golf with important people—one of them a former Governor of Massachusetts. The conversation would often get around to the stock market and to annuities and insurance. I don't know whether my father suspected that de Grote was planning to sell him a large annuity, but that fall, back in Scranton, he received a carefully written proposal. When he turned it down, de Grote wrote an angry letter pointing to all the favors he had shown my father and complaining that an implied promise to buy an annuity had been broken. My father could have been at fault. Like a visitor at an auction who unwittingly makes a bid, he could have given de Grote assurances of which he himself was unaware. There were social conventions he never fully understood.

He remained, of course, a staunch Republican. I had had a sample of his views during that dark year in Scranton when I bought a copy of the *New Masses*. My friend Joe Vogel had a story in it, and I marked it and left the issue on our library table. As I wrote to Percy Saunders, "I nearly forgot it until father brought it to me and said 'Did you mark that? What kind of story do you call that?' Then he read the whole issue and handed down his decision: 'a fine kind of magazine to be buying!' "

In March 1933, three days after Roosevelt's inauguration, he addressed the Chamber of Commerce in Scranton on "The Trend of the Times." He was introduced by Worthington Scranton, and it was the kind of audience with which he was still a spellbinder. One newspaper reported:

> Scranton pride glows, Scranton breathes deeply, the Scranton spirit swells in exultation, at the triumph of the eloquence, thoughtfulness, sense, profound wisdom, and conformity to right, displayed in an address couched in elegance, forcefulness and grandeur of expression. At the beginning Mr. Skinner was accorded the welcome a home town speaker merits. At the end the members assembled rose spontaneously to honor his masterful effort.

That may have been the work of a tongue-in-cheek liberal reporter told by his editor to praise the speech, but it was a theme in which my father deeply believed: "Today all that stands between complete enforcement of [socialism] and the right to own and possess and enjoy property and the fruits of our own industry is the Constitution of the United States. We are secure in our houses, our businesses, and our property, only so long as that document stands."

Two years later he spoke on the same topic at the Kiwanis Club. "A great majority of the people of this country are not thinking about what they can give to their country," he said, "but rather what they can get out of it." This time the newspapers were unkind. The *Scranton Times*, a Democratic paper, ran an editorial:

> Mr. Skinner, by reason of his professional associations, or maybe we should say business environment, naturally falls into the category of defender of the old order. In practically all of his time at the bar he has been a corporation lawyer—counsel for railroad and mining companies. . . . He can not think from the standpoint of the man without a job, his little family suffering for food and clothing and shelter because the old order, of which Mr. Skinner is such a staunch defender, has broken down.

My father apparently learned something from the experience. Two years later, he spoke again at the Kiwanis Club about changes in the workmen's compensation law, and this time he buttered up the newspapers. "They are," he said, "progressive and outstanding and they are a credit to the city and would be to any city. Their influence is great. Here is an opportunity to educate the public and arouse public opinion." But he was not learning quite fast enough. The referees who awarded compensation were, he said, "in the great majority of cases for the past twenty years [appointed] for purely political reasons. Prior experience, legal training or judicial ability were not prerequisites." He would be trying cases before those referees for many years.

IN JULY 1934 I wrote to Fred: "Emerson Hall is all upset. All the younger men except B-Center & Allport have been told to look elsewhere. BC. and Pratt are sick of Boring's dimensionalism. Köhler comes here next year, practically over Boring's dead body and has burned his bridges behind him in Germany. But Gestalt Psych. is dead—as everyone knows now. K. is here five years too late."

Conant had instituted an up-or-out policy in which men who would presumably never be appointed "without limit of time" (the nearest thing to tenure at Harvard) were not to be reappointed at lower ranks. I had written to Percy Saunders to say that it was time Hamilton College had a psychologist on its faculty and telling him that Carroll Pratt was available, but it was too soon for Hamilton to take that drastic step, and Carroll went to Rutgers.

Upon taking over the presidency, Conant had looked at the department and was not pleased. A search was begun for "the best psychologist in the world," and Karl Lashley seemed to be the man. In another letter to Fred I wrote:

Lashley has been shown all over Harvard this week and is being asked to come here (entre nous). Boring is delighted because that would definitely remove the Köhler threat. Boring says Lashley said Watson had expected to come to Harvard before McDougall did, and being shoved out explains J. B.'s bitterness toward McD. Nice gossip. Boring is puzzled over Lashley's friendly feeling toward and admiration of Watson. He explains it as due to W's personality.

Harvard had offered Lashley a professorship in 1929, but he had gone to Chicago instead. Conant now made him an offer he could scarcely refuse, though he first went to New York to talk it over with Watson. The appointment made very little difference. Lashley was given space in the Biological Laboratories rather than in Emerson Hall, and when Boring later described how he held the staff together with a daily luncheon, he added, "Lashley ate with us only on occasion."

I saw Lashley frequently in the machine shop in the Biology Building, and I told Fred that he seemed like "a thoroughly nice chap." But he had a temper, and there were things about the department that brought it out. He was bitterly opposed to psychoanalysis, and was arguing that anyone who had been psychoanalyzed was incompetent to pass judgment upon it. The Psychological Clinic under Harry Murray naturally irritated him. Carroll Pratt wrote to me later that "Lashley flew into a rage over the [Clinic] matter and went to Conant with his letter of resignation. Conant calmed him down, raised his salary, made him a Research Professor of Neuropsychology, and relieved him of all teaching and administrative responsibility. So, as far as the Department is concerned, Lashley is completely out of the picture and Boring resumes his solitary role of lonely authority." Later, Lashley moved to the Yerkes Laboratory in Florida, whence he returned once a year for two weeks to teach the Pro-Seminar. Conant made it clear that he intended to make no other permanent appointments in psychology for a long time.

I called on Lashley when he was still in the Biological Labora-tories and found him not only unhappy about Harvard but about his own work. "I've been barking up the wrong tree recently," he told me. He said he liked my paper on the concept of the reflex, and I suppose in a way it was compatible with his attack on the reflex arc. He had tried to follow a stimulus through the nervous system on its way to becoming a response by training rats to run mazes and then taking out different parts of their brains. Since they could still run the mazes, no one part of the brain seemed to be essential. The brain seemed to work as a whole, a conclusion for which he could find support in Gestalt psychology.

Hunter spotted the flaw: the rats used many cues in learning a maze and Lashley never ruled them all out at any one time. Hunter said as much in a colloquium at Harvard and wrote to me afterward: "I enjoyed the visit very much, and I must say I enjoyed presenting the negative side to Lashley's theory since I knew that Dr. Boring was inclined to take the positive side. . . . Watson wanted to see the MS of the same paper. He has returned it this morning with a comment that he thinks I am right. So there we are."

In 1930 Lashley invented an apparatus in which rats learned the difference between visual patterns by jumping against doors on which the patterns were printed. The door bearing the right pattern flipped open, and the rat landed on solid ground; but the wrong doors re-mained closed and the rat fell into a basket. So far as I was con-cerned, what mattered was not being able to tell a difference, but why the rats jumped at all. When I raised this point with Lashley, he said, laughing, "No one publishes the fact that he whips his rats." (An alternative to whipping once led to a strange mistake. A psychologist "discovered" that when forced to make difficult discriminations on a jumping stand, rats became neurotic. His paper reporting the result at a meeting of the American Association for the Advancement of Sci-ence received a special prize. But instead of whipping his rats, he had used a jet of air to force them to jump, and it turned out that the noise of the air produced "audiogenic seizures," easily mistaken for a neurotic reaction.)

IN THORNDIKE'S LAW of Effect, or what I called Type R conditioning, a reinforcer does not change the particular response it follows. The response has already occurred and cannot be altered. Reinforcement simply makes similar responses more probable. But to have such an effect it must overlap some trace of the preceding response. How long could such a trace last?

I built a timing device in which pressing the lever marked the beginning of an interval, at the end of which food was dispensed. Pressing during the interval reset the timer to prevent reinforcement after a shorter time. When rats were being periodically reconditioned, I inserted intervals of two, four, six, and eight seconds between pressing and the dispensing of food. The rats pressed more slowly, and in general the longer the delay the lower the rate. The biggest reductions were of the order of 30 to 50 percent.

A DISCRIMINATIVE STIMULUS controlled the probability that a response would occur. Could it have another function—as a reinforcer? I set up a discrimination in the usual way, periodically turning on a light and reinforcing the response that followed. Then I waited until a response had been made in the dark before turning on the light (and reinforcing the next response with food). The light had the effect of a reinforcer, and the rat began to press faster in the dark. I expected it to press as fast as it had done before the discrimination was set up, but when I omitted the light and returned to reinforcing with food in the dark, there was a further increase in rate. The discriminative stimulus was a reinforcer, but it was not as powerful as the food that had made it so.

Much earlier I had found that the noise made by the empty magazine worked as a conditioned reinforcer. A rat was adapted to the box and to the dispenser in the usual way, but when it first pressed the lever, the dispenser was empty. The mere noise was reinforcing, however, and the rat began to press fairly rapidly in an extinction curve. In another experiment the sound of the empty magazine proved to be reinforcing even when delayed.

I CONTINUED TO WORK on verbal behavior. Henderson urged me to look at John Horne Tooke's *Diversions of Purley*, published in 1786. Tooke was a political rebel who supported a subscription for the widows and children of the Americans "murdered by British soldiers" at Lexington and Concord, and as a consequence he spent a year in jail. He was also an early behaviorist. Locke's "composition of ideas," he said, was nothing more than the "composition of words." (In 1826 a disciple, John Barclay, published A *Sequel to the Diversions of Purley*, which was an early behavioristic interpretation of words referring to spirit and mind.) According to Boswell, Dr. Johnson said of Tooke, "They should set him up in the pillory that he may be punished in a way that would disgrace him," and Cardinal Newman said, "Grammar . . . at first sight does not appear to admit of a perversion; yet Horne Tooke made it the vehicle of his peculiar scepticism." The book was out of print but I advertised, and several booksellers sent me quotations. I bought two copies and gave one to Van Quine, inscribed V*erbum sat.*

Henderson also sent me to Grose's *Classical Dictionary of the Vulgar Tongue*, a collection of thieves' cant, tradesmen's jargon, and bawdy street talk, from which I took many examples. Later he suggested another motto for my book, from Emerson's *Brahma*, which I used in an epilogue in the final version: "When me they fly, I am the wings." By November I was far enough along to offer a colloquium at Clark University on "Language as Behavior."

In December Van Quine gave three lectures on Carnap's *Logische Syntax*, and after the last one he, David Prall, and I discussed the need for an English translation. Prall agreed to do one with Van's help and we cabled Carnap, with whom Van had worked in Prague. Unfortunately, C. K. Ogden had agreed to publish a translation, and the Countess Zeppelin was said to be preparing one. I wrote to Ivor Richards to see if he could persuade Ogden to change translators. He could not.

In my letter to Ivor I grew rather expansive:

I have written the best part of a book on language, about which I would give anything to have a long talk with you. I begin with a few simple laws of behavior, which I treat as postulates and from which I deduce enough cases to take care of the usual linguistic data. It has all worked out surprisingly well. I get into semantics, of course, and that goes well too. I even get as far as Empson (good work!) and later on to the relation of thought to language, where Carnap comes in. All of this in behavioristic terms, of course, and with what seems to me to be gratifying simplicity. I have tried it out on Eric Trist, who came up from Yale for two days of intensive conferences, much to my profit and I hope to his. I saw Trist again at Yale just before Christmas and we lunched [at Morey's] with Sapir. Sapir is pretty deep in the tradition (or at least his tradition), but he seemed to grant the possibility of my approach, which is all I ask.

Your Mencius on the Mind I liked very much. I have not gone back to it because I gave my copy to a Chinese friend who was leaving America probably forever, but I expect to make good use of it in the last stages of the language book. It is all part of our problem. I am feeling very much encouraged these days with the speed at which the solution is developing. It is good to be in on something as important as that.

I went into basic English quite thoroughly but have pretty much come out again. It is about as perfect as it could be for its purpose, but it is not my purpose.

By January 1935 I was writing even more expansively to Fred:

I'm going into aphasia now, on the pathological side of language. It all comes out very simply. But you should see the boys tie themselves in knots trying to describe aphasia in the old terminology of ideas, sensations, etc. They'll be the last to change—the clinicians. Hope to finish the language book this summer (on my honey-moon?). Behaviorism book I've definitely dropped. One chapter appears in the [1935] Gen.—on stimulus & response.

My apparatus was becoming more sophisticated. I discovered a pen that wrote in red ink on white paper and I gave up smoked drums with relief. The pens were expensive, and I made good substitutes by grinding off the points of hypodermic needles. I bought coils and made my own relays, cutting the frames and armatures from sheets of galvanized iron and the contacts from a thin sheet of silver made by hammering a dime. I made a mechanical lockup relay, in which one circuit was closed by a brief impulse and held closed by a latch until released when another coil was energized. So far as I knew, no one had made such things before.

When I had switched from reinforcing a response every five minutes to reinforcing what I thought was an equivalent number of responses, the rat had begun to press much more rapidly. Possibly it was simply taking advantage of the new arrangement. Why should it wait five minutes if it could press twenty-five times and get a pellet in thirty seconds? But the fact remained that I had chosen the number twenty-five, and there was no reason why I could not have chosen a different one. If the extinction ratio was constant, a larger number should lead to extinction while a smaller number should build up a large reserve of unemitted responses. But was that what actually happened?

I could not use my old apparatus to find out, because the circuit breakers would cause trouble. I had always worked with fairly long periods between reinforcements and with moderately deprived rats, which seldom responded faster than six or eight times a minute, but higher rates would not be accurately recorded if the circuit was broken after each response.

I built four new nonelectrical apparatuses in which a depression of the lever stepped a ratchet mounted on a shaft. It could follow very rapid pressing. The shaft wound up a thread to the recorder and turned a large notched disk. An arm riding on the disk closed a circuit to the dispenser whenever it fell into a notch. By using disks with different numbers of notches I could reinforce the 16th, the 24th, the 48th, the 96th, or the 192nd response.

When four rats are on the same schedule of periodic reinforcement, they must be isolated, because the first to receive a pellet when an interval expires will otherwise provide a discriminative stimulus for the others. Reinforcements which depend upon numbers of responses, however, occur at different times, and I could dispense with ventilated boxes and put my new apparatuses on tables in a quiet room, each with its own kymograph.

I began with the lowest ratio of responses to reinforcements but found that I could move up quickly. To my amazement, I soon had rats pressing 192 times for each pellet! And when I extinguished the behavior by putting on disks with no notches, rats that had been reinforced on a ratio of 192:1 pressed the lever as many as 1500 times in less than half an hour.

When I reported the experiment at the meeting of the American Psychological Association at Dartmouth College in 1936, I spoke of "an experimentally fixed ratio in place of an extinction ratio adopted by the organism," but my abstract shows that an extinction ratio was still troubling me:

> When the fixed ratio is less than the extinction ratio, there is an increase in the store of unelicited responses and the rate increases; when the fixed ratio is greater than the extinction ratio, there is a decrease and the rate falls. In the latter case the organism may, however, develop a temporal discrimination by virtue of which the extinction ratio is increased from about 20:1 to as much as 200:1 [I was rounding my numbers]. The rate of responding between successive reinforcements shows a smooth acceleration which corresponds to a "temporal gradient." The gradient is produced with great uniformity. Extinction curves following the development of the temporal discrimination show characteristic properties, including an initial limb of extraordinarily intense activity.

By a temporal discrimination I meant the effect of a ratio schedule in reinforcing relatively fast responding. According to my notes, I was already planning some research in which I would reinforce a response periodically provided it occurred less than two seconds after another response, moving on to require "three within four seconds, then four in six, etc." In other words, I would explicitly reinforce bursts of fast responding rather than allow a ratio schedule to select them by accident. I also considered the possibility that a group of responses might emerge as a unit of behavior.

As FAR AS I WAS concerned, there were only minor differences between behaviorism, operationism, and logical positivism. My thesis had been an operational analysis of the reflex (taking my cue from

Bertrand Russell), and my suggestion to Beebe-Center that the department let me perform similar analyses of basic psychological concepts in lieu of taking a final oral examination had been perfectly serious. I had published an operational definition of drive, and in 1933 I had added details in a letter to Boring: it was a mistake to call hunger a feeling, as he and Walter Cannon at the Medical School were doing. Hunger pangs were too erratic to explain my smooth ingestion curves.

> On the basis of the covariation of the strength of all reflexes related to the ingestion of food, we may conceptualize a something, and it seems to me that upon historical grounds that something has as much right to the name hunger as have hunger-pangs. Experimentally, as I have said in print, this conceptualization has very little value, since all we can do is to measure one change at a time. That is why the word hunger is only conversational with me, but still very valuable.

In 1934 I gave a colloquium in Emerson Hall on operationism, and I used a different example. Boring had published an important paper on auditory theory, and in the early thirties he had put a graduate student to work on a new device, the electronic oscillator, which produced much more accurate pitches than the steel bars so carefully turned by the old machinist. When the student changed his mind and went to medical school, Boring turned the project over to S. Smith Stevens, who had recently arrived for graduate study after doing Mormon missionary work in Belgium.

Stevens and Boring were now asking a curious question: Was a tone big as well as loud? And in my colloquium on operationism I chose tonal volume as an example. Could one deal scientifically with volume as a dimension of a sensation, or must one look at the instructions to the subject and the resulting verbal or nonverbal responses?

The following March I wrote to Fred:

> Last night I was invited to Boring's evening seminar to answer questions about my paper in the current JGP on S and R ["The Generic Nature of the Concepts of Stimulus and Response"]. It ended up in a pow-wow about the importance of behavior and the unimportance of sensory physiology. There was practically universal agreement with our point of view—at last. Boring contributed a little

historical summary of why there should be discontent with traditional psychology—and he really began to see the light with respect to an interest in behavior per se. Stevens (Boring's star man) has recently come out for a behavioristic epistemology at a colloquium. So we're in at last!

Later in 1935 I would be writing to Stevens:

I am much impressed with your paper on operationism. . . . It is essentially what I have always supposed behaviorism to represent— and what it would long since clearly have represented if psychologists (e.g. Boring) had not shut their eyes to the good in the movement in order to enjoy its flaws.

I do not agree, however, that it is the "sole business" of psychology to test and measure the discriminatory capacities of organisms. That is your heritage from Wundt and Fechner. . . . What is happening in a discrimination, and what properties organisms actually do use in setting up classes (concepts, objects) are far more important questions than what properties they could use or to what extent they could use them. And only by stretching your term pretty far could you include emotion and motivation. That is also a heritage—you need not be concerned with why your observers answer your questions.

My impression is this: it's all O.K., but let's get to work. Enough of us now agree on these matters. The next step is to agree on a framework for a science. If you stick to the sensory field you are not going to be of much help. Your section on the use of language is, as you certainly know, full of ellipses. And that is only one example of the side of psychology that you seem to exclude from its sole business. As I have said so many times that I blush to say it again—if you approached the behavior of an organism as an object of scientific study and set to work, it would be a long time before you would reach the field of discriminatory capacity. All the problems of "association and determination" [the name of one of Boring's systematic courses] would demand treatment first.

I don't expect you to give up the special point of view which, even though determined by historical events, is naturally now the center of your interests. But at least admit the possibility of (and I would say the necessity of) a more general orientation.

In any event, congratulations on a damn good job of exposition.

*   *   *

As soon as I got my degree, Walter Hunter began to treat me as a friend and colleague. He was rather openly cynical of his contemporaries and once said to me, "It only takes one little idea to be a success in American psychology," and he measured the idea with thumb and forefinger. While I was still an NRC Fellow, he wrote to ask me to clear up a "most unusual bit of scandal gossip." He had heard that Crozier was offended when he had failed to turn up at a meeting to discuss tropisms, and he wanted Crozier to know that he had never received the invitation.

There was open warfare between Hunter and Carl Murchison, another member of the Clark department. Murchison once wrote to say that he had noticed that I was a mere Associate Member of the American Psychological Association and wondered if he could make up for Harvard's neglect and propose me for full membership. When I told Hunter, he snorted. "Murchison wants to be president of the APA," he said. "He wants you to be able to vote for him." When I was invited to give that colloquium on language as behavior at Clark, Hunter wrote to suggest that I drop by his house for a drink before the meeting. He was alone, and as we had our drinks, he said, "Skinner, have I ever given you a bum steer?" I said he had not. "Well, I am going to give you a good one now," he said. "Watch out for Murchison." I must have looked surprised. "He'll pick your brains," he said.

It was more than a personal feud. Murchison was an enterprising publisher but not much of a psychologist. When the University pressed him to publish something of his own, as well as so much of the work of others, he cooked up an experiment to "quantify" a social relation. Two fighting cocks or roosters were released in such a way that they ran aggressively toward each other. The weight of each bird multiplied by its speed gave, said Murchison, a measure of its aggression in centimeters per gram per second.

In March 1935 I wrote to Fred:

> The last issue of the J G Psych made me simply ill. I'm going to get out of that journal as soon as my present in-press articles are out (numbering 4). Murchison grows repulsive. He held up the January issue (just out) three times to revise his article after three seminars in which it was picked to pieces. Hunter says "We are hoping he won't make a fool of the whole laboratory." It's Carl's first article, I believe,

and he shows it. Changed the style of the journal to get his name at the top of every [left hand] page. Previously it was the name of the Journal. Oh-hum!

Early in October 1934 Murchison phoned to ask if I could meet with him and a few others on an important assignment. Warren Weaver of the Rockefeller Foundation had asked him how to spend money during the next twenty-five years to advance the social sciences. I drove out to Murchison's house in Worcester early one Sunday morning and joined Leonard Carmichael and Clarence Graham, who had driven up from Providence, and Hudson Hoagland. We had drinks and a good dinner and spent the entire day discussing the problem. Carmichael, Graham, and I agreed that the subject matter of the social sciences was behavior, but Hoagland wanted to pay more attention to physiology.

Murchison asked us to prepare position papers, and in his final report to Weaver the section defining fundamental problems was taken almost verbatim from mine. We should choose a unit of behavior (Murchison softened "reflex" to "stimulus response variables and their interrelationships"), but we should be sure that the examples were typical. Salivation, flexion, and the eyelid reflex (the three conditioned responses most often studied by my contemporaries) were not representative of the behavior of the intact organism. Parameters to be considered were to be found in the fields of conditioning, drive, and emotion. "A scientific language to be used in the description of behavior" was needed.

Among the fields to be studied I put verbal behavior first, but included self-instruction, discrimination, "thinking," volition, responsibility, social and political motives, emotion, prejudice, functional and organic disorders, psychoanalysis, and criminal behavior.

Hoagland was unhappy about all this and wrote directly to Weaver saying that the future of psychology lay with physiology and suggesting how the Rockefeller Foundation might spend its money accordingly. He read his letter to us and I prepared a reply to be added to our report, but Murchison omitted it and told Weaver that I would send a separate statement. Instead, I wrote to say that I did not wish "to enter personally into a controversy of this sort." The truth was, I had grown suspicious of the whole venture. Would Weaver have seriously turned to Murchison for that kind of help? My guess was that in the course of a friendly conversation he had thrown out some such question as "What would *you* do if you were in my place and wanted to help psychology?" That would have been enough for Murchison; the Rockefeller Foundation wanted his help.

I should have published my statement on physiology. I had told Fred that one chapter of the "Behaviorism book" was "anti-physiological" and that I was rewriting it for the *British Journal of Psychology*, but it was never submitted. In my thesis I had redefined the properties of Sherrington's synapse as laws of behavior rather than as properties of the nervous system. And I had scoffed when Boring had tried to escape from mentalism by rushing into physiology, as Lashley had done a decade earlier when he said, "I shall try to show that the statement 'I am conscious,' does not mean anything more than the statement that 'such and such physiological processes are going on within me.'"

So far as I was concerned the physiology of behavior was scarcely more respectable than the physiology of consciousness. It was true that some direct observations of nerve action were beginning to be made, even in the brain in the form of the Berger Rhythm. (The newspapers loved it: "Brain Used as Battery Foretells Approach of Worst Type of Insanity.") But most physiological "facts" were inferences from behavior and should not be used to explain behavior. In *Animal Drive and the Learning Process* E. B. Holt quoted Molière's fatuous candidate who told the learned doctors who were examining him that opium induced sleep because it possessed a soporific virtue. Yet Holt himself could tell his readers that in conditioning "if an afferent path already has connection with a motor path of discharge, then another afferent path, if stimulated simultaneously, or very nearly simultaneously, with the first will tend to acquire the same motor path of discharge," though he had no evidence whatsoever of the connecting of paths.

My report to Murchison concluded:

The argument against physiology is simply that we should get more done in the field of behavior if we confined ourselves to behavior. When we rid ourselves of the delusion that we are getting down to fundamentals when we get into physiology, then the young man who discovers some fact of behavior will not immediately go after the "physiological correlates" but will go on discovering other facts of behavior.

I was recalling my own history. After I had shown an orderly change in the rate of eating with ingestion, friends for whom I had great respect urged me to see whether blood sugar or the physical or chemical properties of the contents of the stomach changed in the same way. And then there was that "autocoid" or hunger hormone to which I myself had appealed in an early note. I had no objection to physiological research, but I wanted to get on with the study of behavior. When, a year later, I spoke at Crozier's colloquium on "Some Properties of the Behavior (or of the Central Nervous System?) of the White Rat," no one who heard me could have supposed that I meant the nervous system.

FRED HAD NOT FOLLOWED my research very closely. His thesis was on a traditional theme, and during his first years at Colgate he and his students continued to work on standard problems like delayed reaction and the sensory control of the maze. Although we promoted behaviorism together, I did not discuss with him the theoretical issues arising in my own work. "Two Types of Conditioned Reflex and a Pseudo Type" appeared early in 1935, and it was almost two years later that I wrote to explain the point.

In January 1935, however, he wrote: "How about one of those sound-proof boxes of yours—with all the gadgets? Can Gerbrands do the job at a reasonable figure?" I had been thinking for some time about a nonelectrical lever and food dispenser. When Julius Wahl was making my clavichord, I had talked with him about the wonderfully subtle yet highly reliable devices used by pianomakers—wooden shafts, leather straps and pads, and felt bearings. Though I would stick with brass, I thought I could build a wholly mechanical "problem box" along similar lines. Ralph thought so too and built one according to my design. I took it to Fred when I drove to Colgate to speak at a meeting of the Upper New York State Psychological Association.

Fred was in charge of the annual meeting that year, and he had invited me to be the principal speaker. He sent some details:

As the surprise note of the proceedings I'm arranging a send-off for Dr. and Mrs. Kline (Skidmore) at the Friday-evening banquet. Kline is getting older and deafer, and is retiring this year at Skidmore, to go to a long-cherished farm in Virginia. He is really a pretty swell old boy and deserves this ovation. Moore (Skidmore's president, the psychologist) has promised to cancel all arrangements to come down here to give the Klines a 5-to-10 minute send-off just before you give your stuff. At the speaker's table (flood-lighted by Donald [Laird], if he has his way) will be, therefore, Moore; Cutten (our president, to welcome the lads and lassies); Dr. and Mrs. Kline; "the noted Harvard psychologist, B.F. Skinner," as the N.Y. papers had it last week; and your affectionate builder-upper. We are to be dressed up, so don't forget your dinner jacket. Most of all, however, don't forget to bring that apparatus.

I replied:

Get Donald off the floodlights and do all you can to stifle publicity. I'm positively not going to announce any new cosmic ray or electrical mindreading gadget. What I plan to do is this: distinguish between certain interests in psychology—chiefly between applied (and clinical) and a pure science. Then emphasize need of (1) rigor of definition (2) care in experimentation (3) and especially work on individuals (not on 2 doz. assorted rats) in a pure field. As example of the sort of thing I'll run off a dozen curves of various sorts and describe them first in the vernacular, bringing in a lot of ideological theories etc. Then go over the same slides (to kid everyone into a feeling of familiarity) and formulate them in terms of reflexes. Object: to show simplicity of assumptions. Summary: a plea for maintenance of a pure science as a basis for technology (with some flattering words for the clinician) + a few smooth curves pour épater les bourgeousies [sic] . . .[*I had some especially smooth extinction curves and I arranged my remarks so that they stayed on the screen for a long time.*]

The Lairds gave a dinner party at which there was a good deal of liquor, as well as a few risqué stories, and afterward I took a charming young psychiatrist from Utica for a drive in my car. When we came back Mrs. Laird met us at the door and wiped the lipstick off my face. I wrote to Fred: "I hope my defective behavior . . . was not too noticeable and that it has not caused anyone any embarrassment."

A RAT PRESSED a lever in many ways, and even though responses became rather similar as an experiment progressed, small differences remained and might be important. Aside from the question of whether pressings made equal contributions to a rate of responding as a measure of strength or to a reserve of unexpended responses, there was the question of how the form or topography might be changed.

I designed (and Ralph built) an apparatus that not only recorded the force with which the rat pressed the lever but selected certain values for reinforcement, and in March 1935 I reported to Fred: "Getting some swell stuff on Discrimination of Force of Response. Pressing lever easily or hard—etc."

A rat normally pressed the lever with a force that varied over a small range around some average value. When I reinforced only responses above a given value, the average rose. Still more forceful responses then appeared, and I could select new values for reinforcement. The average then rose still further, and I could select even more forceful responses.

When I again reinforced regardless of force, the average quickly dropped. In extinction the first few presses were particularly strong, but subsequent presses became very weak. (They also became weak in extinction even when I had not reinforced differentially, but, of course, the ordinary lever selects responses strong enough to move it.) When I selected an occasional forceful response for periodic reinforcement, the rat pressed harder but did not change its rate.

It was hard to reinforce relatively weak responses because the normal force was already low, but when strong responses had been set up, the force dropped rapidly when I required weaker responses.

Another property I could differentially reinforce was the length of time the rat held the lever down, and by requiring that it be held down longer and longer I lengthened the duration to as much as thirty seconds. It soon appeared that there were two conflicting responses: pressing and holding. A burst of very short responses would occasionally break through, as if the rat had to "get rid of a certain number of presses" before it could hold the lever down long enough.

Moreover, the duration did not fall off during extinction, as force had done; instead, the rats tended to hold the lever down longer as pressing grew weak.

Contingencies specifying properties of a stimulus were quite different from those specifying properties of a response, and I began to distinguish the *discrimination* of stimuli and the *differentiation* of responses. (The contingencies could be combined, of course, as by reinforcing strong responses in the light and weak responses in the dark.)

IN 1934 THE Clark University Press brought out a new edition of *A Handbook of General Psychology*, and I undertook to review it *ex cathedra*. I made clear that psychology had not yet fully come around to my way of thinking. Crozier was still talking about tropisms—a concept that was "not extensible upward to the more complex behavior of learning, emotion, and so on, and at the same time . . . not simple enough to be of use in the analysis of such part-mechanisms as those employed in the maintenance of posture." Professor Cannon defined "hunger and thirst as sensations," but "how hunger and thirst 'insistently require the eating of food or the drinking of water or watery fluids,' how they influence the state of conditioned reflexes based upon these 'drives,' is not dealt with." Professor Hunter in a chapter on "Experimental Studies in Learning" "confines himself to the use of the concepts of stimulus and response and of habit. I think it is fair to say that the concept of habit is not an ultimate analytical unit." Professor Lashley's chapter on "Nervous Mechanisms in Learning" had not been revised, but since the author had concluded that "it is doubtful that we know anything more about the [physiological] mechanisms of learning than did Descartes when he described the opening of the pores in the nerves by the passage of animal spirits," it was doubtful whether any recent event could "shake so profound a conviction." I applauded the editors' decision to put chapters on sensation and perception at the end of the book rather than, as in so many texts on psychology, at the beginning. I had something to say about every field—often, as I said, praising the text with faint damns. I struck one low blow: "The chapter on *Chemoreception* by Professor Crozier is practically unchanged except for the withdrawal of

Professor Parker as co-author." Crozier's star had fallen. Conant had never liked him, and as soon as he became President, General Physiology was in trouble. I had written to Fred: "Big shake-up at the lab has scared everybody. Pincus and Castle got reappointments by the skin of their teeth. Others still in air." It was not long before Crozier's great empire was reduced to his own office and laboratory. But I owed him too much to allude in this way to his changing fortunes. Clearly I was not weathering my success or the prestige of my Junior Fellowship very successfully.

IN EARLY JUNE I went back to Monhegan, and a few days after I arrived, I wrote to Fred:

All the Island folk have gone to church, leaving the dark ocean and the night to me. I've been meaning to write for some time. Came up here Monday and expect to stay all summer. So far I've made good a threat to work on the book [on verbal behavior] six hours per day. That means ca. 500 hours this summer—and if I don't finish it with that, why, the hell with it. As a matter of fact it's quite a revelation to me how well you can work keeping a watch on yourself. I calculate my time to the minute. The result is I stick at a thing when ordinarily I would give up as being too tired of it to go on. I now realize that I had fallen into a habit of pampering myself. I've been leaving too much to my subconscious to work on.

The book is going to be good. I'm sure of that. The linguists will laugh at it—most of 'em—and the psychologists won't get through it. But it's good. Underneath what seems like a lot of complexity (which is really only novelty) there lies immense simplification. Much more than I ever hoped for. I'm beginning to wonder why I ever stuck so doggedly to a faith in stimulus and response. It is certainly beginning to pay well now. A lot of it I owe to you, I know that. And probably we both owe something to the obvious stupidity of the opposition.

Fred sent me some results of experiments with his new apparatus. His very first rat had learned to press the lever practically instantaneously although he had not first conditioned it to the sound of the magazine. I was surprised but pleased, and I wrote, "Good for rat number 1! May they all do likewise." By the middle of August I was writing: "I'm taking a week's vacation from the MS, which has given me a pretty severe brain fag. It's not going as fast as I could wish, but it's better than I had hoped so I can't complain."

By the end of summer I had indeed recorded 600 hours of work. Ivor Richards had mentioned my book to Ogden, who said he would like to see the manuscript for the International Library of Psychology, Philosophy, and Scientific Method, but I was far from finished.

The summer was not all work. Remembering that book on the *vita monastica* that I had read during my dark year before coming to Harvard, I started a small garden. I also tried my hand at painting. Rockwell Kent had lived on Monhegan for many summers, and a few of his Monhegan paintings are well known. Less-celebrated artists were still a conspicuous part of the landscape, and the rocky headlands were touched with scrapings from palettes—blues, greens, and the browns of seaweed. During the winter I had attended a life drawing class. (One of the models was a recent graduate with top honors from one of the best colleges for women. She had lost interest in life and was taking on odd jobs to support herself. I gave her some work as a part-time typist, but because she was the friend of a young woman whom I was seeing at the time, I made no move toward a more intimate relation.) I had prepared for the summer by buying oil paints, brushes, canvas and stretchers, and a few canvas boards. I painted standard subjects—the lighthouse, the foghorn building, and Cathedral Woods.

Marianne was not on the island, but I found other friends. A tall dark man with a beard arrived at the Trailing Yew with two charming daughters about ten and twelve years old. At first he was rather aloof and, like the other guests, I was rather in awe of him until, standing on the porch of the Yew in the evening light, he quoted something from *La Physiologie du gout*. I said that I was familiar with Brillat-Savarin, and it was as if two spies had given the right password.

His name was Bill Sewell, and his parents had been among the first artists to spend summers on the island. Recently divorced, he had the custody of his children during the summer, and he wanted them to know the island as he had known it as a child. He played the guitar—not well but adequately for folk songs—and I sent off to Sears, Roebuck for a chromatic mouth organ. A young woman, Eleanor Congdon, came to the Yew and became one of our party. She had a lovely voice but was rather timid. I undertook to bring her out, ordering a book of Schumann's songs and coaching her while playing her accompaniments on a parlor organ.

I made a series of kites, including one based on the Autogiro, a plane with rotating wings that had a brief vogue at the time. My kite spun in the sky like a pinwheel. We sent small Malay kites out of sight on their way to Europe with a number of wooden crosspieces tied a few feet apart near the ends of the strings. In a high wind only one or two remained in the water, checking the kite as it moved swiftly forward. When the wind fell, more pieces dropped into the water and increased the pull to keep the kite aloft. I also made a device attached to a bigger kite that opened a bag of confetti when struck by a small disk carried up the string by the wind.

My hay fever was as bad as ever, and a doctor who was a fellow guest recommended Lobelia cigarettes. I sent for a supply and kept my tiny room full of smoke as I worked. There may have been a psychedelic effect.

THAT SUMMER WAS A FAIR SAMPLE of the pleasant mixture of hard work and relaxation to which I returned in the fall, thanks to the founders of the Society of Fellows. My suite in Winthrop House grew more lived-in and now smelled of turpentine and oil paint. Conversation with tutors and graduate students at dinner and over coffee in the Senior Common Room remained stimulating. Ken Galbraith had moved into Winthrop House and was one of our more articulate colleagues. Every Monday evening a distinguished guest came to dinner at the Society. A cellar of excellent wine had been laid in, and someone had contributed a silver wagon that sped the port around the table after dinner. Among the Junior Fellows, now in the majority, were Harry Levin, George Homans, Bright Wilson (I was best man at his wedding), and John Bardeen (who would eventually get *two* Nobel Prizes). Our exchanges were not always scholarly. One evening after the Senior Fellows had left, we began to exchange bawdy limericks; someone got out a typewriter and we collected more than fifty. We also composed equally bawdy ones about our fellow Fellows.

With all this I still worked hard. I got up early, usually did some writing until the dining room opened for breakfast, walked to my laboratory, and during the morning ran my experiments. I often had lunch with colleagues at a white-tile restaurant in Harvard Square and returned to my office to work on records during the afternoon.

ONE FINE SUNDAY MORNING I went to the Biology Building and descended to my subterranean laboratory. I put the rats in their boxes and started my programming equipment. I was still using circuit breakers, and the friction drives under the four disks emitted a rhythmic pulse: di-*dah*-di-di-*dah*—di-*dah*-di-di-*dah*. Suddenly I heard myself saying "You'll *nev*er get *out*. You'll *nev*er get *out*." Evidently the rhythmic stimulus had had the effect Sherrington called summation. An imitative response had joined forces with some latent behavior, which I could attribute to a rather obvious source: I was a prisoner in my laboratory on a lovely day.

I thought the effect should be studied. Electric phonographs had appeared on the market a few years earlier and, as improvements were made, old turntable motors became available at very low prices. I had already found them useful, and I now converted one into a device that produced an unlimited variety of rhythmic patterns. The rhythms of trap drummers, no matter how ingeniously improvised, follow the natural frequencies of arms and drumsticks. My device generated surprising novelties, and many of them had the effect I was looking for. After listening for a few seconds, I would find myself saying something that matched the pattern. When Jim and Via Agee, then living in New York, came to see me, Jim was intrigued. It was just the thing to trigger the verbal behavior of a young poet.

An improvement was obvious: if the device generated tones as well as clicks, it would create melodic lines, some of them possibly too subtle for human composers or performers. But another improvement was closer to the work at hand—the clicks could be replaced by speech sounds. In a book by Sir Richard Paget called *Human Speech* I had read about organ pipes that played vowel sounds. If my rhythm machine could open the valves of such pipes, it would play patterns much more like speech. By asking people to tell me what I was trying to make the pipes say, I could collect samples of speech which might be "significant" in the Freudian sense. The patterns would be something like auditory inkblots, evoking strong latent verbal behavior.

The organ company that had made the pipes for Paget could give me no help. I went to the Aeolian-Skinner Organ Company in Boston and spoke to its technical director, G. Donald Harrison. I showed him Paget's book and he said he thought he could copy the pipes, but not immediately. I decided not to wait and turned instead to the phonograph. F. C. Packard, an Assistant Professor of Public Speaking, was recording students' voices on 78-rpm disks, and he offered to help. I made up lists of vowel sounds in various patterns. The stressed sounds were long *a, e, i,* and *o* and broad *ah* and *oo.* I mixed them with an unstressed sound like the *u* in "up," to compose samples like *"uh-Oh-Ah-uh,"* or *"uh-uh-I-E-uh."* Played very quietly or against a background noise, they sounded like speech heard through a wall. I designed a gadget to be attached to my portable phonograph that picked up a single pattern and repeated it indefinitely, and Ralph built it for me in the department shop.

I told Harry Murray at the Psychological Clinic about my experiment. He and a team of associates and graduate students were working on thematic apperception, and the "verbal summator," as I called it, seemed to be relevant. Harry gave me a room at the Psychological Clinic and paid for subjects. I found that I could collect a hundred or more responses in an hour simply by asking a subject to listen to a pattern as long as he or she wished and tell me what it said.

What was said was often "significant." When I showed the apparatus to a psychiatrist at the clinic and played *I-uh-uh-A-uh,* he said at once, "Oh, it says, 'I am a traitor,' and I know why. I have just been telling a patient that I can help her and I am not sure I can." One of my more compulsive subjects heard nothing but commands and criticisms spoken by what a psychoanalyst might have called a cruel superego. (One subject heard phrases in Croatian, which he had spoken as a child, and since I claimed to know what was on the record, I was a little embarrassed to ask him to spell his responses.) Apart from the subject matter, there were internal linkages. Some responses seemed to be puns or other kinds of wordplay. Occasionally a sequence seemed to be part of a dialogue.

To Fred I wrote that although the verbal summator was "the result of some theoretical deductions from the language book," it was proving to be "a device for snaring out complexes." It

simply repeats a series of vowel sounds over and over until the subject reads something into them. What the subject reads in is what he has on his mind. In short, the device enables the subconscious to verbalize itself with the aid of summation of imitative reflexes. If it works as well as it seems to at present, it will be a world beater. It ought to become a standard apparatus for any clinical psychiatrist, for it would cut the time required to locate complexes to a mere fraction. I'm going to try it on some nuts at the State Hospital.

Later I regained my scientific detachment. My paper was, I told Fred, "stirring up a lot of comment and is more or less the kind of thing the psychologists like. Quant à moi, ce m'est égal."

Still later I wrote: "The language experiment has paid big. I'll have a paper out within the month, *I hope.*" The paper included some protocols and an analysis of the frequencies of the words I had collected. I had sent it to Murchison, who was starting a journal in which a paper was published immediately upon acceptance and only later issued to subscribers in quarterly numbers. In his reply Fred gave me a tip: "By the way there's an English poet named Auden or Audin who has experimented with some rhyming (or lack of it) of this sort: gay-guy; house-horse. Stuff that may or may not be poetry but is a good example of the sort of spread you get with the summator. Auden is 'ganz modern', communistic, and Gertrude Steinish, but you may find him interesting—if you haven't already."

I FOUND TIME for a good deal of music. In Paine Hall there were string quartets from time to time, and I heard the Boston Symphony in Boston as well as in Sanders Theatre. I saw an opera or two but not especially for the music. Helen Olheim, a house-party girl of mine at Hamilton College, was singing with the Met and came to Boston in the role of Frederick in *Mignon*—a male part often sung by a contralto. (I was in her dressing room when the director came to remind her, evidently not for the first time, to *walk like a man!*) And a year or two later, when I saw her as Micaela in *Carmen* in New York, I could look with satisfaction on my progress as a connoisseur. In fifteen short years I had progressed from that box at the Met in the front of which my brother and I had sat in our new salt-and-pepper tweed sports suits to the dressing room of one of the stars, and when a friend of Helen's dropped by to say, "Is Pinza ever horny tonight!" I knew I had arrived.

(My early expertise as a music critic was curiously confirmed. During that dark year in Scranton when I was writing criticism for a newspaper, I had praised a tenor named Theodore Jones. He could, I said, "turn to the fields of oratorio, opera, or concert at his own choosing." I can be forgiven for not mentioning the movies, for they were still silent, but Theodore Jones changed his name to Allan Jones and I now saw and heard him in the "talkies.")

AT THE END OF 1934 I had my reprints bound and sent copies to my parents and to the Hamilton College Library. I was soon planning a book. I wrote to Fred: "I've had a long and tiring run of experiments —steadily since September 1. But have a lot of new dope. During January I'm going to whip it into shape along with a general outline of the experimental book. I'm going to publish that before the language book for various strategic reasons. Harpers wants to see both of them, but I don't think it's in their line." A month later I was writing to Hull: "I think I never have enough material at hand to corroborate in a general way the scheme of behaviorism that I first sketched in *Concept of the Reflex* (1931) but I hope to bring my researches together within the current year." In April I told Fred: "The book is coming along well. How about reading the manuscript for me in its final form? 'I am much indebted to my former colleague Dr. F.S. Keller . . .' " In May I was asking about an experiment he was doing: "I could use the results very nicely in the book—which, by the way, is exceeding all expectations in the way problems are disappearing (with footnote of gratitude to my distinguished colleague)."

THE FOUNDERS OF THE Society of Fellows must have known that it would help recruit young scholars for the Harvard faculty. Universities across the country would be sending on some of their best men, who after a number of years at Harvard would presumably want to stay. During the second year of my fellowship Dean Murdock wrote to the Junior Fellows asking them to give Harvard a chance to consider them before accepting a job elsewhere. Unfortunately I was in no position to respond to that request, for I had no offers.

Nor had I any a year later as the end of my fellowship approached. I could not be reappointed to the Society because I had been elected as if I were already in a second term. The Depression was at its worst and jobs were scarce. For five and a half postdoctoral years I had been completely free to follow my own interests at my own pace. I had lived in comfortable quarters and had enjoyed the exchange of ideas with other scholars. I could not have asked for a better opportunity to make my way as a psychologist, but now I must pay the piper. My contemporaries—men like Hilgard, Marquis, Wendt, and Graham—were well on their way up the academic ladder, and I was groping for the bottom rung.

My "plan of the campaign for the years 30–60" had not mentioned getting a job. I had chosen my field not because it was popular but because it interested me. I had made no effort to relate my work to that of others in the field, and others had had no reason to relate their work to mine. I had published a good many papers, but they were not in the mainstream of American psychology and were almost never cited. Though Lashley said he liked my paper on the concept of the reflex, he never referred to it in print. Hunter backed me professionally but he did not really understand my research. No one else was doing publishable work with my methods (Fred was just getting started), and the cumulative curve was still a curiosity.

I could expect little help from Crozier—he was not a man to whom one turned when looking for a young psychologist, and his own position was in jeopardy. The Department of Psychology looked upon me as a deserter. Conant and I were uneasy with each other, and the Lashley episode had not encouraged further support of the department. I was not priced out of the market, for no price had been set on me, but I had something of a reputation and departments with Depression budgets were looking for beginners. In addition, there was the almost insurmountable difficulty that I lacked qualifications. I knew almost nothing about psychology. Boring's systematic courses were the vestiges of a dying tradition. I had never had a course in social or child psychology. Harry Murray had not covered abnormal psychology in any exhaustive fashion. Gordon Allport had joined the faculty after I had taken all the courses I needed, and I had learned nothing from him about personality. From Freddie Wells at the Medical School I could have learned about mental testing, and from Walter Dearborn and Phil Rulon (whose offices were in Emerson Hall) about education and mental measurement, but I had not gone that far afield. I had never even read a text in psychology as a whole. Even as an "animal psychologist" I knew little about the errors made by rats in mazes, or the number of choices made in learning a discrimination, or the symbolic processes or insights of primates—nor had I any interest in finding out.

I wrote to Hull, who said that he was disappointed to hear that Harvard did not appreciate "the splendid work you have been doing." In the same mail with my note he had received a request from the Chairman at Northwestern University asking for "a strong man," and he had written to recommend me. (Evidently Yale had placed its own crop of graduate students by that time.) I was to send the Chairman a set of my reprints, but no letter, and "sit tight." I sat tight and later reported to Fred: "Lost the Northwestern job because of lack of teaching experience."

Fred wrote about another possibility:

Talked to [Floyd] Allport's seminar-group in Syracuse last Thursday . . . and put in a few well chosen words about you. They need a man badly there to build up a real animal lab and strengthen their department. . . . Would you object to my writing or interviewing Thelin (the Syracuse head) about their need for a man to build up things there? It really might not be a bad place—although most of the staff appears to be rather dull-witted.

I added a footnote to my next letter to Fred: "Take the Syracuse job yourself, you nut."

I had no feeling that the profession owed me a job or that anything should be done about a system in which I could not find one. I did not complain of my luck. The time had come when I needed a job and I should simply have to keep on looking. I would take whatever I found.

I HAD HAD an early contact with the Worcester State Hospital in Worcester, Massachusetts, when Paul Huston, a former fellow graduate student, wrote to me in 1932 to say that he wondered whether my methods could not be applied to humans. If he had had the facilities, he would have repeated my experiments on rats after injecting them with blood taken from normal and psychotic people, but what about human subjects?

David Shakow and Saul Rosenzweig, also on the staff at Worcester, were interested, and they asked me to come to the hospital and give a colloquium on behaviorism. My room was connected with a ward, and I was given two keys: one to the door of the building and another with which I was to lock the door of my room from inside, to isolate me from the patients. I returned from an evening party at the Shakows' and let myself into the silent building. Then I found that I had been given the wrong key and could not lock the door of my room. I should have to sleep exposed to possible wandering psychotics. I had a simple wish-fulfilling dream: it was early the next morning and I was telling my friends about my amusing predicament.

We discussed the possibility of some lever-pressing experiments with human subjects, and the construction of a suitable room was assigned to a patient who was a skillful carpenter—but only in his better moments. Unfortunately, he went into a deep depression when the room was only half finished and the experiments were never done.

By 1936, Paul had left the hospital, but Dave and Saul were still there and now they wanted to try the verbal summator. To avoid the theoretical implications of "summation," they renamed it the "tautophone." (Boring, too, would soon be complaining about my neologism: "Why call that interesting little business a *verbal summator*?") The "tautophone" might serve as a kind of auditory Rorschach test, with the advantage that the experimenter could easily control both the level of stimulus complexity and the number of repetitions. They worked out a classification of responses to indicate things like suggestibility, rigidity, and human reference. They also found "significant" responses. A patient with a marked feeling of inferiority heard

"You're a failure." He was also somewhat hypochondriacal and heard "They ruined the bile up." He had studied for the priesthood and heard many religious responses, such as "A faith hour," "Each hour of faith," and "Father O'Connor." His problem had centered around emancipation from his mother, and he heard "Obey her."

MY VIEW THAT EXTINCTION was simply the exhaustion of a reserve of responses was threatened by another effect which Pavlov had called "spontaneous recovery." When a conditioned reflex is undergoing extinction in a series of daily sessions, there is a greater flow of saliva at the beginning of each new session, as if the reflex had recovered from "inhibition" overnight. My rats also pressed more rapidly at the beginning of each session when their behavior was being extinguished. I suggested to Fred that if he had some rats that were finishing an experiment in which they had not been extinguished, he should extinguish for four or five days, put the rats aside for several months, then bring them back to the same level of deprivation and continue to extinguish. "If there is much spontaneous recovery, you should get large curves again. I suspect all Pavlov means by complete recovery is that the momentary strength is now back to normal. I.e., the new curves will begin at about the same rate. But they ought to fall off much more quickly . . . ."

Fred did the experiment, as well as a much more elaborate one, and I used his results in "the book."

IN APRIL 1936, nearing the end of my Junior Fellowship, I sent a letter to Fred which is perhaps the best evidence of my theoretical and experimental position, as well as of my personal life at that time. Fred was proposing to do an elaborate experiment on drive, and I began:

> My first feeling is a general one—that you haven't the equipment to do a job that will satisfy you. Old Calvin Stone is at it, with God knows how many rats, and even he gets barely reliable results. It's largely his method (Columbia Obstruction) but I have a feeling that these are among the most variable phenomena. Also you are running up against a lot of medical school work. . . . I read something recently about hunger and sex tie-ups in the oestral cycle, but can't remember

where. I should like to see the thing done by a psychologist as much as you, but I wouldn't do it myself without a lot of money behind me. . . . My feeling is now that hunger curves, such as the rate of eating during ingestion, are useful to us in controlling motivation, but that the central problem is conditioning, and that for the present I want to know only as much as necessary to keep the variable behaving.

The one problem that faces us as behaviorists is a classification of the kinds of drives—which reduces as I see it now to the kinds of reinforcing stimuli that are available. The big drive groups—hunger and sex—are only rather outstanding examples—and are peculiar in that they are hooked up with unconditioned and internal reactions. But the peculiar nature of conditioning of Type I (or as I now have to call it Type R) is that every reinforcing stimulus must be supposed to belong to a drive. . . .

My argument was that when pressing a lever is reinforced with food, the behavior can be subsequently controlled only by changing the level of food deprivation. The lever, as a discriminative stimulus, is important (we can take it away to prevent the occurrence of the behavior), but the control it exerts when present depends upon the deprivation. As an example, assume that a man smokes a pipe because of certain reinforcing consequences; how can we make him more or less likely to smoke? We can prevent smoking by taking the pipe away, but if there is any control when it is available, it will be through some kind of satiation or deprivation. There must be a "pipe-smoking drive." If the probability of smoking does not change, if there is nothing we can do to change it, there is no need to appeal to a drive, as I pointed out in my early papers on drive and reflex strength. My letter continued:

I've made some rather sweeping changes in my system, preparatory to getting out a book this summer. Have two kinds of behavior operant and respondent. No elicitory stimulus for the first (there may be discriminative stimuli). An operant is a castrated reflex with no stimulus. It's controlled only through the drive. Pressing the lever is an example. The lever is a discriminatory stimulus. That is to say, in the presence of certain stimuli (from the lever) certain reaching responses will be reinforced tactually by the lever. The lever is the occasion upon which the reaching response gets an effect but it does not elicit the response in the ordinary sense of elicit. The thing is quite different from a respondent *(e.g. flexion reflex or Pavlovian conditioned reflex)....*

(Fred replied: "I want to get the operant respondent idea clarified in my mind—and would appreciate some dope on it as soon as you have it.")

If you are anxious to make the best use of your apparatus, I strongly suggest taking up certain problems in different kinds of discriminations. That is the big field as I see it now. My distinction between two types of conditioned reflex is only a start toward outlining the various relations that can exist between behavior and the act of reinforcement. I am particularly interested in the number of ways in which behavior can show a differential relation to time. Hoagland's "judgment of time" is elliptical as hell. There are at least a dozen ways in which the passage of time may enter as a discriminatory stimulus. The field is practically virginal (I have not got beyond the vulva yet) and the job could be done with a few rats and, I am sure, with neat results.

I wish to hell you would get interested in this side of the matter. You can control your drive quite well enough to rest easy about it, and there's a hell of a lot more fun and a better chance for results that will make you famous....

Excuse the paternality of the above. I really don't feel the way it sounds.

I'll send you a paper I've been writing in answer to a couple of Poles who take issue with my two types.

The "couple of Poles" were Konorski and Miller. When I first distinguished between two types of conditioning, I did not know that they were trying to get Pavlov to change his formulation in the same way. I learned of their work only when they sent me a paper they were submitting to the *Journal of General Psychology* in reply to my "Two Types of Conditioned Reflex and a Pseudo Type." They also sent a book they had published in Polish, in which they had entered marginal notes in French explaining the graphs and tables. In a typical experiment they shocked the paw of the dog and gave it food when it flexed its leg. Eventually the leg flexed even though the paw was not shocked. The shock as an eliciting stimulus was an essential part of their formula.

My reply was published in the same issue. I argued that true reflexes seldom had the kinds of consequences which led to Type R conditioning. If flexion was a necessary consequence of a shock and if food was a necessary consequence of flexion, then food was a necessary consequence of shock. Such an arrangement could be constructed in the laboratory, but it was extremely rare in nature. An eliciting stimulus could seldom if ever be identified when behavior was acquired through Type R conditioning, and I could now show that stimuli present before a response was made played a different role. The unelicited flexion of the leg that eventually appeared in Konorski and Miller's experiment was not the reflex response with which they began. At best the shock was a way of "getting the behavior out" so that it could be reinforced.

Hull's students were doing something of the sort in their "modified Skinner Boxes" when they smeared food on the lever. The food slowly disappeared as the experiment went on, and the lever became a discriminative stimulus in the presence of which pressing was highly probable. In my reply I used the word "operant" in print for the first time, with "respondent" for the Pavlovian case. It would have been the right time to abandon "reflex," but I was still under the control of the work of Sherrington, Magnus, and Pavlov.

The question of the role of the stimulus had a practical side. Konorski and Miller could elicit the response they wanted to condition, but I had to wait for mine to appear. They seemed to be in a better position to change behavior. But could they find stimuli for all the responses they might want to condition? How would they deal with pressing a lever, for example? On the other hand, how long should I have to wait for the behavior I might want to condition? I answered that question in my reply by describing a process of "successive approximation":

> . . . elaborate and peculiar forms of response may be generated from undifferentiated operant behavior through successive approximation to a final form. . . . A rat may be found (very infrequently) not to press the lever spontaneously during a prolonged period of observation. The response in its final form may be obtained by basing the

In Cambridge, Massachusetts, 1930.

Indiana, June 1948. I'm seated top left with W. K. Estes on my left.
Fred Keller is addressing the group.

Right: With Fred Keller in Cambridge, Massachusetts, 1929.

Below: Washburn Crosby Co. (General Mills, Inc.) identification badge, 1942.

Left: The nonelectrical "problem box" that I designed, and Ralph Gerbrands built, for Fred Keller in 1935.

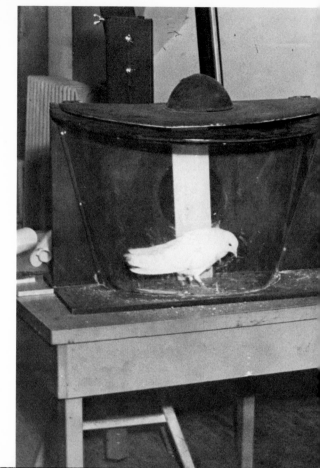

Right: Demonstrating oper-
ant conditioning of a pigeon,
Indiana, 1948.

A pigeon being put into the nose of the Pelican missile.

Right: Pliny dropping a marble down a chute.

With Yvonne shortly after our marriage.

Debbie in the baby-tender being cared for by Yvonne, and playing with toy.

Julie and Debbie in 1945.

With my father in Bradenton, Florida, 1947.

Ceramic statue of me chasing windmills, by William Sewell.

reinforcement upon the following steps in succession: approach to the site of the lever, lifting the nose into the air toward the lever, lifting fore-part of the body into the air, touching lever with feet, and pressing lever downward. When one step has been conditioned, the reinforcement is withdrawn and made contingent upon the next. With a similar method any value of a single property of the response may be obtained.

I do not remember actually shaping lever-pressing in such explicit stages, but I was sure it could be done, and I had certainly changed the "value of a single property" through successive approximation in producing very forceful responses.

My letter to Fred continued: "Have had no luck in an experiment with young Delabarre [Edward Delabarre, Jr.] trying to condition our plethysmographic response according to Type R. We've been trying to contract our arm in order to remove a noxious stimulus. A different angle on the Voluntary business of Hudgins and Hunter."

Konorski and Miller had objected to my assumption that responses of the autonomic nervous system (characteristic of emotional states) could be conditioned according to Type R. The autonomic nervous system, they said, was not under voluntary control. Walter Hunter's student, Hudgins, had taught a few subjects to contract the pupil of the eye "voluntarily." The spoken word "Contract!" was paired with a bright light shone into the eye, and through Pavlovian conditioning it began to elicit contraction in the absence of the light. At least one of Hudgins's subjects was said to be successful in ordering her own pupil to contract simply by speaking the word. But the contraction still was a "respondent." Saying "Contract!" was reinforced according to Type R and was an operant.

A plethysmograph is a metal sleeve enclosing the forearm. The sleeve is filled with water and when the blood vessels in the arm contract or expand, the volume of the arm changes, and a small amount of water is drawn in or forced out of the sleeve and moves an arm writing on a kymograph. Either Delabarre or I would wear the sleeve while the other turned a light or buzzer on or off as the volume changed—an arrangement now known as biofeedback. We found that we could *increase* the volume of our arm on demand, but we soon discovered that we were doing so by breathing more and more deeply; by taking more air into our lungs we were apparently squeezing blood from our chests into our arms. But we did not seem to be able to *contract* the arm, presumably by contracting the blood vessels. My letter continued:

> *Can think of a lot of other stuff to write about, but hope we can talk about it soon. Ought to add a personal report I suppose. My affair of Xmas-time is dead. [In December 1935 I had written: "Have my eyes on a swell dame. Dinner with her last night at Locke-Ober's: oysters after a Bacardi cocktail, Lobster Savannah with a rather sweetish Sauterne, port-de-salut with crackers and a Cointreau. Don't know whether I can make the grade or not but she is damn fascinating and we have a grand time together. I might add she is a widow, twenty-eight, with two very young children—with whom I am equally in love. This is quite entre nous."] Since then I have seen a lot of a young Russian kid, but am now pretty sold on a mezzo-soprano in the Metropolitan Opera. Just got back this morning from a weekend with her. So you see—still nothing permanent. As to you, I am glad you're going through with it and wish you the best of luck.*

As Fred had feared, Colgate proved to be too much for Connie, and she had gone back to Cambridge. The separation led to a divorce, and Fred had fallen in love with a young woman from Utica named Frances Scholl. She had been raised a Catholic, and that had meant problems, but Fred and Frances were now planning a honeymoon in Europe the following summer. My letter continued:

> *Harvard doesn't want me next year, and generous old Garry Boring has recommended me to a Y/M/C/A college in Springfield Mass. He wrote me last week that two universities with $2500 jobs turned me down because of my reputation being too "great" and implies that I will have a hell of a time getting anything unless it's in the upper brackets. Not much consolation there. However, the Brown-Clark shake-up may open up something.*

I met the President of that "Y/M/C/A college" in a hotel in Boston, and I could have had the job. Later I received a good offer from Illinois, but by that time I was negotiating with Minnesota. Walter Hunter was teaching summer school there, and I suspect that it was he who mentioned me to R.M. Elliott, the Chairman of the department. When I heard that I was being considered, I asked Carmichael to write in my behalf and told Boring that I had done so. I learned many years later that, contrary to the impression I had given Fred, Boring wrote a very strong letter in my support. I was, he said, "very anxious to please, and most exceptionally able." And Elliott later reported that his letter had "turned the trick." He offered me the job at $1800 for nine months with the chance to pick up something extra in summer school. His letters were persuasive, the figure was raised to $1960, and I accepted. "I am delighted," Elliott wrote to Boring, "to have a Harvard Ph.D. in the Department at last."

Harvard was celebrating its tercentenary that year, and at a meeting in the Yard I ran into George Birkhoff, the mathematician, who had become Dean of the Faculty of Arts and Sciences and hence, *ex officio*, a Senior Fellow. He knew of my problem, and when I told him that I had found a job at Minnesota, he said, "Well, it's nice to know you are going to be *somewhere*." But that was not the way I felt. I looked forward to Minnesota. Elliott's letters had been urbane and witty, and my only visit to the Midwest, to Omaha, had been pleasant enough. Life would no doubt be different, but the luxury of a Junior Fellowship could not last forever.

It was too soon to say whether the Society had had the effect on me it was designed to have—whether, in addition to support for my work, I had gained much from my association with the other Fellows —but a year later, writing to Henderson about the publication of my book, I added a few words expressing my indebtedness to the Society. His reply was pure Pareto: "It is a great satisfaction to me personally that you feel as you do toward the Society and that in spite of your religion and your theology it comes out. My observation is that a behaviorist can be just as sentimental as a Thomist or an idealist because I think that derivations from one class of residues have little influence upon the residues of another class."

WITH MY IMMEDIATE FUTURE settled, I went back to Monhegan. The Sewells were there, with Bill's new wife, Mary, and I dropped into the old routine, but I was still working on the manuscript, and there was packing to be done at my office and laboratory, and I soon drove back to Cambridge. I was therefore able to accept an invitation that would have important consequences. Dan Smith had married, and he and his wife, Martha, were living in an apartment on Mt. Auburn Street. On July 22 they invited me to dinner. A friend of Martha's from Flossmoor, a small town near Chicago, was visiting them, and I was to make a fourth for dinner. They picked me up at Winthrop House at 6:00. I was wearing a white suit with a dark-blue shirt and white tie. They introduced me to a young woman sitting in the back seat with Martha. Her name was Yvonne Blue. She had light-brown hair cut close to the head in the fashion of the day. Her dress was of gray silk chiffon printed with small bouquets of flowers. It had short, full sleeves and a soft wide belt. She had majored in English at the University of Chicago (she had taken two courses with Thornton Wilder), and we found a great deal to talk about, challenging each other with a bit of name-dropping.

We had dinner at Seiler's "1775" House in Lexington, went to a movie in Boston, and had drinks afterward (alcoholic only for Yvonne and me) at a cocktail lounge. Yvonne spent the next day with an old friend, a reporter who had left his job on a Chicago paper and was doing publicity for Harvard. I picked her up the following evening, took her to Durgin Park for dinner, and persuaded her to spend the next day with me instead of taking the bus to New York as she had planned. We spent much of the day at Walden Pond with a late-afternoon tea at an inn called Hartwell Farm. We came back to Cambridge for dinner with the Smiths, but none too gracefully escaped to spend the evening in my rooms before Yvonne took the sleeper to New York.

We wrote to each other, and I persuaded her to come back to do some typing for me at the Society's expense. There was an exhibition of chess sets at the Semitic Museum, next to the biological laboratories, and it sent us to antique shops in Boston, where I bought two fairly old sets, with which Yvonne taught me to play. I took her to see Harry Levin in his rooms in Eliot House, and he played some avant-garde jazz for us. We picnicked with the Bright Wilsons in Wellesley and spent two days in West Harwich with my family. Then we drove to Monhegan, staying overnight in a cabin on the way. I registered as F. S. Burrhus and Yvonne wore a dime-store wedding ring. We were not very relaxed because laws against fornication were still occasionally enforced. On Monhegan, Joe Davis gave us separate but adjoining rooms, and that was better. I had made a small folding chessboard of pigskin purchased from a bootmaker on Dunster Street. The chessmen—mother-of-pearl collar buttons on which I had painted the chess symbols—could be snapped into holes punched in the leather. We carried it on our walks and played chess while watching the surf. With the Sewells, we cooked lobsters in seaweed on fires of driftwood and swam nude in Gull Pond at night.

We drove back to Cambridge, and Yvonne went on to Flossmoor, where I planned to stop on my way to Minnesota. I packed my books in wooden boxes purchased at the Coop, unscrewed the legs of my clavichord, and called a moving van. I drove up to Dartmouth to comment on Culler's paper in the symposium on conditioning and to give my paper on fixed-ratio schedules of reinforcement. (In a letter that summer, Fred had mentioned the possibility of a variable-ratio schedule, the heart of all gambling systems. "Unless I can find where you did it already," he wrote, "I am going to get data on extinction after 'haphazard' rather than 'fixed' ratios in reconditioning. You know, it's more like human prayer that way!")

I gave Walter Hunter a ride back to Cambridge, and the next day I loaded my remaining possessions in my car and left for Scranton. I spent a day or two with my family and started west on highways that would soon become familiar.

In Flossmoor I met Yvonne's father and mother and younger sister, Tick. They lived in a yellow-stucco Spanish-style house, with a garden and tennis court. Her father, an ophthalmologist, followed a harrowing routine. He rose early, took the Illinois Central to Chicago (an hour's ride), spent the mornings in a hospital clinic and the afternoons at his office near the Loop, came back by train for a late dinner, and went for a relaxing drive in the flat countryside before bed. I also met Yvonne's grandfather, Opie Read, a well-known novelist and Chautauqua lecturer, a tall striking man with a fund of stories. "Nobody here but jest us chickens" was one of his better-known contributions to the genre.

I slept in a room next to Yvonne's and our beds were against the same wall. After we had gone to bed, or early in the morning, we rapped on the wall in a simple code. I learned later that Yvonne's mother had been quite unhappy about these communications. She would have been unhappier still if she had decoded them.

We decided to get married. We had known each other only a little more than six weeks but had spent much of that time together. The Christmas holidays seemed to be the right time for a wedding. I wrote to my parents, who must have breathed a sigh of relief, and drove on to Minneapolis a fiancé.

ELLIOTT HAD ARRANGED for me to live at the Faculty Club, where I had a pleasant room with space for my clavichord and free use of the Common Rooms, except at noon when the faculty swarmed in for lunch, bridge, and billiards. Two fellow guests were Richard Hocking, the son of the Professor Hocking I had known at Harvard, and Willard Everett, both philosophers. I saw a good deal of them.

Elliott in person matched his letters. He spoke with an upper-class Massachusetts accent and great precision. He dressed punctiliously and his office was in perfect order. (He put a book or a pair of scissors back in place as soon as he had finished using it, something I had never learned to do.) His wife, Mathilde, was young, soignée, and active in the Institute of Fine Arts. They lived in a contemporary house, and a portrait of a Chinese mandarin in their living room could have been of Elliott himself. His friends called him, incongruously, "Mike."

The introductory course in psychology, taken by about 800 sophomores, had been carefully engineered. The senior members of the staff lectured in their fields of specialization, and the multiple-choice examinations had been carefully evaluated. By using two arrangements of true and false items, it had even been possible to determine the direction in which students tended to look when cribbing answers from their neighbors. Mike Elliott would later describe my role in the course in this way:

> Each year I announced in the first lecture of the big introductory course that Skinner would take charge of a small segregated [intellectually!] section of students whose previous scholastic standing had been especially high. He personally interviewed those who volun-

teered, told them how different their assignments would be, and invited the ones who impressed him to join his section, which they were free to do or not to do, as they wished. Partly through this device and in general through the appeal of his originality, Skinner quickly surrounded himself with a highly motivated group of students, many of whom were thus snared for advanced work.

Much of what was "original" about me was due to the fact that I was wholly unprepared for the job. The Minnesota staff was not entirely unaware of my deficiencies, and Donald Paterson in particular was worried. He insisted that I use the same texts as the larger section, and he would have been happier if my students had had to take those carefully engineered multiple-choice examinations. One text was by R. S. Woodworth, the highly respected psychologist whom Fred would not, in a calmer moment, have called an ass. The other was a text in developmental psychology by a local figure, Florence Goodenough. Near the end of the course we also used a small book called *The Psychology of Insanity* by Bernard Hart. It was the first time I had read anything of the sort, and the fact that I was keeping a jump ahead of the class that first year must have been obvious. My students were certainly not in awe of me. We often argued quite violently—in part because, though I did not mention my own research, I took a strong behavioristic line.

The rest of my "load" for the fall and winter quarters was a section of the laboratory course. Students working in pairs did simple experiments with simple apparatus. I accepted and taught what the course was designed to teach. By looking back and forth from one dot to another, the students were to discover that the eye is blind as it moves, and I refrained from asking them to look from the right to the left of a neon bulb and observe the sixty-cycle track recorded by the "blind" eye. In one experiment rats learned a complicated elevated maze with all the students recording right and left turns, and I kept my opinion of the maze as a research instrument to myself.

Minnesota had promised me an annual research budget of only $200, but the Society of Fellows had given me my old apparatus, including four of the nonelectrical pieces I had designed for Fred. In Cambridge I had ventilated the boxes with an air pump belonging to the Department of General Physiology, and I now made a substitute of an automobile-tire pump driven by an old phonograph motor. The department had living cages, water bottles, and other equipment for the care of my rats.

A member of the department, William T. Heron, was interested in animal behavior, and he and I set up the four nonelectrical apparatuses for an experiment on hunger. We periodically reinforced responses for an hour each day but gave the rats no other food. Day after day they grew hungrier and pressed faster, until they grew weak. Their rates reached a very high level.

In October, Delabarre wrote that he had gone over our data and that we had indeed conditioned a reduction in the volume of our arm as an operant. I had not been a good subject, but "in my case," Delabarre wrote, "I gave a fairly sizable response every time and then, when you abolished the correlation between the arm-volume response and the showing of the red light, the response dropped out in about ten trials and the series went on for thirty-two more trials with no return of the response." When the decrease in volume turned off a buzzer, the evidence was better. "If we . . . take ten succcessive trials with a response occurring every time as . . . a criterion, we got conditioning even in your case; and you will remember what a time we had trying to get it."

Delabarre wanted to go on with the experiment for his thesis but was having trouble with his advisers. He asked me for "the names of the two fellows who wrote that manuscript saying that this could not be done," and three weeks later he reported: "I was successful in pushing the general subject through and getting its acceptance for thesis purposes. I did run into snags of one sort or another however. . . . They seemed to object to accepting your formulation of the two types of conditioned reflex."

Yvonne came to Minneapolis for a weekend, and I showed her the campus and took her to tea at the Elliotts'. She seemed unsure of herself. Perhaps she was not convinced that she should be a faculty wife. A rather unsatisfactory correspondence followed, and we decided to postpone the wedding. When I told my family, my mother wrote a long letter with an appendix typed from my father's dictation. It was a mistake to postpone our marriage. Surely we could find a place to live (I had given a shortage of apartments as one of our reasons). They had told their friends, and no doubt Yvonne and her family had done so, too, and it would be embarrassing to explain the change in plans. I should not expect to figure out what life with Yvonne would be like as scientifically as I figured out a problem with my rats. If I waited, I would probably never marry Yvonne or any other girl.

As one grows older [my father dictated], his or her habits and opinions become more fixed and therefore more difficult for readjustment. While you are not old in years, you are old enough and have studied enough to have fixed views and strong opinions. You have had a life practically free from responsibilities. It strikes me that you are the one who will have to give up your fixed notions and adjust your life to your wife's. You will have to surrender your bachelor independence. If you care enough for Yvonne to sacrifice some of that independence and fixed ideas to meet hers, and be willing to adjust views so as to make life harmonious, and if she is a girl who is willing to meet you halfway, then I think there will be no doubt as to your successful married life.

Yvonne and I continued to debate the question, and when a letter of mine seemed to imply that I, too, was not sure that she was faculty-wife material, she sent a card saying "I am breaking the engagement," and told her family and friends that she had done so. I persuaded her to let me come to Chicago to talk things over. I went down by sleeper on a Friday night and checked into a hotel. She came to my room and we not only made up, we decided to be married right away. We reached City Hall just in time to get a license, bought a wedding ring, and took the train to Flossmoor.

Her family was out. I phoned my father and mother and they left for Chicago by the first train. During the afternoon we listened to a football game on the radio and heard Northwestern break Minnesota's three-year winning streak. Yvonne's father and mother and sister had not known that I was in Chicago, and when they came home they were understandably surprised to learn that we were to be married the next day. Friends were called and Yvonne's mother went shopping. It was Halloween, and the only cakes available for the reception were decorated in orange and black. A local minister was found. (Hearing that I was a psychologist, he asked whether we minded if he mentioned God during the ceremony, and we said we did not.)

My father and mother arrived on Sunday morning, and we were married that afternoon. A few friends had been rounded up, and Yvonne's grandfather came and charmed my father and mother with reminiscences of Chautauqua. We dispensed with bridesmaid and best man. The minister stood at one end of the living room near the piano and Yvonne and I simply walked in together. Yvonne wore a dress that her sister had bought the day before.

My father and mother could not have been happier. Their son was married at last, and married, moreover, to the daughter of a well-to-do, conservative American family. In addition, the Roosevelt regime was coming to an end. A poll conducted by the *Literary Digest* predicted a sweeping victory for Alfred Landon, and after the ceremony they hurried back to Chicago so that they could get to Scranton in time to vote for him.

Among the guests were some old friends of Yvonne's, Lou and Ken Mulligan. They took us to Chicago for a drink and put us on the train to Minneapolis. The next morning a taxi rushed us to the University campus on a bumpy back road to avoid traffic. I left Yvonne in a drugstore with a cup of coffee and got to my class just in time to discuss emotion.

We found a pleasant one-room apartment at 515 Delaware Street. Yvonne had accumulated as many books as I, and I bought lumber and paint and made three floor-to-ceiling bookcases. Just enough wall space was left for the clavichord. In Cambridge I had painted a chessboard, with chess figures from *Through the Looking Glass* along the ends, and we kept it set up on a small stand ready to play. A hasty wedding had meant gifts of money rather than things, and in Minneapolis we bought silver, china, and linen. A chest of drawers belonging to Yvonne was sent up from Flossmoor.

We soon acquired an *objet d'art*. Bill Sewell had proposed that he make a ceramic portrait of me. I had never seen any of his work but he spoke intelligently about art, and we agreed upon a modest fee. He took photographs of my head from various angles, and in his studio in New York he made a small ceramic figure showing me on the back of a rather undersized horse. Six hundred hours of work in one short summer had suggested extreme dedication, and he portrayed me as a young Don Quixote. The caparison of my horse was decorated with large white rats, and a smaller rat was on the cover of the book that I held as a buckler. In my right arm I held a rather phallic lance, and I leaned forward with what Bill called "an expression of bitter tenseness." My horse, however, was in a different mood. It was looking back, its head swung around by my left knee.

I HAD CONFINED MYSELF to studying some of the pleasanter consequences of behavior, but the unpleasant were probably commoner in daily life, and I decided to look at them. Electric shock, delivered to the feet through a gridlike floor, was the standard punishment in animal experiments, but I did not want to shock my rats. Instead, I arranged a hammer that knocked the lever upward and slapped the paw that pressed it down. I had sketched such a device in 1931, noting that one could "adjust strength of blow by changing weight and voltage." I called the contingent slap "negative reinforcement," a usage I later corrected. Reinforcement implied strengthening, but I was interested in how behavior could be weakened or, more specifically, how responses could be "subtracted from the reserve." I built up a presumed reserve through periodic reconditioning and then extinguished the behavior for seven days. Shortly after the beginning of the third day I slapped all responses. The rats pressed more rapidly for a few moments but then stopped for the rest of the hour. On the following day all pressings were again slapped, though few occurred. On the fifth day I stopped slapping, but responding resumed only slowly. Punishment of all responses for nearly two hours had, I said, "exhausted the reserve."

In a different experiment, however, responses were slapped only during the first ten minutes of a fresh extinction curve, and the rats soon recovered. By the end of the second day's session (a total of four hours) they had emitted as many responses as a group that had not been slapped. The slaps had suppressed the rate but had apparently not "destroyed the responses in the reserve." Punishment was not the reverse of reinforcement.

In another experiment responses were periodically reinforced but also periodically slapped. Responding was temporarily suppressed, but the rats quickly adjusted and eventually responded at a normal rate even when every response was slapped. (I suspect that they had learned to press the lever very quickly and avoid, or at least greatly weaken, the effect of the upward blow.)

I MAY HAVE REPAID my debt to one of the rats in the starvation experiment when I brought it back to normal weight and helped it acquire a certain fame. I had chosen to work with rats because their behavior was relatively simple, but other psychologists were studying "almost human" apes, investigating higher mental processes presumed to be beyond the reach of a rat. There was, for example, an experiment in which a chimpanzee earned poker chips and spent them on food and other goods. Did the chips have a symbolic value to which a mere rat would be insensitive?

I decided to teach a rat to spend money. Poker chips would be hard to handle, and I chose glass marbles instead. The rat was to release a marble from a rack by pulling a chain, pick the marble up, carry it across the cage, and drop it into a tube standing about two inches above the floor. I could not, of course, wait for this complex sequence to appear before reinforcing it. I had to construct it step by step through "successive approximation," each step being something the rat would do at the time so that it could be reinforced.

I began with a platform about a foot square. A bottomless wire cage was held far enough above it to permit a marble to roll off any edge. As the marble fell it tripped a switch that operated a food dispenser in a corner of the cage. A number of marbles were put on the floor and any move the rat made that knocked one off the edge was reinforced. Moves of various kinds were strengthened. I then put a rim on three sides of the floor and the rat learned to push the marbles off the free edge, eventually quite quickly. A marble had meanwhile become a conditioned reinforcer, and when I added a rack and chain to the roof of the cage, the rat quickly learned to release a marble by pulling the chain.

I added a slight lip to the free edge, over which the rat had to push each marble, and as I made the lip higher, it began to grasp the marble in its paws, lifting it up and out over the edge. It did not drop it, however. It would hold it over the edge, its forelegs trembling, and wait for it to fall. Evidently rats are not inclined to drop things "to have an effect." For a time it solved the problem by knocking the marble out of its paws with its nose. It often shot the marble so far that it missed the switch below, and I added a backstop. Eventually, simple letting go appeared as an operant, and I slowly altered the edge of the cage until the rat was dropping the marble into a small box standing about two inches above the floor.

By this time the student newspaper, the *Minnesota Daily*, had run a story, naming the rat Pliny the Elder. The local newspapers picked it up and then the wire services, and *Life* magazine published a series of pictures in its issue of May 31, 1937, showing Pliny at work. A writer to the *New York Herald Tribune* saw some relevance to the human condition: "Maybe, as Professor Skinner says, all this proves nothing of importance, but if I were a sales manager seeking a topic for next Monday's pep meeting, I should certainly call the achievement of Pliny to the attention of the sales force."

I later replaced the box with a tube just big enough to accept the marble. Pliny was awkward as he (the impersonal "it" will no longer serve for a rat with a name) walked across the cage with the marble in his paws, but I could see no other difference between him and the chimpanzee. When not very hungry he would occasionally pull the chain to release marbles which he did not immediately spend, though I doubt whether he was "hoarding money for its own sake." When Hull visited my laboratory, he noticed that Pliny licked the marbles as he carried them across the cage and he called it an "anticipatory goal reaction."

A cameraman came to get the story for Pathé News. He turned up unannounced when Pliny was enjoying a vacation and was fully fed. I said that he would not perform for a day or two, but the man said he knew all about animals and had captured many great moments just as they occurred. I should just leave him alone with Pliny. He set up his camera and stayed there all day, smoking cigars. I dropped in from time to time to see how things were going. Whenever Pliny moved toward the chain the photographer began cranking his camera, stopping as soon as Pliny turned away. Then he waited to begin cranking only when Pliny approached the chain and stood up on his hind legs, stopping when he came down on all fours. Most of the time Pliny slept and the cameraman smoked. Eventually all his film was exposed, and Pliny had not yet pulled the chain. The company had agreed to let me know when the feature would appear on the screens of the country, and one day Heron received a garbled message to the effect that the story had been dropped because rats were "repugnant" to movie audiences.

IN THE EARLY THIRTIES I had come across a monograph in a second-hand bookstore that contained a plot of Chinese word frequencies on logarithmic coordinates. It may have been the thesis of George K. Zipf. In 1935 Zipf published his *Psychobiology of Language* and I learned more about his "law." In any large sample of verbal behavior, words occur with certain frequencies, and if you put them in rank order according to frequency and plot the frequencies against the order on logarithmic paper, you get something close to a straight line. I published a Zipf plot to show the "normality" of the words I had collected with the verbal summator.

At Minnesota I somehow acquired a copy of a monograph by Kent and Rosanoff on word association. It listed the words associated with 100 stimulus words by 1000 psychotics, together with their frequencies. It had been published in 1910, several years before Carl Jung had more explicitly treated word association as a thought process. (By 1936 the "significance" of associated words was so well understood that Kaufman and Hart used it in *You Can't Take It With You.* Why should Mrs. Kirby say "dull" in response to "honeymoon?") The frequencies given by Kent and Rosanoff looked as if they might obey Zipf's Law.

One of the projects in Roosevelt's New Deal was the Federal Youth Administration, which paid students seventy-five cents an hour to serve as research assistants, and I hired an undergraduate named Nathan Gage to help me with the data. The commonest response to a stimulus word occurred on the average about 25 percent of the time, the second commonest about 12 percent, the third a little less than 8 percent, and the others in slowly declining percentages. When averaged, the percentages gave a straight line on logarithmic coordinates, except that the commonest responses to vaguely defined words like "justice," "religion," or "comfort" showed slightly less than the predicted agreement.

AFTER OUR MARRIAGE, I continued to follow my established routine, but Yvonne found herself with little or nothing to do. She had never been interested in housekeeping, and when the weekly cleaning woman came, she simply got out of the apartment. Our precipitous wedding had interrupted the cooking-school program upon which she embarked when we became engaged, and she had not advanced beyond breakfast; her competence was limited to orange marmalade, popovers, and various ways of cooking eggs. It was not a serious problem, and she soon became an excellent cook.

In the evening we played chess and began to take it seriously. We subscribed to a chess magazine and occasionally went to a chess club in Minneapolis. A game Yvonne played against a visiting master was published in a local paper. Playing together, we kept a record of who played white and who won. In January Yvonne was six games ahead of me, but in March only one, and as I drew even, we began to compete too aggressively for marital peace. We turned instead to reading aloud. Henderson had put me on to Trollope, and we went through the Barchester series. We also caught up on each other's collection. Yvonne had all the volumes to date of Jules Romain's *Men of Good Will* (which Henderson had also strongly recommended). She also had a copy of Morton Prince's *Dissociation of a Personality*, and I astonished my class by recounting the strange story of that Boston spinster with the charming but mischievous alter ego.

My father and mother had urged me to adapt my ways to Yvonne's, consider her point of view, and be fair to her. Possibly I had profited from their advice, for by spring I was writing to Fred: "Yvonne is proving the absolutely perfect wife. A perfect foil for an old scientific crank who likes his own way altogether too well. Not that I get my way, but I don't mind not getting it."

Our social life was not exciting. Dick Hocking had a set of bells, and we occasionally recruited a few friends and rang changes in peals of modest length. We exchanged Sunday-evening suppers with some of the younger people in the department, particularly the Longstaffs and Hathaways. Yvonne was soon making an excellent crabmeat St.

Jacques, which she served on a large blue plate received as a wedding present, and we shopped in a Chinese store for canned lichee nuts and dragon's eyes. At these parties we played parlor games, and Yvonne read handwriting. She had worked as a stenographer for a newspaper handwriting expert, but she could not always read her stenographic notes, and had therefore learned something of the art in order to be able to substitute her own analyses.

My father and mother made the two-day trip from Scranton to visit us, and I showed them around the department. I made the mistake of having them try a paper-and-pencil test of mechanical ability. My mother, the daughter of a carpenter, had finished the test when my father, almost exclusively verbal, was still struggling with the first items.

I did not find it easy to make friends with colleagues outside the department. I was invited to join a Faculty Dining Club, which met once every three weeks. No drinks were served, and perhaps that is why I found it hard to break into established friendships. I talked mostly with, and usually sat beside, a lonely little man whose ancient connection with Harvard gave us something to talk about. A surprising number of my acquaintances spoke critically, if not hostilely, of Harvard, some of them, perhaps, because they had been at Harvard and had not been kept on. I began to speak of a Pan-Harvard Union, and at times I no doubt sounded like a member. (Several years later a friend took me to a club of younger faculty men. I suppose I was being looked over as a member, but I was ill at ease and told a story—the old chestnut about *le capot noir*—which, it was clear, everyone had heard before.)

With respect to professional matters, Minnesota was satisfactory enough. "My position here," I wrote to Crozier, "is all that could be desired. My teaching duties are light, my students interesting, and I have all the facilities for research that I need." And to Fred: "I find I like to teach! This place is really grand and I tink I bane one lucky Swede—as they say out here."

HERON AND I THOUGHT that behavior under periodic reconditioning might serve as a baseline against which we could observe the effects of certain drugs. We reinforced pressing a lever every four minutes and then injected various compounds. Moderate doses of caffeine and Benzedrine nearly doubled the rate, although large doses of caffeine depressed it. Adrenaline produced a quick rise followed by a sharp decline. Phenobarbital suppressed the behavior within a few minutes. A small amount of insulin administered one hour before testing brought a substantial increase, but a combination of insulin and Benzedrine abolished almost all responding.

Fred was using rate of responding under periodic reconditioning as a baseline in a series of experiments on oxygen deprivation at high altitudes, and Heron and I did some work on cerebral anoxia. I thought that oxygen deprivation and drugs should have the same effect as a change in drive—"a momentary decrease [or increase] in rate . . . no lasting effect upon reserve." But after prolonged extinction, caffeine and Benzedrine produced rates far higher than any observed before extinction began, and my concept of a "reflex reserve" was strained to the breaking point.

I HAD NOT FINISHED the book that I would call *The Behavior of Organisms* by the end of my Junior Fellowship, but it was rapidly taking shape. Though I was teaching for the first time and had set up my laboratory and was conducting experiments (and was starting life as a married man), I found time to make graphs of the data that I had not published and to put together not only an account of my research but a "system."

I had come to psychology devoted to Pavlov, and I had soon discovered Sherrington and Magnus. They seemed to be closer than any of their contemporaries to a true science of behavior. The concept of the reflex had served them well, and in my thesis I had said that it was all that was needed in the study of behavior. I knew better by the time I began to write my book. My field was the operant rather than the respondent, and my measure of strength was probability (or at least rate) of responding rather than magnitude of response or latency or after-discharge.

I could not break my chains, however. I went on talking about reflexes. "The term reflex will be used," I wrote, "to include both respondent and operant even though in its original meaning it applied to respondents only. A single term for both is convenient because both are topographical units of behavior and because an operant may and usually does acquire a relation to prior stimulation." I did add that, in general, "the notion of a reflex is to be emptied of any connotation of the active 'push' of the stimulus." My book would, I hoped, be "beyond the reach of current criticisms of oversimplified stimulus-response formulae." Stimulus and response would "refer here to correlated entities, and to nothing more." It was necessary to move beyond mere narration to the lawful connections between behavior and environment, but the mere collection of reflexes (the "botanizing of reflexes") was not enough.

My definition of behavior as "the movement of an organism or its parts" was misleading. It assured the reader of my objectivity: my rat pressed the lever and that was all I saw; I did not see its motive, intention, or purpose or the meaning the action had for it. But to predict, and especially to control, behavior, I needed to know the situation in which it occurred and the consequences that followed, and these should have been mentioned in my definition. I did point out that "neither a reflex nor a group of reflexes appropriate to, say, a drive or emotion can be identified from topographical features alone." (I would make the point quite explicit in my analysis of verbal behavior. The speaker's response did not possess meaning; its meaning was in the circumstances under which it now occurred. The meaning for the listener was to be found in what the listener subsequently did.)

When relevant variables were identified, a behaving organism could be regarded as a system, rather like those "encountered in physical chemistry . . . an aggregation of related variables singled out for the sake of convenient investigation and description from all the various phenomena presented by a given subject matter." There were "laws" to be established—"static" laws such as threshold or latency, and dynamic laws such as reflex fatigue, refractory phase, and inhibition. The book was mainly concerned with the dynamic laws of operant behavior, which was emitted rather than elicited. Its strength at any moment was determined by stimuli which "evoked" behavior because of a preceding history of reinforcement and by operations in the fields of drive and emotion. A "reflex reserve" had no "local or physiological properties."

I could not put the concept of operant behavior in its proper historical setting, because I did not know enough about the long struggle to define a unit of behavior. Except for structuralism, in which a unit was defined in terms of organization, some sort of appeal had usually been made to the consequences of behavior. "Intention" and "purpose" alluded to consequences, and "persistence until a goal was reached" did so more explicitly. The maze began to serve a theoretical function (for Tolman, in particular) because the behavior was physically oriented toward a goal. But when it was implied or asserted that "behavior occurred because of its consequences," the reference was to the consequences which were to follow. An operant, defined as behavior that has a specific effect upon the environment, might seem to suggest the same thing, but the experimental contingencies made it clear that the strength of behavior was due to *past* consequences. The strength of behavior was determined by what had already happened rather than by what was going to happen in the future.

Much earlier I discussed another issue about a unit of behavior with Köhler, and in December 1937 he wrote:

> *I agree with you in the conviction that there is no science without analysis. But I know of many cases, in physics for instance, where phenomena are analysed, but not into independent units. . . . You say, quite rightly "We must analyse if anything at all is to be said about behavior"; but if you add to the verb "analyse" "into units," and if units are supposed to be independent, elementary facts, then I do not see the necessity of the procedure because Physics is full of other cases where the procedure is analytical but does not yield independent units.*

Nevertheless, *The Behavior of Organisms* would be "frankly analytical." There was nothing arbitrary about the operant as a unit. As I had argued in my paper on the generic nature of stimulus and response, I would not, with Watson, define a response as "anything the animal does, such as turning toward or away from a light, jumping at a sound, and more highly organized activities such as building a skyscraper, drawing plans, having babies, writing books, and the like." A unit would have to prove itself by yielding orderly changes in "reflex strength."

Köhler had objected to that too: "I do not think that we are through with our discussion, although I like very much what we did. One of the main questions which I should like to discuss is the term 'orderly.' As a Gestalt psychologist I feel allowed to use such a term, but I do not yet see how you can introduce its meaning into your science of behavior. . . ."

NEAR THE END of the book I briefly discussed its relation to the work of Hull and Tolman, the two giants in the field. Hull had grown up in Michigan, had taught at Wisconsin, and remained loyal to the Midwest. Whenever he returned there for psychological meetings, he delighted in showing his young Eastern friends that Midwestern milkshakes were so thick that you had to eat them with a spoon. A victim of polio, he needed a cane, but he was energetic and enthusiastic.

I first saw him at a meeting of the American Association for the Advancement of Science in the Boston area at Christmastime, 1933. I gave a paper and when I finished, he stood up and said he wished to call the attention of the audience to "the work of this young man." A week later he wrote, "I was particularly interested in your paper. . . . I was very sorry that I did not have an opportunity of meeting you after the meeting. I have a rather strong conviction that the rational or deductive approach characteristic of the work of Crozier and his group on the one hand, and that of Hecht at Columbia fits in very well with the similar approach which is being developed by myself and a number of my associates at Yale." He asked me to send him reprints, and when I did so, he wrote that he was having them bound. He asked me to come to New Haven, and I said I hoped to do so the following year. That spring he visited my laboratory and afterward wrote that he was "much impressed."

The following December, when Eric Trist arranged for me to meet Edward Sapir, I asked Hull if I might drop by his laboratory, and he invited me to talk to his seminar. A last-minute announcement said that I would presumably talk about some "free conditioned reflex work," where "free" seemed to mean that my rats, unlike Pavlov's dogs, were not harnessed.

Hull put me up at his home, and I dined there with a few of his students. The seminar was friendly and the discussion stimulating. I was not, however, impressed by the Institute of Human Relations. I reported to Fred, "Came away with a sore lip to keep from laughing. Hull was damn nice, and in earnest too. Nothing smug about him at least. But the Yerkes and Gesell outfits are unspeakable." The institute had been designed to bring together a number of distinguished people in the field of behavior. They were given separate parts of the building, and the connecting doors were soon locked. Hull was the only one to show an ecumenical spirit. His Wednesday seminars, which began in the early thirties, were attended not only by most of the psychologists at the institute but by logicians (e.g., Woodger), philosophers of science (e.g., Northrup), and anthropologists (e.g., Murdock). Mimeographed reports were mailed to interested people.

Hull's students soon began to use what he was the first to call a "Skinner Box." In June 1935 I wrote to Fred: "Did I tell you Hull is going to change his laboratory over entirely and work on motivation? He told Kemp at Clark that he didn't think I realized the extent to which my method could be exploited. As Kemp said, that's the right word." But a year later Hull was working with Neal Miller, O.H. Mowrer, and John Dollard on psychoanalysis, and in May I wrote to Fred: "Just got the latest broadside from Hull's seminar on psychoanalysis and conditioned reflexes. I'm afraid the old boy is lost."

By the time I was finishing *The Behavior of Organisms* Fred wrote that Hull had offered to lend him some "modified Skinner-boxes" if Fred would do some experiments in which Hull was interested. I replied: "Your news about Hull made me damned mad. I don't mind his cribbing apparatus—but to bribe you into doing his exp.—that's a little too much. However, if you can screw him for apparatus, why not. Get anything you can . . . you prostitute, but keep your fancy free. Have you seen Hilgard's recent summary of the conditioning problem? It looks as if the Hull faction were going to make the fight for a single kind of process." Hull, I told Fred, had "promised Elliott his book in 2 1/2 years. I'm going to take a healthy crack at him in my last chapter so it may be 3 1/2." But all I said was that Hull had "failed to set up a system of behavior as distinct from a method of verification." Most of his definitions were drawn from various inexhaustible sources. Several hundred acceptable definitions of the same sort could readily be obtained, and a dismaying number of theorems could be derived. . . . Deduction and the testing of hypotheses are actually subordinate processes in a descriptive science. . . . A science of behavior cannot be closely patterned after geometry or Newtonian mechanics. . . . If Hull had chosen experimental physics or chemistry as a model, the place of deduction in his system would have been much less important.

MY PARAGRAPH ABOUT Tolman had a footnote: "The essential aspects of the present system which enter into the comparison were described in my paper on the concept of the reflex in 1931." I added it because I felt that Tolman had failed to acknowledge his indebtedness to that paper when, in February 1934, he addressed the Kosmos Club at the University of California in Berkeley on "Psychology *versus* Immediate Experience." He presented an equation very much like mine representing behavior as a function of certain independent variables and asserted that "the determination of the actual form of this function . . . will constitute the final goal of . . . behaviorism."

That was very different from his position only a year before in *Purposive Behavior in Animals and Man* (a book which in his paper he called "a less completely thought out statement" and which, in a letter to me in October 1937, he would describe as " 'cute' five years ago but decidedly passé now"). His new position, he said, had been anticipated by Russell and Bridgman. But he had not mentioned Bridgman in *Purposive Behavior* nor Russell except for an opinion expressed in 1912 which was scarcely Tolman's view at any time. There was no reference to the fact that I had discussed both Russell and Bridgman with him at length in 1931 or that he had read "The Concept of the Reflex in the Description of Behavior" with its similar equation. (He had not only read the paper, he had discussed it with his students.)

In my last chapter, I pointed to an important difference: "What has here been treated as a 'state,' as distinguished from the operation responsible for the state, is called by Tolman an 'intervening variable.' " By attaching names to these intervening variables, he suggested that they were initiating agents and capable of being modified by internal cognitive activities. I also criticized Tolman's use of behavior at a choice point as an experimental datum: "No measure of the strength of [turning right or turning left] is provided by maze behavior, since a 'choice' reveals only the relatively greater strength of one. Instead of measuring behavior directly, Tolman is reduced to determining a 'behavior ratio,' which is of little use in following the various processes which are the principal subjects of investigation."

I HAD NOT ABANDONED verbal behavior. As I neared the end of *The Behavior of Organisms*, I told Fred that I was "skimping on the section on drive to get the damn book finished, because I'm very anxious to get to work on language. Have had a seminar on it this [spring] quarter and various people are interested." I had defined the field as "that part of behavior which is reinforced only through the mediation of another organism."

To make a little extra money I taught a summer school course described as follows:

The Psychology of Literature. Fundamental processes involved in the creation and enjoyment of literary works. Descriptive and emotive uses of language. Psychological basis of style; nature and function of metaphor; techniques of humor, etc. Unconscious language processes and their use in the production of literary effects. Modern trends in the uses of literary materials and devices.

It was only a small part of the field of verbal behavior, but it was easy to teach because it took me back to my old love. I could talk about Gertrude Stein, T. S. Eliot, Ezra Pound, and James Joyce. Empson's *Seven Types of Ambiguity* had put multiple meaning in the air, though I found an earlier treatment by an American critic, F. C. Prescott, whose *Poetic Mind*, published in 1922, had a wider range of examples.

Unfortunately many of my students found these issues technical and dull. I had already met the problem when the Women's Club of Minneapolis had invited me to lecture. I had prepared a fifteen-page paper on "Literature Without Meaning," using examples from e. e. cummings, Joyce's *Two Tales of Shem and Shaun*, and Gertrude

Stein's *Tender Buttons*. I thought I had pitched it at a popular level, but when I finished, the Chairman thanked me for my "scholarly lecture." My class was also unhappy about scholarship, and, to entertain them, I "psychoanalyzed" Lewis Carroll, J. M. Barrie (Oedipal mother-love in *Margaret Ogilvy*), D. H. Lawrence (ditto in *Sons and Lovers*), and Dostoevski (Oedipal father-hatred in *The Brothers Karamazov*), devoting a full lecture to each.

(One of my best students was Sister Annette Walters, who smuggled Joyce's *Ulysses* into her living quarters under her habit so that she could do a term paper on it. Yvonne and I invited her to lunch with a young historian, William Aydelotte, who was teaching at Minnesota that summer and had that day received the first copy of his first book, *Bismarck and British Colonial Policy*, which he showed us with pardonable pride. Sister Annette would not smoke, but we tempted her successfully with a dish of candies.)

WHEN SUMMER SCHOOL was over, Yvonne and I drove up to the Arrowhead country in northern Minnesota. We stayed in a cabin and ate at wayside restaurants. I painted a water color or two, but the swimming was not good and nature was unkind. At night we fought the occasional mosquito that penetrated the netting over our bed, and one day walking along the shore we were attacked by gulls—presumably because we were close to a nest.

Mike Elliott had recommended Hungry Jack's, an expensive summer resort, and we decided to have one luncheon there. To our surprise, considering the name of the place, all the guests seemed to be university professors, and they and their wives were dressed as if for a faculty tea. We were wearing very old clothes, and we slunk into and out of the dining room as quickly as possible.

At one of the restaurants where we ate there were slot machines, but, as in wayside restaurants in general, they were set at very poor odds, and we lost a bit of money. Hoping to have the same fun more cheaply, I made a cardboard wheel and marked it with cherries, lemons, bells, and bars. We took turns spinning it, three spins at a time. We lost no money but did not win any either, and we soon threw it out.

We came back to Minneapolis in time for the annual meeting of the American Psychological Association, held that year at the University. I was put in charge of publicity. There was only one well-known science writer at the time, and he ignored the young upstart who was supposed to arrange interviews and made his own contacts. There were not very many well-known psychologists at the meeting. Edward Thorndike was an exception. He was an impressive figure with a walrus mustache, and everyone knew who he was, but when I first saw him he was carrying his tray to a small table in the cafeteria, and stretching out his hand to the startled young man sitting on the other side, he said, "I'm Thorndike." Tolman gave the presidential address.

FRED WAS WRITING a book on psychological fields and from time to time sent me pages for comment. Here are a few of my reports:

> In the midst of a busy morning I stopped to read the section on functionalism and found it grand. . . . I really didn't think you could do it, old man, and it gives me a hell of a kick.

> This is nothing short of brilliant! I couldn't resist giving it to Elliott and he is much impressed. He'll write you about it, I think.

> I am unsatisfied with the great space given to Titchener but I dare say your later chapters will put him in his proper place. Your summary of his system is the best I know of. I wish I had had it before my PhD!

Elliott accepted the book for the Appleton-Century Company, and when it was published, under the title *The Definition of Psychology*, I sent one last comment:

> I think your book is even better in print than MS. Garry wrote a postcard to Elliott saying smugly—What do you think of Keller's book? When Elliott said he naturally thought it was good or he wouldn't have published it, Garry wrote back saying he saw no excuse for it! We got a good laugh out of that! All the old Boring prejudices. . . . His paternal interest in Psychology is amazing—going out of his way to approve or disapprove everything.

✻ ✻ ✻

IN THE FALL of 1937 Bernard DeVoto, whom I had met when I was a Junior Fellow and who had taken over the editorship of the *Saturday Review of Literature*, asked me to review J. B. Rhine's *New Frontiers of the Mind*. I was not impressed by it. Rhine contended that extrasensory perception was a "delicate and subtle capacity," something like writing poetry, and that one could not expect to examine it under rigid controls.

> The experimenter must be "friendly, almost fraternal" and the experiments "casual and informal." The situation must appeal to the subject; he must not be reluctant or feel hurried. There must be a spirit of play; a monetary reward is destructive. Strong emotions, illness, fatigue, over-intellectual analysis, or pre-formed beliefs may interfere. And so on. Many of these conditions, one suspects, must have entered first as *ad hoc* explanations of failures. Some of them remain that. It is true that the phenomena *may* be thus seriously constrained, but this only adds to Dr. Rhine's burden of proof. It is too easy to regard his conditions as a list of alibis, not only for himself, but for the failure of other investigators who attempt to confirm him.

Rhine had published his famous ESP cards and was encouraging people to test themselves. One of my younger colleagues, Ken Baker, had several packs, and we all ran off experiments from time to time. There was talk of the need to keep an open mind; as scientists we could not dismiss the matter out of hand. The statistics were certainly impressive. Then one day I discovered that I could read the cards from the back. The ink in which the symbols were printed had warped the cards slightly and by glancing across the back one could detect the patterns. I made a few perfect runs in the presence of witnesses, had them sign a paper to that effect, and sent it to Rhine.

I also played a trick on Yvonne. She was out when I went home that afternoon and when she returned I appeared to be distraught. "Something terrible has happened," I said. "I have discovered that I have ESP!" She was naturally skeptical, and I offered to demonstrate. I asked her to shuffle the cards, and I then dealt them face down in five piles. They were all perfectly matched, and she was so alarmed that I hastened to explain. I gave a talk in the Student Union on mental telepathy and displayed my newfound powers there.

I had explained my perfect performances to Rhine and asked him if he was aware of the warping. He replied: "You will understand now why it is that we rely upon screening, sealed packs, distance, and the like, for our conclusions regarding ESP; particularly so since for various reasons we have had to have our cards manufactured." He said, however, that the defect in the printing "had caused us enormous misery," and the manufacturers were experimenting to overcome the difficulty. He appreciated my calling his attention to it, "even though we have known of the defect."

I wrote to ask why he had not warned potential users, and he replied:

Just how would you have had us inform the public of the defect in the cards? By press release or by publication in a psychological journal? We have considered the situation and summarized it somewhat as follows. Those who wish to test themselves need not deceive themselves with these cards, and probably not one in 1,000 will ever discover the slight warping. Those who wish to test others and to do so under conditions which will allow them to draw conclusions of scientific value will want to follow the precautions prescribed in our various writings, either following our own examples or using screens or distance, or following our instructions in the Pratt and Stuart Handbook *which recommends such precautions.*

I did not ask about the possibly more than 1 in 1000 who might get positive results without "discovering the slight warping" which had enabled them to do so.

In our apartment one evening Yvonne and I and a few graduate students tested our extrasensory powers. One of us would leave the room while the others agreed upon a scene to be visualized. We would then comment upon the subject's guesses until some final version was reached. When one graduate student was out of the room, we agreed to accept his guesses as correct and show increasing astonishment as he produced a complete and accurate picture of what was on our minds. Before we had a chance to explain the joke, it was all too clear that he had convinced himself that he was extrasensorially percipient.

A young woman in one of my classes had a friend in New York who knew Dunninger, a magician then attracting attention with his "psychic" powers on the radio, and she asked me for advice in conducting a test. Her friend had suggested that at an agreed-upon hour she was to think of something in St. Paul, and Dunninger would tell the friend in New York what it was. How should she conduct the experiment? Yvonne and I went to her home, and I chose a word by opening a dictionary at random and taking the tenth word on the page. We all sat around for five minutes and "concentrated" on it. We then put through a call to the student's friend. Dunninger's guess had no conceivable relation to the word we had chosen. But it was said that the air waves were not clear that day, and so we tried again—with no better luck.

IN 1937 I RECEIVED a grant of $150 to study "the avoidance of undesirable consequences"—a phrase chosen for its effect upon the Dean. The hand slap would not serve, and I steeled myself to the use of a stronger aversive stimulus. I put grids on the floors of my boxes so that I could shock my rats through their feet. On a shaft driven by a Telechron motor I arranged four arms, each of which moved through a ninety-degree arc in fifteen seconds. At the end of the arc, it made a contact that sent current through the grid, but it was whipped back to its starting point whenever the rat pressed the lever. By pressing a little oftener than once every fifteen seconds, the rat could keep itself free of shocks.

Under these conditions some of my rats pressed often enough to take only an occasional shock. When they were doing so, I discontinued the shock, and the rate declined in a typical extinction curve. But when I began extinction in a new session without any exposure to shock, there was no responding at all. It appeared that no "reserve" had been built up. Avoiding shock was not like food-reinforced behavior, and I was puzzled. I was late in applying for a renewal of the grant the following year and dropped the experiment.

IN THE SPRING OF 1937 a student at Wesleyan University in Connecticut, John B. Carroll, was admitted for graduate study in psychology at Minnesota. He was also admitted at Yale, where he could work with Sapir in linguistics, and at Indiana, where J. R. Kantor had recently published his *Objective Psychology of Grammar*. I wrote to Carroll to congratulate him on his other chances: Sapir's book on language was highly regarded and I thought Kantor was "on the right track." I summarized my own position:

> *Your collateral interests . . . are practically identical with my own. The Meaning of Meaning is an old friend, and I have spent many pleasant hours with its co-author Richards talking about the problems it raises. . . . It was something of a surprise to find that you had also looked into Logical Positivism. My first acquaintance with it came through a friend of mine, W. V. Quine, who studied with Carnap in Prague. Since then Carnap has come to this country and I saw something of him last summer with Quine. [Carnap had given some lectures in the Harvard Department of Philosophy.] He is the only European I have ever met who grasps the significance of modern behavioristic psychology and its implications for the problem of thought. I have little hope of reconciling logic with psychology, however, except by convincing the logician that most of his problems are essentially psychological—and that is not likely to be successful!*

Carroll chose Minnesota, and I crowed to Fred: "I've got a grand graduate student coming out here next year from Wesleyan to work with me on language. I snared him away from Sapir at Yale and Kantor at Indiana. Has a brilliant record and sounds as mature as a Harvard Professor."

Carroll was the first graduate student with some prior commitment to work with me personally, but the commitment did not last. I turned over to him an apparatus I had designed to see whether "unconscious cues" played a part in concept formation. Subjects were to learn to name abstract figures displayed in an apparatus that "accidentally" threw slightly different shadows on them. They could name them correctly only if they took the shadows into account, but did they need to know that they were doing so?

Unfortunately Carroll was not much interested in the project or, for that matter, in a functional analysis of verbal behavior. He preferred a statistical approach, and I arranged for him to work with some of Thurstone's people at Chicago. Thurstone's factor analysis of scores on a series of mental tests had revealed certain "vectors of mind," and Carroll designed tests to identify other verbal factors.

I HAD ADDED "An Experimental Analysis" to the title of my book, and I began to refer to the whole enterprise as "the experimental analysis of behavior." It differed from other work on animal psychology mainly because I did not average data. I had four apparatuses and usually published results from four rats in each experiment, but I considered each rat separately. Minnesota was statistics country, however, and the department was strong on validation and reliability. I wrote to Fred: "Heron has been pounding away at me as to the necessity of larger numbers of observations. 'Do you feel that the records you have enable you to predict with considerable certainty just what four other rats would do?' " Fred said that groups of four were too big, but unfortunately I allowed myself to be persuaded of the contrary.

And, of course, there was more to statistics than averaging cases. R. A. Fisher had published his *Design of Experiments*, and Heron among others saw the chance to explore the effects of several variables in a single experiment. He applied for a grant to build an apparatus with twenty-four boxes, all to be used at the same time in one experiment.

MIKE WANTED MY BOOK for the Century Psychology Series, which had published Boring's *History* and was the most prestigious in the field, but he had published Tolman's *Purposive Behavior* and had a contract for Hull's *Principles* and was unhappy about urging the company to take on "another rat book." Another publisher had shown an interest. Mary Louise White had married Edward Aswell and they had left the *Atlantic* and gone to New York, where Ed was an editor of *Harper's*. He had written to say that he was interested in my "magnum opus." But the Century Series seemed the right place, and I eventually got my contract, although I agreed to forgo royalties on the first 1000 copies.

As the manuscript progressed and the number of figures increased, Mike grew desperate. "He feels," I wrote to Fred, "that he has put over a dirty one on A. Century since it . . . can not possibly make expenses. He appeals to me practically with tears in his eyes to cut out figures, make as few changes in proof as possible, and so on."

I felt I needed at least 148 figures, but half of them had already been published, mostly by the Clark University Press, and money could be saved if the old cuts could be used. Earlier I had written to Murchison asking for permission to reprint the figures. When he specified that I should cite the source under each one, I asked Hunter if he thought it was really necessary, and he wrote: "Inasmuch as the copyright to the Journal is held by Clark University, there is no need, I think, to follow Murchison's suggestion concerning full acknowledgements under each cut, since your book will be appearing after Murchison has ceased to be editor." But Murchison bought the journals and took them to Provincetown, where they continued to be published by his Journal Press. When I asked him about the cuts, he said they had been thrown away.

I turned to the Society of Fellows. Henderson agreed that since most of the work had been done while I was a Junior Fellow the book was "entitled to everything in the way of support that it would receive if it had been finished during the period of your fellowship." The question was, however, one of general policy about which there had been a good deal of discussion, "the upshot of which is that in the first place we can't make a decision . . . until the whole book is completed."

Early in December I reported to Fred: "The long silence is due to what amounted to a vow to ignore everything else until the ms. was finished. Elliott is going through it now for the last time and since he is working slowly (poor fellow, it's hard going) the pressure on me is somewhat lighter. Although I have some continuity to put into the last chapter, it's about all finished. Around 150 figures and about 600 pages of MS." I had lost the first draft of my last chapter (it turned up a year later in a manila folder among some clavichord music), and I had pressed rather too hard in replacing it. The "continuity" was in response to a comment of Mike's: "The degree of your impatience to be done with the book surprises me. . . . I've seen other authors who, once their ideas are embalmed in cold print beyond recall, would give anything to add that 10% difference between the good and the better (or the excellent and the superlative). It'll be a long time before you see another fundamental book of your writing in print. And 4 weeks —28 days—are *nothing* except to JUVENILES!!"

When I finished the manuscript and sent a copy to Henderson, he wrote, "Everything is all right and I hereby authorize a payment of $500 to permit the publication of your book. This will give me great satisfaction, and I'm sure that everyone else will feel as I do." In February Mr. Ferrin wrote that "we can handle the book in its present form and, taking into account the $500 subsidy from Harvard, with a fair chance of breaking even on the venture."

I knew nothing about the publication of a book, and in April I complained to Fred: "The manuscript is only now actually being set up. If I had known of the delay I'd have spent more time on it and given you a chance at it. For the past three months I haven't thought about the thing at all. A jumbled copy lay around the office unlooked at. I'm gradually beginning to think it may be a good book after all, however. As time goes on I may be glad I wrote it."

WHILE I WAS IN LABOR with *The Behavior of Organisms*, Yvonne was also gestating, and I reported to Fred that she "is fairly well, everything considered. Having a baby is certainly no fun no matter how you look at it. Every now and then she gets scared as hell. Is just now feeling terribly self-conscious about her figure. She went to a young Faculty Wife's club yesterday and some fool made the five pregnant women present sit in a row. Poor Yvonne burst into tears in telling me about it."

Early in April I wrote: "Three weeks more ought to turn the trick. We're tired of waiting but it's about over. Yvonne keeps up extraordinarily well. Has been attending the aesthetics course regularly and getting around a good deal. We have a new car (Plymouth standard in beige) with a radio and we go out into the countryside, which is especially beautiful this time of year, and listen to music."

Three weeks turned the trick, and after one fruitless dash to the hospital, Yvonne went into a not too difficult labor. I was allowed to be in the delivery room. A month or two earlier, Yvonne's grandfather had been given a birthday celebration and we had sent a telegram from his as-yet-unborn great-grandchild, ending, "If I am a boy

I shall be signing myself—Opie Read Skinner." Fortunately it was a girl, and we named her Julie.

Yvonne stayed in the hospital for the prescribed ten days, while I did some last-minute shopping. Somehow we had never really believed that a third person would be joining us, and there were many things we needed. When we brought Julie home we hired a nurse to care for her for a few days, and after she left we were both unnecessarily solicitous. Yvonne had never had any experience with babies, and the first time she was alone and Julie cried, she called the doctor. I weighed Julie each time Yvonne nursed her to find out how much she had taken, and when bottle supplements were needed and we eventually abandoned breast feeding, I continued to weigh her, evidently not trusting the graduations on the bottle. Julie survived these attentions. Yvonne had planned to fly to Chicago with her to spend a few days with her parents in Flossmoor while I closed the apartment, but a plane crashed and burned in Cleveland, and we canceled the reservation. (A few days later I received the last two or three pages of proof of *The Behavior of Organisms* with burned edges marked "Damage due to air mail interruption" and a letter from another B. F. Skinner then living in Minneapolis to whom the airline had mailed the refund.)

The superintendent of our building let us use a small room in the basement to store our possessions—except for the clavichord, which I left in the Music Department at the University.

Early in November, Boring had written to ask if I would teach at Harvard that summer. He did not mention salary and I replied that, with a baby due in the spring, finances had to be carefully considered. He sent a telegram to say that I would get the minimum of $500 and added "CONGRATULATIONS BABY. ARE YOU MARRIED?" I would be teaching the introductory course, and a young instructor, Dr. Leo Hurvich, would assist me. I began to worry about a text. In his own course Boring used one he had written in collaboration with two friends, Langfeld and Weld. It was much too traditional for me, and when I expressed reservations, he wrote, "Heavens! There is nothing sacred about B. L. W." He would be glad to have me use the text I had suggested, by Dashiell. For a second course I would teach the Psychology of Literature, and a graduate student, D. V. McGranahan, had asked to be assigned as my assistant.

We stopped for a day or two in Flossmoor, heard Joe Louis knock out Schmeling in spite of Hitler's assurances of Schmeling's racial superiority, and drove east with Julie lying in a basket in the back seat. We stopped at restaurants or bars to have her bottle warmed and spent the nights in tourist homes. (Highways still went through towns and the hearts of cities, and families refurbished spare rooms and hung out signs. Babies were viewed with suspicion; did they cry, and what was done about diapers?) We stopped for several days with my family. My grandfather Skinner had died a few months before, and we drove to Susquehanna to let my grandmother, my only surviving grandparent, see Julie. Eventually we found ourselves in Cambridge in a faculty house sublet for the summer. We borrowed a baby carriage from the Quines, but it was one of the rainiest summers in the city's history, and we spent most of it indoors.

Two years of introductory teaching had given me confidence if not competence, and the description of my introductory course was as unlike Boring's as I could make it:

> The fundamental problems of psychology, including the relation of psychology to the sciences, the arts, and the affairs of practical life. The facts and principles of general psychology receive primary consideration, although materials from abnormal, social, animal, and child psychology are also included.

My course in the Psychology of Literature was by now old stuff.

On my way back to Minnesota, we stopped again in Scranton, where my father, always generous and anxious to throw a little business in the way of a fellow Kiwanian, bought us a sofa with matching armchair for the duplex we had rented on Oak Street in Minneapolis. In our living room they proved to be much bigger than on the floor of the store and left little space for clavichord and bookshelves. A phonograph that I assembled had a bad hum, but a Black Forest cuckoo clock that Yvonne's parents had received as a wedding present worked with high fidelity in Julie's room.

FRED'S SITUATION at Colgate had become desperate. I had written a letter for him to a teachers' agency, and I passed on word of possible openings. Carmichael was leaving Brown to become Dean at Rochester, Walter Hunter would take his place at Brown, and Fred had his eye on Hunter's spot at Clark. Then a job opened at Columbia: Ross MacFarland, a psychologist specializing in aviation medicine, was going on leave and might not come back, and Fred took his place, with no guarantee of a future. He was soon reporting:

Affairs march satisfactorily here as far as I can tell. My courses are well under way, I am making all the proper contacts, and I am getting quite an education. There is only one fly in the o., Warden. Everyone cautions me not to step on his toes or expect to do much animal work on my own in his laboratory, and for God's sake not to plan to give any problems to the Ph.D. candidates. Since I have between fifteen and twenty pieces of research that I'd like to do something about fairly soon, I feel somewhat depressed with all the warnings; but in the meantime, I am doing my level best to ingratiate myself with the King of the Brutes. . . . If only I knew more about golf and the stock market. . . .

The Behavior of Organisms, dedicated to Yvonne, was published on September 2, 1938. Eight hundred copies were printed but not all of them were bound. I received a few copies gratis and sent one to my father and mother. A few days earlier, I had received a copy of the third edition of my father's book on workmen's compensation law. It was inscribed:

To my son Frederic and family.

This book represents many days and nights of hard work and study. It was written with the thought always present that I wanted to contribute something to my profession and to be something more than just an ordinary lawyer—soon forgotten. It is well received now, but its permanent value will be greatly affected by future changes in the law.

Due largely to this book I have, considering my meager advantages as a boy, been able, fortunately, to provide for ourselves the necessary means to live comfortably and to finance your education. It is this book therefore which to a great extent has made possible your

*book which will undoubtedly have a greater lasting value and longer
recognition.*

> *With love to you all*
> *Father*

It was a graceful gesture if not quite supported by the facts. My
Hamilton College education was paid for before any royalties were
received from the first edition, and my *Digest of Decisions of the
Anthracite Board of Conciliation* and two fellowships paid for my
graduate study. Nevertheless the inscription nicely fitted two arche-
typal patterns—my father's that successive generations move on to
better and better things and my own that life should be *une course du
flambeau*, a relay race in which each generation receives from the
past and gives to the future.

I sent a copy to Bugsy Morrill at Hamilton College, who, as I
wrote in an inscription, "put Loeb's *Physiology of the Brain* and
Pavlov's *Conditioned Reflexes* into my hands and is hence probably
responsible for this book." I sent another to L. J. Henderson of the
Society of Fellows ("Its substance seems to me very interesting, and
within my limited capacity I judge it excellent") and another to John
Tate, my Dean at Minnesota, a physicist ("I admire the scholarly
method of analysis you have adopted and your insistence that behavior may be treated as a subject matter of a science").

These were not rave notices, but I had also heard from Fred:

> The book is great! *Woodworth managed to grab it from the library
> before I got it, but he turned it over to me for the weekend and I have
> already read several chapters. It is the most exciting thing that has
> ever robbed me of well-earned and much-needed sleep. It comes up
> to, and goes beyond, everything I had anticipated, and I had Great
> Expectations! In my humble opinion it is the most important single
> contribution that this century has seen in the field of psychology. As a
> beautiful example of inductive method and operationalism, it puts to
> shame the Hullites, the Titchenerians, et alii with their high-powered
> deductions, their narrow applications, their physiologizing, and their
> vague dreamery of psychology-as-science. The exposition is crystal-
> line, and the criticisms are incisive beyond words, without any
> polemicizing or pretence. Hell! You know what I mean without all
> this big talk. . . .*

Hunter sent congratulations and, perhaps remembering how much trouble I had had getting a job, said that it "should be a great professional asset." He had written an entry for *Psychological Abstracts* and said, "I hope you don't feel that I stressed too much the minor role of neurological data in a science of behavior!" When I saw the abstract, I felt that he had done so.

Tolman wrote to Dana Ferrin:

> *It was really "swell" of you (if you will forgive the vernacular) to send me Skinner: The Behavior of Organisms. I consider it a most outstanding book both because of the very important experimental findings which it presents and because of the clear and, to my mind, extremely significant "system" which it presents as its skeleton for these findings. It will always have a very important place in the history of psychology.*

I soon heard from him directly:

> *I haven't been so intellectually excited in a long time as I am now perusing your book. It is, of course, a very major contribution to "real" psychology....*
>
> *I think the two words* operant *and* respondent *are swell. Your analysis of the four functions of stimuli is also terribly important and the whole thing clears up a lot of the questions which have always worried me....*
>
> *I congratulate you on coming through Harvard so beautifully unscathed!*
>
> *P.S. And of course I was pleased as hell to be mentioned in the Preface.*

(Had he not reached the last chapter, in which I compared our positions?)

The following May, Van Quine wrote:

> *It's a tremendous thing . . . a masterly job of cold, clear writing and thinking. And the utter freedom from hedges is a great relief. Typical source of satisfaction:*
>
> *"We can neither assert nor deny . . . If, nevertheless, the author . . . is expected to hazard a guess publicly, I may say that the only*

differences I expect to see revealed between the behavior of rat and man (aside from enormous differences of complexity) lie [perfect build-up for a hedge] in the field of verbal behavior [thud!]."

But by then I was hearing from the critics, and their views were less reassuring.

HERON GOT HIS GRANT from the Ford Foundation and by the end of 1938 we had built a monster of an apparatus, each of its twenty-four boxes containing two levers, a grid floor wired for shock, a light and an earphone for discriminative stimuli, and a pellet dispenser. (We had found a company that converted dog biscuits, mixed with some kind of presumably digestible glue, into small spheres.) The University machine shop built, according to our specifications, a huge cumulative recorder with twenty-four strips of paper passing over cylinders, and twenty-four pens driven by rotary solenoids and screws. We tinkered with it for a long time. I wrote to Fred: "Heron and I are still changing our apparatus and he is such an infernally constant worker that my conscience is always howling at me to put in every minute I have to spare. Things are just about as we want them now, and I wish you could see how impressive the set up is." Later I wrote: "The new apparatus is certainly impressive and it looks like a good year next fall. We've reduced the effort of experimentation to an almost absolute minimum."

In our published report we boasted:

> An experiment upon 24 rats, treated individually, can be carried out with little more attention than that required to put the rats into the apparatus and remove them at the end of the experimental period (typically, one hour). Because of the ease with which the apparatus may be adapted to a given type of experiment, it can be used practically continually throughout the day upon a number of different researches. The possibility of using large groups of animals greatly improves upon the method as previously reported [a reference to *The Behavior of Organisms*], since tests of significance are provided for and properties of behavior not apparent in single cases may be more easily detected and studied.

The Industrial Revolution had come to the study of animal behavior.

We had trouble from the very start. Some of it was mechanical;

the pens drew slightly wavy lines when driven at a constant rate, and it was almost impossible to keep twenty-four boxes in good working order. There was trouble with the rats, too. We reported that "as one consequence of improving the technique of measurement, the variability of behavior comes into greater prominence." That was all too true. It was nearly impossible to keep a group of twenty-four rats, divided among carefully matched groups, in good health and at given levels of deprivation day after day.

When everything worked well, a different problem arose. We got the data needed for a large experimental design, but the problem of analyzing them so that the next day's experiment could be planned was overwhelming. To solve it I added a "summarizer." Twenty-four fine steel wires attached to the pen carriages were led to a system of pulleys on a panel at one end of the apparatus. The pulleys converted the movement of the pens into averaged curves for four groups of six rats each, for four groups of twelve rats composed of any two groups of six, and for all twenty-four rats. In other words, it was a mechanized version of the statisticians' Latin Square. The curves were beautifully smooth and immediately available in planning the next stage of an experiment.

Experiments could be, as we reported, "extremely complex (for example, twenty-four individuals may be grouped according to at least two factors which remain constant, and submitted to changes in other variables, during the course of the experiment)," but very little research was ever done in which that was the case. In January 1940, Crutchfield and Tolman, also enamored of R. A. Fisher, published a paper on multiple-variable design citing an "experiment in progress" on vicarious-trial-and-error at a choice point, and I believe it remained in progress. Heron and I started our apparatus, as I wrote to Fred, "on her maiden voyage" by comparing the performances of maze-bright and maze-dull rats in extinction and discrimination, and I did one experiment (with W. K. Estes) using all twenty-four boxes, but I soon dropped to the old magic number of four in each experiment.

ALTHOUGH MINNESOTA WAS OFF the beaten path, we had interesting visitors from time to time. Bertrand Russell spent the academic year of 1938–39 at the University of Chicago and lectured at other universities in the Midwest. When he came to Minnesota, a few philosophers and psychologists arranged a luncheon, and at table Russell was flanked by the Head of the Philosophy Department and Mike Elliott, the Head of Psychology ("The first time I've ever sat beside an earl," said Mike, rather characteristically). I sat across from Russell, and when I had a chance, I told him that his *Philosophy* had converted me to behaviorism. "Good heavens," he said, "I thought it had demolished behaviorism." I let him believe that it had done so.

Karl Bühler, the distinguished psychologist from the University of Vienna, now an émigré, had found a place at a small Catholic college in Minnesota. He gave a colloquium in the department on homing behavior in pigeons. According to Tolman, who had spent a year in Vienna, Bühler's students used to write their theses and then go through them and "garnish with Bühler." Bühler's wife, Charlotte, also a psychologist, made her presence in the Midwest more clearly known.

Kurt Lewin (we still pronounced it L'veen) gave a colloquium in the department. Later I wrote to Fred:

> *Lewin was up here a month or so ago. The Germans were blackmailing him at the moment for the support of two relatives (whose property had all been confiscated) but he carried on in heroic style. Have you seen his new book? He diagrams several lever-pressing situations, and did the same for me for two or three hours. He is sure we agree, but fundamentally there is the same old ghost of purpose standing between us. I am getting througher and througher with any talk about goal-directedness.*

I REPORTED TO FRED that I was "getting a big thrill" out of a study of Shakespeare's sonnets. I was interested in the more general fact that we tend to repeat sounds we have just heard or used. We pick up words from each other in a conversation and use a particular word again and again. We do so in part because of the subject matter, but single sounds, syllables, and other bits of speech show the effect. Given a choice of synonyms, for example, we are likely to choose one we have just used even if it is not now quite right, or one that begins with the same sound as a word we have just used, or rhymes with it. The formal devices of poetry—alliteration, rhyme, and assonance— were conspicuous examples, and in my lectures I usually quoted a few strongly alliterative lines to prove my point. When Shakespeare begins a line with "Borne on the *bier*" should we be surprised if he continues with something like "with white and *bristly beard*"?

It was almost too easy, and I became suspicious. Some instances of alliteration should arise from chance, and it seemed important to know how many should do so before claiming to have demonstrated a verbal process. I decided to test the first hundred Shakespeare sonnets, and I turned again to that low-cost student power supported by the Federal Youth Administration. I worked out a way of scanning lines by rule, emphasizing nouns, verbs, adjectives, and adverbs. The average number of stressed syllables per line turned out to be almost exactly five, in agreement with the pentametric form of the sonnets, though the range was from three to eight. My assistant then tallied the stressed initial consonants, and, using a binomial expansion, I calculated the number of lines that should contain no occurrences of each consonant, one occurrence, two occurrences, and so on. I explained the point of the project in a letter to Thorndike:

> *If Shakespeare used alliteration and assonance as literary devices, his sounds could not be distributed at random but must be grouped. Using either the line or the sonnet as a unit, I am comparing the occurrence of each initial consonant or vowel with the expectations from a random order. I hope to do something of the same sort for samples of spontaneous speech in the hope of discovering just what effect the occurrence of a sound has in facilitating or suppressing subsequent occurrences.*

Thorndike wished me "good luck with the Shakespeare" and added that his brother Ashley in 1898 (his Ph.D. thesis in English at Harvard) used various counts as a test of Fletcher's cooperation in some of Shakespeare's later plays.

To my surprise I found that Shakespeare showed almost no evidence of the deliberate use of alliteration. He tended to repeat a whole word within a line, and this had to be taken into account, but except when he did so, he lengthened a series of three like consonants into four not more than once in twenty-five sonnets, and no oftener than once in twenty sonnets did he lengthen a series of two into three. So far as I could see, he supported the philosophy of the Duchess who said to Alice, "And the moral of *that* is, 'Take care of the sense, and the sounds will take care of themselves.'"

(I made a practical test of my mathematics. I mounted a large tin drum on a shaft and put in anagram counters bearing letters in the right proportions—from a great many *s*'s to a very few *qu*'s. My wage slave then generated 1400 five-consonant "lines" by reaching into the drum for a counter, copying the letter, putting the counter back, rotating the drum a few times, and choosing another counter. The numbers of "lines" containing four, three, two, one, or no instances were *very* close to my predictions using a binomial expansion.)

BY THE END OF 1938 things were going very well. I was happily married, the father of a charming daughter, and the author of a book. I wrote to Fred: "Julie is wonderful. So is Yvonne and life is very good. J. is acquiring new tricks daily and beginning to stretch the seams of the old behavioristic garb of my dream-world. (What a metaphor!) Still—I haven't needed to appeal to insight yet."

At Christmas we drove Julie through parts of the city where houses were decorated with great strings of colored lights, and we had our own Christmas tree. I cut small wings out of cardboard, covered them with cotton batting, fastened them on Julie's shoulders, and photographed her as an angel. And on December 31 I wrote to Fred, "The last day of my best and happiest year! . . . The Skinners are a very happy family, even if not quite living within their income. Julie is a model baby and gives us no more trouble than she can help. Our duplex is small but very comfortable. My teaching load is light."

But I had not yet "made over the entire field to suit myself," and late in May, after attending a meeting of the Midwestern Psychological Association, I wrote:

The damn science is folding up, as far as I can make out. Went to some depressing meetings at Lincoln last month. No papers of any merit. Training school for graduate students, getting used to saying chi-square in public. Had several long talks with Muenzinger, who is sold on the book, and with whom I am arranging a round-table at Stanford on the place of the C.N.S. in Psychology. Saw something of Krechevsky [David Krech], who has written a scurrilous review of the book for Social and Abnormal, and was trying to prepare me for it. Spence made a bad impression on me with an enormous amount of pretence, and no stuff on the ball that couldn't be called either back-biting (Tolman) or back-scratching (Hull). Old Harvey Carr sat in the main lounge solidly for two days and beamed on the youngsters—having ruined the damn science completely at Chicago. [Elmer] Culler thinks the nervous system works according to latency—a sort of "prior entry" theory—and insists its all psychology.

If this weren't damned nice country to live in, and if Yvonne and Julie didn't continue to be wholly satisfying, I'm sure I'd be trying to sell insurance.

HERON HAD REPEATED Tryon's experiment in breeding strains of "bright" and "dull" rats. Using a simple maze, he had mated rats which made the best scores and those which made the worst. The next generations differed in average scores, and the brightest of the bright and the dullest of the dull were again selected for breeding. Some physical differences, as in the shape of the head, were becoming obvious, but was there a difference in some identifiable behavioral process? If, for example, one strain extinguished more rapidly than another, some of the difference in scores could be explained.

Using nearly a hundred rats in our big apparatus, we found that under periodic reconditioning the bright rats pressed 36 percent faster than the dull. It was possible that the standard feeding schedule made them hungrier, and that could have had an effect in the maze experiment. When corrected for this difference, the extinction curves were similar.

RETURNING FROM SUMMER SCHOOL at Harvard we had stopped in Columbus, Ohio, for a meeting of the American Psychological Association, where I gave a paper suggesting that the Zipf curve might have a bearing on the way in which verbal behavior was stored. "The relative frequencies of words evoked by a stimulus word may show its 'associative capacity' under normal usage." In any given category one associated word occupies a certain percentage of the available space, a second then gets a certain percentage of the remaining space, and so on.

L. L. Thurstone had seen the advance notice of my paper and wrote to ask if we could meet to discuss it. He said he had once encouraged one of his students "to make an analysis of the relation between relative frequency and rank order of words in word counts," but because of illness the work was never finished. (The student was presumably not Zipf.) The point I was making was valid only if the relation held not for responses to a word collected from many people, but for responses to the word collected from one person at many different times. It would presumably be impossible to get completely independent responses under such circumstances, but there might be relevant facts in recorded verbal behavior.

I put another FYA student to work on a Shakespeare concordance. She was to look up all the words in various categories—such as colors, plants, or animals—and count the number of times each occurred. The samples were small but when I tallied the most common word, the next most common, and so on, and averaged across categories, the plot was a fairly straight line. The result seemed to indicate something about the organization of concepts or the very structure of categories in Shakespeare's behavior, and I was excited. Zipf had been excited too and was carried much farther away. He suggested that the data could be thought of as reflecting the availability of tools in space, possibly the main principle of organization in the world as a whole. Representing this as a generalized harmonic series, he proposed that "the values of t from minus ∞ through 0 may well represent the organization of stellar bodies . . . the values of t from 0 to 1 inclusive, biological organization . . . and the values of t from 1 to plus ∞, mental organization." My own theory was considerably less proud, but great was its fall. The discovery was too good to be true, and I sent my student to the concordance again. This time she was to count the number of instances of the fifth word on each page, the tenth, the fifteenth, and so on, and when I treated these numbers in the same way I got the same result. The logarithmic plot was some kind of distribution curve, as significant, perhaps, as what I once heard Whitehead call the cocked-hat curve of Gauss, but no more useful in telling me why the frequencies were as they were. By assigning categories to my student I had simply called for random samplings of frequencies. I had discovered nothing about the storage of concepts in a verbal repertoire.

I GAVE MY COURSE on the Psychology of Literature in the spring term, and when I offered it again in summer school, it was broadcast by the University radio station. My class met in a studio at the station, and I received a weekly analysis of the comments from listeners across the state. The broadcasts were recorded, and a student, Marian Kruse, typed them as they became available. One day I discovered the importance of a visible audience. The air conditioning in the studio broke down and I was put in a small cubicle with a microphone, while my students were left to listen (I hoped) over the radio. It was an ordinary lecture, and I had plenty of notes, but I could scarcely force myself to speak to an audience I could not see.

The broadcast brought an invitation to dinner by a Minneapolis businessman interested in literature. He played a recording of James Joyce reading *Anna Livia Plurabelle*. I could have used it in my course, but the record was not for sale in the United States. I canvassed several other people at the University and found a few who would be glad to have a copy for instructional or experimental purposes. I borrowed the record and had matrices cut, from which a number of records were pressed. Requests for copies soon began to come in, but I decided to stay out of the business of pirating disks.

I published a paper on alliteration in Shakespeare in the *Psychological Record*, a journal founded by J. R. Kantor, of which I was an associate editor. To remedy the serious delay in publication which was then common, a paper was published immediately upon acceptance and later included in a bound issue distributed to subscribers. I sent a reprint to a retired Minnesota professor, E. E. Stoll, a specialist in Shakespeare, and he published a criticism. Shakespeare had not drawn his words out of a hat! I wrote to ask whether we might discuss the matter, and he replied, "I am of course glad to have a talk with you but I don't see much use in our conferring on this particular subject. If in writing we make so little impression on each other what prospect is there of our doing so by word of mouth. Writing is the exacter and clearer medium, and yet you (naturally enough) are of your own opinion still and so am I of mine. I frankly have no faith in your undertaking so far as I understand it."

WHEN SUMMER SCHOOL was over, Yvonne and I left Julie with Yvonne's parents and took a long vacation. The American Psychological Association would be meeting in the San Francisco area early in September, and we went first to Glacier National Park and then to Vancouver, Victoria, and the Puget Sound area. Don Marquis had come to Minnesota early that spring and had told us about Orcus Island. We stayed there for a week at an inn catering to academic people (a brother of E. R. Guthrie, the psychologist at the University of Washington, was a fellow guest). England and France were on the point of declaring war, and early in the evening we crowded around the radio to listen to the news. One day we heard Hitler himself direct from the Sportspalast in Berlin.

I had once talked with Ivor Richards about an interest in world affairs. I could either give up psychology and spend all my time on the Depression at home and Nazism abroad or give all my time to my work, and I had decided on the second course. I was betting that the world would survive into the near future, and if I could speed the day when people would be better able to solve their problems because they knew more about themselves, we should all come out ahead. Our friends at Minnesota were not political, and the geographical isolation was real. Hubert Humphrey's campaign for mayor of Minneapolis was more interesting than international affairs. But times were changing, and with the rise of Nazi Germany an exclusive dedication to research grew harder to defend.

The Marquises were on the island for the summer and invited us to a supper of salmon steak cooked over an open fire. With Ernest Hilgard, Don was writing a book, *Conditioning and Learning,* the manuscript of which I had seen. I suggested to Don that we draw up a statement about the field. In January Hilgard would be writing to say that he thought "some sort of statement representing attitudes upon which Guthrie, Hull and Tolman might agree" was possible, but nothing further was ever done.

At the meetings Heron and I reported our experiment on extinction in maze-bright and maze-dull rats. Two young graduate students from the University of Washington, Fred Sheffield and Eleanor Maccoby, who had read *The Behavior of Organisms*, looked me up and we had a good discussion. Ross MacFarland, whose position at Columbia Fred had taken, was now in aviation psychology, and he took us to see one of the great Clipper seaplanes then flying the Pacific. We came back by way of the Grand Canyon. Gordon Allport and his son were on the train, and Yvonne and I played chess with them on my collar-button board. We were running short of money. We had allotted a certain amount for each day's meals, but a heavy rain washed out a section of the track, and we were rerouted (into and out of Mexico at one point) and our arrival at Chicago was delayed by a full day. We began to order the cheapest items on the menu, and once when we sat down at a table that had not yet been cleared and saw the remains of a meal that had scarcely been touched, we were tempted. In the end I was reduced to getting off the train at stations to buy bags of peanuts. It would never have done to ask Professor Allport or our other friends for a loan.

When reviews of *The Behavior of Organisms* began to appear, I saw for the first time how it looked to the profession rather than to my friends. One reviewer (F. Nowell Jones) thought that I had done my job well and that "surely the basic position should always deserve respectful consideration." But while other reviewers agreed that my methods and data were sound enough, most of them thought the book had serious, if not fatal, flaws. I thought I could answer most of their complaints:

Item: *The title was pretentious.* "Experiments with white rats are certainly not enough to establish a system of behavior." A better title would have been "Properties of Certain Specific Complex Reflex Mechanisms in the White Rat." I was surprised by this because I had only followed Pavlov, who had not added *in the Dog* to his title, and

Sherrington, who had not added *in the Cat*. One critic went even further: the book was about *only one strain* of rats, but I had used two or three strains, long inbred, and had kept my eyes open for genetic differences.

Item: *I neglected other work on learning and motivation*. "At almost no point does [Skinner] seem to have been aware of the rather overwhelming fact that hundreds of other experiments have been done in the field of psychology." "No serious attempt is made to relate the results to the accumulated literature on learning and conditioning." But, as one reviewer noted, I had warned my readers that "I have had little luck in finding relevant material elsewhere because of differences in basic formulations and their effect upon the choice of variables to be studied." With rate of responding as a basic datum, I could make no use of the number of errors made or the time consumed in running through a maze or the ratio of right to wrong responses at a choice point or the mere extent of flexion of a leg or the number of drops of saliva secreted. One reviewer claimed that "studies from Hull's laboratory find rate of response to be an extremely variable measure of conditioned behavior and tend to indicate that the total number of responses, or the total time consumed during responding, yields a more precise index of behavior." But as I had complained to Fred, Hull's variability came from stopping his experiments when arbitrary criteria were reached. And if number and time were both important, then number divided by time, or rate, must be important, too.

Item: *There was nothing new in my contention that a science of behavior should not be burdened by physiological hypotheses*. Tolman, Guthrie, Lewin, and Hull had taken the same position. But I could have pointed out that Hull's postulates were becoming heavily neurological and that Tolman had defined hunger as "an initiating physiological state . . . in the nutritive alimentary tract."

Item: *The book did not cover many important fields of psychology, such as perception and thinking*. But I had at least implied that all traditional fields, *when redefined operationally*, could be brought within reach. If anything remained to be treated, it lay within the field of verbal behavior.

Item: *My claim to have dispensed with hypotheses was unjustified*. My "laws of the reflex were surrogates of hypotheses." "Despite

Skinner's intention to hew to the line of the strict positivist and opera-tionist, he really does not (and I would say he *can not*) get along without hypotheses." So far as I could see, however, my only hy-pothesis (which I should have called merely an assumption) was that behavior was lawful—that it was free of caprice and could be de-scribed as an orderly system.

Item: *My book lacked the "fortification of statistical conven-tion."* "Most psychologists will not agree that 'an averaged curve is of little use,' or that 'the appeal to a number of cases is unfortunate.'" Pavlov had used single cases and all his work would now have to be done over again statistically. But I was getting data from single rats that were more orderly and reproducible than the averaged data of my contemporaries.

I did not, at the time, formulate these answers in any definite way. In fact, I paid little attention to my critics. But I was glad to get reassurance from Fred: "I am now definitely on the Skinner band-wagon. The book was the last straw; and I like it better all the time. . . . I've got a dozen problems and I have thrown up all other interests —abstracting, etc.—to get some research done this year."

In his review, Hilgard had mentioned my failure to acknowledge my indebtedness to Thorndike, and in 1939, writing to thank Thorn-dike for a copy of his *Studies in the Psychology of Language*, I said: "Hilgard's review of my book in the *Bulletin* has reminded me of how much of your work in the same vein I failed to acknowledge. . . . It has always been obvious that I was merely carrying on your puzzle-box experiments but it never occurred to me to remind my readers of that fact. I don't know why I mention this, because I can't imagine that it bothers you in the least." Thorndike replied, "I am better satisfied to have been of service to workers like yourself than if I had founded a 'school.'"

Mike's pessimism about the book as a commercial venture proved to be justified. Neither Fred nor I would make any money for the Century Series. When I used *The Definition of Psychology* in my small introductory class (the department having given me somewhat greater freedom), I reported that it was "very stimulating as to dis-cussion and the kids liked it. I'll write Ferrin a quotable note shortly." But I also had to add that "Elliott says the sales have been disappointing though you have one big adoption for next year at Tennessee. My sales are so-so with no adoption."

I BEGAN TO USE only four units of the big machine. I had started my experimental life with four boxes and felt at home with that number. In one experiment I looked again at the way in which hunger affected extinction. I gave eight rats the major portion of their food every forty-eight hours. I recorded performances under periodic reinforcement every day—which meant twenty-two hours after the major feeding on one day and forty-six hours on the next. On the forty-six-hour days the rats pressed about twice as fast as on the twenty-two-hour days. I then extinguished the response on every other day, in one group on the day on which the rats were only slightly hungry and in the other on the day on which they were very hungry. The extinction curves had the same curvature, but one contained about twice as many responses as the other.

That was not what I had said about drive and extinction in *The Behavior of Organisms*. If the reflex reserve contained a fixed number of responses, the rats should press the lever the same number of times in extinction no matter what the level of deprivation, although they would empty the reserve more slowly if they were not very hungry. The facts supporting that view were sketchy, and my new ones were quite clear. When I reported them at a meeting of the American Psychological Association, I said that "the 'reserve' cannot . . . usefully be given the dimensions of a number of potential responses." I was not willing to abandon the concept entirely: "The simplicity of the concept of a reserve is somewhat reduced by this additional consideration, but it still represents a useful synthesis of a number of well established facts."

I had abandoned my rather amateurish attempts to analyze my data mathematically. The orderly changes in strength in my experiments depended upon too many different conditions to be plausibly described by simple equations. It was easy to fit curves to data if you used enough of those things that can be given different values and hence are called constants. A German physicist once said that with three constants one can draw an elephant and with a fourth make him lift his trunk. There was, nevertheless, great pressure on psychologists to be mathematical, and graduate students with mathematical facility came looking for data to be mathematical about. I offered them the smooth and reproducible extinction curve obtained after a brief exposure to periodic reconditioning. (I performed one mathematical analysis myself in a practical way. I plotted the curve on a large vertical board and held a fine gold chain against it. When I tilted the curve upside down at just the right angle, it was covered by the chain. In other words, the curve was a catenary.) One graduate student, Calvin Mooers, played with it in a much more sophisticated way but, alas, with no greater contribution to theory.

ALBUREY CASTELL, a philosopher whom I had come to know, asked me if I would like to spend a day or two at St. John's Abbey at Collegeville, Minnesota, a Benedictine community, and we drove up together on a cold winter's day. My guest room was spartan; a single crucifix was not enough to make it attractive. We dined alone, our meals served by nuns of a German order who cooked for the abbey; their bread was delicious. After lunch we met in the quarters of the abbot and talked about theology while smoking excellent cigars and sipping excellent brandy. An evening was planned in which the prior would explain the proofs for the existence of God. We went for a walk across a frozen lake to a grotto, and when I returned I took a nap. I was awakened by a rude pounding on my door. I opened it and found two lines of young monks pressed against the walls of the hallway, waiting to move into the church for a service. No one seemed to want to speak to me and I could only conclude that I had been snoring and disturbing the serenity of the occasion. We were not impressed by the proofs for the existence of God, but later I told Alburey that I rather liked the *vita monastica*. "Would you sign on the dotted line?" he asked sternly. It was a rhetorical question.

Mortimer Adler came to the University to lecture, and the head of the Philosophy Department asked a few of us to spend an evening with him. He told a story about Gertrude Stein. She and Alice B. Toklas were invited to dinner by Robert Hutchins and as they were leaving, Alice Toklas said to Mr. Hutchins, "Gertrude Stein has said things here this evening that it will take her months to understand." Afterward I sent Adler a reprint of my article about Gertrude Stein and followed up something he had mentioned in our discussion by saying that I had had a graduate seminar go through the latter half of Roget's Thesaurus—"the whole body of English words referring to psychological subject matters"—and evaluate the adequacy of contemporary academic systems or texts in dealing with them. "No system or text," I reported, "showed the slightest promise of dealing comprehensively with simple psychological facts," but I said that I was not sure that I subscribed to the "Aristotelian framework" which he had presented in his book *What Man Has Made of Man*. "God knows we need something of the sort. I take it that you have no objection to improving upon the master, but I wonder what sort of improvement you anticipate." Adler said he would like to see our collection of words. Possibly he was interested because he himself was then engaged in identifying the 101 great ideas.

In February I had received a wire from Fred about a job at Columbia. Gardner Murphy was leaving and they needed someone either to take charge of undergraduate teaching or to teach two graduate courses. The salary would be between $3600 and $4500 with certain extras. "Animal research problematic [Warden again!] tenure uncertain." A letter followed with more details. Mike thought they would not want anyone in my line, but I told Fred I was interested. I saw no quick way to the top at Minnesota because I had my own Warden problem. Heron was becoming "disgruntled and distant." I had to avoid talking about my "system" with graduate students who were interested in working with animals.

In December I was officially asked to come but just for the spring semester, presumably to be looked over. Mike was not happy about letting me go, and there were financial problems. At Minnesota the year was divided into quarters, but at Columbia into two semesters and a summer school. I should have to miss two quarters (and the salary that went with them) in order to teach one semester. Moreover, in two years I would be in line for a sabbatical, and Mike, who knew Henry Allan Moe, head of the Guggenheim Foundation, thought I could get a fellowship that would give me a year to work on verbal behavior. One semester at Columbia would mean postponing my sabbatical for a full year. I said no.   ,

I HAD FOUND little or no evidence of alliteration in Shakespeare, but there were other poets who were surely alliterative. I tested five hundred lines of Swinburne's *Atalanta in Calydon* and found that where we should expect two lines with four instances of the same initial consonant, Swinburne had thirteen, and where we should expect thirty-one with three instances, he had fifty-four (of which only two were on the same word). There were slightly too many lines with two instances (where Shakespeare had a shortage). (A similar tabulation of a small sample showed Wordsworth far below chance. He was self-conscious about ornament and clearly discarded many words which happened to be alliterative.)

With the Swinburne material I could even discover how long the alliterative tendency lasted. In that sample from *Atalanta in Calydon* he showed a strong tendency to use an initial consonant again in the very next stressed syllable, the tendency falling off until it was no longer significant after four intervening syllables.

ONE OF MY FIRST EXPERIMENTS using the new apparatus attacked an old problem: how to make sure a rat would be at the same level of hunger at the time of an experiment day after day. Since rate of responding varies with hunger, it should be possible to solve the problem by letting the rate control the amount ingested. I had failed to do this by reinforcing a given number of responses (and had discovered the peculiar effects of fixed-ratio schedules in the attempt). Another possibility was to vary the amount fed at each reinforcement, but that might change the effectiveness of the reinforcer. A simpler system was to change the size of the supplementary ration given at the conclusion of a daily session.

As a target rate I chose 450 responses per hour under four-minute "periodic reinforcement" (as I was now calling it, rather than "periodic reconditioning"), and at the end of each session I gave each rat additional food according to how fast it had responded. If it had pressed more than 450 times during the hour, it got more food and was less hungry and pressed less often the next day. If it pressed less than 450 times, it got less food and therefore pressed faster the next day. By working out a formula for the amount to be fed according to the departures from 450 responses, I produced a group of rats all of which responded at much the same rate day after day. If the rate could be said to define hunger, they were all equally hungry, but I noted that some rats pressed rapidly although maintaining a nearly normal weight, while others grew thin. I thought of breeding a strain of rats that pressed the lever rapidly when not very hungry in a nutritional sense.

IN THE SPRING TERM, I again taught a course in the psychology of aesthetics which I had given two years before, and I began to be interested in the field. An instant authority, I was invited to discuss Picasso on the radio and to write an article on "The Psychology of Design" for *Art Education Today*. Guy Buswell had published records showing how people looked at a picture, their eyes darting from one point to another, and it occurred to me that successive fixations should produce the apparent movement called the Phi Phenomenon. Pictures with lines at different angles should appear lively, and those with parallel lines quiet. The movement might even be related to the subject. As one looked from one figure to another in Daumier's "Don Quixote with Sancho Panza Wringing His Hands," for example, Panza seems to pull back (in anguish?) and Don Quixote to throw himself forward on his horse in part because of "Phi." Either figure is less active if looked at steadily. Moreover, since Panza is the larger, Don Quixote shrinks into the distance because of a similar process as one looks back and forth.

I also dabbled in music. I worked out a new kind of notation, using a staff of parallel lines on which the position of a dot indicated the relation of a note to the preceding note. If a dot was on the center line, the note was to be repeated; if on the line above or below, it was to be a half tone higher or lower; if two lines above or below, a whole note, and so on. I transcribed some melodies and, to my surprise, found a woman in my class who could read them at sight.

*   *   *

THOUGH I HAD COMPLAINED to Fred that I had "too god-damned many irons in the fire," I could not say that I was overburdened by our social life. We continued to go to parties—but only with a few young members of the department and the same few time after time. A dancing club was a monthly trial: I struggled to fill my card in the cloakroom, looking for the men Yvonne liked to dance with while ducking those with whom she suffered (and meanwhile getting reasonable partners for myself). Yvonne began to study writing with Meridel LeSueur, who invited us to a Communist meeting where we heard a young woman incorrectly explain Marx's views on costs and prices. Once a week we went to a neighborhood movie theatre, while a student who came to help with dinner stayed on as baby-sitter.

We put Julie in the University Nursery School, but she was often absent because of colds and sore throats. I wrote to Fred: "Everybody just says that's what you have to expect the first year out in the world," but twice it was a strep throat and quite serious. (It was not yet the day of antibiotics.) "Very painful. Pathetic example of ambivalence as she would try to eat and then throw food away from her crying 'Hurt!' . . . Yvonne lost five pounds in one week worrying about her." One night her temperature went dangerously high and in desperation I took her clothes off and splashed cold water on her to cool her down.

"She's a swell little kid," I told Fred, "and very verbal. So far, she has not successfully assailed my behaviorism." Later I would be writing, "Julie thrives. Her verbal behavior is all out of hand now. She surprises us every day with new words out of the blue. Largely imitation but surprisingly correct usage. Lots of interesting 'slips,' blends, etc. which suggest a lot of needed research." She was turning my attention to education. "Believe it or not, I'm writing a textbook for the fifth or sixth grade on non-arithmetical thinking—a sort of puzzle-book designed to teach the bright boy or girl the fundamentals of scientific thinking . . . a sort of pastime for quiet evenings but lots of fun. I'm not too serious about it."

The book was designed to draw young children into more and more complex verbal and spatial problem-solving through "successive approximation." At first I thought it should be printed cheaply and sold through the dimestores, but when it developed into something more substantial, I wrote to Dana Ferrin at the Century Company to ask if he would be interested in a book to teach children to think. A good title might be *Something to Think About*. It could be sold simply as a puzzle book but "might be used as a textbook in progressive schools in a new kind of course in thinking. It should be extremely interesting because of its similarity to puzzles, word play, and other things which interest children. In fact, it would just about teach itself, and this should also recommend it to schools." It could "serve as an excellent differentiator of good and poor students."

WHEN W. K. ESTES TOOK my introductory course, he was in the Engineering School, but he changed to Arts and Sciences and two years later applied for graduate study in psychology. I had a hard time persuading the department to take him. His grades and test scores were very high, but several members thought he could not possibly teach. He was naturally diffident and particularly so when speaking to an audience. In giving a report in class he would stand rocking from side to side as he shifted his weight from one foot to the other. He was accepted by a narrow margin but began at once to do brilliant work, filling in some weak spots in *The Behavior of Organisms*.

Early in my graduate-school days I had bought and read the famous papers by James and Lange on emotion. I preferred Lange because he tried to describe the behavior that is characteristic of given emotions, whereas James found such descriptions boring. I had also been impressed by some early experiments by Robert Yerkes in which he bred strains of violently aggressive or fearful mice. But I had done nothing myself, and I treated the subject rather casually in my book. Estes took it up, and I was soon reporting to Fred:

> *Under low hunger he has been studying the effect of a tone which precedes a single shock. The shock itself is not enough to upset the periodic curve, but after a few trials the rats quit entirely while the tone is on which precedes the shock. Anxiety? Estes is out to study*

emotion through its effect upon normal behavior. . . . This is his first try and he's getting great stuff. It can't be conditioning in the Pavlov sense, since the effect of the conditioned stimulus is not the effect of the original shock. If you leave the tone on and don't shock . . . the animal gradually comes back to his job and gives a swell compensatory curve.

Fred had done some pioneering work in which pressing a lever turned off a bright light, and we suspected that a tone preceding a shock might have a different effect on such behavior. I wrote for further details: "What we had hoped was to match the periodic rate which is the base of this experiment with your light drive, on the hunch that the rat would not stop during the tone but would on the contrary press all the faster. That is, fear of shock (?) weakens hunger but strengthens the darkness drive. So far we have nothing conclusive."

IN APRIL 1940 the Nazis had invaded Norway and Denmark, and on a train to Chicago to attend a meeting of the Midwestern Psychological Association, I recalled the bombing of Warsaw and the way in which the airplane had been converted into a weapon. What was to prevent the destruction of any city at the whim of a ruthless leader? Was there a counterweapon? Could a shell or missile be designed to home in on a bombing plane? I knew nothing about radar, but what about the noise of the engines or the heat of the exhaust?

I was looking out the window as I speculated about these possibilities, and I saw a flock of birds lifting and wheeling in formation as they flew alongside the train. Suddenly I saw them as "devices" with excellent vision and extraordinary maneuverability. Could they not guide a missile? Was the answer to the problem waiting for me in my own backyard?

In Minneapolis a few days later I bought some pigeons from a poultry store that sold them to Chinese restaurants and began to see how they could operate a mechanical device. Feet and wings would be hard to harness, but the head and neck might be used. The pigeon's eyes could pick out a target, movement of its neck could produce signals to steer the missile, and its head and neck together could pick up grain as a reinforcer. I found that I could conveniently package a pigeon in a man's sock with its head and neck protruding through a hole in the toe and its wings and legs drawn together at the back and lightly tied with a shoestring. The jacketed bird could be strapped to a block of wood and put into an apparatus.

I built a system in which the pigeon steered by moving pairs of lightweight rods alongside its neck—a horizontal pair above and below the neck that moved up or down and a vertical pair that moved from side to side. By lifting or lowering its head the pigeon closed electrical contacts operating a hoist, and by moving its head from side to side it drove the hoist back and forth on an overhead track.

I would put a bull's-eye on a far wall of the room, with a few grains of food in a small cup in the center, and push the apparatus toward it. By moving itself up and down and from side to side, the pigeon could reach the wall in position to take the grain. My pigeons became quite adept at this, and I pushed them faster and faster across the room until they were operating the moving hoist as fast as the motors permitted. (By holding a harnessed pigeon in my hand and responding to the movement of the rods, a very easy form of a "cold reading," I could carry it "wherever it wanted to go." Given this opportunity, it would explore various spots on the walls of an empty room.)

In great secrecy I told a professor in the Department of Aeronautical Engineering what I had done, and he came to see a demonstration. He thought he could design a small plane for a test, but he was involved in something else at the moment and there would be a delay. I went to see Dr. John Tate, Dean of the Minnesota Faculty, who was already involved in defense research, and told him that I had a system in which a living organism could guide a missile to a target with considerable skill. He saw a demonstration and wrote to Dr. R. C. Tolman (the brother of the psychologist), who was Chairman of Division A of the National Defense Research Committee. Tolman asked how many pigeons were available, how conspicuous the target would have to be, and how flak and other planes in the sky would affect the birds. I could reply that there were millions of pigeons in the country and that they could see whatever an antiaircraft gunner could see, but I had no idea about how they would respond to flak or other planes. Experiments would be needed. He said he could not support them.

I HAD DECLINED an invitation to teach summer school at Harvard in 1939 because our trip to the West Coast would have meant too much traveling, but on the train coming back after the meetings Gordon Allport had asked about the following summer, and it was more or less understood that I should be invited again. Late in October, however, he wrote to say that the director of the summer school was insisting upon some retrenchment. The course in the Psychology of Literature would be given by my former assistant, McGranahan. Gordon recalled our chess games and reported "acute images (verbal responses?) of collar buttons," thus indicating that he was not quite clear about (or disdainful of?) a behavioristic interpretation of images.

Since we badly needed the money, Mike agreed that I could teach summer school again at Minnesota. Early that spring, however, my father, who wanted to see more of his adored granddaughter, offered to pay my summer-school salary if we would come and spend the time in Scranton. As I wrote to Fred, "Elliott was a good sport and went to work to find a substitute. We finally got MacKinnon of Bryn Mawr to give one of the courses I was signed up for plus a (we hope) drawing card in pussonality."

The transcription of my radio course suggested a plan for the summer. The material was not very important, nor was much of it original, but it had attracted attention. Harry Murray had asked about it and had said he hoped I would write "some kind of text that would start the ball rolling in that direction." Why should I not "get a book out of" my lectures? We drove to Scranton, taking with us as nursemaid a young student who had worked for us during the year. I set up a table in the basement (as far as possible from the attic study in which I had attacked literature in a different way during that dark year) and wrote for three or four hours every morning.

I took time off from literature for a small venture in the language of politics. My father was still a political orator, and that summer I could for the first time share his enthusiasm for the Republican candidate for President. Wendell Willkie had been nominated against the wishes of the old guard, and I did not like a third term for a President, even Roosevelt. But Willkie's speeches were disappointing, and I thought I knew why. I wrote to Governor Harold Stassen at Minnesota, who was close to Willkie and might pay some attention to a professor at his University. I said I had heard that Mr. Willkie was proud of writing his own speeches but that

> it may well prove an expensive pride. It would be a great pity if his unwillingness to provide himself with what is coming to be considered an indispensable technical service were to make all the difference in a close race. . . . It is my conviction that Mr. Willkie's style, if it is not changed during the early part of the campaign, will count heavily against him. This is also the opinion of good Republicans with whom I have talked [my father!].

I sent Stassen my revision of a short speech reported in the *New York Herald Tribune*. Willkie had said:

> It is difficult for me to believe reports of the President's press conference. I cannot believe that the President meant to say that he has never commented on pending legislation. Did he have nothing to say about legislation which was intended to pack the Supreme Court while that legislation was pending in Congress? Did he not tell Congress to pass the Guffy Coal Act irrespective of doubt about its constitutionality? If my memory serves me correctly the President has commented many times on pending legislation.

I argued that "for me" was unnecessary and objectionably egocentric, "I cannot believe" repeated what he had just said. "Legislation" was repeated unnecessarily and "irrespective of doubt" was awkward. "If my memory serves" was a cliché. A better version (shorter by fifty words) would be:

> It is difficult to believe reports of the President's press conference. Does the President contend that he has never commented on pending legislation? Did he have nothing to say about the legislation intended to pack the Supreme Court? Did he not tell Congress to pass the Guffy Coal Act in spite of some question of its constitutionality? It is a

simple fact that the President has commented upon pending legislation many times.

I never heard from Mr. Stassen, and without my help Mr. Willkie lost the election.

My summer was no more successful in other ways. Scranton was not the place for me at any age. I had brought only a few books with me, and most of the library my father had accumulated in Susquehanna had been left in my grandfather's barn. I found a dictionary of similes, presumably acquired for use in speechwriting, and made a rather pathetic study of some examples. I nibbled away at the transcription of my radio course until very little survived. I was not happy with the manuscript that had taken its place, but I went over it with Fred and later wrote: "Reading it with you has helped a lot and I am confident that it has reached a reasonably final form. Getting it out should do something for the cause in interesting those who don't care about rats."

But I was tired of it. I had borrowed the psychoanalysis of Lewis Carroll, J. M. Barrie, D. H. Lawrence, and Dostoevski from other writers, and my own work on alliteration and metaphor was concerned with the decoration rather than the content of verbal behavior. As I wrote to Fred, "What I have written ought to be followed by [a book] on Scientific Verbal Behavior to straighten out the Logical Positivists, Semanticists, etc." Six months later I would be writing, "I'm almost ready to undertake a five-year plan and convert the whole thing into a complete treatise on Verbal Behavior, instead of literary manifestations only . . . . However, I don't know whether the old ego would survive not getting another book out until then."

FOR MANY YEARS the American Psychological Association met early in the fall on college campuses. Students had not yet returned, and members stayed in the dormitories and ate in the college cafeterias. At the meeting at Pennsylvania State College in 1940 it was clear that the practice could not last. As I wrote to Fred: "There were 1200 or more there and all cooped up in a dinky little town with nothing to do but talk to each other. I never talked so much shop in my life." I gave a paper rescinding some of my earlier conclusions about the reflex reserve and its relation to drive, but the interesting events were unscheduled. I described one to Fred:

> *Lewin was there and asked me to lunch. I brought Yvonne and he brought Köhler. We had a hell of a violent argument. I don't know what they were trying to do—convert me, I guess. Strangely enough we finally located our difference pretty clearly, and that was that. At one time I caught K. off guard in a surprising way. He had, of course, brought up visual perception. (When I suggested that we talk about a blind organism, to simplify things, he shouted, "Ah, ha! He admits he cannot handle perception!") K. was contending that a hell of a lot of things were "given" in perception. You can see aggression, friendliness, etc. I argued that that clearly depended upon one's experience— that you saw merely the behavior of two or more people and that you inferred the friendliness. And so on—well, anyway I suddenly asked him if, when you looked at a familiar picture, the familiarity was part of the perceptual pattern. He got pretty flustered for a moment, then rallied and said yes. When I contended that the familiarity could not be in the stimulus but was obviously related to the past experience of the observer, he said, in plain language that surprised me, that he didn't care where the thing came from genetically. If this is what they've been saying all along I've had a wrong idea.*
>
> *I tried a little experiment on K. with startling results. I asked him about Goldstein (see my review in J. Soc Abn) and he confessed that Goldstein was an embarrassment to them all. He said Goldstein called himself a Gestaltist but no Gestaltist ever knew what he was talking about. "Gestalt psychology in the colloidal state, I call it," said Köhler. Then I tried my experiment. In reading Goldstein I suddenly realized how much of it comes out of Goethe. It's part and parcel of Goethe's biological views, but Goldstein is the only one I know who has acknowledged this. So, watching Köhler very closely (D[ick] Tracy speaking), I said I was surprised to notice the similarity to Goethe. Instantly his face was a mass of tics! There wasn't a muscle that he didn't twitch. Afterwards when I told Yvonne why I had said it, she said she had noticed his face and had wondered whether he had had a bad tic all along which she had missed.*

THAT FALL I MADE a Plastalene head of Julie and cast it in concrete. The first cast was defective and I took it across the street and rolled it down the embankment into the Mississippi. Would it turn up in some future dredging operation? Mound Builders? Sioux Indians? No, a marked Greco-Roman influence.

Julie learned to talk at an early age, and we began to teach her nursery rhymes. She began to stammer slightly, but we eased up on the verbal contingencies, and the stammer disappeared. She began to want a particular rag doll with her when she went to sleep. I had heard of children becoming dependent upon things of that sort, one of them carrying a fragment of an old blanket about for years. A friend of ours kept a bit of woolen thread wound around one finger and agreed that it was a similar dependency. Something should obviously be done about the doll. I found that Julie would go to sleep happily enough if it were on a small table close beside her bed, and after leaving it there several nights I began to move the table a little farther away, a few inches at a time. Her interest in the doll as a nighttime companion diminished without incident.

I HAD HAD a not very good offer from the University of Chicago. As I reported to Fred, "I told them 'not interested' as the offer stood, but [Dael] Wolfle thinks they may try again and that I should stand out for a promotion in rank, a juicy experimental budget, and guaranteed chances to take graduate students. (We have had two or three applications for the last couple of years from men wanting to work with me.)" Something might also open up at Indiana "where a new young president is out to boost the research status of the place and where I have a certain drag with Kantor. At present it's just a question of 'would you be interested if—' "

In April I received an offer from Columbia—an "upper grade Assistant Professorship." (According to Fred, Thorndike, who was at Teachers College rather than in the Department of Psychology at Columbia, had favored something of the sort instead of a one-semester sample the year before.) But there was a problem: I should have to begin at once to teach Social Psychology. I knew nothing about the field and there would be no time to learn anything, because I had agreed to teach at Chicago that summer. If I could stall for a year by teaching the Psychology of Language and Literature in the fall (clearly branches of Social Psychology) and hope to know more about the field the following year, I told Fred I was interested. Teaching Social Psychology might be "good for me." But the offer was not, I said, what I should have called handsome. Though it was possibly the entering wedge of a better deal, I hoped that the book on language and literature would give me greater bargaining power. I do not remember whether my terms were accepted; in any case I did not go to Columbia.

I WAS OBVIOUSLY MOVING toward a book on verbal behavior as a whole. The psychology of literature was not the field I had embarked upon as a Junior Fellow, and in the spring term I gave a course called "The Psychology of Language," covering "the nature and forms of verbal behavior; motivational and emotional influences in the emission of speech; the problem of reference or meaning; internal language processes, etc." I was encouraged by a letter from Thorndike: "I am very glad that at last we shall have in you a specialist in the psychology of language. It is a most alluring field, and satisfying also. Waste no time on Korzybski. He is learned, but not in linguistics, and seems to me definitely insane."

A new friend also helped. Herbert Feigl, a member of the Vienna Circle of Logical Positivists, had joined the Minnesota Department of Philosophy. An article of his had appeared in the first issue of *Erkenntnis*, to which I subscribed in my early enthusiasm for scientific method and epistemology. As I wrote to Fred, "I suppose Feigl's presence is responsible for [my change in plan] because all the stuff that I had dumped into a folder under Scientific and Logical Verbal Behavior to be saved until the book was finished, is now yelling for help."

In an earlier letter I had written:

> *The operationists continue to get in my hair. Slipping into behaviorism through the back window. Stevens' article in the Bulletin was good, though, I thought. Still, why don't they get down to work. If psychology is what they say (and I'd say it is, approximately) there is a hell of a lot to be done, and, if we are going to hold our jobs in the face of criticism, done damned soon.*

My ambivalence about what others were doing with operationism may explain a Christmas card that I made and sent to my
psychological friends. It was a linoleum-block print of a graph in
which "Number of Christmas Cards Received" was plotted against
"Days in December." It was labeled "An Operational Definition of
Christmas."

I tried to recruit another logician friend. A year or so before,
Quine had complained of a heavy teaching load at Harvard, including
a course on Leibniz, and I had told Elliott I thought he might come to
Minnesota if asked. Recently his department had recommended him
for promotion, but the administration had turned him down, and he
would remain an instructor for at least another year. He would, he
wrote, accept an offer elsewhere "with unbounded delight." I asked
for his latest reprints and tried again, but with no luck.

A T   T H E   U N I V E R S I T Y of Chicago that summer we sublet the apartment
of Joseph Schwab, a biologist whom Yvonne had known before we
were married. There was a yard in which Julie could play, and other
children to play with, and I could walk to my classes. I taught, badly,
a course in physiological psychology—badly because there was no
good text, because I had not kept up with the field, and because my
few students consisted of an aging physician who had forgotten how
to study, a few undergraduates, and one or two graduate students
who knew more about some branches of the field than I.

I had plenty of material on literature and language, but for the
first time I ran into criticism. When I said that a word that is only
slowly recalled is pronounced more forcefully the longer the delay,
two of my students measured the latency and loudness of responses to
a list of questions and found that their subjects did not speak more
loudly when it took them longer to answer. I should have specified the
contingencies more accurately. It is only in a conversational setting,
where a listener is waiting and one must say something, that a longer
pause builds up a more aversive situation from which one is more
strongly moved to escape. An auditor in my course on language was
Thomas A. Sebeok, already an accomplished linguist, and I had to
watch myself when I strayed into that field, though it was not close to
my own. Tom arranged for me to speak to the Linguistics Club.

*   *   *

JULIE GREW MORE ACTIVE, and our duplex on Oak Street was soon too small. My father offered to help us buy (he meant, of course, to buy) a house. In St. Paul we found one of venerable age, recently rebuilt, with a winecellar, three fireplaces, a two-car garage with hayloft, and a lawn running down to a lake. Because it would be expensive to keep up (my father had not offered to pay for maintenance), we turned instead to University Grove, a large tract near the agricultural campus where members of the faculty owned homes on land leased to them by the University. A trolley shuttling between the two campuses stopped at the Grove.

A professor at the Medical School was getting a divorce and wanted to sell his house. My father advanced the down payment, and we undertook to pay off a mortgage in lieu of rent. We bought some furniture, and my father and mother, who were moving into a suite in a hotel, sent the grand piano. There was a room for a live-in maid.

We became substantial householders. I put a loudspeaker in the bookshelves in the living room, and we began to listen to the radio on a regular schedule—Fred Allen, Jack Benny, "Henry Aldrich," the opera with Milton Cross on Saturday, and the Philharmonic on Sunday afternoons. On Sundays, we had a rather elaborate tea. At the university theatre we saw a fine performance of Kurt Weill's neglected *Johnny Johnson*—strangely fitting because there were many John Johnsons in that outpost of Scandinavia, and the pacifism fitted the isolationism of the Midwest. The Minneapolis Symphony played on the campus in a large auditorium, under which there was a warm garage in which we could park on cold nights.

I HAD NOT GIVEN UP my research. I broke off one letter to Fred:

> *Must start some rats! (Yes, I'm really running off a few things with the aid of my assistant—this chap Guttman.) I intend to get Horn and Heron's "disinhibition" with ninety seconds of shock before any conditioning whatsoever. [Heron, working with a graduate student named Horn, had questioned my failure to get disinhibition. They claimed that rats which were undergoing extinction started to*

respond again after being shocked.] It's obvious that the rats climb all over the lever and only seem to be reviving their responding. . . . After that, I'm going to try "reinforcing not-responding." Get some basic extinction curves, and into one group work a number of free pellets following at least a minute of no-responding. Will this curve flatten out? I.e. if you reinforce not-responding, are responses subtracted from the reserve? Tell you later.

IN 1940 the Zenith Foundation experimented with telepathy on the radio. A group of "senders" met in a studio, a coin was tossed five times, and each result was "sent" to the radio audience, who were asked to mail in postcards reporting the calls they "received." In the very first experiment a surprisingly large number of listeners reported the correct sequence, the odds against their having done so by chance being astronomical. Rhine is said to have written to congratulate Commander MacDonald, head of the Zenith Foundation. A week later the result was just the opposite: there were far fewer correct calls than expected from chance. I believe Rhine said that this too was significant; telepathy worked in mysterious ways.

The explanation was soon clear. To most people certain patterns —for example, heads, tails, heads, heads, tails—look like chance, while others—for example, five heads in a row—do not. A radio audience reports the same distribution of patterns week after week, and when the coin in the studio happens to hit a preferred one, the result seems highly significant, as in the first Zenith experiment. When the toss yields an unlikely pattern, the results are "negatively significant."

Two published analyses pointed to certain elements of "symmetry" in the guessing patterns, a type of structural explanation I distrusted. Behavior is discovered to have certain organizing principles which are then used to explain the behavior. The structuralist movement in linguistics and anthropology had not yet bloomed, but Gestalt psychology was taking that line.

For me guessing was simply a kind of verbal behavior distinguished by the fact that responses were not under the control of identifiable discriminative stimuli. I could not accept five guesses as a unit to be explained by structural principles. What stimuli determined each call? The first of five calls might be due to miscellaneous factors

—heads oftener than tails, perhaps, because we say "heads or tails" rather than "tails or heads"—but the second should be under the additional control of the first, and the third under the control of the second and perhaps the first.

I published an analysis of the Zenith data in which I attributed the actual sequences "received" to tendencies to alternate calls. A long history of "chance" events is presumably responsible for the fact that after one has called heads, there is a slightly greater tendency to call tails, and if one has called heads twice, the tendency is stronger. But once a call has been changed, the tendency to change drops to the original value. (When the paper was submitted for publication, I listed among the references: "*Verbal Behavior* [Manuscript].")

IN COLLEGE I had smoked only on occasion and usually only Pall Mall Ovals in red-and-gold boxes when I was wearing a black tie and tuxedo. In Scranton I became a fairly heavy pipe smoker, favoring a meerschaum with a brass cap or a briar with a stem a foot long. In graduate school I discovered Leavitt and Peirce in Harvard Square, where tobaccos were mixed according to personal recipes, and in Minnesota some of the younger men in the department took me to a shop where I bought blocks of briar and hard-rubber pipestems, and I began to make my own pipes, drilling and carving the blocks in various shapes. There were two schools of thought about the stems: the "tars" should vaporize and be taken into the mouth or collected in a soggy mass in the bottom of the pipe. I made pipes on both principles.

Three years later I gave up smoking—for several reasons. In an article in *Science*, March 4, 1938, Raymond Pearl published some results of his long-term research on survivorship. He had followed a large number of people for many years, recording their habits as well as their medical conditions, and when they died, he looked at their ages and the facts he had accumulated. He published survivorship curves showing that "usage of tobacco by smoking" led to early death by several years. Of course, some unidentified factor might have caused people both to smoke and to die early, but moderate drinkers did not show the effect, and I was inclined to agree that smoking was injurious. (Pearl had not, however, distinguished among kinds of smokers, and his early deaths were almost certainly due to cigarettes rather than pipes or cigars. As a pipe smoker I was probably not threatened.)

In 1941, I decided to see whether I could give up smoking for a week. I put my humidor and pipe rack on the mantel in my study, and there they stayed. The week grew into a month, and still another month, and eventually I gave my better pipes to my friends and threw the rest away. I do not think the change was due to a mere statistic. I had been experimenting with different tobaccos, and a month before I stopped I had tried a rather aromatic blend. I began to have headaches (presumably an allergic reaction), which stopped when I stopped smoking. I had unintentionally arranged a kind of aversive therapy.

Another possible contribution should not be neglected. I often listened to broadcasts of evangelical preaching, which I found fascinating simply as verbal behavior. I liked to listen to a preacher named Luke Rader, who specialized in distinguishing between controlled and controlling selves. One day he was denouncing the demon rum. Someone had complained that he could not control his drinking, and Rader said something like this: "What do you mean you can't control it? Isn't it your arm that raises the glass to your lips? Do you mean to tell me you can't control your arm?" I found the theme helpful in self-management. And so it could be said that I gave up smoking for cognitive, Pavlovian, and religious reasons.

THE FIRST WEEK of December 1941 was eventful. On the 4th I received an encouraging letter from Tom Sebeok. "Your lecture at the Linguistics Club last summer," he reported, "certainly stirred up a lot of healthy controversy: it is still constantly popping up and, as a matter of fact, it has spread to Princeton, as my friends there tell me. We all look forward to your book. When will it be out?"

On the 5th I wrote letters of introduction for a young graduate of the University who was leaving for New York to find work as a writer—possibly for the radio. His name was Max Shulman. I gave him letters to Hutch and to Max Wylie, a Hamilton College friend. To Wylie I wrote:

For the past two years I have started the day by picking up my copy of the (undergraduate) Minnesota Daily and looking first of all for Shulman's column. He has let me down only once or twice. His stuff is really very funny—consistently so and, for an undergraduate, uncannily light in touch. He has tried his hand at practically every brand of humor and seems to be equally good at all of them. I have been lecturing on humor (God help us!) off and on for a number of years, and while that may not make me an authority with a radio scriptman, in my opinion Shulman has got what it takes.

Several years before, Hutch had left the *Times* for the *Boston Transcript*, where he had taken the place left by the death of "H.T.P.," a music and drama critic whose reviews were highly respected by his New York colleagues. When the *Transcript* folded, Hutch went back to the *Times*, which, he wrote,

never seemed so safe, so Gibraltar-like. There will never again be an office or a job so pleasant as that weird and screwball place at Washington and Milk Streets; but there is something to be said for being certain of a check week after next. Middle age, no doubt. It was something to have lived through, those last three years of the Transcript—*exciting and harrowing and, at the very least, tragic. The more so because the paper never should have failed.*

Max Shulman's career in New York was brief. A friend who was equally impressed with his work persuaded a publisher to give him a contract for a book called *Barefoot Boy with Cheek*.

On the 6th of December there was a meeting of the Psychological Roundtable in New Britain, Connecticut. Members of the Roundtable were required to resign at forty, but Fred Keller, just overage, was present because the symposium was on operant behavior. The roster was impressive. Fred discussed the differences between operant and respondent conditioning. Carl Hovland of Yale talked about the acquisition of conditioned operants, and Clarence Graham of Brown their extinction. Clifford Morgan discussed discrimination and differentiation, and O. Hobart Mowrer the role of drive in operant conditioning. Donald Marquis summarized the session. I had been invited but could not afford the trip.

On the 7th something rather more serious happened. I was listening to the afternoon symphony on the radio and finishing an answer to a criticism of my position on the nervous system. To celebrate the opening of new psychological laboratories at the University of California at Los Angeles, the Chairman, Knight Dunlap, had organized a Symposium on Physiological Psychology, and Roger Brown Loucks had been asked to discuss the chapter on the nervous system in *The Behavior of Organisms*. I had sent Loucks some comments on an early draft of his manuscript, and at the last minute I was asked to send comments on the final version but had no time to do so. When Loucks's paper was published, however, an answer seemed necessary. The concert was interrupted by news of Pearl Harbor.

The next day I resumed work on the pigeon project. Two graduate students, Keller Breland and Norman Guttman, offered to help, and the University gave me money for better apparatus. Since I had been told that the United States had no guided missile, we abandoned ground-to-air systems and turned to a steerable bomb, to be dropped straight down. We found that pigeons would work when held in a harness pointing down, and if the bomb rotated slowly, it would be enough if they simply steered back and forth.

We studied the presumed behavior of a bomb by dropping a dart from a high ceiling in the basement of the psychology building. We put a small round-head iron nail in the end of the dart among the feathers and hung it from an electromagnet on the ceiling. We could release it in precisely the same way time after time, and with equal precision the point of the dart went into the same hole in the floor again and again. But by the time we put vanes on the bomb to make it turn, things became difficult, and we decided to leave that part of the project to experts. We would confine ourselves to the behavior of the pigeon.

Rather than rotate the pigeon in its descent, we built a table that turned the target area, and rather than move the pigeon back and forth, we moved the target on the rotating field. The pigeon descended eleven feet, and as it did so the table turned and the target moved back and forth according to the signals it sent.

We tried to let the pigeon steer in a more natural way by striking plates with its tail feathers, but its flight behavior was badly disrupted by the harness, and we settled for parallel rods alongside the neck. All our pigeons maneuvered well during fairly rapid descents, within the limits imposed by the speeds of our motors, and brought the target into position so that they could get the grain it held when they reached it.

In February I again asked Dean Tate to see a demonstration, and he suggested that we make a film. He wrote to Dr. Tolman: "If you have a steerable bomb, I feel fairly confident that a bird's vision and head movement constitute an instrument for guidance which is probably superior to anything which can be produced by the hand of man." (Dr. Tate soon took over Section C-4 of the National Defense Research Committee and offered me a job in antisubmarine work. Much earlier I had filled out a manpower form listing the languages I read or spoke and the experience and skills I had to offer, and some item I checked brought an invitation to study cryptanalysis. In March 1942 I went to a heavily guarded building on Fulton Street in New York to discuss the antisubmarine position. Later I wrote to Dean Tate that I still believed in the pigeon project and asked to be excused. He said he "fully appreciated my reasons." The man who took the job was killed when a blimp from which he was making observations near the New Jersey coast fell into the ocean.)

Near the end of March, Dr. Tolman reported that the National Defense Research Committee "would not be able to justify the use of funds." I had told Fred that if we were turned down, I was going to write an article about the experiment for *Life, Look,* or the *Saturday Evening Post,* but I still thought of it as a military secret and could not bring myself to expose "our failure to get through to the brass hats."

To Dean Tate I wrote:

> *My plan for directing bombs was shelved as "perhaps feasible" but not sure enough to warrant further investigation. This has not altered my faith in the plan and I wanted to tell you that I have put aside all other research and am giving all my time exclusively to going on with this work. With a limited budget I cannot reach the stage of a field test but I am quite sure that I can put on a laboratory demonstration that will convince the doubting Thomases. If you can get a chance to mention it to anyone who may be in the slightest way interested, I will be eternally in your debt.*
>
> *This morning's (unconfirmed) news of the sinking of the Prince of Wales [in the Bay of Bengal] looks as if the Japs were using men*

rather than birds. Perhaps we can get American morale that high, but if not, I can provide perfectly competent substitutes.

THE SOCIETY OF Experimental Psychologists, exclusive and self-perpetuating, had been founded by Titchener. I had been made a member in 1938 but I could not afford to attend the meetings because they were always held on the East Coast. In March 1942, however, I went to New York to receive the Society's Howard Crosby Warren Medal. There I ran into Charles Bray, best known for his research with Glenn Wever on the physiology of the ear. He had moved to Washington and was active in military affairs. I told him about our project, and he made an appointment for me with Commander Luis de Florez. I wrote about the meeting to Fred:

> *Just a note to report on the state of the war. I got a free trip to Washington last week to discuss with the Navy. De Florez (chief of Special Devices section) is all on our side and wants to see a field test. But his group can't do it. [He had recently backed two similarly outrageous proposals and both had gone wrong.] He's going to try to sell it to other branches. Tolman (NDRC) turned it down flat; said it might do for the next war but not for this. Bray thinks his (T's) lack of respect for his brother may be the trouble.*
>
> *De Florez is grand. Just the right sense of humor about the whole thing. Feels it is a mistake to table any suggestion till the next war. [One of Tolman's reasons for turning us down was that as yet we had no missile, but De Florez made short work of that: put an automatic pilot in a Piper Cub, fill the plane with dynamite, and feed the pigeon's responses into an automatic pilot.]*
>
> *Meanwhile a UP dispatch from Moscow says the Russians are using dogs to blow up tanks. I hope to hell the Nazis don't get too many ideas.*

During the summer a young man came to the department looking for an animal psychologist. He wanted to use dogs to steer torpedoes by responding to auditory signals from submarine engines. I said I thought that dogs could do so but that acoustic and electrical devices could do as much with the same signals. Moreover, I said I didn't think he would get very far with the Navy. Word of our project had got around (a colleague had heard a professor at Northwestern University tell someone about "a damn fool who was trying to get pigeons to steer bombs"), and I saw no reason why I should not describe our abandoned project.

I did not discourage our visitor. He had been unsuccessful before. (His first name was Victor and as we heard more of his story, Keller Breland and I began to call him Vanquished.) He went to several companies in Minneapolis looking for support for his submarine project, among them General Mills, Inc. To make his own project plausible, he described our work with pigeons, and the Vice President in charge of research became interested. He was about to leave the company to take over the I. G. Farben Industries in the United States, but he asked me to tell him about my project, and I did so just before he left. His place was taken by Arthur Hyde, who was also interested. He brought our project to the attention of James Ford Bell, Chairman of the Board of General Mills, and together they consulted two mechanical engineers who were working for the company. One of them had invented the Toastmaster and was developing a series of household appliances which the company planned to market after the war; the other was working on a hydraulic brake for airplanes. They said they could design a missile that could be controlled by a pigeon, and Mr. Bell appropriated $5000 to develop our device "to the point at which support could be obtained from a government agency."

In January I had been granted a sabbatical furlough from the University and in March I had got my Guggenheim. If I could not take it up that year, the fellowship would be waiting for me when the war was over, and I now wrote to ask for a postponement. Charles Morris had received a Guggenheim on a similar project, and he wrote that he hoped we might get together, but the pigeon project was absorbing all my time, and once again verbal behavior would have to wait.

Keller Breland and Norman Guttman had kept in touch, and we were joined by Keller's wife, Marian (née Kruse), the student who had tabulated the alliterative consonants in the Shakespeare sonnets and typed my broadcast course in the Psychology of Literature. Later Bill Estes joined us for a few months. We could begin work on September 1, on the top floor of a flour mill in downtown Minneapolis. We became employees of General Mills, Inc., and were issued wartime identification buttons bearing our pictures. The top floor was the twelfth and could be reached by first going as far as the tenth on a "Humphrey," a long vertical leather belt passing straight up through holes in the floors. Cleats and hand grips were fastened to the belt, and with a little practice you took hold of a grip and stepped onto a cleat as it came up through the floor, rode straight up on the belt, and stepped off at just the right time. If you did not step quickly, it was too late, and for a while we got off at the eighth or ninth floor to give ourselves a second chance. Norman once went over the top, tripping a safety switch that stopped the belt.

We began to redesign a controlling system. Our demonstration had revealed a serious weakness: only when the target was conspicuously out of line did the pigeon work to bring it within reach. It did not fly an interception course. We worked out a different method in which the pigeon pecked a translucent plate on which the target image was projected by a lens. Pecking the image was reinforced on an intermittent schedule by dropping grain directly onto the plate. To pick up the location of the pecks we tried dividing the plate into pie-shaped segments, each making its own contact when pecked. A better system proved to be a cardboard cone, with the plate fastened across the large end and the lens fitted into the small. The cone hung, lens down, on bearings which permitted it to swing in any direction against a light friction. The harnessed pigeon was held head down in an enclosure above the plate, on which a picture of the illuminated target below the lens appeared.

If the small end of the cone was pointing straight at the target, the image was in the center of the plate, and the pigeon's pecks did not tilt the cone, but if the target moved out of the center, the image moved in the opposite direction, and the pecks tilted the cone until it pointed at the target again. As we moved the target about, the cone rather jerkily continued to point to it. If you did not know what was inside, it was quite mystifying.

Something more substantial than a cardboard cone was needed in a missile, and we turned to electrical controls. A translucent plate tilted slightly as the pigeon pecked it, and contacts at the edges controlled motors which moved the target—as they would eventually, we trusted, move a missile. We used a variety of visual patterns, and found schedules under which a pigeon controlled a moving target for several minutes without stopping.

We advertised for pigeons. A few racing fanciers sold us culls, and a farmer brought in a boxful collected at night as they roosted in his barn. We also considered crows, which probably learned more rapidly and could operate more sophisticated controls. We asked Cedric Adams, a columnist in the *Minneapolis Star Journal,* to say we were looking for tame crows, and we bought three that had been trained as pets. They were amusing to work with but not very cooperative. (A farmer called to say that he would catch some crows for us but never delivered them. Years later I learned that he had brought several to a Professor Skinner at the Medical School who did not want them and who knew nothing of our project. The farmer concluded that he had been the victim of a student prank and was rather violently angry.)

We built an apparatus to train four pigeons at a time, using whatever materials we could find under wartime shortages. (At one point we were puzzled by an intermittent failure, as the whole system went on and off unpredictably. We had picked up some sockets at a five-and-ten, one of which we eventually discovered was designed to turn Christmas tree lights on and off.) Each pigeon was snugly gripped in a jacket (still made from a man's sock) and held in a harness at a forty-five-degree angle facing a four-inch opening through which it could strike a translucent plate. The target pattern was thrown on the plate by a cheap slide projector. Two beams of light crossed at the spot at which the pigeon was to strike and were intercepted by the beak when a response was correct. A contact then operated a programming device resembling my old apparatus for the study of fixed-ratio schedules, except that it reinforced on the powerful variable-ratio schedule that Fred had characterized as "more like human prayer." For reinforcement a shallow tray of grain swung into the middle of the target opening. The housing in which the pigeon was mounted moved slowly about the plate so that the spot appeared in different positions in the four-inch opening. From time to time the slides were changed to show the target at different distances and angles.

We heard nothing further from the National Defense Research

Committee, and in December I urged Mr. Hyde to appeal to them again. A Dr. Letchfield was sent to inspect our project, but we heard nothing more until we again pressed for a hearing. In February we were asked to bring a film to Washington. (I carried it in a new brief-case, a present from my colleagues, who thought my old academic model would not impress the committee.) I summarized our situation in a letter to Fred:

I'm going down to show off our new film and give NDRC one last chance to use their scientific heads. I'll be bolstered by a vice-president of General Mills and an engineer. It'll be our last chance in that quarter and I'm going to give them the works.

The story is about as follows: G.M.I. undertook to back us on the opinion of their engineers that a suitable bomb could be built. We have spent 6 months very profitably in advancing way beyond where we were with our "gadgets" [I meant "pigeons," of course, but I was protecting security], but the engineers have fallen down. Priorities, designs calling for too-high tolerances, loss of enthusiasm—have all played havoc. One engineer has been dawdling along with a balsa model to be dropped off a bridge! We (my two side-kicks and I) have tried to rush things (although so far as I can see we could go on drawing a check . . . and nobody would remember to fire us!) because we want action rather than a safe job for the duration. Last week I went to the V. President in charge of Research, said I didn't think our chances of working with a bomb of our own design in the near future were good, reminded him of NDRC's promise to visit us (nearly 3 mos. ago!) and asked him to use G.M.I.'s rather considerable prestige to force a hearing. He phoned Washington and got it set for next Friday. Our line must now be this—we have a unit ("never mind what's inside it—you know, but you don't know how well it can be controlled except through our results—which stand on their own feet") which will steer toward a target which is as little as 2° off the center of a field and which is so small that it fills no more than 1" of visual angle (a battleship at 3 mi.). The steering signals come out at the rate of 3 or 4 per second without interruption for more than 2 minutes—and we can even run it 30 minutes if you allow a 5 sec rest every 30 sec running time (the latter in the case of surface craft sneaking up on a Navy). These signals are independent of conditions A,B,C, etc.—a long list. The unit can be adjusted to pick up any type of target (say, a ship, bridge, railroad line) or it can be specially adjusted within a week to pick up a particular target (U-boat garage at Lorient, etc). What do you say?

Heretofore there has been nobody on deck to answer the simple-minded question that came up in such a meeting. I'm going loaded for bear! Including prepared memoranda, photos, etc. & a 15 minute film. Also a special statement in case of a brush-off—to this effect—Would you or would you not support further work if we walked in with an electronic device that would do the same thing? If you would, then your refusal is simply another instance of ignorance and neglect of a contemporary but distant field of science.

I've never had greater faith in the idea. I'll send our film as soon as possible. If NDRC says no, G.M.I. may withdraw support (with a 60 day notice) or it may not, I can't tell. We would probably try the services directly, a local company making gyro-pilots (who would have a financial interest in the scheme if it worked with such a plane), and maybe a couple of private sources. If nothing happens, I go back to the Guggenheim till next fall and then take up teaching. My sabbatical won't keep and I can't live on the fellowship alone.

The meeting called for no histrionics. We were told that a missile was under construction, although little was known about how it would be steered. Various types of signals were discussed, and a member of the committee, Frederick Hovde, suggested that someone visit our project to see whether our pigeons could be installed in a grounded vehicle to test their control. In March 1943, H. H. Spencer, an electrical engineer, and Fred Cummings came to see us. We demonstrated the control of targets of various sizes, shapes, and degrees of contrast, with distracting "cloud patterns," and at different speeds in sustained runs up to more than five minutes.

As a result the newly formed Office of Scientific Research and Development voted to support the project, but before approving that action the Director asked for measures of the bird's accuracy. We sent data and heard that "computations were going forward to determine the effect on the steering mechanism." Three weeks later we were asked for an estimate of the number of pigeons in the country. Eventually, in June, a contract in the amount of $25,000 was awarded to General Mills, Inc., "to develop a homing device" under the name of Project Pigeon.

Two representatives of OSRD came to Minneapolis to tell us more about the missile. It had the code name "Pelican"—and for good reason: the controlling equipment was so bulky that there was no room for explosives, and someone had been reminded of the limerick about the pelican whose beak can hold more than its belly can. It was a small wing-steered glider, and it approached its target slowly and at a low angle. Six or seven possible methods of picking up the signal from the plate were discussed, and we were given approximate specifications. The adequacy or inadequacy of the signal was to be determined from photographs taken during actual test flights.

We had been told to prepare for a target in Florida, of which we were shown photographs, and we constructed a large replica on the roof of the mill, using colored sawdust, sand, and blocks of wood, and made slides for our apparatus. But the target was abandoned, and we were asked to prepare for one near Toms River, New Jersey. It would be necessary to wait for winter coloring before taking photographs.

I reported to Fred: "It's a hell of a strain—especially the weary waiting. But hold on, old man, there may be a break in the clouds. I'm afraid the war is a long way from over. We're sort of counting on Europe in the summer of '44 for our theatre. For a while I thought we might get left, but with only 850 casualties in Italy so far and 1,999,150 still to go I'm afraid we'll have plenty of chances."

In due time I went to Toms River, where I found a group of people working on the Pelican Project. We were lodged in a small hotel run by a German couple, who, I was warned, had not been cleared. My "psychosomatic" stomachache had returned, and I spent some free time walking the streets of the town intensively relaxed (to take care of the psyche) and looking for a drugstore that would sell me paregoric (for the soma). A young naval officer was to take me up in a small plane. (He was an intelligent man, but handicapped by a bad stammer. "Project Pigeon is not a very secure name," he said. "You are obviously going to train pigeons to guide missiles." That was classified information and I said nothing.) I strapped on a parachute, and we walked out to the plane, the parachute swinging itself and me from side to side in an embarrassing way. The target proved to be a large stirrup-shaped pattern of white sand, where a bulldozer had scraped away the topsoil and its scrubby vegetation. I had made a box with a translucent screen and lens through which I could see what the target would look like to the pigeons. We made a number of approaches, weaving in like a badly controlled missile, while I did my best to look at the image in my box. Later, photographs were taken to be used in conditioning the pigeons.

Meanwhile, the Mechanical Engineering Division of General Mills, Inc., had gone to work on ways of picking up the signal. A pneumatic system seemed best. A venturi cone on the outside of the missile would provide a vacuum, and four small ballistic valves on the edges of the translucent screen would pop open whenever the screen was struck, allowing a little air to enter a system of pipes leading to two diaphragms. When the pigeon pecked the center of the screen, all the valves opened to the same extent, but if the pecks were as little as a quarter of an inch off center, some of them admitted more air. This altered the pressures on the diaphragms, and changed the electrical input to the missile control. (The space occupied by the pigeon could be pressurized, but the Pelican operated at low altitudes.)

When we were given a sample of the plywood nose of the missile, we found that there was room for three pigeons. Three pneumatic systems could easily be yoked together to give a joint report—much more sensitive and accurate than that of a single bird. We could even use a majority vote. If the missile were approaching two ships at sea, for example, all three pigeons might not choose the same ship, but at least two must do so, and the system could be arranged so that the third would be punished for its minority opinion and would change to the other ship. Any pigeon guilty of deviationism thereafter would be quickly disciplined. (Eight years later von Neumann would publish the solution of a similar problem—how to build reliable processing systems from unreliable components—using probabilistic logic.)

The company also built a trainer, rather like the Link Trainer used to teach pilots. It was a tilting table that banked and yawed like the Pelican. Our three-pigeon unit, attached to the table, quite accurately pointed toward a target moved about on the far side of the room. The fact that we thus "closed the loop" in the system was significant in later discussions.

In our laboratory, meanwhile, we investigated many of the conditions that might affect the pigeons' behavior. We needed a powerful reinforcer, and we had read that pigeons were almost fearless when feeding on hemp seed. We got a supply, heat-sterilized, and found, indeed, that our pigeons worked faster when it was used in place of our standard grain. (Tincture of marijuana sprayed on grain had little effect.)

To be sure that the birds would not be distracted, we adapted them to a variety of disturbing noises, and eventually they went on pecking even when a pistol was fired a few inches away. We centrifuged them at the end of a five-foot arm, and studied their behavior under the atmospheric pressure encountered at 10,000 feet. (One day the glass window of our pressure chamber blew in when my face was pressed against it. It knocked my glasses off, and as I searched for other possible damage, I was rather surprised to find that Keller and Norman were looking at the pigeon. It had gone on working.)

We injected nitrous oxide into the apparatus to see how quickly pigeons would resume responding as they recovered from its effects. We reduced the amount of light on the screen and found, to our surprise, that a jacketed pigeon would continue to peck a panel in total darkness. Some pigeons lived a forty-eight-hour day, with twenty-four hours of light and twenty-four of dark. Some lived continuously in the light.

Pigeons have different systems for distant and close-up vision, and we were probably working with the latter, but there should be an optimal distance from the target plate, if not for vision, then for convenient pecking. We held a jacketed pigeon at different distances from the plate and found that it pecked most slowly when it could barely reach the plate and most rapidly when it was very near.

A crucial question was how closely the training pictures must resemble the target as seen in the missile. To what extent did pigeons generalize from one pattern to another? In one experiment we reinforced pecking a yellow triangle and built up a high rate under periodic reconditioning. When we presented a red triangle and stopped reinforcing, the pigeon responded very slowly, but fifteen minutes later, when we restored the yellow triangle, it pecked at a high rate and recorded a typical extinction curve.

We explored ways to get a pigeon to peck harder. We held it vertically over a small disk on one end of a balanced bar. Pecking drove the end of the bar down and made a contact that dispensed food. By sliding a weight along the other end of the bar, as in a counter scale, we required more and more forceful pecks. Very slight differences proved to be extremely important. Too quick a change would lose the behavior, but under careful programming the pigeon struck so hard that the base of its beak became inflamed.

YVONNE AND I continued to live our daily lives. We had met a few new friends in the Grove, though we entertained very seldom. A wartime community garden was opened on some nearby land, and some of our neighbors zealously tended their plots, but we settled for a small garden in the rear of our property, part of which slid down toward the trolley tracks during a heavy rain. Yvonne took Julie to dancing school, and I helped prepare her for a recital in which she and a dozen other pupils danced a Polka Dot Polka, wearing a red-and-white polka-dot dress, with metal taps on her slippers. She was not much interested in dancing, and I must have played "Sweet Sue" a hundred times, at gradually increasing speeds, as she practiced.

One of the General Mills engineers, Irving Boekelheide, played the viola, and we organized some chamber music. The Minneapolis public library had a fine collection of scores, and there were many talented young string players in the Twin Cities for whom I had only to suggest time and place—which meant our house and usually Sunday morning. We began with piano trios and quartets. I was not up to the standards of the best players, but they were tolerant. As we forged through a new and difficult piece one day, our first violinist not only played her part flawlessly but called out to me, "B-*flat*! B-*flat*!" It was a kind of musical behavior, verbal as well as nonverbal, that was quite beyond me. As our competence increased, we moved on to things like the Schumann Piano Quintet, and one Sunday morning we tackled the Dvořák Piano Sextet at sight. I was at the time reading a book called *Sight Without Glasses*, which Aldous Huxley had recommended, and I did the Dvořák sextet with my naked eyes. The tolerance of my companions survived.

Some of the graduate students began to meet at our house to discuss operant behavior and its implications, among them the Brelands, Norman Guttman, Howard Hunt, and Paul Meehl, with Herbert Feigl dropping in occasionally. We ranged widely, and one evening my economist neighbor, Arthur Marget, came over to talk to us.

MANY OF THE EXPERIMENTS we did while waiting for Washington to make up its collective mind had little or nothing to do with the project. The pigeons were there, crude apparatus was available, and we had all the time in the world. I reported to Fred:

> *The way we are turning the stuff out these days is making it absolutely impossible to go back to the old schedule. I'd get no sense of achievement out of it at all. As it is, we are fast filling a sizable book. Almost complete repetition of the B of O (with a different species) plus oodles of new stuff. Some work on discrimination that would put your eye out. A new trick with* variable *periodic reinforcement that eliminates the steplike effect of a temporal discrimination. . . . New work on reinforcing a* rate *of response. Complete survey of drive. Etc. Etc. and* beautiful *records. Every one like an average for four to twelve rats.*

We were using a method in which a pigeon, held in a jacket, closed a circuit by pecking a small strip of translucent plastic exposed through a hole about an inch in diameter—an early version of the standard pigeon key. Colored lights could be turned on behind the key. We also tried to set up two simultaneous operants in a single organism, reinforcing both pecking a key and pulling a string attached to one foot.

In another experiment we used food to reinforce drinking. The pigeon was hungry but not thirsty and could get food by drinking a small amount of water from a dish. It outwitted us by developing ingenious ways of operating the food dispenser. The dish was on the end of a balanced arm and it rose and closed a contact when a small amount of water was taken out, but the pigeon learned to strike the bottom of the dish so that it bounced up and closed the contact. When we made the dish too deep for that, the pigeon learned to dip its head into the water and bring up water on its feathers. If necessary, it would shake the water from its feathers and dip a second time.

We taped a pigeon's beak so that it could not take grain into its mouth. One pigeon with a long history of responding to the plate under periodic reinforcement pecked rapidly at a dish of grain for as much as two hours, although no grain was eaten. Grain in the food dispenser proved to be reinforcing for a long time even when covered by transparent plastic. We designed a dispenser in which the grain was covered during nine out of ten presentations, hoping to be able to work for many hours with little or no satiation.

We taught a pigeon to play a simple tune ("Over the Fence is Out, Boys") on a four-key "piano." We reinforced by hand, beginning with the first note and adding others as the pigeon's behavior permitted. In the final performance the pigeon pecked while executing a rather pronounced dance movement.

Possibly our most impressive experiment concerned the shaping of behavior. I had used successive approximation in my experiments on the force and duration of lever-pressing, and we had seen how important it was in teaching a pigeon to peck hard. Pliny's complex behavior had been put together step by step by making slight changes in the ap¡aratus. But one exciting day on the top floor of that flour mill we programmed contingencies by hand.

We put a pigeon in a large cardboard carton, on one wall of which was a food dispenser operated by a hand switch. We put a wooden ball the size of a Ping-Pong ball on the floor and undertook to teach the pigeon to knock it about the box. We began by reinforcing merely looking at the ball, then moving the head toward it, then making contact with it, and eventually knocking it to one side with a swiping motion. The pigeon was soon batting the ball about the box like a squash player. We had shaped a very complex topography of behavior through successive approximation in a matter of minutes, and we "gazed at one another in a wild surmise."

I remember that day as one of great illumination. We had discovered how much easier it was to shape behavior by hand than by changing a mechanical device. Yet Thorndike had shaped the behavior of a cat by hand, and I had published that explicit account of the process in my reply to Konorski and Miller.

Our research did not take all our time as we waited for action in Washington. Bill Estes liked to play chess, but he was the slowest, most cautious player I had ever known, and I could not maintain my interest in a game—or win. After he went into the Army Air Forces, we turned to a game of skill I had seen as a child at a summer resort. A ball hanging from the ceiling on a string is swung in such a way that at the top of the swing it drops into a cup. We competed for the longest string of successful swings.

One of our more amusing diversions involved that balsa model glider I had mentioned to Fred. It had a lens in the nose, and the airfoils and rudder moved when the pigeon pecked a translucent plate. The engineer who built it proposed that we teach a pigeon to peck at a picture of the dam in the river below the mill and then release the glider and pigeon from a window. Fortunately we never reached that stage. We let the glider slide down a long tightwire and watched the airfoils and rudder as we moved a target about at the lower end. It was sheer play; there was no chance that the pigeon could ever guide the missile to a target.

We were not always intellectually idle. The *American Journal of Psychology* asked me to review Hull's *Principles of Behavior*. Hull had once advised me to read Newton's *Principia*, and now his own *Principia* was out. In 1941 I had written to Fred:

> *Hull hasn't yet broken his record of complete silence about the book* [The Behavior of Organisms] *and about his own work with the method. The mimeographed reports of his seminar indicate that he is still hiring mathematicians but that he still can't make it clear to them what the hell he wants. They now refer to their multitudinous sets of postulates by date. "This week all papers handed in should use the postulates of Feb. 15" etc. I've been contending all along that there is a perfectly good way of finding out which basic concepts are most convenient, but he still prefers to get his postulates from somebody's theories.*

In the *Principles of Behavior*, however, the postulates described an internal mediating system in which stimuli entered the organism, underwent various changes, and emerged as responses. It was not far from the Conceptual Nervous System I had rejected in *The Behavior of Organisms*. Many of the experiments offered in support of the analysis were carried out with "Skinner Boxes," and the "Skinner bar-pressing habit" was also mentioned, but there was almost nothing else from *The Behavior of Organisms*. On the contrary, Hull tended to play leapfrog over my work. For example, in discussing the effect of a delay of reinforcement he began by describing some old experiments in which rats, upon arriving at the end of a maze, were held in a retention chamber before being fed. He then continued, "the most recent experiment in this field [using a "modified Skinner box"] is reported by Perin," with no reference to the experiments on delay of reinforcement reported in *The Behavior of Organisms*. When Norman Guttman came to that part of Hull's book, he exclaimed, "How can he *do* that?"

But Hull was not deliberately suppressing my work. He was the only established person in the field who had shown any interest in it, and, except for Fred, his students were almost the only ones working along similar lines. But he could not have included my results without giving a detailed account of a great deal of new material with which he was probably not very comfortable. He was not alone in being puzzled by cumulative records and schedules of reinforcement, nor was he ready to give up "habits" and other "learning processes." Perin's work was a good example. Where I examined the effect of a delay in reinforcement on rate of responding, Perin looked at its effect on rate of learning—a throwback to Thorndike and the learning curve, for which there was no place in my formulation.

I could scarcely complain, because I myself never made any use of the work of Hull or his students, particularly Kenneth Spence and Neal Miller. My results did not fit their theories nor their results mine. It was not, I think, a self-centered isolation on the part of anyone; the science had not yet found a generally accepted formulation.

We discussed Hull's book at length in our idle moments in the flour mill, and I wrote my review. When it was published, the editor of the journal, Madison Bentley, wrote to thank me, and I replied:

As you may have discovered between the lines, I was pulling my punches. The fact of the matter is, the book is an unbelievable muddle, though I did not feel (in view of Hull's past contributions) that a more vitriolic treatment was called for. . . . I hate to think of all the useless theorizing and experimentation which is bound to follow if such a work is presented to young men in the field of psychology with Hull's own evaluation attached to it.

Unfortunately, I also wrote, "I was rather disturbed by a considerable garbling of my text. My copy was none too clear, as I was trying to make a January date line, so I suppose I am partly to blame; but someone made a lot of fussy sophomoric changes (e.g., 'Professor Hull' to 'our author') which made me blush."

Bentley replied, "Your note of the 12th confirms my suspicion that your final opinion of Hull's book was less favorable to the work than the published expression," and then he added, "In your manuscript you had a great many 'Professor Hulls.' For the sake of critical readers, I introduced variants. One of these variants was 'our author,' commonly regarded as an innocuous mode of reference. I doubt very much whether careful readers will share your emotional reaction to it, but 'a lot of fussy sophomoric changes' is fairly violent."

OUR PROJECT MOVED toward a decision. The question of phase lag had come up. Our pigeons, like human operators, were a little slow in reporting the position of a moving target. We were asked to drive the target back and forth in a sinusoidal motion at various speeds and to record the position of the table as the pigeons followed it. We were told to expect a phase lag of about ninety degrees when the target was moving at one cycle per second, but we did better than that. At high speeds our signal was rather jerky, but we could adjust the pneumatic system to get a compromise between speed and a well-modulated signal.

After many tests we felt that we had fully met the specifications. We had, of course, one great advantage: we were working on visual targets, which were the most difficult to mask or jam. Hugh Dryden, who was familiar with our project, said that we had no competitors in the field of land targets. Nevertheless, we ran into trouble. Specifications were changed, and recommendations were made and canceled. It became clear that the issue was not the actual properties of our system. The physicists and electrical engineers on Project Pelican simply did not trust pigeons.

A final presentation in Washington was arranged. We went first to meet engineers at the Radiation Laboratory at MIT in Cambridge. One of the people at that meeting was Harold L. Hazen, an authority on feedback control and servomechanisms, who took one look at our data and said, "Hell, that's better than radar!" But a young engineer, A. C. Hall, insisted that there was a "discrepancy" between our phase-lag data and the relation of amplitude to frequency. We knew that our signal showed the phase lag at the amplitudes and frequencies we reported, and if this was impossible according to Dr. Hall's equations, something was wrong with the equations. We spotted one possible source of trouble: the effect of a peck on the screen was not strictly proportional to the distance from the center because the pigeon struck a glancing blow near the edge. The difference could be corrected electrically, and at the end of our meeting Dr. Spencer agreed to recommend a further contract in the amount of $50,000.

The following day he did so when we appeared before some of the top brass of the Office of Scientific Research and Development in Washington, with Frank Jewett, director of the Bell Telephone Laboratories, presiding. To our surprise Dr. Hall again brought up the question of a discrepancy, but when he predicted that our device could not control the missile when we "closed the loop," Dr. Spencer pointed out that we had closed it with our tilting table. But it was no use. There was an air of ill-concealed joviality in the meeting. We were being judged not on the properties of our signal but on the use of pigeons.

I had foreseen the problem and had brought a jacketed pigeon in a box, facing a translucent screen on which the New Jersey target could be thrown by a projector from across the room. The pigeon had been in its jacket for thirty-six hours, and we had checked the box into and out of the baggage window at Chicago and had carried it with us on two long train rides. If the image on the screen was to be clear, the box would have to be closed, and I had installed a tube through which the pigeon could be watched without admitting too much light, but it would take too long to look down a tube, one person at a time, and I was asked to open the box. That meant that the pigeon saw a very faint image—and with strange members of the division peering down at it. Nevertheless, it performed beautifully, pecking steadily as we moved the target about. Someone put his hand in the beam from the projector and the pigeon quickly stopped. It started again just as quickly when the hand was withdrawn. There could scarcely have been a better demonstration of the extraordinary predictability of behavior, the keenness of a pigeon's vision, the accuracy of its responses, and its freedom from distraction, but there were smiles and a bit of laughter, and someone told me about an experience he had once had with his dog.

Mr. Hyde briefly summarized our position. We had a homing device suitable for a wide range of visual targets. It used no materials in short supply and could be put into production within thirty days. The committee thanked him, and we were dismissed. As we left the building, he said to me, "Why don't you go out and get drunk?"

On April 8 we were told that "further prosecution of this project would seriously delay others which in the minds of the Division have more immediate promise of combat application." If they meant the atom bomb, which might make pinpoint bombing unnecessary, they were right. (I had heard that the bomb was on its way; that secret was not as well kept as many people have supposed.) But if they meant other projects with guided missiles, no evidence was ever forthcoming of anything with "more immediate promise of combat application." It would eventually appear that the United States had not only no way of guiding a missile but no missile worth guiding. The Germans were far ahead. In September 1943, long before our final meeting in Washington, they had used missiles controlled by radio from mother planes to wreak havoc on the American fleet landing soldiers at Salerno.

There was nothing really outlandish about our project. As I had reported to Fred, the Russians had taught dogs, carrying incendiary bombs, to run under enemy tanks, the bombs being detonated either magnetically or when upright arms struck the tanks. A Swedish sociologist taught seals to attach small devices to moored mines which, after a short delay, blew up the mines. (The seals began their education when very young and were fed rich cream as the nearest thing to seal's milk; there was a shortage of cream in Sweden during the experiment.) And when our project came to the attention of Frederick A. Lindeman (Lord Cherwell), who was scientific adviser to Winston Churchill, he is said to have "regretted its demise." It would have found a place in Churchill's "Toy Shop"—a collection of ingenious devices developed by the British during the war, an example of which was the Limpet, a hemispherical mine to be attached to the side of a ship by a swimming saboteur, which exploded when an aniseed ball had dissolved.

General Mills, Inc., could do nothing more. Mr. Hyde had stuck by us loyally, but the company could not continue to support a project officially declared of no value to the defense of the country. My co-workers and I were given a month's notice. I wanted to complete some of our research, but the others felt they deserved a vacation, as they certainly did. They helped store the big training device in the basement of the psychology building (it would later be discarded unused), and twenty-four expert pigeons were set aside to be installed in a dovecote that I would build in our garden. Then my colleagues took off.

A young woman more recently employed, and hence not eligible for time off, stayed with me in the mill, and we went over our records and made figures for a published report of our research. I had told Fred that it would be a better book than *The Behavior of Organisms*, but I was wrong. We had not kept good records, and the topics we covered had been selected for miscellaneous reasons with no coherent plan. Some of our graphs found their way into a paper that I published later on learning theory, but the rest have long since disintegrated.

Project Pigeon was discouraging. Our work with pigeons was beautifully reinforced, but all our efforts with the scientists came to nothing. My verbal behavior with respect to Washington underwent extinction, and the effect generalized. My co-workers told me after it was all over that toward the end of the project I was not finishing my sentences.

It was not a total loss. The project demanded an extraordinary control of behavior. We could not make any use of "the average pigeon." We needed a real pigeon upon a real occasion, and we explored almost every condition that had any bearing upon its behavior. The research that I described in *The Behavior of Organisms* appeared in a new light. It was no longer merely an experimental analysis. It had given rise to a technology.

I COULD AT LAST take up the Guggenheim. In the basement of our house there was a fairly large playroom, and I converted it into a study and a shop. A four-by-eight-foot sheet of heavy plywood mounted on two sawhorses served as a desk at one end, and I put an assortment of small tools salvaged from the project on a workbench at the other.

One of the first things I made had an early deadline. In the uncertainty of the war years we had postponed having a second child, but by 1943 the future seemed clearer and we decided to go ahead. When Yvonne said that she did not mind bearing another child but rather dreaded the first year or two, I suggested that we simplify the care of a baby.

The human species evolved in a tropical climate and certainly without benefit of clothing. As the temperature changed, or as the species moved into colder climates, clothing began to be used, and in a modern house babies were kept warm by insulating them with several layers of cloth. Julie had worn a diaper, shirt, and nightgown, had slept on a thick mattress covered with a pad and a sheet, and was zipped into a flannel blanket, her head protruding through a collar, her arms in flipperlike sleeves. It was impossible for her to turn over. The commonest alternative was a top sheet and one or more blankets. All this was not only inefficient and confining, it was unnecessary. In a modern house the temperature of the space in which a baby lived could be controlled in a better way. Other problems could be solved at the same time.

For our second child I built a crib-sized living space that we began to call the "baby-tender." It had sound-absorbing walls and a large picture window. Air entered through filters at the bottom and, after being warmed and moistened, moved upward through and around the edges of a tightly stretched canvas, which served as a mattress. A strip of sheeting ten yards long passed over the canvas, a clean section of which could be cranked into place in a few seconds.

By the end of August the baby-tender was nearly finished and so was the baby. We dashed to the hospital early one morning on a false alarm. A day later we dashed again, and again the labor pains stopped after we arrived. The obstetrician was sure the baby was full-term, and he gave Yvonne an injection to induce labor. Our second daughter, Deborah, was born within an hour or two.

While Yvonne and the baby remained in the hospital, I added some final touches to the baby-tender. I discovered that I had almost committed that classic blunder of the man who builds a boat in his cellar and cannot get it out. The baby-tender was within an inch of being too large to go through the doors in our house. Moreover it had become surprisingly heavy. My neighbor and colleague, Miles Tinker, and I were barely able to inch it up two flights of stairs into a bedroom.

When Debbie came home, she went directly into this comfortable space and began to enjoy its advantages. She wore only a diaper. Completely free to move about, she was soon pushing up, rolling over, and crawling. She breathed warm, moist, filtered air, and her skin was never waterlogged with sweat or urine. Loud noises were muffled (though we could hear her from any part of the house), and a curtain pulled over the window shielded her from bright light when she was sleeping.

In July a group of thirteen prominent psychologists circulated a statement to members of the American Psychological Association. It began: "We have been told by competent advisers that the enclosed 'Statement,' if signed by a large number of psychologists and if released at the proper time, might have considerable influence on public (and even official) opinion. At the very least it would serve an educational purpose in leading people to think about the conditions essential for a sound peace." The statement began, "Humanity's demand for lasting peace leads us as students of human nature to assert ten pertinent and basic principles which should be considered in planning the peace. . . ." Among the principles were these: War can be avoided. It is not born in men; it is built into men. Racial, national, and group hatreds can, to a considerable degree, be controlled. If properly administered, relief and rehabilitation can lead to self-reliance and cooperation; if improperly to resentment and hatred. The trend of human relationships is toward ever-wider units of collective security.

We were asked to sign the statement and send comments. It was the kind of psychologizing that I loathed, and my reply was blunt:

> While I subscribe wholeheartedly to every one of your ten points as a citizen, I will not put my name to them as a psychologist. It is a plain question of intellectual honesty. I do not believe we have the slightest scientific evidence of the truth of at least nine of these propo-

sitions. I do not propose to join in an effort to make the public believe we have. They may seem self-evident in the light of recent history, and they are undoubtedly essential articles of faith in a working conception of democracy, but they are nevertheless still opinions, not facts. Yet how else will the laymen interpret "a statement by psychologists" than as a scientific pronouncement? Why otherwise mention the fact that the men who sign it are psychologists?

Your whole case is given away when you say that competent advisors have told you that the statement "might have considerable influence on public (and even official) opinion." There are the men to sign your statement—your competent advisors. If their prediction is worth a damn, they obviously know more about opinion than we do.

I was not unconcerned about peace. I had grown tired of war and of my part in it, and I had begun to think about a more benevolent application of behavioral science. On one of my trips to Washington I had outlined a program "to increase strength of 'moral' or 'ethical' verbalisms in the behavior of the inmates of a penal institution." A radio drama would be broadcast at a given time of day in dining room or dormitories. Among the characters in the drama would be a parental figure who would "eventually establish authority and court imitation." At first the program would be almost wholly musical with no more than one or two minutes of dialogue. But the story line would be gradually lengthened. The views of the boys or men would be learned by inquiry or questionnaires, and characters would be introduced into the drama to represent them. The episodes would dramatize useful principles such as "The first step toward trouble doesn't look like trouble," or "Be smart; get what you want, but stay within the law." Reactions could be gauged by distributing leaflets or putting up posters about the programs and noting the extent to which they were destroyed or defaced, and new programs could be adjusted to take these reactions into account.

The project would be evaluated from the records of former inmates.

JULIE CONTINUED TO THRIVE. She had a large second-floor bedroom and alcove to herself, in which I put the cuckoo clock. She developed an elaborate fantasy of another world—a pleasant flower world that she told us about quite freely. Perhaps it was her own version of heaven, for we gave her no religious education. I had suffered from the religious teachings of my parents and my grandmother Skinner, and Yvonne had had a rather similar experience. Though her father said grace at meals, he never went to church, and her mother had no religious beliefs at all. Yvonne might have been spared a religious experience if she had not found a copy of Dante's *Inferno* in her grandfather's library. It contained Doré's illustrations of the agonies of hell. She began to make inquiries, and when she found that she had never been baptized, she looked into the practices of the local sects. It appeared that the Baptists washed away sins most thoroughly, and with her parents' consent, and as they watched, she was purified by total immersion.

Julie's religious education came from her friends. One of them took her to an Episcopal ceremony, and she reported that "they had candles and God was there." A neighbor's child made a more dramatic attempt to proselytize. One morning, two or three days after Debbie was born, I found Julie missing. I had made a kind of jungle gym in our backyard by tying a ladder against a clothes pole, and the ladder was now against the window of Julie's room and her bed was empty. I could not see that she had taken any clothes with her, and the ladder against the window reminded me of the Lindbergh case. When Yvonne called from the hospital, I said that Julie was playing outside, but I had no idea where she was. I was on the point of calling the police when she came home. The neighbor's child had taken her to early Mass—surreptitiously because she assumed that I would object. Julie had worn her dancing pumps with their metal taps and a filmy fairy costume on the skirt of which I had dropped globs of hot solder, which splashed out as bright spangles. Over the years two or three other children took Julie to Sunday school, but when she found they *had* to go, she lost interest.

That fall Julie would be starting in first grade, and we were rather concerned about reports that the teacher in her school was something of a martinet. Julie was well behaved, but not because she was disciplined. When she was quite young we had occasionally punished her, rapping her knuckles lightly if she reached for a breakable object or spanking her for other tabooed behavior. At five she had reached the stage when she would apparently ask for punishment, and I thought it was time to put my science to use. Bill Estes had extended the experiments reported in *The Behavior of Organisms,* and although strong punishment evidently "reduced the reserve," the eventual rate of engaging in punished behavior was not much affected. I proposed to Yvonne that we simply stop punishing Julie, and she agreed. I did not even want to profit from past punishments, and we told Julie that we were never going to punish her again. For a month or two she tempted us, beginning to act in punishable ways and watching us closely, but it did not last. For one thing, having abandoned punishment, Yvonne and I looked for and found better ways of treating her, using positive rather than negative reinforcement. But would a strict disciplinarian now cause trouble?

ALTHOUGH OUR PIGEONS never had the chance to be heroes, they established themselves as excellent laboratory subjects. As I said to Fred, there were "lots of 'engineering' problems in controlling routine, but once you get 'em you've got 'em." My commitment for the year was to verbal behavior, but I did a certain amount of unauthorized experimenting. I had long been interested in memory. In 1936 I had written to Fred, "I have . . . done the following: condition as usual, *no* extinction, put away for 45 days, then extinguish. Result: just about the same curves you would get without waiting 45 days (i.e., no 'forgetting')." But rats did not live very long, and aging was a problem if the period of retention was much longer than 45 days. Pigeons were different; they lived for decades. I now found myself in possession of two dozen birds with a long history of a rather subtle visual discrimination on a variable-ratio schedule of reinforcement. They offered, I told Fred, "a swell chance for retention studies." If extinguished at once, they would peck the target thousands of times. How long would they "remember" to do so, and how many responses would remain in the extinction curve after a period of time?

I made a dovecote in our garden for the pigeons. As test equipment I would use the portable demonstration box that I had taken to Washington. (I kept the colored slides under lock and key to be absolutely sure that no one tested a pigeon in my absence. Pavlov had had to withdraw a claim that he had demonstrated the inheritance of acquired behavior when he discovered that an overzealous assistant had fudged his results.)

I had no way of knowing how fast the behavior would disappear, and I squandered pigeons by running my first test too soon—at the end of six months. I put four birds in individual cages and reduced them to approximately 80 percent of their normal weight. Then for several days I put each one in a harness in the darkened box, so that it became accustomed once again to being handled and to eating grain dropped into a small trough beneath the screen. For the crucial test I arranged the slide projector so that I could turn it on while watching the pigeon through a small opening.

When the target appeared on the screen for the first time in six months, each bird pecked it accurately and at once and then proceeded to give a large extinction curve. The original behavior was essentially intact. I tried again with four more pigeons at the end of the year (as I would be trying again with the remaining pigeons after two, four, and six years). All of them accurately struck the target, although the extinction curves were smaller.

With the same apparatus I tried a Lamarckian experiment. In the dovecote the pigeons mated and raised beautiful squabs. I thought it worthwhile to see whether they had inherited any tendency to strike a target to which their parents had responded vigorously for many months. I chose one of the most handsome pairs and reduced them to 80 percent of their normal weight. I put them in jackets and harnesses and conditioned them to eat food dropped into the tray in the demonstration apparatus. On the day of the test I watched carefully when the test pattern appeared. An exploratory peck or two might have been expected, and the target, as the most important feature of the pattern, might well have been singled out. I should then have had to run controls with pigeons whose parents had not had the earlier experience. But neither bird pecked the plate at all during a full hour.

I tried another experiment that year with crude equipment. Two xylophone bars, struck by magnetic plungers, could play sixteen four-note patterns, among them the opening phrase of Beethoven's Fifth Symphony—the Morse Code dit-dit-dit-dah for the letter V, which everyone then knew stood for Victory. Once a minute and in random order a pattern was played. A pigeon could peck at a disk at any time, but a response was reinforced with food only after V-for-Victory. The pigeon lived in the apparatus and got all its food by responding around the clock. I devised a crude method of counting pecks, but, alas, by the end of the year I saw no evidence that the pigeon preferred V-for-Victory.

THE FIRST FEW MONTHS of that Guggenheim year went to manual labor, as I built the dovecote, finished the baby-tender, and built apparatus, but after that I settled down to intellectual work. Rebounding from the chaos of Project Pigeon, I fell into a strict routine. For four or five hours each morning—Saturdays and Sundays included—I worked at my improvised desk on verbal behavior. In my application for a fellowship I had defined the field as "the actual behavior of the individual in emitting speech." It was a "relatively undeveloped subject," though several established fields were related. Comparative and historical linguistics "threw some light on the verbal behavior of the individual but were not themselves within the scope of the book." Classical grammar and syntax were not very useful but "traditional material in these fields . . . is reinterpreted." The elaborate vocabulary of classical rhetoric was "of little use though it deals with many of the present problems." Literary criticism was relevant and so were logic, semantics, and scientific method. "With respect to these fields it may be said that no one deals exclusively with the present subject but that no one can avoid it." I was proposing "an acceptable psychological treatment which is in accord with other facts of human behavior and at the same time useful for special purposes." It would be based upon "the systematic position developed in *The Behavior of Organisms*."

I did not expect to have too much trouble with everyday or literary behavior. The "latent speech" from the verbal summator, alliteration and assonance, word associations, guessing, wordplay, and a growing collection of slips of the tongue and other distortions fitted into my formulation well enough. Logic and the verbal behavior of scientists would be more difficult. Russell, Bridgman, Carnap, Reichenbach—I had discussed all of them with Cuthbert Daniel, Ivor Richards, Quine, and Feigl, but their positions had not really coalesced.

Bloomfield had been aware of the relevance of logical positivism. In 1930 he had written that linguistics had not yet reached the stage at which science can "win through to the understanding and control of human conduct," but in 1936 he noted that "the logicians of the Vienna Circle have independently reached the conclusion of *physicalism*: any scientifically meaningful statement reports a movement in space and time. This confirms the conclusion of A. P. Weiss and other American workers: The universe of science is a physical universe. This conclusion implies that statements about ideas are to be translated into statements about speech-forms." Weiss was an early and influential behaviorist, but John Horne Tooke had converted ideas into speech forms a century and a half before him.

I had collected a lot of experimental data on verbal behavior—on how people learn strings of nonsense syllables, or the nonsense names of nonsense figures, and I had my own results on verbal summation, alliteration, and guessing. They began to clutter up the manuscript without adding much by way of validation. They threw the book as a whole badly out of balance because I could not find experiments for the greater part of the analysis. I was still the empiricist at heart, but I did not think it would betray that position if my book were not a review of established facts. I was *interpreting* a complex field, using principles that had been verified under simpler, controlled conditions. Except for certain aspects of the solar system, most of astronomy is interpretation in this sense, its principles being derived from laboratory experiments. I decided to leave out all experimental data. (An interesting question then arose: what survived to reinforce writing or reading the book? Was not confirmation the be-all and end-all of science? It was a question concerning my own behavior, and I thought I had an answer: "February 2, 1945. What is motivational substitute for thing-confirmation? Pretty important in teaching method to graduate students. Resulting *order* instead of *confirmation*?" My reinforcers were the discovery of uniformities, the ordering of confusing data, the resolution of puzzlement.)

THOUGH I WORKED WELL and happily on verbal behavior, I was anxious to get back to the laboratory. My experiments on retention and Lamarckian inheritance scarcely touched the potential we had uncovered in our research in the flour mill. The pigeon should be more widely used as an experimental subject. It had excellent color vision, it lived for a long time, its level of hunger or thirst could be easily controlled, and because it had been domesticated for several thousand years, it was resistant to human diseases. I spent a good deal of time planning experiments to be done the following year.

One was on hunger. I had been puzzled by the fact that we get hungry at certain times of the day, more or less independently of any physiological condition. The strength of ingestive behavior seemed to be under stimulus control. I designed an experiment in which pigeons would peck a red key (under periodic reinforcement) on days when they were very hungry and a green key on days when they were only slightly hungry. After many days, or possibly weeks or months, I would see whether they slowed down on hungry days when the key changed to green or went faster on not-so-hungry days when the key was changed to red. The experiment was never done.

I also tackled theoretical issues, including the redefinition of some traditional terms. *Remembering* could mean either responding to a fragment of a discriminative stimulus or to the original stimulus after a period of time. *Believing* referred to the strength of one's behavior with respect to a less-than-adequate controlling stimulus. *Thinking* also sometimes suggested a behavior weaker than *knowing* but could also be taken to refer to all behavior, a point I developed in the manuscript on verbal behavior. I also considered terms like *desiring, avoiding,* and *getting* and *spending.*

Another theoretical note was on certain "by-products of operant conditioning." One learned to play a tune on the piano by, let us say, simply striking a succession of keys where only the right pattern was commended by a listener. In doing so one also "learned how the tune went." One could learn this when someone else played the tune, and if one could say right or wrong when someone else played, then one's own playing was presumably automatically reinforced by the same consequences.

WHEN I FIRST MET Robert Kantor at a meeting in Urbana, Illinois, I was impressed by his scholarship and intellectual vigor. He was a behaviorist, though of a very special kind. A footnote in *The Behavior of Organisms* reads: "The impossibility of defining a functional stimulus without reference to a functional response, and vice-versa, has been especially emphasized by Kantor." He spoke of "interbehavior," in which stimulus and response were reciprocally related. In 1940 Kantor had asked whether I would consider coming to Indiana, and now, with the war approaching an end, I was offered the chairmanship.

I went to Bloomington and talked with the President and the Dean and met the other members of the department. A former Chairman at Indiana had once stated a rule: To find the Department of Psychology in any university in the late thirties, simply look for the oldest building on the campus and go to the top floor. At Indiana the department was indeed on the top floor of an old building. It was called Science Hall, although all the other sciences had fled. I was assured that other space would be made available.

I should have to assume the chairmanship, but I could have an administrative assistant. The Dean asked me what salary I wanted, and I named what was at the time a rather high figure, $7500 a year with summers off. He agreed so readily that I was sorry I had not asked for more.

I stayed with the Kantors, in their pleasant house, about a mile out of town in a wooded area, with cows in a pasture beyond. They had built the house when they first came to Indiana many years before; they had not expected to stay, but they were still there. The house was full of books and newspapers, many in French or German, and on the walls were large oil paintings by their daughter on themes from the Old Testament. It was a small intellectual and cultural oasis in the university community, not untouched by sadness.

I met some of the younger members of the faculty and their husbands or wives at a performance of *Hedda Gabler*. The players read their parts on an improvised stage at the end of a living room. By the rule of the group, there had been only one rehearsal, but the performance was surprisingly effective. There were drinks and a supper afterward, and the friendliness was unlike anything I had known in Minnesota.

I took Yvonne to Bloomington. We looked for houses and found nothing we liked. When we were alone, Yvonne was often in tears. The professional advantages meant little to her, and she would be giving up a pleasant house and leaving old friends. The Kantors, with whom we stayed, were aware of her reluctance and gently assured her that she would enjoy life in Bloomington.

I discussed the offer with Mike. Indiana would give me a full professorship, of course, but Minnesota could do no better than an associate professorship with a salary of $5000. Mike pointed out that no one but Lashley had advanced so rapidly to the Associate Professor level in the department, but he could not promise me a professorship in the near future. When he reminded me of the advantages of living in the Twin Cities rather in Bloomington, I said, "You don't think much of Indiana, do you?" He said, "I think it is a dump," and it was then that I decided to go.

When I reported my decision to Robert Kantor, I suggested some rather drastic changes in the introductory course. The Dean had told me that students were taking psychology as an easy way to satisfy a science requirement and that other departments were proposing that it be dropped from the list of science courses. I suggested a sweeping reorganization and proposed that someone like Fred Keller be brought in to take charge. I had touched on a sore spot. Kantor himself and two of the other tenured members of the department taught independent sections of the introductory course. It was sacred territory, and a strong letter from Robert sent me back to Mike for advice. In the end I let the matter drop. I should be teaching only graduate seminars myself, and I did not like to meddle in something with which I should have little to do. Fred was not interested in coming, and I did not know of anyone else whom I could trust with the assignment.

I ACCEPTED INDIANA'S OFFER in part because I was feeling rather out of things. I liked the Twin Cities, but they were not only in the Midwest, they were on a spur track off the east-west routes. Under wartime restrictions I had attended no professional meetings and had lost contact with my old friends in the East. Psychologists were too busy with the war to pay any attention to rat experiments or a book like *The Behavior of Organisms*—only eighty copies of which had been sold during four war years—and no one seemed to be taking up the study of operant behavior.

In 1941 Hilgard was on sabbatical leave at Chicago and came

to Minnesota to give a colloquium. As a full professor at Stanford University, he was one of those contemporaries who had started up the academic ladder without delay and were now far ahead of me professionally. As we were walking across the campus, he said he was sorry that my research was not better known and that others were not using my methods. I gave him the answer Crozier had given me when I complained that psychologists were neglecting important issues: "Why should you care? It gives you all the more to do yourself." The answer was good enough at the time, but I was no longer satisfied with it. I wanted to be part of an expanding field.

Walter Hunter, busy with the war, had sent me "an impertinent note precipitated by thoughts of recent vigor. You have so far done some of the most intelligent and careful research in psychology. Don't let down, even in wartime. Keep up the record and plan to relax only when you are 60 or more! Psychology is developing serious lacunae at the top." I was not going to let down, but I should be moving ahead. My position at Indiana would carry more professional weight. I could build a new laboratory to take advantage of what we had learned on Project Pigeon. I could escape from that shrine to the memory of R. A. Fisher—our twenty-four-box behemoth—and study one rat or pigeon at a time. I could have my own graduate students.

I began to write notes as a prospective Department Chairman. I reviewed ways of reducing a teacher's load. "Remember that the student teaches himself. Provide every encouragement. Library with good facilities. Discussion groups. Journal club. Courses by examination only? (Reading lists and examinations.) Practical courses with results substituting for examinations. Group reading courses." I wrote a note about the support of research by administrations and foundations. Research was often not appreciated until long after it had been done. "How much more difficult must it be to determine the value of research which has not yet been performed?" One trouble was that "we have no adequate scientific knowledge of scientific thinking."

I watched Debbie carefully, of course, but although the baby-tender would have been an ideal place for experiments, I did very few. At one point I attached a thread to the canvas that served as a mattress and made a kymograph record of her activity. There was seldom a period of more than a few minutes when she was not moving about, even when asleep. I made special toys. When she was still quite young, she could grasp and pull a ring hanging from the ceiling of the baby-tender to sound a whistle, and grasp and turn a T-bar to spin a pinwheel of brightly colored pennants. Later I rigged a music box so that she could play a tune by pulling on a ring, note by note. She would lose interest in one of these toys but would immediately play with a different one that replaced it. There was some kind of fatigue that deserved further study.

One day when I had opened the window of the baby-tender and was talking to Debbie, I wrinkled my nose. To my amazement she immediately wrinkled hers. At the time I was not convinced that there was any innate tendency to imitate, but it seemed impossible that she could have *learned* that the muscles she moved produced an expression on her face like the one she had seen on mine.

Naturally I began to look more closely at early behavior and I wrote a note about

habits [that] can be established in the first year. Are the important cases specific acts to specific patterns of stimuli or second order effects, such as sustaining high ratios?

1. Emotional "reactions." (a) Love, etc. conditioned to person who feeds, bathes, clothes, etc. the child. Strong "adience" [E. B. Holt's word] to certain faces, places, etc. Best to avoid? E.g. by changing faces and places, voices, etc. Masks. (b) Fear, etc. of faces and places. Doctors, etc. Avoid—adapt out. Combine with (a)?

2. Operants. (a) crying for attention (b) other R's → attention (Attention = food, change of diapers, etc. play, etc.) (c) Achievements with toys, etc. (d) Achievements with body, turning over, etc. (e) Successful exploration (curiosity)—things that produce results.

3. Adaptation to (a) novel places (b) mild annoyances— discomfort, dressing, rough handling, noise, etc. Gradual build-up. Radio [as a source of noise]? (c) foods not liked.

4. (part of 1.?) Tolerance for frustration—get operant. Extinguish briefly. Reinforcing at fixed ratio going over to high ratio.

5. Eliminative habits. Routine = Retention. Release at S^D?

6. Discrimination. Pitch, color, etc.

7. Eating and sleeping habits. Follow schedule?

I soon had some information about elimination. In a standard crib, urination is first followed by a reinforcing warmth; it is only after several minutes that the diaper becomes cold and clammy. In the baby-tender urine around the edges of the diaper immediately chills the skin, and urination is apparently postponed under mild aversive control.

When Debbie was old enough to be put on the toilet, I found a mechanical solution to a related problem. When a parent stands by until a child urinates before taking it back to crib or playpen, the child may postpone urination because contact with the parent is thus prolonged. If, instead, the child is left alone on the toilet, it may be left much longer than necessary and taken up with a red ring around its bottom. I attached to the toilet seat a music box that began to play as soon as a few drops of moisture struck a strip of paper under the seat. (The tune was "The Blue Danube.") We planned to leave Debbie on the toilet until we heard the music and then come and take her off, but the music proved to be reinforcing; in other words, she quickly learned to urinate at once "to make the music box play."

When she was six months old, we heard that a famous pediatrician at the Mayo Clinic, Dr. C. A. Aldrich, had criticized the baby-tender, and I sent him some facts. When Debbie first came home from the hospital, we had set the temperature at 85° F. At six months we were keeping it between 76° and 78° during the day and between 78° and 80° at night. At a low temperature she was pale and held her arms close to her sides as if too cold, but that was no more than 4° below the temperature at which she was pink and moist and possibly too warm. The baby-tender kept her within an acceptable range much more effectively than wrapping her in shirts, nighties, sheets, and blankets.

The baby sleeps in a variety of postures and changes posture during sleep with ease. The danger of smothering or strangling is entirely eliminated. . . . During the first six months her exercise consisted largely of a violent snapping action executed by lifting the legs at the hips and then suddenly straightening so that the feet strike the mattress with great force. This has developed strong stomach muscles. . . . The baby is obviously strong. Our pediatrician has commented upon this when examining her.

Filtered and humidified air reduced the danger of airborne infection and kept the baby clean. "We usually bathe her twice a week. Once a week would suffice. Her ears and nose are pink and clean, and require very little care."

Because of the partial soundproofing, Deborah was not disturbed by doorbells, telephones, or other children, and "has maintained highly regular sleeping habits. If it is objected that a baby should learn to sleep in a noisy environment, noises can be gradually added at a rate which enables the baby to adjust to them easily."

A similar argument could be made with respect to infection.

Our baby is, of course, handled at feeding and playtime, so that she is exposed to infection during part of each day. . . . The neighborhood children come in to see the baby but see her through glass. The filter probably removes most of the water droplets in the air. She has not had a cold. [She did not have a cold for many years. Warnings that she would not be able to withstand extreme temperatures were answered when we were invited for Christmas dinner by our friends, Stacy and Margaret French. Debbie was then four months old, and we drove several miles in subzero weather and brought her home again with no ill effects.] If, however, a gradual exposure to infection is advisable, why not carry it out according to some schedule, rather than allowing the neighbors to sneeze on the baby?

The baby is not at all isolated socially. She is taken up for feeding, of course, and at six months spends about one and one-half hours per day in a play pen or teeter-chair. One whole side of the compartment is safety glass, through which we all talk and gesture to her during the day. She . . . greets us with a big smile when we look at her through the window. I cannot see that she is any more isolated than in the standard crib.

She has never shown any sign of not wanting to be put back and simply does not cry. For the first three months she would cry when wet, but would stop immediately upon changing. . . . The only times she has cried in the past four months (and this is literally true) have been when she had diphtheria shots (and then only for a minute or two), when I nipped the tip of her finger while trimming her nails, and once or twice when we have taken her bottle away to adjust the nipple!

I hope to be able to put a number of these apparatuses in homes under normal conditions and compare the development of the babies with others raised in the traditional fashion. If no harmful effects are noted, then I should like to see such devices supplied commercially. I am quite sure that many beneficial effects will follow, not only in easing the lot of the young mother but in building happy and healthy babies even in otherwise unfavorable circumstances. I do not doubt that babies can be properly raised without such a device, but if we can make it easier to do so without depending so much upon the intelligence and infinite patience of the mother, then it will be possible to make a real contribution to child health. . . . The problem is two-fold: to discover the optimal conditions for the child and to induce the mother to arrange those conditions. The latter is frequently the more difficult.

I must confess also to an ulterior motive. If, as many people have claimed, the first year is extraordinarily important in the determination of character and personality, then by all means let us control the conditions of that year as far as possible in order to discover the important variables. . . . It should be possible to conduct experiments in private homes but with a minimum of interference from the household routine and to begin to accumulate some significant data from the subsequent history of the children involved. This however is a project for the distant future.

Aldrich replied that he still had "some reservations when I come to think of the average person using it and misinterpreting the purpose. It might very easily become the means of not giving the very attention that you so carefully give and I have many fears that other people would misconstrue your motives just as I did at first."

Cuthbert Daniel had had some industrial connections and I wrote to him for advice about the commercial development of the baby-tender, but he and Janet had moved to Oak Ridge and were working on more important things. I turned again to General Mills, Inc., and two of their engineers came to see the baby-tender. They submitted a memorandum to the management clearly not intended for my eyes. "This particular thing could be a flop for many reasons, and again it could be a very successful money-maker." It would need full-time demonstration or subsidized part-time demonstration in baby specialty stores. The patent situation should be checked. "It shouldn't cost a great deal to rig up a better-looking set-up than the inventor of the device we saw had. His looked like a forbidding quick-freeze display case. He apparently put his device together on the basis of a few dollars out of pocket cost. It would seem that it shouldn't cost a great deal more to do the right kind of job, designing and all." Cost figures should be worked out on the basis of 10,000–20,000 units. "We also would like to point out that this whole thing—which involves babies at a very tender age—is a very ticklish subject for a lot of novices to play with. One underdone baby, one frozen youngster, or one smothered child or something of that sort charged to General Mills, could be a pretty bad thing from a publicity standpoint." One handicap would be "the possible psychological reaction against the device by the average mother who may not care to raise her baby in this way or may not trust the gadget. The thing, as I saw it, was a surprise and somewhat of a shock at first sight. It didn't seem to comport with my idea of the warm-hearted mother whom I envision as wanting to tote her youngster everywhere; also listen to his howls at night, but maybe there are enough long-haired people and cold-hearted scientists such as the professor who invented this gadget, to make a market for it."

I consulted two of the people I had worked with at General Mills, and they said it could probably not be patented. It was simply a small heated room, and there was nothing new about that. Special features that might be patented could be "designed around" by competitors. I abandoned my plans to promote a commercial model. If I were to do any research, I should have to apply for a grant.

Research was clearly in order. One baby proved little or nothing about a method or a device. I needed the help of prospective parents who would volunteer to follow a routine and keep records, in return for the loan of a baby-tender. I wanted to know about sleeping and feeding patterns, illness, weight, appearance of new behavior, and so on. In a proper experiment only half of those who volunteered would get baby-tenders; the other half would agree to follow the same routine in standard cribs. But I began to see a problem, which became all too clear when someone from the Census Bureau offered to alert me to the birth of twins, whose parents might be persuaded to raise one baby in a baby-tender and the other in a crib. Suppose a significant difference appeared in the health or well-being of one child? Suppose one twin was sleeping better, having fewer colds, growing faster, or simply being happier? How long could the parents be asked not to give the other twin the same treatment?

Mrs. Alfred Pillsbury, known to her friends as Gretchen, was the unchallenged social leader in Minneapolis. She loved the theatre and gave talks about current plays, which she saw on occasional forays to New York. She saw them from the front row, because she was almost blind. With published plays she needed help, and Yvonne began to read to her. She liked Yvonne's voice and style, and we began to see something of Alfred and Gretchen Pillsbury. They invited us to dinner on the evening of a false report of a European armistice. I sat next to a friend, Mrs. Pierce (Hilda) Butler, whom we had met through the Elliotts. She had a son and a son-in-law in the South Pacific, and we were, of course, greatly cheered by news of the armistice.

I began to talk about what young people would do when the war was over. What a shame, I said, that they would abandon their crusading spirit and come back only to fall into the old lockstep of American life—getting a job, marrying, renting an apartment, making a down payment on a car, having a child or two. Hilda asked me what I thought they should do instead, and I said they should experiment; they should explore new ways of living, as people had done in the communities of the nineteenth century. She asked for details.

As a child I had read stories about the Shakers and other perfectionist sects, and I had grown up only two or three miles from the spot where Joseph Smith had dictated the Book of Mormon. I had gone to college near the site of the Oneida Community. Yvonne had encouraged me to read Louis Bromfield's *The Strange Case of Miss Annie Sprague*, about the stigmatized daughter of the leader of a religious community. And I had recently read *Freedom's Ferment*, a history of the perfectionist movements in the United States by a colleague, Elizabeth Tyler. Most of the communities of the nineteenth century had come to an end but often, I thought, for irrelevant reasons. I told Hilda Butler that young people today might have better luck. They could build a culture that would come closer to satisfying human needs than the American way of life.

Hilda insisted that I write it all down. Young people needed help in the postwar world. When I said that I could scarcely advise them to do something that I myself was not doing, she said, "But you have found your place. They still have to find theirs. You must write it down." I protested that I was working hard to meet a June 1 deadline and had promised to write another paper during the summer. Hilda said I should simply tell the editors that I could not do the papers. But that was scarcely possible, and I gave the matter no further thought.

WHEN DEBBIE WAS perhaps nine months old, I was holding her in my lap. The room grew dark, and I turned on a table lamp beside the chair. She smiled brightly, and it occurred to me that I could use the light as a reinforcer. I turned it off and waited. When she lifted her left hand slightly, I quickly turned the light on and off. Almost immediately she lifted her hand again, and I turned the light on and off again. In a few moments she was lifting her arm in a wide arc "to turn on the light." She had behaved as our pigeon had behaved that day in the flour mill, and I was amazed. But why should I have been? If I had put a rattle in her hand and she had moved it slightly and heard the noise, I should not have been at all surprised if she had then shaken it vigorously. But there was a difference. The contingencies which reinforced rattle-shaking were built into the rattle. I had *contrived* my contingencies, and their effect was therefore surprisingly conspicuous.

BY THE SPRING OF 1945 the baby-tender had more than fulfilled our hopes. Debbie, a healthy nine-month-old baby, was enjoying a new mode of child care, and so were we. I thought the experiment should be reported, and I sent an article to the *Ladies' Home Journal*. After a rather long delay an editor wrote to say that it "has aroused such controversial interest among the *Journal* editors that we are still in the process of heated discussion." Would I send photographs of the baby in and out of the baby-tender and answer a few questions: Could we hear the baby from another part of the house? Must the laundering of the ten-yard sheet wait a *week* if it happened to be badly soiled? What would happen if the current went off? Was it really true that a daily bath wasn't needed?

My answers were evidently satisfactory, and the article was accepted. A photographer came, and for a good part of the day Debbie smiled at the camera, allowed Yvonne to change her diapers unnecessarily, and played with the gadgets in the baby-tender as the lights flashed. (A picture of Julie and Debbie playing together in our living room reminded me of Sir Thomas Lawrence's "Calmady Children" in the Metropolitan Museum, which I used to sit and look at when I was living in Greenwich Village.) Debbie failed as a model in only one assignment. The photographer had been told to get a picture of her asleep, and when he had taken all the pictures he wanted, he set up his camera and lights and left the room, planning to tiptoe in and shoot a picture after she had succumbed to the long day. But with a room full of photographic equipment, Debbie simply sat up and waited, and when we occasionally looked in on her, she smiled expectantly. The photographer finally gave up and took down his equipment, and he had scarcely left the room before Debbie was asleep.

THE PAPER WITH the June 1 deadline was on operationism. Boring had proposed that a special issue of the *Psychological Review* be devoted to the subject, and I was asked to contribute. I adapted part of the manuscript of *Verbal Behavior* and called it "The Operational Analysis of Psychological Terms." In it I raised the question of how a verbal community can teach a person to describe stimuli to which the community has no access. We respond to stimuli inside and outside the body in ways which are traceable to selective contingencies in the evolution of the species, but for the most part we emerge from what William James called a "blooming buzzing confusion" when our behavior with respect to stimuli is differentially reinforced. As children we learn to respond to colored objects, but we "know our colors" only when people ask us about color and reinforce our responses to color as distinct from the other properties of an object. We also come to "know" the private events which play a part in our internal economy only when people ask questions about them. But just as a colorblind person can teach a person with normal vision to name colors correctly only if other information about the colors is available, so other people can teach us to describe events taking place within our skin only if they have other (necessarily public) information. I listed four kinds of public information that could be used, none of which guaranteed an exact knowledge of private events.

Consciousness or awareness, generated by the differential reinforcement supplied by a verbal environment, was a social product. It was not a matter of observing the nervous system, as Lashley and Boring had tried to show. The events observed through introspection were physiological (all behavior was physiological), but they were stimuli and responses, not nerve impulses or states of the nervous system. Adrian had written, "Perhaps some drastic revision of our system of knowledge will explain how a pattern of nervous impulses can cause a thought, or show that the two events are really the same thing looked at from a different point of view," but such a double-aspect theory was fudging. The *evidence* that a person was "having thoughts" was behavioral: there was nothing psychic or mental to be explained.

The papers were circulated to the contributors, so that their comments could be published in the same issue. I criticized those who defined mental states operationally while continuing to believe that the states existed. The operationism of Boring and Stevens was "an attempt to acknowledge some of the more powerful claims of behaviorism (which could no longer be denied) but at the same time to preserve the old explanatory fictions." It was a case of "Galileo's *E pur si muove* in reverse."

There was another surprising difference. If the operationists (or logical positivists) could study only things observed by two or more people, introspection was ruled out. Ironically, however, radical behaviorists could deal with descriptions of private events, with the provision that the descriptions were inaccurate and perhaps never to be trusted, and that the events described were physical. I made the point with a bad pun. Where Boring's operationism limited him to an account of my external behavior, I was still interested in what might be called Boring-from-within.

I HAD NOT TAKEN Hilda Butler's suggestion seriously and had finished my paper by June 1, but the next day I began to write a book about an experimental community. I revealed still another source of my interest in a designed life when I called the community Walden Two.

I first read parts of Thoreau's *Walden* at Hamilton College and found them dull, but when I discovered Walden Pond and began to go swimming there, I took another look. I read and reread the copy with which I absolved my guilt in owning a car, and in a secondhand bookstore I found a leatherbound set of Thoreau's works. I also bought Odell Shepard's collection of Thoreau's notes and a copy of his translation of the *Transmigration of the Seven Brahmins*. I began to make an annual pilgrimage to the pond late in the fall, picking up after the summer visitors near the site of Thoreau's hut.

I adopted a standard utopian strategy: a group of people would visit a community and hear it described and defended by a member. There would be a chapter on labor: following Thoreau, the community would reduce consumption by reducing needs; and if everyone worked (women as well as men, the young and aged according to their abilities), only four hours a day would be needed. There would be chapters on food—growing, storing, cooking, and serving in common dining rooms—and on supplies and services, including medicine and dentistry. There would be chapters on child care, education, ethical training, and the (minimal) family. There would be scattered glimpses of diversions—music, theatre, art, sports—and a daily life rather in the style of a nineteenth-century English country house without the servant problem. A chapter or two would go to religion and politics, or their absence.

It was a reasonable plan if I were simply to describe an imagined community, but a few characters were needed, and they soon asserted themselves. I did not know until I had finished the book that I was both Burris and Frazier. Burris, the narrator, is a pedestrian college teacher, particularly unhappy with his lot because he has just returned from an exciting wartime experience. (I had written, but not submitted for publication, a sketch called "Cincinnatus 1946" in which a young biologist meets his first class after the war in a similar mood.) Frazier, the founder of Walden Two, is a self-proclaimed genius who has deserted academic psychology for behavioral engineering, the new discipline upon which the community is based. Some of his mannerisms are Henderson's and some are Crozier's. (Was "Frazier" a blend of "Fred" and "Crozier"?) Castle, a philosopher who voices objections to the community and its principles (which

Frazier answers, perhaps too easily), is a not very accurate portrait of Alburey Castell, the friend whom I had joined in retreat at the abbey in Collegeville. The community would be seen through the eyes of two young couples, for one of whom it meant little, for the other almost everything.

I wrote with great speed. I once calculated that my thesis cost me two minutes for every word, and I could say the same for *The Behavior of Organisms*. I had records showing a similar figure for the manuscript-in-progress on verbal behavior. But I wrote my utopia in seven weeks. I would dash off a fair version of a short chapter in a single morning. I wrote directly on the typewriter, as I had not done since my college days, and I revised sparingly. Except for a bout of dramaturgy during my junior year at Hamilton, when I wrote a three-act play in one morning, I had never experienced anything like it. There are a number of possible reasons.

I did not need a great deal of imagination. Much of the life in *Walden Two* was my own at the time. Frazier played the Schumann Piano Quintet about as well as I did, and his relations to the other players were mine to my talented young friends. I had seen the solemn procession at the children's birthday party on Julie's third birthday in the University Nursery School. The baby-tenders were, of course, copies of Debbie's. Fergus, who conducted the chorus from the B Minor Mass, was Donald Ferguson of the University Music Department, who had just put on the whole Mass in the University auditorium. The architects were Winton Close and Lisl Scheu, two young friends who had appraised the house we almost bought in St. Paul and with whom we had discussed building a house before we found one we liked. Mrs. Olsen was my Aunt Alt.

The issues Frazier discusses with Castle I had discussed with a group of philosophers and literary critics, among whom, in addition to Castell, were Joseph Warren Beach, a professor of English, who usually arranged the meetings, Herbert Feigl, Donald Oliver, J. W. Miller (a philosopher who spent one year at Minnesota), and Robert Penn Warren, the novelist and poet. In discussing the implications of a science and technology of behavior with these friends, I took a fairly extreme position—one that I should not always have wanted to defend publicly—but in the book, I could go much further. I could enjoy poetic license. I let Frazier say things that I myself was not yet ready to say to anyone. During the winter, for example, I had written a note:

> *The alternative to popular vote:*
> Government by specialists, to include (1) Accurate and adequate ascertaining of "will" of people—i.e. results of governmental measures. (2) Planning (which can't be done by "majority") so the will can be carried out. (3) [Counter-] Control. Eventually through—
> *Constitutional guarantees of rights and freedoms.*
> Occasional plebiscites on satisfaction with management.
> Psychological Principles (1) People really don't want to vote. Witness enormous efforts to "get it out." (2) [not completed]

This was pretty much Frazier's line, but it was not a popular one, and I should not have published it at the time over my own name. (Eventually I became a devout Frazierian.)

I may also have written easily and rapidly because my verbal behavior was generously reinforced. I read pages to Yvonne as I finished them, and once a week Feigl and some of the younger psychologists came over to hear the latest episodes. It must also be relevant that I wrote some parts with an emotional intensity that I have never experienced at any other time. There is a scene in which Burris and Frazier discuss the disparity between the chaos and turmoil in Frazier as a person and the order and serenity of the community he has founded. I composed it as I walked the streets near our house, and I came back and typed it out in white heat. "Can't you see?" Frazier says to Burris,

> *I'm—not—a—product—of—Walden—Two!* . . . Isn't it enough that I've made other men likable and happy and productive? Why expect me to resemble them? Must I possess the virtues which I've proved to be best suited to a well-ordered society? Must I exhibit the interests and skills and untrammeled spirit which I've learned how to engender in others? Must I wear them all like a damned manikin? After all, emulation isn't the only principle in education—all the saints to the contrary. Must the doctor share the health of his patient? Must the ichthyologist swim like a fish? Must the maker of firecrackers pop?

And I am always deeply touched by the scene in which Steve and Mary ask Burris whether they have the facts right about Walden Two. If they joined, could they get married and move into the community immediately? Would their children just naturally go to the schools they had seen—and with the other children they had seen? Would they be free to enjoy everything in the community like everyone else? There should be (and I almost believe there could be) a world in which the answers are yes.

I decided to call the book *The Sun Is But a Morning Star*, from the last paragraph of Thoreau's *Walden*, which I eventually added to the text: "I do not say that John or Jonathan will realize all this; but such is the character of that morrow which mere lapse of time can never make to dawn. The light which puts out our eyes is darkness to us. Only that day dawns to which we are awake. There is more day to dawn. The sun is but a morning star."

I was never more active than during that Guggenheim year. I built and used the baby-tender and followed Debbie's development day by day. I conducted two or three interesting experiments. I nearly finished a manuscript on verbal behavior and extracted from it for immediate publication the paper on operationism. To cap it all, I wrote the book that would be published as *Walden Two*. It was a productive year but an exhausting one, and perhaps it is not surprising that as Burris looks forward to his new life in the community he dreams of "time to write! Time to think would be nearer the truth. Time to evaluate. Time to plan. But first—and who knows for how long—I would have time to rest."

But I was moving into a far from restful world.

IN BLOOMINGTON, we had succeeded in renting a rather interesting furnished house for at least a year. We could not take much of our furniture with us, and misjudging our affluence, we sold the rest rather than store it for later use in a house of our own. (We did not have our possessions evaluated, and unaware of what the war had done to prices, we sold many things too cheaply.) A neighbor would keep our piano until we sent for it.

Yvonne was beginning to feel better about the move. She had never found life in Minnesota very exciting. As a minor gain, she could make a long-desired change. Her novelist grandfather had chosen her name and those of her two sisters, Charmian and Norma, whom everyone but their mother soon called Boo and Tick. Yvonne had remained Yvonne, and it was especially inappropriate for a down-to-earth surname like Skinner. When we reached Indiana and new friends, she would be Eve.

For Debbie continuity was the thing, and to avoid breaking her experience in the baby-tender during the move, I made a portable model. It had padded canvas walls and clear plastic hinged windows and could be collapsed and carried like a large suitcase. Yvonne took it with her on the train to Chicago, where her mother was living after her father's death, and where Yvonne and the children would stay while I finished packing. There was much to be done, and I was barely ready for the movers when they arrived.

Number 824 Sheridan Road, Bloomington, had been built for a former Dean of Music by Ernest Flagg, a New York architect who had developed an inexpensive way of making fieldstone walls. The house was a hollow square with a breezeless patio in the center. Sloping slate roofs were vaguely Norman-French. A large living room with open-trussed ceilings had a tall copper fireplace at one end. All the floors were tiled, and a dropped dish not only broke but shattered. Debbie was just learning to walk; fortunately she was not easily broken.

Minnesota was famous for its agriculture, and it was a special kind of agriculture that depended for its very existence on intensive research at the University. The dependency, and with it a bit of deference, rubbed off on the rest of the faculty. Bloomington, on the contrary, was a small town in a poor part of the state, and an expanding University intruded upon the lives of its citizens. Many of them believed that the faculty held cocktail parties which were little short of drunken orgies, and some of its members even belonged to the NAACP and were trying to desegregate the movie theatre, where blacks were allowed only in the balcony.

Members of the faculty were thrown upon each other for their social life. We made new friends with surprising speed, and they entertained frequently and lavishly. We found ourselves going to two or three cocktail parties (but not orgies) every weekend, as well as a monthly dance at which no one bothered to fill out a card. In November I wrote to Mike that we were giving a cocktail party with which we were returning eighteen invitations.

Among our new friends were Roland and Francis Davis. Roland was a member of my department. In the Medical School I found T. J. B. Steir, whom I had known in Crozier's laboratory at Harvard. He and his wife, Evelyn, whom we called Pete, had restored an elegant old house on a large tract of land outside the city. Joseph Low was teaching in the Art Department, and his wife, Ruth, was Clark Hull's daughter.

When Robert Yerkes learned that I was going to Indiana, he wrote to say that he hoped I would "promptly make the acquaintance of Professor Kinsey," whose work was being supported by a committee of the National Research Council, of which Yerkes was a member. Everyone seemed uneasy about the project. Kinsey himself was rather defensive. In a colloquium in the Department of Psychology he explained how he had come to study sex. He was a biologist who had specialized in the gall wasp or, more particularly, in the variability displayed by gall wasps. When he was asked to participate in a new course on marriage for Indiana students, he had discovered to his astonishment that there was more variability in sexual behavior than in gall wasps and had, therefore, changed to this more promising field. He never smiled, let alone laughed, when discussing sex, and I could never decide whether he was humorless or simply making sure that no one could suspect him of ribaldry.

Eve and I found a bit of relevant evidence when we were invited to one of his musical evenings. He had a large collection of records and had chosen several to compose a program. Standing beside his floor model of a 78-rpm Victrola, as Caruso had done in the advertisements, he told us that thanks to the magic of the phonograph we were to be privileged to hear in a single evening the Vienna State Symphony Orchestra playing in Vienna and the Philadelphia Orchestra playing in Philadelphia. (The other wives, aficionadas, had brought family sewing or socks to darn as they listened, but Eve, who hated to listen to music at any time, had nothing else to do.) Most of our new friends had given their sexual histories to Kinsey, but we were not asked to contribute ours because his academic sample was already large.

Though Bloomington, like Minneapolis, was out of the main east-west route, and was a much smaller city, it was not without its culture. Concerts were frequently held in a large auditorium on the campus. Horowitz played there and puzzled his audience by pounding out "Stars and Stripes Forever" as an encore (was he condescending to provincial tastes?). Melchior missed a performance when he ran into bad flying weather out of Chicago and accepted a ride from another stranded traveler who had rented a car, only to find himself several hours later, just in time for his concert, in Bloomington, Illinois. Marshall Stearns, a member of the English Department, had a celebrated collection of early jazz records, and Hoagy Carmichael, or so it was said, had composed "Stardust" in a drugstore just across the street from the Administration Building.

The chairman of the Art Department was Henry Hope, and an artist in residence was Robert Laurent, the sculptor, whose wife, Mimi, lent me a French novel or two. We met a few celebrities at Henry and Sally Hope's, among them Frank Lloyd Wright, dressed in outmoded formal attire with a gold chain across his waistcoat, as if Frank Lloyd Wright had never lived. There was no theatre, but we joined the play-reading group and saw many plays, often surprisingly good. Eve, as she was now to be called, and I soon began to take part, and our stage presence slowly improved.

I MOVED INTO the Chairman's office and hung up my autographed portrait of Pavlov and a small oil painting I had made of the foghorn building on Monhegan. For the first time I had a secretary, and I found that I was rather embarrassed when dictating to her or asking her to perform standard services. A few departmental problems had to be solved. A member of the staff, returning from the war, found himself paid slightly less than he thought he had been promised, and I went into action. Mike Elliott had always seemed too much on the side of the administration, and I resolved to be on the side of my men. I protested strongly and the salary was readjusted.

The faculty was in the process of changing the curriculum. (It was my first brush with that ancient mode of educational reform:

when students are not learning much, make them take different courses. You must not ask how well any course is taught, because a teacher's classroom is his castle.) The Chairman of the Astronomy Department was a strong man on the faculty, and with the proposed curriculum all freshmen would take astronomy. Psychology would lose many students, and the department would be weakened.

My response was rather utopian. In a memorandum to the faculty I argued that we had not analyzed the present situation, had no guarantee that the proposed changes would have the effects predicted, and had made no provision for evaluating the results. I proposed, as an alternative, that we try to measure the intellectual and cultural behavior of the students. What magazines and books were to be found in fraternity and sorority houses? How many students attended concerts, lectures, exhibitions, discussions of current affairs? What were the topics of conversation in the Union Cafeteria? Records should be kept for a year or two, and an index of intellectual and cultural interests worked out. Behavioral scientists would then be called in to raise the index. As I might have expected, nothing was done—nor, in the end, were any substantial changes made in the curriculum.

I found that I was not quite through with Minnesota. The Comptroller of the University was named Middlebrook. He was a powerful figure, and under the name of Mittelbach I had promoted him to President in *The Sun Is But a Morning Star*. Now he was writing about my sabbatical leave, to which the University had made a small contribution. "The rules," he said, "provide that the member of the staff will continue service with the University after the furlough for at least one year. Will you kindly advise me what plan for return of the sabbatical furlough payment would be most acceptable." Our new affluence had already vanished, and I consulted a former member of the Minnesota faculty now at Indiana, Oliver Fields. He said that Middlebrook was always appealing to "rules" which were never public knowledge until Middlebrook needed them. I did not answer the letter and heard nothing more.

MY ARTICLE APPEARED in the October issue of the *Ladies' Home Journal* under the editor's title "Baby in a Box," with a pink border around a two-page spread, showing Debbie in the wrong box, the portable model. There were half a dozen other pictures and a subtitle: "The machine age comes to the nursery!"

The editors, not quite sure of themselves, had called in an Associate in Psychiatry at Johns Hopkins University, who contributed a meager supporting note. "Naturally, it should be tried out first, scientifically, before it is adopted by the general public; even a project with ten babies under scientific observation would tell a good deal; but I think there is a possible beginning here for interesting experiment [sic] in baby care." Dr. Stoesser, an allergist who had treated Julie, was even more cautious:

> I am interested in pediatric allergy cases, and the Skinner family has much allergy. Therefore, I volunteered to follow their new baby as closely as possible. It was during my visits to their home to watch and prescribe for the baby, that I observed the functioning of the baby compartment which Professor Skinner had designed and built. I could see nothing wrong with it, although I did not spend much time inspecting it. It certainly did not do the baby any physical harm.

Nor would Dr. Stoesser's grudging testimonial do him any harm professionally.

Newspapers and the radio picked up the story, and Pathé News was not far behind. In the film, Eve and I were shown sitting on opposite sides of the great copper fireplace in our Norman-French home. I was holding Debbie on my lap and Eve was playing chess with Julie on a low coffee table. I put Debbie on the floor and, predictably, she crawled to the chessboard and pulled it off the table. Eve picked her up, left the room, and was shown putting her in the baby-tender and pulling down the shade. Only when I saw the film in a local theatre did I realize that we were giving the impression that we used a baby-tender to keep Debbie out of the way as a trouble-maker. The sequence ended, however, with Julie in pajamas pulling up the shade and saying good morning to a smiling Debbie.

Hundreds of pregnant women or their husbands wrote to ask me how to build a baby-tender, and I sent mimeographed instructions. (In due time I got photographs and clippings from scores of local newspapers showing the results.) A few readers misunderstood the point. An anonymous writer from Pasadena, California, sent me a copy of his letter addressed to "District Attorney, Bloomington, Indiana."

> *This professor who thinks he can rear his little child by depriving her of social life, sun and fresh air. Can't you people of the law do something about this? These crack-pot scientists. They say they will probably keep her caged in this box until she is three. If they want to rear her to be so healthy, come down to California. Little children are happy here, out in the sunshine, playing in yards with their dogs and other children and enjoying the flare for living. If I lived in the same town as these people I would be tempted to tell them what I thought of them. Caging this baby up like an animal just to relieve the Mother of a little more work.*

Another letter began, "Your Artical in Better Homes and Gardens was awful. . . . If you don't care what happens to your baby, *why have one?* If you have to go out so much why did you 'dicide to have a baby?' "

As people began to hear of the baby-tender by word of mouth, misunderstanding spread. Details of Debbie's actual life and the care we gave her were lost in the retelling. The editors of the *Ladies' Home Journal* had put the word "box" in my title, and it caused trouble. As Mike Elliott wrote, "The only time that human beings are subject to boxes is when they are dead." It was inevitable that the baby-tender would be confused with the apparatus I had used in the study of operant conditioning—the device Clark Hull and his students had named the "Skinner Box"—and it was natural to suppose that we were experimenting on our daughter as if she were a rat or pigeon.

I HAD TROUBLE in setting up a new laboratory. Relays and timing devices were hard to get because of the war. Universities were offered masses of surplus equipment, some of it captured in Europe, but little was useful. I had brought some of my old apparatus from Minnesota, but it had been designed for rats, not pigeons. I began to use single pieces rather than sets of four (let alone twenty-four!), and ran pigeons in tandem if I wanted more than one case.

We took a giant step forward in the design of operant equipment when Norman Guttman turned up as a graduate student. In his military training he had discovered the snap lead—with which one put together various electric circuits on instructional breadboards. With them we could quickly assemble and reassemble complex contingencies of reinforcement.

I had brought my Project Pigeon birds with me in order to test them for retention after longer periods of time, and they were soon joined by a local volunteer. I was in my office one day talking on the telephone when a pigeon came in the window and landed on my desk. I was by then an experienced pigeon trapper, and I slipped my open fingers over its feet and pinned them to the desk, the pigeon flapping its wings as I finished my call. I kept it in isolation for a few days and then used it in an experiment in which it learned to play a single tune on a toy piano.

I OFFERED a small graduate seminar in the analysis of behavior. It was a laboratory course, and in a letter to Mike, I boasted that I was using no text and no reading list. My students were not to memorize anything: they were to learn to control behavior. It was the kind of course I had described the year before, "with results substituting for examinations." I had no time to build good equipment, especially with wartime shortages, but my students carried on well enough without it. They reinforced behavior by dispensing food by hand, but only after rapping with a coin on the side of the pan in which the pigeon's cage rested. The event which is immediately contingent upon behavior in the usual experiment is the sound of the dispenser, and the rap took its place.

My introductory teaching at Minnesota had been richly rewarding. I did not like what was being done at Indiana, but I wanted a peaceful department. I envied Fred his freedom, for he and Nat Schoenfeld were making revolutionary changes at Columbia. In October 1945, he had written about a book that they were planning to write.

I've had it in mind for quite a while, as you know—a Skinner for Beginners. It became more and more clear that something had to be done about a text for the General course; Schoenfeld alone of those hereabouts really understood the viewpoint and was cooperative and critical enough to help me undertake the job; and finally it came to a point where something had to be started. Last Summer I tossed the texts out of the window and started out on my own, with very encouraging results. Beginners get the point if you don't let 'em read the junk that is now marketed as psychology.

The next development is related to the book. I am trying to put over a new deal in General here beginning next year. Essentially, this is it: a one-year, 8-point course, two lectures weekly, and four hours of lab. . . . Experiments will parallel text and lectures and they will be few in number, say 8–10 major experiments. Rats will be our subjects, the slant being "biological," and 15 or 20 all-purpose Skinner boxes will constitute our first standardized equipment. Every basic principle in the course will be demonstrated by actual experiment. No apology, incidentally, will be made for using rats as subjects; human experiments can come into the next course. The boys will never take an "aptitude test," calculate a threshold, map a touch spot or a color zone, etc., etc., but they will get their general principles. Just to show you how crazy I am, I'll tell you what I have in mind beyond the General. At present, a single "experimental" course, with the usual offerings in Social, Abnormal, et al, for which the General is not necessarily prerequisite. Later, and it may be much later, an experimental course in Discrimination, another in Conditioning, and another in Motivation, each ultimately with its own laboratory space and assistants. I'm going cautiously and avoiding toe-treading at present, but I'm going ultimately to force a good course in Social (or Verbal Behavior) and Abnormal; and I may even see the Graduate Offerings compelled to become Graduate in content as well as name. And so forth and so on. I'm half-cracked, but much happier that way, and I find the younger men extremely sympathetic. There's a remark that has passed around recently to the effect that Keller and Schoenfeld are the only men on the staff who have anything to say that they believe in; and I already have more candidates who want to work with me than I can handle. And these men are our best ones.

There was a touch of envy in my reply: "The new course sounds wonderful. I wish I had the same freedom and backing here, but I don't feel like jamming what looks like my own stuff down the throat of this Department. I don't suppose I can ever do it, as you are working things out there." Later Fred wrote: "Rumor hath it that you are bending over backwards in your attempt to give freedom of action and belief to your staff. Everyone approves, and I think you are right, but I suppose it will retard the day when you will have the 'model' department. We're really pretty lucky here, and I think that working up from the bottom may be more possible for us in the long run than trying to produce ideas from the top."

In October I received a handwritten letter on blue paper with "Display Associates" in red-and-black letters across the top. At the bottom were the names of the associates, identified as "fabricators" or as involved in "design and store planning" and "window and interior backgrounds." The author, J. J. Weste, said that he and his wife, together with three friends and their wives, were interested in the baby-tender. His wife had called me "the greatest thing for women since Amelia Bloomer." Were plans and specifications available? If I would permit, they would like to build a few to sell on a special-order basis. He suggested the name "Heir Conditioner."

I replied immediately, telling him about the doubtful patent situation, but pointing to the presumed advantage of an early appearance on the market with a registered trademark and a chance to keep ahead of competitors by making early improvements. I liked the name Heir Conditioner and hoped a commercial model would be produced for a number of reasons—I believed the baby-tender was good for mother and child, I could use more of them for experimental work, and I was not unwilling to make some money. What sort of organization had he, and what arrangements would he suggest? Weste replied that he was glad I liked the name and wondered why, as a conditioned-reflex man, I had not thought of it. It would be, he hoped, a household word before long. He and his associates would be glad to form a company to produce the Heir Conditioner and would, in return for any rights I had and for help in the design of a good model, give me ten models for research and pay a royalty on those they sold. They would expect help in publicizing the device but only as far as professional ethics permitted. They had a shop for the manufacture of displays and display fixtures, with all the power tools and spraying equipment needed to produce Heir Conditioners in lots of fifty at a time. They would distribute them by direct mail, a simple model costing no more than $100, with a possible deluxe model available at $200. Materials were still in short supply because of the war, but Weste thought he could get everything he needed. Could he come to Bloomington and talk things over?

Eve had an uncle living in Cleveland, and I wrote to ask him if he knew anything about Display Associates. He reported that they were not in any local directory, but perhaps they were new to the city. Weste came to Bloomington, and I liked him and agreed to put things in his hands. From that point on I referred those who wrote to me asking for information about the baby-tender to him.

When I first met Henry and Sally Hope, Sally was pregnant. I told them about the baby-tender and they said they wanted to try one. Early in November their baby was born, and we lent them our portable model. Sally had a wealthy relative living in Indianapolis who was intrigued by the device and thought that he and a friend might invest in it. I arranged for them to meet Weste.

Weste sent news of progress. Supplies were a problem, but it could be solved. He would know about the price after the first two or three had been completed. He thought the company would gross $100,000 during 1946, and after that they would be manufacturing about 3000 Heir Conditioners every year. He was closing out his interest in Display Associates and would be giving full time to the project.

I did not go to Cleveland to see the plant because rail communications were inconvenient, and a trip would have taken at least two days away from my busy first year as Chairman. I continued to forward inquiries, including one from Edward L. Thorndike, who wanted an Heir Conditioner for his grandchild, and one from the British Committee on Domestic Engineering.

Weste worked out an interim arrangement with the people in Indianapolis. Ten samples were to be finished, and if they were successful, further capital would be available. The *Ladies' Home Journal* asked me to send a letter reporting the results of my article, and when it was published, another flood of inquiries came in. I continued to forward letters to Weste, but I began to hear that they were not being answered. One customer in Chicago told me that five letters had gone unanswered. In each case I said I could not explain Weste's delay and assured the writer that Heir Conditioners were being manufactured as rapidly as supplies permitted.

THE REACTION-TIME EXPERIMENT has had an important place, and a long history, in psychology. In a simple arrangement, a subject is instructed to release a telegraph key as quickly as possible upon hearing a signal. The time taken (measured in thousandths of a second) depends upon many things. The subject takes longer, for example, if a choice must be made between two signals. Hence it has been argued that reaction times may be significant properties of thought processes —an impressive notion. J. McKeen Cattell, an early worker in the field, once said that psychology must be a science "because it measures things in thousandths of a second." I decided to see how a pigeon could be "instructed" to respond as quickly as possible, or, alternatively, how human subjects actually come to follow such instructions appropriately.

I fed a hungry pigeon when it pecked a disk shortly after a noise was made, giving it plenty of time to respond, as in the discrimination experiment. The period during which a response was reinforced was then gradually shortened. Slow responding was extinguished, and the pigeon began to respond more and more quickly. A ready signal was added by illuminating the disk from one to three seconds before the noise occurred. The pigeon soon began to hold itself "at the ready," standing with its beak very close to the disk. It also began to peck hard and therefore rapidly. The final reaction time was almost certainly shorter than that of a human subject tapping or releasing a telegraph key in response to a sound, but my rather crude timer was strained beyond its limits. (A shorter reaction time is to be expected for anatomical reasons, since the distance from the pigeon's ear to its neck muscles—no doubt via the brain—is much shorter than that between the human ear and the forearm, and conduction time must enter into the final figure.)

In another set of temporal contingencies only slow responses were reinforced. I gradually extended the length of the required delay, and the pigeon began to mark time, often by pacing away from the key.

MY EXPERIMENTS WITH RATS and pigeons were often assigned to a field called "learning." I myself used the term only in casual discourse, because it covered too much territory to have any scientific value. My rats first "learned to press a lever." (They did so in a single trial, and there was no learning curve because the change was too quick to follow.) In extinction they "learned not to press the lever" (and did so more slowly, the course of the change being shown in those wavelike extinction curves). When the dispenser was empty, they "learned not to respond even though the dispenser sounded." In forming a discrimination they "learned to respond to one stimulus and not to another" (and the process, much like extinction, was easy to follow). When I reversed the contingencies, they "learned to respond the other way." They "learned to press the lever hard or to hold it down" (and the speed of learning depended in part upon the promptness with which I changed the selective contingencies).

I had itemized these kinds of "learning" in a passage omitted from *The Behavior of Organisms*, in which I concluded that "no two of these processes have the same properties, nor should we expect them to have. The idea of a single learning curve is absurd." I could have added that Pliny had "learned to perform a complex sequence of responses" (at a rate which, again, depended upon the skill and speed with which I changed the contingencies). And now, under special temporal contingencies, a pigeon learned to peck either as quickly as possible or after a delay usually achieved by "marking time." Again, how quickly they learned to do so depended upon my skill in changing the contingencies.

Not only was an organism said to learn all these things, it was said to *know* them, and it is often said even today that "what the rat learns is that pressing a lever brings food." The contingencies are thus moved into the rat in the form of "knowledge," rather than left in the environment in the form of facts. "Knowledge" was the subject of my *Sketch for an Epistemology*, but I was moving from theory to an empirical analysis. The experimental evidence for "the possession of knowledge" seemed to dictate only one course: the concept should be abandoned.

In traditional terms, both "learning" and "knowing" neglected "motivation." The maintenance rather than the acquisition of behavior could perhaps be said to involve "an inclination to make use of what was known," but the facts themselves could be dealt with in a simpler way.

I WAS SOON TACKLING still another kind of learning and knowing. When Tolman wrote to me about *The Behavior of Organisms,* he said:

> *I do think, as I have said so many times before, that what you ought to do next is to put in two levers and see what relationships the functions obtained from such a discrimination set-up will bear to your purified functions where you have only one lever. No doubt you are right that the "behavior-ratio" is a clumsy thing for getting the fundamental laws, but it is a thing that has finally to be predicted and someone must show the relation between it and your fundamental analysis.* ·

He was interested because he was continuing to use a T-maze in which the important thing was a choice between two paths: did a rat turn right or left?

When Heron and I completed our twenty-four-box behemoth, I wrote to Tolman, more or less whimsically, "You should be pleased to know, I hope, that we are just putting into operation twenty-four new apparatuses containing *two* levers each. At present one lever is *hors de combat* but we may get around to some 'choice' problems yet." We never got around to choice, but it was something that needed to be studied, and I now began with a simple experiment.

A hungry pigeon could strike either of two keys, and pecking was reinforced once a minute. I reported the results in a paper called "Are Theories of Learning Necessary?" in the following way:

> By occasionally reinforcing a response on one key or the other without favoring either key, we obtain equal rates of responding on the two keys. The behavior approaches a simple alternation from one key

to the other. This follows the rule that tendencies to respond eventually correspond to the probabilities of reinforcement. [This is now called the "matching law" but I turned immediately to the momentary contingencies.] Given a system in which one key or the other is occasionally connected with the magazine by an external clock, then if the right key has just been struck, the probability of reinforcement *via* the left key is higher than that *via* the right since a greater interval of time has elapsed during which the clock may have closed the circuit to the left key. But the bird's behavior does not correspond to this probability merely out of respect for mathematics. The specific result of such a contingency of reinforcement is that changing-to-the-other-key-and-striking is more often reinforced than striking-the-same-key-a-second-time. We are no longer dealing with just two responses. In order to analyze "choice" we must consider a single final response, striking, without respect to the position . . . of the key, and in addition the responses of changing from one key . . . to the other.

When reinforcement was made contingent on responses to the left key only, responding to the right declined and responding to the left accelerated. The combined rate remained the same, appropriate to one reinforcement per minute. Eventually all responses were made to the left key. When the contingencies were then reversed and responses only to the right key reinforced, nearly an hour elapsed before the change to the other key was complete. The combined rate again remained constant as the preference changed.

The preference was remarkably stable. During a change from one key to the other, I stopped reinforcing altogether when the pigeon was responding twice as often to the right key as to the left. As responses to both keys underwent extinction, the pigeon continued to respond twice as often to the right, even when responding had dropped to a mere trickle.

THE BABY-TENDER was safer than a crib because there was no danger of smothering, nor could a lively baby fall out, but Debbie was putting on weight and soon revealed a defect in my construction when she began to treat the tightly stretched canvas as a trampoline. I had dealt with wartime shortages by making the frame of old broomsticks, and one morning one of them broke, dropping Debbie a few inches into the pan beneath. There was no danger, except temporarily to her comfort, but Julie, who was recovering from an operation for appendicitis, rashly got out of bed and lifted her out of trouble.

One of the first letters in response to my article on the baby-tender was from Mrs. Armand Denis at the Anthropoid Ape Research Foundation in Dania, Florida. She said they had a month-old human baby "for whom we want to adopt your method"; they also had thirty-nine chimpanzee babies and expected more. The chimpanzees were treated exactly like human babies, and the baby-tender (now, unfortunately, beginning to be called the Baby Box) would help in protecting them from the respiratory infections to which they were particularly susceptible. I sent the letter on to Weste, who wrote to the foundation. Armand Denis replied that he thought the Baby Box would be a most important part of the model nursery they were planning in a special chimpanzee exhibit. He pointed out that it would mean a tremendous amount of publicity for Weste's product (though I doubt that a picture of an Heir Conditioner occupied by a tiny chimp would induce many mothers to use one for their own babies).

The Hopes still had our portable model, but early in February Weste wrote that their own Heir Conditioner was finished and had been picked up by the express company. The Westes' own baby had gone into theirs (and was enjoying it immensely). A third was waiting to be shipped to a customer in Memphis, Tennessee. When the Hopes' did not arrive, I wrote to Weste, who replied that he had investigated and had found it badly damaged at the freight office. A worker had concealed his carelessness by stashing it out of sight in a corner. The Hopes took their disappointment in style, but Eve's sister would need our portable model in March.

Near the end of March a new one for the Hopes arrived. It had been shipped before the paint was quite dry and the finish was marred. Moreover I was soon writing to Weste that it was not working well. The thermostat was badly located and not responding accurately because air was not passing by it. Weste had made the cabinet large enough to cover the sheet locks, and it was unnecessarily bulky. There was a strong smell of paint, apparently from the acoustic tile in the ceiling. The Hopes tactfully suggested that they would be willing to part with it in case anyone else "urgently needed one," and I was inclined to take them up on it and get the thing out of town.

The whole venture was in trouble. Only a very small number of Heir Conditioners had been built, correspondence had gone unanswered, a potential market was slipping away. I wrote Weste a strong letter. "I have lost a lot of sleep trying to see a way out of the whole mess. I can't see that any progress has been made during the past six months." As "a reasonable program" I thought Weste should fill present orders with the units now under construction, hold off other orders with a statement about redesign and change in production methods, and cancel orders for excess materials.

Within a week one of Weste's former associates called. Weste had disappeared. I went to Cleveland immediately and talked with his wife and his associates. There had been no Heir Conditioner damaged in the freight office, the Westes had never had one for their own child, and none had been sent to the Memphis buyer. Two models were under construction in the shop—a shop so small that fewer than five Heir Conditioners could have been made in it instead of fifty as Weste had said. He had borrowed money ($500 from me), and the lending companies were after him. Worse still, he had taken advances from a number of potential customers. (I discovered later that, after he left Cleveland, he stopped in Chicago, looked up a prospective buyer there, and collected still another advance.) His former associates (who had closed out their interests in Weste rather than vice versa) told me that they would try to finish the models in the shop for two of those who had sent cash. One was eventually delivered, but the purchaser complained of poor construction and refused to pay more than half the amount still due.

I was no doubt partly to blame. Weste's first proposal, to build a few to sell on a special-order basis, was reasonable enough with his facilities. It was my reply that had sent him off into a managerial world in which he was incompetent. The more difficult the situation became the less he had to offer. His associates told me that he would often come to the shop and simply lie down and go to sleep. To cover his inadequacies, he began to lie, not only to me but to the potential buyers from whom he had taken advances. Eventually it became too much for him and he skipped. (I was least inclined to forgive him for collecting that advance in Chicago, since he knew then that he would never deliver an Heir Conditioner. The Chicago buyer held me responsible and threatened to send an abusive letter to the *Ladies' Home Journal* if I did not reimburse him.) I went back to Bloomington and sent letters to hundreds of correspondents, telling them that Weste was no longer in business.

I had received letters from several large companies interested in manufacturing the baby-tender (and one from the makers of a table-highchair called the Baby-Tenda asking me not to use the name), and the people in Indianapolis had suggested setting up an independent company. I had stuck by Weste in spite of growing evidence of his incompetence, but now I was free. One man who had written was Dan Caldemeyer of Evansville, Indiana. He had been a basketball star at the University and had inherited a large furniture company. He was interested in building a baby-tender for a prospective heir, and he would be interested in making a few to see if they could be sold at a reasonable price. I told him I had assigned my rights to Weste (though I had not actually signed any papers), and he wrote to Weste and asked about a franchise.

When Weste disappeared, I wrote to Caldemeyer, and Eve and I drove down to Evansville. We did not see much of the factory because it was being reorganized and modernized after the war, but Caldemeyer and his wife took us to dinner at a country club, and in the evening we played poker with two of his managers and their wives. (The managers had been in the company longer than Caldemeyer and were obviously skeptical of the baby-tender as a product.)

Caldemeyer came to see me (arriving in a private plane at the small Bloomington airport), and things moved rapidly. He consulted electrical engineers, a filtering corporation, and plywood companies. To replace both the stretched canvas and the sheeting, he found a woven plastic called Lumite which felt like linen and could be washed and dried instantly. We tried it and liked it. He looked into patents and trademarks. We had discussed "Aircrib," and it could be registered as a trademark, but only after a year's use.

By July, 80 percent of the items needed had been assembled, but low power motors for fans were in very short supply and plywood was not available because of the high priority of new housing. A honeycomb panel which would have been ideal because of its light weight was too expensive. Caldemeyer felt that the best material might be pressed steel. I recalled the "deep freeze" problem, but bright colors might solve it.

In November I received a blueprint of a steel model. It was disappointing. The working height for the parent was wrong, the baby could easily roll out, a filter on the side of the cabinet rather than the bottom could be easily damaged. Changes were made, and by March a model was almost ready for testing. I went down to see it and found other things wrong. Caldemeyer's designer had misunderstood the problem of ventilation and had put two or three small floor registers at the mattress level, where the baby would be exposed to unmixed, dangerously hot air. Meanwhile the price had gone up to $420.

WE WERE ANXIOUS to have a house of our own, and we paid too much for one on South College Avenue, only a block from an expanding business district. There was a spare bedroom and bath, and we could once again have a part-time, live-in student maid. The house had recently been redecorated but would have to be furnished, and furniture was in short supply. We had the piano sent from St. Paul and haunted auction sales for other things. The rooms were large, the ceilings high, and we needed pictures. Robert Laurent, the sculptor, who was an artist in residence at the University, had a fine collection of paintings with no place to hang them. He lent us three Marsden Hartleys, which we hung in the dining room, a lovely Jules Pascin for the living room, and two Chinese silk paintings for the upstairs hall.

My father paid for the house. I had saved no money at all up to that point and had, as a matter of fact, closed out a small locally financed retirement fund upon leaving Minnesota. With my appointment at Indiana I began to make payments to a national teachers' annuity fund, but I was carrying no insurance and was in effect giving my father responsibility for my wife and children. My father once noted how little I had in my checking account and gave me $1000, suggesting that I keep my balance roughly in that range while enjoying a little flexibility. He never asked me about it again, and it was soon gone. For me it was the theme of the torch race—one generation passing the torch on to the next—but as a self-made man my poor father passed it both ways. He supported his own father and mother for two decades and was responsible for the fact that Eve and

I and our children lived for many years more comfortably than would otherwise have been possible.

The following spring he sent me a copy of the fourth edition of his book. Again, in an inscription, he noted that it had been responsible for "the acquisition and possession of most of the things we all hold dear." And he added: "Your success in life—your happy marriage—our dear grandchildren, are full reward for all our efforts, and as I turn back my thoughts over the past and review our lives, I feel that we truly owe a lot to this book and the inspiration which prompted me to undertake writing it." The "inspiration" had been the death of my brother. I am sure my father did not mean to say that Eve and I, if not he and my mother, owed our good fortune to the accident of my brother's death.

WE WENT EAST during the summer, and at a meeting of the American Psychological Association in Philadelphia I gave a paper on the differential reinforcement of responses with respect to time, covering my reaction time experiments and reinforcement only after a delay in a discrete trial arrangement.

That fall my administrative chores were considerably lightened by the arrival of a new member of the department, William S. Verplanck, who had taken his degree under Hunter at Brown. He served as the administrative assistant that I had been promised. Just out of the Navy, he knew how to run a trim ship and seemed to enjoy doing so. Bill Estes was also back from the war. He had taken his degree at Minnesota, and I now hired him at Indiana. He had suffered a curious "service-connected disability." On patrol in the South Pacific he had had time to spare and had read mathematics. His brilliant career as an experimentalist soon yielded to mathematical model-building, from which he suffered for many years.

In their revolutionary changes at Columbia, Fred Keller and Nat Schoenfeld began to use *The Behavior of Organisms*, and the resulting sales came just in time. Two hundred and fifty copies of the original printing of 800 were left, and they were now being bound. Reprinting, however, was in doubt. The plates had gone into a scrap drive during the war, and a photographic process would be needed. It was a close decision, and the "adoption" at Columbia saved the day. Another modest batch of copies was printed.

In another graduate seminar, this time on "self-control," I asked my students to do what Frazier and "a young man named Simmons" (Fred Simmons Keller?) had done in *Walden Two*—search the literature of religion, ethics, morals, education, and folk wisdom, as well as their own lives, for techniques of self-management. Do people control their own behavior by exercising willpower or by redesigning their personal environments? We were all surprised by the ease with which ethical principles could be reduced to simple environmental practices.

LIKE OTHER BIOLOGICAL PROCESSES, operant conditioning presumably evolved because it had survival value. When the environment was not stable enough for the natural selection of innate behavior in a species, a rather similar "selection by consequences" was needed to build an effective repertoire in the individual. But when the point was reached at which a single reinforcement built up a substantial tendency to respond, a new problem arose. It did not matter *how* a response produced its consequences; when one thing followed close upon another it was usually caused by it, and temporal proximity was all that was needed in the evolutionary process.

But not every event that follows a response is caused by it, and an organism so highly evolved that it is changed by a single reinforcement is, therefore, vulnerable to accidents. Its behavior may be changed by consequences which follow "for no good reason." We call the result superstition.

I looked for the effect in pigeons. I arranged to have a dispenser deliver food every fifteen seconds, regardless of what a pigeon was doing. Superstitious operants quickly developed. The pigeon was necessarily doing something when food appeared, and it was therefore slightly more likely to be doing it when food appeared again. Two or three hits were enough to establish the behavior in strength. One of my pigeons turned around several times between "reinforcements." Another kept thrusting its head into an upper corner of the cage. Two swung their heads and bodies from side to side like pendulums. When the contingencies remained in force for some time, the topography of behavior slowly changed. A pigeon that first moved its head slightly to one side began to turn its body, then to take a step or two, and finally to hop from one foot to the other. All this, the pigeon might have said, "to make the dispenser operate." Once a response had been strengthened, "reinforcements" could be spaced out. One pigeon maintained its superstitious behavior when food was delivered (quite independently of its behavior) no oftener than once a minute.

MATCHING TO SAMPLE was another "higher mental process" to which a good deal of attention was being paid. Could a pigeon match colors? I arranged three keys in a row, each of which could be illuminated with either red or green light. The center key was the sample, and the side keys were kept dark until it had been pecked. The pigeon was thus induced to "look at the sample." When the side keys were then illuminated, pecking the matching key was reinforced, and correct matching quickly followed. With a minor change in the contingencies, the pigeon learned to choose the opposite of the sample.

A pigeon that has learned to match red and green will not necessarily match blue and yellow, but such a match can also be quickly taught, and as the number of matches increases, any new stimulus will have more in common with stimuli already matched, and a general ability to match novel stimuli should emerge.

I HAD ABANDONED but not forgotten that experiment in which a rat avoided a shock by pressing a lever slightly oftener than once every fifteen seconds, and I decided to try again with a different species. I put a pigeon in a jacket and fastened wires to two toes of one foot. A light shock made the toes flex. (The extent of the flexion was a useful gauge of the strength of the shock.) Shocks were delivered once a second. In front of the bird was a plate that could easily be pecked, and pecking terminated the shocks for a period of time. To expose the pigeon to the contingencies, I first reinforced pecking with food and then added the aversive conditions. When the delivery of food was discontinued, the pigeons pecked often enough during extinction to postpone the shock many times, and for a while pecking seemed to be sustained by that consequence, but eventually the pigeon simply took the shocks indefinitely without responding.

I put the plate back of the pigeon near to its feet, so that it could strike at the site of the stimulation, as it would "naturally" have done if it were, say, being bitten by a predator, but the new location did not help. Pecking did not seem to be sustained by what I had once called the avoidance of undesirable consequences or what I should now call negative reinforcement.

I had first used the term "negative reinforcement," incorrectly, to mean "punishment." I had assumed, along with almost everyone else, that punishment was simply the opposite of reward. You rewarded people to make them more likely and you punished them to make them less likely to behave in a given way. In my paper on two types of conditioning I said that reinforcing stimuli may be positive or negative "according as they produce an increase or a decrease in strength." But "reinforcing" means "strengthening," and in *The Behavior of Organisms* I began to hedge. Consequences produced a change in the strength of an operant, "which may be either an increase or, *possibly* [italics added], a decrease." I said that the strength of pressing a lever may increase if the consequence "is, for example, food and it may decrease if it is, for example, a shock," but a footnote referred the reader to a later section on "negative reinforcement" called merely "The Possibility of Negative Conditioning." Elsewhere I put the term "negative reinforcement" in quotation marks and questioned whether "a reduction of this sort actually occurs." My experiments had seemed to indicate that there was no effect on the reserve.

PUNISHMENT WAS ONE FIELD in which I worked on a technical problem. The standard apparatus was a floor of parallel bars wired alternately as positive and negative poles, through which a shock to the feet of a rat was delivered. It did not work if the rat was standing on bars of the same sign, or if feces on the bars shorted the circuit. A graduate student, Sam Campbell, and I made a commutator that changed the pattern of polarities. Any two bars were of opposite poles at least once every second, and if any two were shorted, the others worked most of the time. In addition, a motor slowly rocked the bars through ninety degrees so that feces passed between them. Aversive stimuli could then be reliably administered for long periods of unattended research.

Another technical problem was not so easily solved. On Project Pigeon we had improvised a kind of cumulative recorder in which a pen was drawn across a moving strip of paper by a taut string. The ratchet driving the string was made from an old gear. I thought it was time to standardize a recorder for general use; graphs from different laboratories would then have the same dimensions. Materials were still in short supply, but I found a small standard circular saw blade that had the right number of teeth for a ratchet, and I designed a paper drive mounted on a chassis of sheet aluminum. Unfortunately, the saw eventually cut into the pawl that drove it, as I might have expected, and there were other problems. I asked Fred if he thought that we could get firm orders for twenty or thirty instruments (from Yale, say, as well as from Columbia and Indiana) to encourage a company to develop a good model. I was soon reporting that a company was willing to go ahead without committed orders, and Fred and I eventually tested a prototype. It proved to be not only expensive but inaccurate. As in our behemoth, the pin was driven by a screw, and when we operated it at a steady rate, it drew a slightly wavy line.

I made another small move toward standardization. We usually labeled our graphs with a lettering guide and pen, but it was easy to smudge or otherwise spoil them. Researchers with big grants could pay for professional work, but papers on operant conditioning were often shabby. I had a number of the commonly used legends (RESPONSES PER HOUR, TIME, CONTROL, EXPERIMENTAL, DAYS, MINUTES, etc.), together with the alphabet and some useful numerals, printed on sheets of gummed paper, from which items could be cut and pasted to produce a reasonably professional job.

WHEN I RECEIVED the Warren Medal from the Society of Experimental Psychologists, Boring wrote to say that he regretted having got away without congratulating me,

*particularly because I was much in favor of the award. I have actually
nominated you for it on two previous occasions. Since you know that
I do not believe that psychology is only skin deep, or that these
institutional distinctions about what is psychology and what is physiology are important, it is especially desirable that I should say to you
how much I appreciate the contributions that you are continuing to
make to psychology. They are first rate and the Medal was very well
bestowed!*

(The typed word was "unimportant" but he had crossed out the "un,"
and when I showed the letter to Mike Elliott, he returned it with a
marginal notation: "Just what he does think, this secretary knew.")

It was an encouraging letter, but Boring and I were not yet
warm friends. (When I applied for my Guggenheim Fellowship in
1941 I gave Thorndike, Carmichael—who had become President of
Tufts—and Tolman as my references, omitting all Harvard connections. It would have been too easy for Boring to remember me as the
behavioristic *enfant terrible* of the early thirties.)

Our relations were about to improve, however. Indiana was
nearer the East Coast in a financial as well as a geographical sense,
because the University paid the expenses of its department chairmen
when they attended meetings. In the spring of 1946, the Society of
Experimental Psychologists met, courtesy of Professor Boring, at the
Harvard Club in New York, and I was able to go. Boring's special
issue of the *Psychological Review* on operationism was very much
in the air, and although he had probably been responsible for my
invitation to participate, I was not sure he appreciated my pun on
his name. (When I was having a cocktail with Herbert Langfeld of
Princeton, a close friend of Boring's, he said he liked the symposium
except for the paper by that chap . . . whose name he could not . . .
quite recall . . . and stopped recalling when it came to him that I was
the chap.) At luncheon the next day I sat beside Boring, and for the
first time since my postdoctoral days we had a long talk. The ice
melted, and a few months later he wrote to ask whether I would be
able to give the William James Lectures at Harvard if I were invited. I
asked Robert whether the department could get along without me for
a term, and he thought it could, and so I said yes and soon received
the invitation. I would give ten lectures during the fall term, together
with a seminar.

Obviously my topic would be verbal behavior. Except for one seminar I had done no further work on it since coming to Bloomington; I had not even discussed Kantor's *Objective Psychology of Grammar* with its author. I could plead the exigencies of a chairmanship, but I had undoubtedly digressed. Fred had justly sent a note of complaint: "Report reaches me that you are doing too goddam many things. The 'goddam' is my insertion! I want from you, sir, a book on language, and a few thousand psychologists need one badly. As second choice, I'll take rats or pigeons, but I'm not interested in Ethics, children's books, chess, baby-tenders, cryptanalysis, or what have you!"

When I wrote to ask Fred if he had seen the announcement of my appointment as William James Lecturer, I offered some reassurance: "I have turned my laboratory over to my research assistants and am spending a number of hours each day at my desk working on what I'm sure this time will be a final draft of *Verbal Behavior*." And I added: "Boring has made a complete about face and is fantastically chummy in all his letters." (He had signed a letter "Garry" with a handwritten note: "You will surely get to use this name when you come. Why not now, as Smitty [Stevens] and Eddie [Newman] do?")

Bertrand Russell had given the William James Lectures in 1940. He had called them *An Inquiry into Meaning and Truth*. As far as I was concerned, that meant verbal behavior, and now I should have the chance to prove it. Ten lectures would not cover the whole manuscript (Boring said I could give more than ten if I liked, though he could not guarantee an audience), but perhaps I could publish a longer book with the parts that were the lectures identified as such. The Harvard Press was interested (and Elliott wrote that Dana Ferrin would be happy to be released from an implied agreement to publish a book that would have such a small readership). What should I call the lectures? "Verbal" was not yet a common word (but commoner than "phatic" or "phemic," the alternatives I had once considered!). I wrote to Boring:

> *Language suggests the field of the linguist, which is scarcely my field at all. "Speech" has got tied up with vocal behavior, the theatre, rhetoric, and the speech clinic. "Sign" and "symbol" are pretty much the property of the logicians. "Words" is noncommittal but suggests*

Hamlet and has other pejorative connotations. That is why I am happy to confine myself to "verbal behavior," which has little tradition behind it, and is relatively descriptive of the actual subject matter. I think it ought to be used in the title of the book, but almost anything could be used for the lectures. I would be glad to settle for Smitty's "Words and Behavior."

It was clear, however, that I preferred "Verbal Behavior," and that was the title we used.

I proposed that my seminar be called "The Analysis of Behavior." I warned Boring that it would be pretty much about my own work, but he said that that was just what they wanted.

I WAS NEVER able to come very close to Robert Kantor's way of thinking about behavior, although our differences were trivial compared with our similarities. We gave a joint seminar in which we held doggedly to our own positions—essentially giving two semi-seminars in parallel—to the dismay of the students who were trying to find out what it was all about. One of them, Paul Fuller, later compared our styles in terms we ourselves might have used:

> Skinner emphasized positive reinforcement in his teaching as well as in his writings. If a student was floundering when asked a question, Skinner would shape his verbal behavior into more nearly correct paths until through the social reinforcement of successive approximations, the correct verbal behavior was obtained. Although Kantor used some aversive control techniques on occasion, the preponderance was positive. When a student's verbal rate approached zero and remained at or near zero for some time, Kantor reconstructed the situational variables, reran the crucial series of behavior segments, and administered strong social reinforcement.

We were never really in intellectual contact. For example, I had continued to defend my position on physiology. On my sabbatical leave I had written a note on the concept of brain center and the absence of any useful behavioral parallel, and I had recently published a review of *Mathematical Biophysics of the Central Nervous System* by Householder and Landahl, in which I began: "This book is not about the nervous system. It is about behavior. It considers data taken for the most part from classical psychology—sensory and motor processes, conditioning, and so on. The explanatory hypotheses which the authors set up contain only vague references to neural anatomy, and there is no reason why they should contain any at all."

At more or less the same time Robert was teaching a course in physiological psychology. It was Roland Davis's course, but Roland had had a serious operation and was taking the term off. Robert soon published his *Problems of Physiological Psychology.* Our positions were quite close, but there was no sign in my review or in his book that we had ever discussed them. And in fact we had not.

We differed quite clearly on one point. Robert seemed to be the pure environmentalist. When a pair of robins nested outside his study window and hatched and raised their young, he told me with great satisfaction that they drove the young from the nest, not "by instinct," but quite obviously because the nest was becoming crowded. Though most of my research was on the role of the environment, my first experiments were in what was coming to be called ethology, and I was currently studying a bit of behavior that seemed to occur before it could be affected by any consequences.

HULL'S STUDENTS had smeared food on their levers so that their rats would press more quickly, and Konorski and Miller had shocked the feet of their dogs and then reinforced the resulting flexion. In Project Pigeon we had sometimes fastened a grain of corn to the target plate so that pecking could be quickly reinforced. But if something of the sort was not done, why *did* a rat press a lever or a pigeon peck a key? There were no identifiable, let alone manipulable, stimuli at work as an organism explored an apparatus.

I designed an experiment in which I hoped to tease out a bit of innate or "phylogenic" behavior. I put a translucent plastic plate across the upper half of one end of a box, with a food dispenser below it at the right. A spot of light could be projected on the plate at the standard height of a pigeon key. It appeared at the right edge of the plate and moved across it in about four seconds. When it reached the left edge, food was dispensed. Exposed to these conditions, a hungry pigeon began to peck the spot and to do so as if it were driving it across the plate. I recorded the behavior by lightly greasing the plate and "lifting a print" after one pass by dusting it with powder. The prints showed slashes, an inch or more in length, all of which were made as the beak moved from right to left in a driving motion just behind the spot. As the experiment continued, the slashes became less specifically directed toward the spot and swung down toward the dispenser when the spot neared the edge.

Driving the spot seemed to be innate behavior, possibly only one part of an extensive repertoire of "moving things about" that could be shaped by the contingencies in natural selection. But had I eliminated all possible reinforcement? Since the movement of the spot across the screen was followed by the appearance of food, it became a conditioned reinforcer. I could, for example, have arranged to have the spot move when the pigeon pecked an adjacent key. It would peck the key "to make the spot move." Possibly, the slashing behavior was thus (adventitiously) reinforced, but its appropriateness would still not be explained. The same consequences could adventitiously reinforce strutting about the box, for example.

DEBBIE HAD CONTINUED to use the baby-tender for sleeping and naps. Once her bowel-movement pattern was established, she slept nude, and urine was collected in a pan beneath the plastic, in which a few crystals of borax had been spread. We were warned that she would be a bed wetter, but she learned to keep dry in her clothing during the day, and when she started to sleep in a regular bed (as she did when she was two and a half), she treated it like clothing. Except for one night when we had been traveling and were all very tired, she never wet a bed. She also remained remarkably resistant to colds and other infections.

I moved the abandoned baby-tender to the laboratory and converted it into a living space for pigeons.

IN THE *American Scientist* Dr. Evelyn Hutchinson wrote a rather favorable account of some experiments by S. G. Soal on card-guessing, and I wrote to protest:

Two conditions must be fulfilled before the readers of the American Scientist can be asked to spend much time on card-guessing experiments. In the first place it must be shown that "every precaution it is possible to devise" has in fact been taken. In the Soal experiments this was not by any means the case. When the extraordinary claim is made that human behavior can be influenced by a future event like the position taken by a shuffled card, the demonstration must be rigorous. In experiments of the Soal variety, cards are shuffled by hand, cards are placed in compartments by hand, counters are drawn from a bag by hand, positions of cards are recorded on a tally sheet by hand, a "percipient" makes calls orally to be tallied by hand or tallies them himself, either along side other tallies or on a separate sheet which must then be placed against other tallies in order to check "hits." Even "extreme precaution" will not guarantee the absence of inaccuracies and artifacts, especially when we remember that experiments of this sort last many hours and frequently become almost hypnotically tiresome.

Hutchinson sent my comments to Soal, who replied at length, ending as follows: "During the past three years I have demonstrated over and over again the telepathic powers of Mrs. Stewart of Richmond to numerous men of high academic standing and, as was the case with all those who saw Shackleton, they have expressed perfect satisfaction with the way in which the experiments were carried out."

But not everyone was satisfied with the way in which Soal conducted the experiments I had criticized. One subject claimed that she saw him change 1's to 4's to increase the number of hits, and a careful statistical study of the tabulations later showed that this must have been done.

I became involved in another kind of Extraordinary Sensory Perception when someone in the Department of Terrestrial Magnetism at the Carnegie Institution in Washington raised the question of whether birds were affected by radar. He sent me a film in which a camera followed a flight of migrating ducks; a light at one edge of the frame flashed when a radar beam went on or off. The V-formation clearly broke up and re-formed, but although I ran the film forward and backward, fast and slow, I was never sure that the radar was having any effect. I was offered microwave equipment to be loaned to the Department of Physics at the University, so that I could try to disrupt a pigeon's behavior in the laboratory, but the University had no license to operate it. I did put a large coil around a pigeon box, and found no evidence that responding to a key was disturbed by a strong magnetic field. Nor did the pigeon discriminate between the presence and absence of the field when reinforcement was contingent upon its presence.

TWO YEARS HAD PASSED and *The Sun Is But a Morning Star* was still unpublished. During my first year at Indiana I had gone over the manuscript, and a daughter of Professor Kinsey's had typed a fair copy. I sent it to Dana Ferrin, editor of what had become the Appleton-Century Company, but he turned it down; he thought it was too talky, and the prose rather creaked. A traveler for Houghton Mifflin read the manuscript when he was in Bloomington and suggested that I send it to their editors. They also turned it down, to his great regret.

I should have been discouraged if I had not sent a copy to Fred, who replied in characteristic fashion: it was "tremendously exciting" and "ought to be the most talked of book in the country when you finally release it." ("Release it" was so much more encouraging than "get it published!") After a second reading, he said it was the most "upsetting and inspiring thing he could recall having read at any time" and that he and Nat Schoenfeld were already talking about setting up a Walden Two.

The college editor at Macmillan, Charles Anderson, was looking for an introductory text in psychology. Young men and women recently in the services were flocking to colleges, and the government was paying for their books. Two or three publishers with new texts in psychology were cleaning up. Would I do a text? I told him about my problem with *The Sun Is But a Morning Star,* and he asked to see the manuscript. He gave it to two readers, neither of whom was enthusiastic about it. It was far too long; one reader thought it could even be cut to half its length. There was too much direct discourse; Burris should summarize many of the points Frazier makes and let Frazier stop talking. More human interest was needed. I had committed "a technical blunder of the first order" in getting the reader interested in the young people visiting the community and then letting them drop out of the story for a couple of hundred pages. Possibly the book could be converted into a story of the conflict within Frazier's own being, showing how he "becomes a man working himself out." More should be done with Castle. One reader concluded that "the novel is by no means illiterate" and "certainly something could be done with it," but "how well the result would sell is anybody's guess." The other pointed out that successful utopias had touched on important current issues, and that there were some elements in my book "that might have a strong appeal in our times," but he thought "any spectacular success was doubtful."

I had neither time nor inclination to revise the book in any important way, but I offered to shorten it by taking out two chapters, in one of which I had described how Frazier started the community, and in the other how the problem of race was treated, using some of Pei Sung Tang's experiences in America as an example of what could be avoided. (The chapters were inadvertently thrown away.) Anderson said Macmillan would publish the book, in spite of misgivings, if I would give them first refusal of an introductory text. When the contract was signed, I was still calling the book *The Sun Is But a Morning Star*, but there was another star title on the market, and we changed to *Walden Two*.

WITH THE WAR at an end, research along the lines of *The Behavior of Organisms* was being done again. Some of Hull's students were active, but the centers were still at Columbia, where the rat was the principal subject, and Indiana, where the pigeon was king. We had trouble getting our reports published in the regular journals. We used very small numbers of subjects, we did not "design our experiments" with matched groups, our cumulative records did not look like learning curves, and we were asking questions (for example, about schedules) that were not found in the "literature." At meetings our papers were mixed in with others we seldom wanted to hear.

As a temporary solution, Fred, Nat Schoenfeld, and I organized a conference. Indiana University made some dormitory space available and paid Fred's and Nat's expenses. The meetings were informal. We simply took up different topics and spoke from the floor when we had something to say. We called it a conference on the "experimental analysis of behavior," taking the "experimental analysis" from the subtitle of *The Behavior of Organisms.*

It was not a wholly satisfactory name for a field. What should we call ourselves? "Students of behavior"? "Behavior analysts"? And what adjectives could we use to identify our research, our theories, or our organization? "Behaviorism," "behaviorists," and "behavioristic" were not quite right. They were too closely tied to John B. Watson. To most people "behaviorism" meant a denial of genetic differences. Watson's famous challenge ("Give me a dozen healthy infants, well-formed, and my own specified world to bring them up in, and I'll guarantee to take any one at random and train him to become any type of specialist I might select") had attracted far more attention than his immediate disclaimer ("I am going beyond my facts and I admit it, but so have the advocates of the contrary and they have been doing it for many thousands of years"). It was a connotation to be avoided, and in an interview I said that although as a psychologist I was concerned with behavior, "that did not of necessity make me a behaviorist."

One of our specialties, the shaping of behavior, reached into an established field that summer. Jack Hilgard was teaching at the University of Washington, and he told three experts in the field of learning, Guthrie, Loucks, and Horton, about a demonstration I had described at a meeting of the Society of Experimental Psychologists. A pigeon is habituated to a small semicircular amphitheatre where it can be fed from a dispenser with a hand switch. A bit of behavior is chosen as an objective—for example, the pigeon is to hold its head as high as possible. Sighting along the top of the head, the demonstrator chooses a slightly higher mark on the opposite wall. The first lifting of the head above the mark is reinforced. The pigeon soon holds its head slightly higher, and a higher mark is chosen. Eventually the pigeon walks about with its head and beak stretching upward, and it may even topple over backward. If the objective is turning around, the demonstrator first reinforces a very slight turn, but then gradually increases the extent required until the pigeon goes all the way around.

By shaping both clockwise and counterclockwise turns, it may be induced to pace a figure eight.

Hilgard said they wanted to try it "just for our own instruction, without any thought now of trying to obtain scientific records," and would I send details? I did so, and at the end of the summer he wrote enthusiastically: "You can actually see learning take place!"

SINCE WE SHOULD BE coming east for the fall term, Fred arranged to have me teach at Columbia during the summer. We found a camp in the Poconos for Julie, and Debbie spent some time with my parents and some with us in a Morningside Drive apartment, sublet from a Columbia professor. I gave two courses: "Theories of Learning and Conditioning," a title, like the published description, supplied by the Chairman, and "Verbal Behavior" (the Chairman had suggested a "fairly general title" such as "The Psychology of Semantics"). The material in the latter was taken from my courses on the Psychology of Language and the Psychology of Literature, as well as from the William James Lectures in preparation. Ralph Hefferline, a member of the department, had once been a court stenographer, and he recorded my lectures in shorthand. Later he summarized his notes in seventy-six single-spaced pages and distributed mimeographed copies. They covered much more ground than my William James Lectures.

Jim Agee and I had lunch together. He was writing movie criticism for *Time* and was rather defensive about it: he insisted that he had greater freedom than if he were writing for the *New Yorker*. He did not seem like the Jim I had known. He may have felt that I judged him harshly for his treatment of two of my friends. Via's brother, Blake Saunders, whom I had tutored when I was at Hamilton College (we then called him Frisk), had become engaged to a young woman in Utica named Alma. One fatal summer, when Jim and Via were spending some time with the Saunderses, Jim fell in love with Alma, and they ran away together. I knew the story of this double desertion, but it had happened long before, and I do not think I recalled it when I saw Jim.

Someone on the *New Yorker*, writing for "Talk of the Town," came to see me. He wrote that he had paid me a call because he had "heard from a philoprogenitive friend that [I was] the inventor of a mechanical baby tender, counted on to revolutionize the rearing of children and enormously diminish parental strain." He reported that "Skinner confessed, rather uneasily, that he'd put some of his theories into practice by writing a novel, which will be published next spring. His confidence returned when he started talking about his mechanical baby-tender." The interview concluded: "A commercial model . . . will probably be on the market late this year, selling for something over $200, which is a good deal cheaper than the cost of a crib, blankets, sheets, baby clothes, and so on. As might be expected, Lewis & Conger are interested." In September, however, Caldemeyer sent me an account of what he had done, and the problems he had met, and said that he could not produce a commercial model.

When we left for a brief vacation on Monhegan, I wrote to Fred: "Haven't really told you how much I've enjoyed the Summer. You've got a fine gang. I'll never teach with as much enthusiasm again—or as well, God help me. You are doing the best job of graduate teaching in the country and the histories of the future will refer to the 'Columbia group' as the turning point in American psychology. And I'm not kidding!"

HARVARD HAD PLANNED to give us an apartment in some temporary housing called Jarvis Court, but it was not yet available, and we stayed for more than a month with our old friends Ken and Lou Mulligan, who were now living in Wakefield, half an hour's drive from Cambridge. Their three daughters were more or less the ages of ours. I drove to Cambridge every weekday morning and dropped Julie off at the Shady Hill School. I knew the school well because the Davises had been staunch supporters and Marian Stevens had spent a year there as an apprentice. I had persuaded the headmistress, Katherine Taylor, to take Julie on for a single term.

A month or so later we moved into Jarvis Court and found a small nursery school for Debbie. She was showing early signs of *Wanderlust*. In Indiana early that spring we had received a phone call from a woman who had found two small, very tired children walking along a country road two or three miles from Bloomington. One of them was Debbie, not yet three. Soon after we moved into Jarvis Court, she struck out by herself on a Sunday morning. She wandered into and across busy Massachusetts Avenue, went into a drugstore, helped herself to a pack of cough drops, and was about a mile away when Julie and a friend found her quite by accident. The baby-tender had not made her timid about open space. Perhaps it had made open space particularly attractive.

I was given an office in the Department of Psychology in Memorial Hall and soon met its new members, some of whom Smitty Stevens had assembled in the Psycho-acoustic Laboratory during the war—Georg von Békésy, Walter Rosenblith, Robert Galambos, Fred Frick, and George Miller. With Boring, Smitty, and my old friend Beebe-Center, we ate lunch together every day, and the conversation was of a high order.

Week by week I wrote my lectures, and Kitty Miller typed them. I delivered them on successive Friday afternoons. On the first day my audience was fairly large, and then it settled down to the size characteristic of a lecture series. Ivor Richards was now on the faculty of the School of Education and not only came but read my lectures as I produced them. Bridgman came and often had something to say afterward. Once, when he agreed that much of the time he thought in words but at high speed, he broke off: "No, that can't be right. The pitch would be too high." Edna Heidbreder came in from Wellesley and sent a good report to Mike Elliott.

More than a dozen years after Whitehead's challenge, I was presumably finishing a manuscript on verbal behavior, but I was taking it from a much longer version, and I wrote my lectures knowing that they would probably not be published as such. Nevertheless they covered the main themes. When people spoke, wrote, or gestured, they were not expressing ideas or meanings or communicating information; they were behaving in ways determined by certain contingencies of reinforcement maintained by a verbal community. The contingencies had properties which were responsible for the special character of verbal behavior.

Thanks to the invention of the alphabet, verbal behavior could be described well enough for the purposes of my lectures by direct quotation. The probability that a speaker would utter a verbal response could be estimated from its rate of emission. Verbal operants were to be classified according to contingencies of reinforcement, a classification resembling the "moods" of the grammarian and traditionally said to show the intention of the speaker. For example, a "mand" was controlled by its normal reinforcing consequences, and special kinds of mands were distinguished by the conditions under which listeners responded. A "tact" was determined primarily by a discriminative stimulus, the reinforcing consequences being generalized as far as possible. Stimulus generalization explained metaphor, metonymy, and some malaprops and solecisms, while a special feature of the contingencies maintained by a verbal environment explained concept formation and abstraction. Some verbal operants were under the control of other verbal behavior—overheard or read, and the audience was another important controlling variable.

Once verbal operants had been thus classified one could move on to the actual emission of speech. Many unusual processes arose because one controlling variable could be related to many responses and one response could be related to many variables. For example, a speaker acquired different verbal repertoires with respect to different audiences, and when two audiences were to be addressed at the same time, common elements were more likely to be emitted. Multiple variables led to "significant" choices of synonyms and to wit, wordplay, alliteration, and assonance. Word games, puzzles, and conundrums also showed the multiple determination of verbal behavior. Making sentences was a matter of putting raw primordial verbal behavior into some kind of order and of qualifying, asserting, denying, and otherwise editing the behavior in the process of emission, in such a way that it had a better effect upon the listener.

In my early notes and in my course at Columbia I used "hearer" instead of "listener." Russell used it in his review of *The Meaning of Meaning* in the *Dial*. It is a more comprehensive term because there are instances in which we hear a verbal response though we are not listening, but it was hard to pronounce and "listener" was taking over. The behavior of the listener required separate treatment. It was not true, as Watson, Russell, and others had said, that one responded to words as if they were the things the words stood for. That was true only of conditioned reflexes, most of them emotional. The kind of control exercised by a discriminative stimulus was the key to a more effective analysis. Nothing passed from speaker to listener in "communication"; the speaker merely supplied stimuli which enabled a listener to take effective action with respect to circumstances available only to the speaker.

Understanding was something more. We understood in the sense that we said the same thing for the same reasons. If we possessed similar behavior already in strength, listening or reading was a waste of time. If we were unlikely ever to say what we heard or read, we dismissed it as abstruse or incomprehensible. We tended to listen to or read what we ourselves were almost ready to say and could now say with the help of speaker or writer. However, a tendency could be built up in the listener or reader to say what the speaker or writer then went on to say, and formal devices, particularly in poetry, could generate a spurious sense of understanding.

In a final lecture I analyzed my own behavior as lecturer:

> Putting the matter in the most selfish light, I have been trying to get you to behave verbally as I behave. What teacher, or writer, or friend, does not? And like all teachers and writers and friends, I shall cherish whatever you may subsequently say or write in which I think I can detect my "influence." If I have strengthened your verbal behavior in this way with spurious devices of ornamentation and persuasion, then you will do well to resist, but I plead not guilty. . . . This seems to me to be a better way of talking about verbal behavior and that is why I have tried to get you to talk this way too. But have I told you the truth? How can I tell? A science of verbal behavior makes no provision for truth or certainty. We cannot be certain of the truth of that!

(The question of truth had come up years before when I was discussing my thesis with Boring. I had said that I was not writing to state truths but to have an effect upon my reader. He sent me a note the next day telling me that he was shocked. But my subsequent analysis led to much the same conclusion. Wittgenstein would later say the same thing: "I am in a sense making propaganda for one style of thinking as opposed to another.")

I concluded my lectures by recalling the challenge that had plunged me into the field. Could I now explain Whitehead's behavior as he said to me, "There is no black scorpion falling on this table"?

Certainly not in any adequate sense. But was it perhaps a metaphor? Was Whitehead perhaps assuring himself that the behaviorism I was describing was no black scorpion? Was behaviorism to be feared because it destroyed the notion of a controlling self? I did not think so:

> There is no reason why scientific method cannot be turned to the study of man himself—to the practical problems of society but above all to the behavior of the individual. . . . If we can eventually give a plausible account of human behavior as part of a lawfully determined system, human power will rise even more rapidly towards its maximum. [People] will never become originating centers of control, because their behavior will itself be controlled, but their role can be extended without limit. The technological application of such a scientific achievement cannot now be fathomed. It is difficult to foresee the verbal adjustments which will have to be made. "Personal freedom" and "responsibility" will make way for other bywords, which in the nature of bywords, will probably prove satisfying enough.

OUR TERM IN CAMBRIDGE was not all work. Hudson Hoagland, whose course, General Physiology, had clinched my allegiance to a science of behavior, had left Clark University to establish the Worcester Foundation of Experimental Biology, and he invited us to visit the laboratory. Gregory Pincus was there, and we saw work in progress on the effect of certain ketosteroids in suppressing ovulation in cows. A contraceptive pill was not too far in the future.

I confessed to Hudson that I had once played a prank on him. Although I admired his dedication to biological science, I had not liked his experiments on the effect of temperature on one's judgment of time ("Elliptical as hell," I had told Fred). When we first moved to Bloomington, the papers were reporting a follow-up study in which Hoagland had talked about a chemical clock, and I wrote a letter in pencil on cheap paper, giving our Bloomington address—

Dear Doctor,

Have read in Indianapolis Times of your expiraments on chemistry of Time and wish to tell you my wife's peculiar condition if you can use her in any way. About ten years ago she first complained of a ticking sound in the chest. At first I or the doctor's couldn't hear it but it is plain to all lately. It is like a kitchen clock. It runs slower at night. It ticks when she holds her breath. Not on heart side, so not heart. Anyway too fast. Doctors can't help us out.

If you can tell my wife is it chemistry of Time we will be much obliged. Lately ticking has been slower, causing my wife to worry she is running down. What can be done, doctor?

Jerry Davis

Hudson replied that he was completely baffled, but he assured Mr. Davis that it was a good sign that the ticking was getting slower. "Whatever the cause," he wrote, "it is decreasing."

I gave a colloquium at Clark University on "The Processes Involved in Self-Control," a subject I had first explored in that seminar in Bloomington. When I gave the same lecture at Mount Holyoke, I had a very large audience—not, it turned out, because of some special need for self-control among the students but rather because Tom and Ellen Reese were teaching in the Department of Psychology, and Tom had been a student of Fred's at Columbia. The students had been, as critics might have said, indoctrinated.

The baby-tender was still talked about, and Bronson Crowthers, head of Children's Hospital in Boston, invited Eve and me to his house for an evening. I reported to Fred:

I had a wonderful session last Saturday night with about forty pediatricians, child psychiatrists, and child psychologists, at the home of the head of Childrens Hospital. Baby Box, of course. They started out very skeptical but before the evening was over they were shouting each other down to suggest new uses. It seems it would be a Godsend in children's wards—to prevent overheating the ward (costly) and cut down nursing needs (costly). When I said I was glad to hear all that but thought there was a manpower shortage and money shortage in the home, too, they said "Oh, but the mother does it for love."

HUTCH HAD BECOME editor of the Sunday *New York Times Book Review*, and he asked me to review *The Reach of the Mind* by J. B. Rhine. In writing about another book by Rhine and his associates, *Extra-sensory Perception after Sixty Years*, I had argued, "If extrasensory perception is as readily available for study as the authors contend, then little is to be gained from quibbling over experiments performed several years ago under conditions which have not satisfied many qualified observers. . . . The authors only weaken their case by making so much of the early evidence." In reviewing Rhine's new book I brought up other issues. Anecdotes and poorly conducted laboratory experiments were used to build a convincing case for "psi," even though Rhine admitted that it was safer to regard such evidence as "more suggestive than conclusive." He tended to answer an objection to one experiment by citing another to which it did not apply but to which a different objection could be raised. He characterized "psi" as a sensitive power "hampered as the experiment is made complicated, heavy, and slow moving," and hence "destroyed in the very act of trying to demonstrate it" (and hence beyond the reach of scientific proof?).

Rhine sent Hutch a bitter protest. My studies of *rat* behavior did not qualify me to review a book on *human* capacities. He doubted if I knew any more about his field than he of mine and he would consider it "professionally a little unethical to pose as an adequate reviewer of a report of [my] researches." He said I resorted to ridicule and misrepresentation, smeared him, and made him out an inconsistent and ridiculous figure. Instead he felt I should have said, "In all professional honesty: I do not pretend to know anything about this business, but I'm agin' it. Either it or my physicalistic philosophy of man is the bunk!" At Hutch's request I sent Rhine a disclaimer, but he wanted his letter published, and so I wrote an answer to be published with it. Hutch answered the charge that I was only a rat psychologist by noting that I was "currently delivering the William James Lectures on verbal behavior and had published technical papers on automatic writing, the statistical analysis of frequencies of speech sounds, and the Zenith Radio Telepathy experiments."

ONE DAY, Garry Boring dropped into my office and sat down in a chair against the wall. "Smitty and I would like to have you in the department," he said. He was speaking quite precisely. I was not being invited, but if I said I might come, they would put up my name, and the administration would ask an *ad hoc* committee of outsiders to evaluate me. If the President and Fellows then appointed me, the appointment would still have to be approved by the Board of Overseers.

The old Department of Psychology had broken apart. Gordon Allport and Harry Murray had chafed long enough under the standards imposed by Boring and Stevens in the name of science and had joined sociologists and social anthropologists in founding a new Department of Social Relations. Psychology was left with "experimental psychology" in a very narrow sense, and Stevens and Boring covered only a small part of it. In particular they needed someone in the field of learning. They had invited Hilgard, he had refused to come, and now they were trying me.

I warned Garry that if I came, they would be taking on more than a professor. The experimental analysis of behavior was flourishing, and I was sure that I would soon have dedicated graduate students and an expanding laboratory. Garry said they would not ask me if they were not expecting that.

We discussed salary and support for my laboratory, and I talked with the Provost. I told him I thought I was worth more than the $9000 they were offering me, and he made it $10,000. He authorized the department to spend $4000 from one of its funds to provide for my initial equipment and $1000 a year to maintain it. He would make another $4500 available each year for five years to support my research, but from that point on I should have to find other support. There was really no question that I should accept. I had begun at Harvard two decades before and had done almost all the research reported in *The Behavior of Organisms* there. I felt that I belonged at Harvard and said yes.

I had already begun to revise the lectures, and although parts were nearly illegible, I sent them off to Fred, and we prepared to leave Cambridge. My father and mother were now spending their winters in Bradenton, Florida, and they invited us (all expenses paid, as usual) to visit them for a week before returning to Indiana. It was a long train ride with two young children, and once there, Julie and Debbie were not always well behaved according to my mother's standards. Nevertheless, we got some sun, played shuffleboard, and did a bit of swimming.

When we returned to Bloomington, we found that our house had been badly treated. We had sublet it at a very reasonable rent to a young couple who were to serve essentially as housesitters. They had a small child and were expecting another, but they had assured us that they would take good care of the place. Our better china and silver were put aside, not to be used. As soon as we left, they moved themselves into the living room and rented all the bedrooms, in some of which grease stains on the walls now testified to cooking on hot plates. An oriental rug in the front hall and the stair carpet had been badly worn, some of our good china was broken, and several ceramic flowerpots, a rather good white leather wastebasket, and a number of other things were missing. Yvonne spent a week with a cleaning woman, and we put the house on the market. We had paid too much for it, and we (that is, my father) now sold it at a loss.

YVONNE AND I had enjoyed our life in Bloomington, and professionally I had learned a few lessons. I had seen the political side of university administration and resolved never to see it at close range again. Except for two seminars, I could not say much for my teaching. I had turned out some interesting research—on choice, matching, reaction time, and superstition, among other things—but the laboratory I had dreamed of when I accepted the Indiana offer never came into existence. Wartime shortages had been too severe, and I had kept to the improvisations of Project Pigeon.

I was in the mood for a clean sweep. At Harvard I should have the use of a departmental library, and I saw no reason to move the journals I had accumulated. I gave my copies of *Isis* to Robert, sold the rest, and left great quantities of early reprints to be thrown away.

I HAD MADE UP for my slow start in the profession. I was returning to Harvard as a full professor. I had been proposed for membership in the two most prestigious learned societies for which I was eligible and had been elected to what Hunter called the better one—the American Philosophical Society, founded by Benjamin Franklin. (I would make the other, the National Academy of Sciences, the following year.) Woodworth had asked for a photograph for a new edition of his *Contemporary Schools of Psychology.*

I was also halfway through "the years 30–60," but my "plan for the campaign" had not been closely followed. A year earlier, in a note called "What I have to say, as of January 13, 1947," I listed four items, two of which were as follows:

> *Verbal Behavior*—top level—a rigorous construction of a science of VB. The missing link between animal and human behavior. Part of large construction of a rigorous science of behavior.
> *Verbal Behavior Lectures*—An *interpretation* of a causal analysis of VB. No details at all. Examples of rigor, but not full analysis.

I was now close (or so I thought) to finishing the book I had planned in response to Whitehead's challenge. Verbal behavior as such was not on my list in 1932 but my lectures at Columbia and at Harvard (and particularly the manuscript in progress) covered much of what appeared under "Theories of Knowledge" both scientific and nonscientific, as well as "Behaviorism versus Psychology."

My paper on operationism had been taken from my manuscript on verbal behavior, and it had, I thought, reduced the problem of privacy to a simple analysis of contingencies. Feigl had called it "a very important paper." He and I had never fully resolved the differences between logical positivism and behaviorism, and each of us, as Feigl put it, continued to cultivate his own garden, but Mike had recently written: "Feigl is certainly enthusiastic about your consistently behavioristic analysis of the 'private world problem.' Apparently you have practically convinced him that his garden is a plot within yours."

The fourth item in 1932, the "experimental description of behavior," had become in 1947:

> *Experimental Work on Animals and Men*—Rigorous advancement of a science of behavior.
> Question of unit, e.g. comes here. Prob. of R=rate.
> Complex acts.

I defended its importance at a conference at the University of Pittsburgh in March 1947 on "Current Trends in Psychology." A great deal had happened to trends since I had entered the field. The conference made it clear that psychology was now important in daily life. Robert Sears discussed child psychology, Lowell Kelley clinical, Carl Rogers psychotherapy, John Flanagan personnel, Clifford Morgan human engineering, and Rensis Likert the sample interview survey, none of which had been taught in Emerson Hall in my day. I had studied nothing but "experimental psychology," and that was what I was asked to discuss. I acknowledged the diminishing relative importance of a laboratory science but defended its general relevance. Its task was to develop a theory that would be useful in every field of human behavior. Theories were simply statements about organizations of facts, and "whether particular experimental psychologists like it or not, experimental psychology is properly and inevitably committed to the construction of a theory of behavior." The development of an effective theory should restore experimental psychology to its proper position.

There had been a change in emphasis in my experimental work. When Garry Boring wrote to Mike Elliott to support my appointment at Minnesota, he said that I had been "sheltered" by five years of research fellowships. I was only just beginning to see an important effect. Almost all the experiments reported in *The Behavior of Organisms* were done to follow up leads arising from the work itself. I answered questions, clarified points, and solved practical problems raised by my own research. Once out of my shelter and in contact with other people, I turned to other questions: at Minnesota, to how fast rats pressed at maximal hunger, whether maze-bright and maze-dull rats differed in extinction, whether a rat could use tokens, and what effect drugs had on behavior; and at Indiana, reaction time, choice, and matching. These were a kind of technological application of the operant methodology. I was *using* an experimental analysis of behavior rather than furthering it. The results were interesting to many more people, but they were digressions.

I had kept to basic issues in some discussions with Arthur F. Bentley, a disciple of John Dewey's who lived in Paoli, Indiana, and who came to see me soon after I arrived in Bloomington. As a young man in the 1890s he had dropped in on a class of Dewey's at the University of Chicago and had been interested in him ever since. They were now conducting a long correspondence that would eventually be published.

I gave Bentley some of my papers and later he wrote:

I do not know why I never, until now, became acquainted with your work. If I had known of it, there are several things I have said in recent papers that I would have altered. This applies strikingly to the word "stimulus." I am saying, even in the paper to appear in a couple of weeks, that there is no use as yet, so far as psychology goes, in trying to specify the word. But right on the opening page—as approached with my kind of eyes—you have the makings of specification through bringing the word in system with reflex. Your approach to reflex—though not your particular phrasing—is a joy to me. Your type of experimentation is something I understand 100%. . . . In fact, except for Pavlov, it is unique to my eyes. . . . Your treatment of operant behavior under reflex, your refusal to spread stimulus over everything, your manner of putting drive in its place, your manner of pushing away both the mechanical and the mental with one common slap—all are up my alley. . . . If I had been aware I would have built directly on your procedure. Until some ten years ago I always expected that when the time came I would find a psychology I could use. When it appeared [that] I could not, and that I had to dig in a little myself, it set me back a long way.

MY PLAN FOR THE CAMPAIGN had made no provision, of course, for other products of time and chance. I could not have foreseen the accidents which led to the verbal summator, Project Pigeon, and *Walden Two*. It is only because I had to scrape up a course on the psychology of literature to fill out my teaching load that I got into sound patterning in poetry. The baby-tender was a solution to a practical problem.

There was also nothing in my plan for the campaign like the fourth and final entry in 1947:

> *Controlling Human Behavior*—A book for the educated layman on implications of a science of behavior—with enough on such a science at work to serve as an introductory text. Title?: The Control of Man.

The word "control" had begun to turn up in my notes at Minnesota, and the nearly complete control of the organism achieved in Project Pigeon had left its mark. At Indiana I spoke of control so often that when the graduate students put on a skit about the staff and Norman Guttman played Skinner, he said little more than, "Control . . . control . . . control . . ."

I knew the word was troublesome. Why not soften it to "affect" or "influence"? But I was a determinist and control meant control, and no other word would do. I did not mean punitive or aversive control, of course. On the contrary, I thought I had demonstrated effective alternatives to those objectionable modes. The only course I had taught on the subject had been on "*self*-control," which could scarcely be called threatening.

Control was no doubt at the heart of Frazier's behavioral engineering, but Frazier was not "treating people as if they were pigeons." Certain behavioral processes, like new drugs, surgical procedures, and artificial organs, are tested on animals before they are applied to people, but that does not mean that there is anything inhuman about them. Like the humanity of an artificial kidney, the humanity of behavioral engineering does not lie in its origins but in its use.

The behavioral engineering in Frazier's community is not aversive or punitive. The citizens of Walden Two behave well, productively, and creatively for *positive* reasons, which are, moreover, the natural consequences of their behavior. There is no "token economy." The only credit is a labor credit, and even the contrived social reinforcer "Thank you" is taboo. No one "intervenes" in the lives of anyone else. The community has been designed in such a way that the behavior needed for its successful functioning is *naturally* reinforced. The social environment, self-maintained, is as natural as the nonsocial. (Frazier, who designed it, is no longer in control. Emulation is confined to peers. There is no hero worship because there are no heroes.)

I WAS SATISFIED that I had solved the major problems inherent in the control of human behavior, and when I received my first copy of *Walden Two*, I was pleased. It seemed to demonstrate the success of a number of principles underlying the construction of the good life. As I would say later in the preface of a new printing:

Five of these are to be found as well in *Walden* (*One*) by Henry David Thoreau: (1) No way of life is inevitable. Examine your own closely. (2) If you do not like it, change it. (3) But do not try to change it through political action. Even if you succeed in gaining power, you will not be able to use it any more wisely than your predecessors. (4) Ask only to be left alone to solve your problems in your own way. (5) Simplify your needs. Learn how to be happy with fewer possessions.

Those principles could be enunciated without the help of a science of behavior, but *Walden* described only a Walden for One. Thoreau asked only to be left alone as an individualist. The problems of society called for something more, and that was where a behavioral technology could make its contribution. Five other principles were needed:

(6) Build a way of life in which people live together without quarreling, in a social climate of trust rather than suspicion, of love rather than jealousy, of cooperation rather than competition. (7) Maintain that world with gentle but pervasive ethical sanctions rather than a police or military force. (8) Transmit the culture effectively to new members through expert child care and a powerful educational technology. (9) Reduce compulsive labor to a minimum by arranging the kinds of incentives under which people enjoy working. (10) Regard no practice as immutable. Change and be ready to change again. Accept no eternal verity. Experiment.

Upon these ten principles Walden Two was founded and *Walden Two* written, and when the book was published I was more than ever convinced of their validity.

The early reviews seemed to back me up. Lewis Gannett in the *New York Herald Tribune* wrote that "spinning utopias is one of mankind's oldest parlor games, and Professor Skinner's has some ingenious new psychological twists." Charles Poore in the Sunday *New York Times* called the book "a brisk and thoughtful foray in search of peace of mind, security, and a certain amount of balm for burnt-fingered moderns." Bergen Evans in the *Chicago Sunday Tribune* wrote, "*Walden Two* is not a magic mountain, but it is a sunlit hill with an extensive view in many directions." And the *New Yorker* called it "an extremely interesting discourse on the possibilities of social organization."

There were a few disturbing notes. I had dedicated the book to my father and mother, using their initials only, but I was not surprised when my father told me that he thought the only sensible things in the book were said by Castle, Frazier's foil. Orville Prescott in the daily *New York Times* took the same line. He felt that life in my "land of milk and honey would be just as intolerable as in any of [Walden Two's] renowned predecessors." And then I saw the June 28 issue of *Life*:

THE NEWEST UTOPIA IS A SLANDER ON SOME
OLD NOTIONS OF THE GOOD LIFE

The making of utopias by literary people has been with us since the days of Plato, but of late the habit seems to be more contagious than ever. Within the past month at least two new ones have been published, one of them—by B. F. Skinner—bearing the entirely presumptuous title of *Walden Two*. In spirit *Walden Two* is as much like Thoreau's original *Walden* as a Quonset hut is like a comfortable and properly proportioned Cape Cod house.

Dr. Skinner is the professor of psychology who is responsible for the invention of something known as "the mechanical baby tender" (*Life*, Nov. 3). This air-conditioned palace for infants consists of a glass-walled cage which shuts out viruses and keeps the child from encountering splinters and other menaces to cranium and skin. In a world in which the common cold is still rampant, we would predict a low immunity to respiratory infections for any baby brought up amid Skinner gadgetry once it emerges into workaday surroundings. But the menace of the mechanical baby tender is as nothing compared to the menace of books like *Walden Two*. For Dr. Skinner's utopia is a triumph of "cultural engineering" and "behavioral engineering" where the conditioned reflex is king. Boards of Planners unobtrusively tell every big and little Skinnerite exactly what he or she must do. Once they are trained, the inhabitants of *Walden Two* have "freedom." But it is the freedom of those Pavlovian dogs which are free to foam at the mouth whenever the "dinner" bell invites them to a nonforthcoming meal. The very possibility of random personal choice has been eliminated from Dr. Skinner's world by a hierarchy which alone has the right to experiment. The desires, not the sins, of the fathers are visited upon the children to the third and fourth generation. Such a triumph of mortmain, or the dead hand, has not been envisaged since the days of Sparta.

If Dr. Skinner wants to imagine such a utopia, that is his privilege. But what should really be held against him is the egregious liberty he has taken with the title of Henry David Thoreau's original *Walden*. For the truth of the matter is that Thoreau's book is profoundly antiutopian; it does not belong in the long line of antiseptic literature that began with Plato's *Republic*. Far from trying to escape into a "brave new world," Thoreau, the cosmic bum, set out resolutely to make the best of what he could find right around home. Where Samuel Butler traveled to Nowhere from his *Erewhon*, where Edward Bellamy marched ahead to the year 2000 A.D. for his *Looking Backward*, Thoreau set up housekeeping by the edge of a duck pond outside of his native village. As Elliot Paul has said, he "got away from it all" by moving just a little farther from town than a good golfer could drive a ball. The lumber of Thoreau's cabin was taken from a shanty that had belonged to James Collins, an Irishman who had worked on the Fitchburg Railroad; the beans that Thoreau hoed and ate were Yankee beans, grown in recalcitrant New England soil.

Briefly, Thoreau was perhaps the greatest exponent of the old Yankee virtues of "use it up" and "make it do." He made a philosophy of the Here-and-Now, not the Far Away. There were no gadgets in the original *Walden*, and there was no "conditioning" for a "freedom" planned long in advance according to the rigid specifications of a gang of hierarchs. In the argot of 1948, in Walden One there was simply freedom, period.

Books like *Walden Two*, then, are a slur upon a name, a corruption of an impulse. All Thoreauists will properly resent them, and if Dr. Skinner comes around with any of his advice the good Thoreauist will, like Diogenes when confronted with the proffered largesse of the Macedonian king, tell the author of *Walden Two* to stand from between him and the free rays of the sun.

The editorial was not signed, but Ken Galbraith, whom I had known in Winthrop House, and who was working for *Life* at the time, told me that it was written by John K. Jessup. Though he called himself a liberal (he granted me the privilege of imagining a utopia), Ken thought he would have burned every copy of *Walden Two* if he had had the chance. It was my first contact with the rage sometimes elicited by the application of a scientific analysis to human affairs. I did not mind the strong language ("a slur upon a name, a corruption of an impulse"); it was the misrepresentation of what I had said and done that bothered me. The baby-tender was not a "glass-walled cage," and it did not leave the baby vulnerable to colds. In Walden Two the conditioned reflex was not king. (Except for the Pavlovian desensitization of emotional responses, most of the behavior was sustained by operant reinforcement.) People felt as free in Walden Two as anywhere else (no one was told "what he or she must do"), and it was not the freedom of those dogs which "foam at the mouth whenever the 'dinner' bell invites them to a nonforthcoming meal." (Dogs do not foam at the mouth when food is not forthcoming; they simply secrete less saliva.) A "gang of hierarchs" was experimenting, but the only promising kind of experimentation demanded rather than denied "random personal choice."

I myself had made many of the points Jessup urged against the book. Walden Two was not an escape to a distant island, to "Nowhere," or to a future time. As Frazier said, it differed from the classical utopias precisely because it was to be found (and could be believed in) here and now. It employed very few new gadgets, and Frazier was as much concerned as Thoreau to "use it up" and "make it do." Both asked of government only to be left alone. As Thoreau examined his own behavior, so Frazier examined the behavior of people in general, and both designed new ways of life to conform to what they found.

The *Life* editorial was only the beginning. A kind of behavioral engineering demonstrably effective in daily life would soon begin to replace my fictional account, and I should have many more opportunities to adjust to the rage, and, in turn, the misunderstandings that followed.

I ARRANGED A SECOND conference on the experimental analysis of behavior, and then we left Bloomington. We stopped to see my parents in Clarks Summit, a suburb of Scranton near the country club and golf course, to which they had moved when my father retired. In Cambridge, we looked for houses. I did not want to commute to work, and Eve had known the isolation of a suburb when she lived in

Flossmoor. Eventually, we hoped to build or buy near the university, but until we got the feel of the city, we would rent. We found a small house on Ellsworth Avenue within walking distance, though on the wrong side, of the Yard. Then we went on to Monhegan.

The preceding fall we had looked at, and through the windows into, a cottage that was for sale. It had been built in the first decade of the century for an artist, a Miss Hood, who had given the local carpenter a postcard showing a Swiss chalet and asked him to build a house that looked like it. An extra bedroom, kitchen, and shop had been added. Rockwell Kent, a friend of Miss Hood's, had carved a balustrade. As soon as my appointment at Harvard was confirmed, we had made an offer and purchased the house.

Jo Davis had married a fisherman, Dinty Day. She was still running the Trailing Yew, and except for breakfast we took our meals there. The ocean was still too cold for swimming, though Julie and Debbie did not seem to mind. We explored the far side of the island, studied the life in tidal pools, picked raspberries and wild strawberries, and built fires of driftwood on which we cooked lobsters wrapped in wet seaweed.

In September we went back to Cambridge. I had arrived there twenty years before in a different role, and I could now look forward to a different life.

NOTES

PAPERS CITED IN THE TEXT

ACKNOWLEDGMENTS

NOTES

14 "polemics against literature"
    A sample:

> The literatus delights in boulevard restaurants for it gives him oppor-
> tunities to study his beloved human nature. Street observation is, indeed,
> the best source of material for the fictionist, because one sees in a passing
> crowd only those universalized traits and physiognomies which trans-
> planted to a book bear witness to a supposed depth of penetration. It can
> be stated almost without reservation that in a work of fiction what passes
> for an understanding of human nature is merely a highly refined mimicry
> which because of its uncanny accuracy in reproducing a physiognomy is
> given credit for detailed knowledge of the underlying anatomy. In the case
> of a Dostoevsky, the mimicry (or for the sake of good manners, the redu-
> plication) extends to complicated relationships which indicate extraordinary
> perceptions; universally, however, Dostoevsky is given credit for an under-
> standing. There is no indication that he ever tried to understand, above a
> very religious wondering.

Other notes were prompted by Bergson's *Sur les Données immediates de
la conscience,* which I had read just before coming to Harvard. What I wrote
about Bergson's theory of perception is quite unintelligible to me now, and
much of my analysis of meaning was a heady mixture of sense and nonsense,
of reflexes and introspections, not necessarily respectively. Here is a sample:

> If all thought can be attributed to processes of perception and reflex,
> "meaning" in its wider sense may prove to be an expanded aspect of
> "essence." The sound of running water is conveyed in a quick succession
> and overlapping of several clicking and chirping sounds. We should say it
> would have no meaning to a person who has not learned the sound of run-
> ning water. It might seem not only unintelligible to such a person, but
> without a central unity of any kind. It is the part of the analyzers or syn-
> thesizers (the integrators) to interpret these sounds; and this can only be
> done when associations (conditionings) have been set up. Once done, the
> *sounds* of running water become the *sound.* In addition, the cause intro-
> duces liquidity into the effect, and in combination with other senses, de-
> velops the *meaning.*
>   If this be true, the question of naive realism cannot be neglected
> since it may be in the most direct relation to the perception of meaning.

On the boat coming back at the end of summer I had been sitting on deck
reading something of Bergson when a steward standing just behind me blew
a bugle to announce dinner. When I returned to the book, I could "feel the

blast of the bugle coming" as I read down the same page. Now I could specu-
late about an experimental test:

> Since the perception of the words leading up to the introduction of
> the stimulus did not take place simultaneously with the perception of the
> stimulus, there could be no chance for association (unless the question of
> time as being only apparent is raised). The only possibility of a relation
> between the two lies in the persistence (by memory or continued excita-
> tion) of an effect of the words.
>
> The climactic character indicates the importance of short time. Sup-
> pose the [bugle to have blown] at the end of line ten. Line one has no
> conscious pull towards a memory, nor have lines two and three. Line four
> however brings the feeling that precedes definite recollection, and by line
> eight I have analyzed the strangeness and discovered the association. Lines
> nine and ten are definitely powerful and the word upon which [the bugle
> sounded] stands out prominently. There is thus a greater suggesting power
> nearer the stimulus, which makes it possible at least that there is some
> *trace* from the stimulus of each word (independent of meaning?) which
> has associative power. . . .
>
> A possible experiment on the dog: some stimulus which is constantly
> changing in a definite progression is necessary; a disc of light climbing a
> silhouetted staircase, jumping from one step to a higher. The dog is shown
> the disc as it climbs from steps A to B to C and so on. At K food is pre-
> sented.
>
> Note should then be taken of the flow of saliva *for each step*, as the
> conditioning develops.
>
> A succession of unrelated stimuli would be better.
>
> If a physical or mental monism is tenable, then the process of learn-
> ing in perception may parallel a racial sense education, just as the foetus
> recapitulates roughly the racial evolution of form. Histories of art are
> therefore valuable as suggesting the course of sense education. (Roger Fry,
> "Plastic Color," *The Dial*, November, 1926, Volume LXXXI, no. 5.) In
> illuminated manuscripts, the *role* of color was mainly decorative, its ref-
> erence to natural appearance scarcely going beyond that of following the
> local colors of nature such as flesh tints, the green of trees, the blue of sky,
> and this *only in the most generalized way*.
>
> The history of music offers a parallel. Congenital color blindness and
> tone deafness may be simple reversions.

Some of my notes were little more than topics to be investigated:

> Surprise following looking where a mirror has been.
>
> By drawing a percept out of shape, its distortion is read into the thing
> perceived. Pressed eyeball, tongue sucked through the space between teeth
> which gives the effect of protruding edges on the teeth.

Two other notes written at about the same time:

> A single typographical error in a typewritten letter which I was read-
> ing casually threw my whole system back to a depressing emotional tone

of the evening before when I had been typing a letter, hastily and badly, which involved a great deal of gut reaction. I noted that the type was the same style and size and that I had a strong tendency to fall into that mood anyway.

I turn out a light, slightly burning my finger, and cross the room. My hand feels a current of warm air which pours from a heating pipe. Instantly I withdraw the hand, for the former slight burn is revived and I have the feeling that my hand has come dangerously near a *very* hot surface, as of a stove.

15 *Flying from Vienna:*
My note about the color of the Danube continued:

(I am not sure that the force of this memory was not borrowed from my surprise at the sudden association; yet it is easy to picture the image of the film waiting on the threshold as I looked from time to time at the river, the memory struggling to assert itself, and suddenly emerging, with a terrific bursting, at a certain moment.) The discussion increases in interest when the intersection theory is applied. Shortly after the experience I searched my mood, my state of mind, my surroundings, and my most recent thoughts for traces of a possible second association. On the wall in front of me was an advertisement which used facsimiles of 30 or 40 flags of many nations. When I was a child I played a game with small flags and learned to identify those of some 50 countries. Flags have strong meanings, or strong characters, and could easily have taken me back to the older period, as, indeed, they did when I began to notice them. Likewise, the country over which we were flying continually reminded me of the country in which I had lived as a child.

It should be noted that a factual memory of this sort occurs completely at one instant, just as the point of intersection occurs precisely at a given moment when two converging lines meet. Often in recalling a word which we remember vaguely we search for other associations, as if one line needed another to cross it before it determined a point. This geometric analogy can do no particular good, and perhaps great harm, but it will serve to crystalize my feelings about the inevitability of recollections, given the necessary (probably two or more) stimuli. The feeling of identity between the water and the film was at first generalized beyond the mere color. It was almost as if I were seeing again the actual film. The *blow* was one of recognition, beyond a mere recognition of color.

51 A *tunnel of galvanized iron:*
All the sheet-metal parts of the apparatus were beautifully made by an old tinsmith named McGee. He had worked for a local hardware store, and when it went out of the tinsmith business, he set up his own shop—with equipment purchased largely on time. He was a fine craftsman and taught me a great deal about soldering and working sheet metal, but the Depression ruined him. When Prohibition was repealed, he began to drink and finally shot himself in a hunting shack.

90 stimulus . . . varies considerably:

I gave further details in another letter:

> The rat does not go on eating [responding] with full strength because his chances of getting into such a position that the stimulating energies will be identical with this first case are pretty small. Actually let us say he comes at the lever again in such a way that some of the first (and now conditioned elements) are effective but some not. His second response will be made a little quicker than his first because of the operation of common elements. Moreover the new elements in the second case will now become fully conditioned so that his chances of getting more and more common elements on subsequent occasions will steadily go up until a point is reached at which, no matter how he comes at the lever he will receive conditioned *stimulation which is to all intents and purposes maximal.*

93 his Wednesday seminar:

H. D. Kimmel, "Notes from 'Pavlov's Wednesdays': Pavlov's Law of Effect," *American Journal of Psychology*, 89 (1976): 553–56.

95 wavelike form:

I explained the wavelike character of the extinction curve in this way: failure to receive reinforcement not only leads to extinction, it makes the rat "frustrated" or "angry" and in doing so depresses the rate. But fewer responses then go unreinforced, there is less "frustration," and the rat begins to press faster. Another cycle then follows. I had appealed to a similar emotional effect in explaining the rate to which a rat returns after it has been prevented from eating pellets for a period of time.

97 single pellet reconditioning:

My letter to Fred describing my attempt to measure the effect of a single reinforcement continued:

> Then, I begin putting in two pellets (ensemble) every 15 minutes. The slope immediately goes up. . . . I haven't calculated the ratio, but it is not due simply to the extra pellet being added in. There seem to be two chief factors at play (1) The inhibition (which finally yields [a sharp break followed by no responding] and lasts till next pellet is put in) and (2) reconditioning and extinction. With 2 pellets there is more conditioning and the inhibition is warded off for a longer time. What I want to know is whether the rat will "learn to push twice and leave it alone." It did not learn to push only once during twenty hours of exp. And if it does get its slope down to about 2 or 3 pushes per 15 min, what will happen if I begin to give 3 pellets every time? Etc.

98 Pavlov was experimenting:

H. D. Kimmel, "Notes from 'Pavlov's Wednesdays': Partial Reinforcement as a Test of Mobility," *American Journal of Psychology*, 90 (1977): 529–32.

103 discriminative . . . stimulus:

I had anticipated the role of the discriminative stimulus in my thesis. My equation, $R = f(S,A)$, gave the stimulus no special status among the variables of which reflex strength was a function. The letter A stood for any "third variable" such as might be found in the fields of conditioning, drive, or emotion. Thus, to make a rat more or less likely to press a lever you could condition or extinguish the response, change the level of deprivation, or affect the rat emotionally. You could also present or remove any stimulus which had been present when the behavior was reinforced.

The role of the discriminative stimulus is subtle. Let us say that a child is playing quietly until someone appears with a dish of candy and that it then stops playing and insistently begs for candy. It is easy to call this a change in "drive"; the child has suddenly "become hungry for candy." But the change is in the situation, not the child. It is now a situation in which begging for candy is likely to be reinforced. Hence the strength of the behavior.

I wrote a rather confusing note about another case in which a discriminative stimulus could be confused with an increase in deprivation:

Let us suppose that a man who is breaking off smoking does not feel his desire to smoke until he sees his old pipe. Is this an intensification of drive? Not at all. The presence of the extraordinarily well conditioned reflex means that an unusual effort is required to repress it. [I identified the "reflex" by listing three things: a stimulus (the old pipe), a response (reaching), and a reinforcing stimulus (contact with old pipe).] The response of reaching into one's pocket for a pipe varies with the pipe drive (pipe drive varies with what fundamental drive?).

Or a man sees another man smoking and then reaches into his own pocket for his pipe. What about this? (Old question of reinf. vs. having facilitating effect.) Suddenly questioned a man may say I did not feel a desire for tobacco until you mentioned it. I.e., I was not making any response or inhibiting any response to tobacco until you supplied a discriminative stimulus.

I was using "drive" uncritically (though I saw that we needed to know more about the "pipe drive"), and I was still using "facilitation" and "inhibition" to explain changes in reflex strength, but the last paragraph makes an important point about the discriminative stimulus.

Another mistake is to confuse a reduction in "drive" with improved discrimination as shown by a lower rate in the presence of S^Δ. In one example I noted, mistakenly, that "the rat discriminated better as the strength of reflex dropped," although all I had observed was that the pause after reinforcement (under periodic reconditioning) was longer when the rats were less hungry.

103 "Further Properties of Discrimination":

In a later experiment I reversed the stimuli. If I had been reinforcing an occasional response when the light was on, I now left it on and reinforced after it went off. The rats stopped responding in the light and began to respond in the dark. When I switched conditions again, they returned to the original pattern. I planned, but never carried out, an experiment in which a response would be reinforced only after the change from light to dark, but not after the change from dark to light.

The process of discrimination explained some earlier observations. When I reinforced all responses on some days and extinguished them on others, the extinction curves contained fewer and fewer responses as the experiment went on. Now I could see that a few unreinforced responses were functioning as S^Δ; the rats were distinguishing between good and bad days. I could now also explain the "inhibition" seen under periodic reconditioning. The small extinction curves appearing in the first few intervals between reinforcements grew flatter and reinforcements were eventually followed by short pauses. Now I could see that the receipt of a pellet was functioning as an S^Δ. I confirmed this interpretation by grouping reinforcements in pairs, reinforcing after intervals of eight and two minutes instead of five and five. The rate was conspicuously lower after the two-minute interval. Two reinforcements were a more effective S^Δ than one.

104 *"time interval effect"*:

If a response could be made to a "time interval," there were two stimuli present when a response was reinforced: the light that had just been turned on and the end of a period of time.

117 *my marginal notes:*

Here are some other examples of my marginal comments in C. I. Lewis's *Mind and the World Order*:

Lewis: Suppose we talk of physical things in physical terms and our discussion involves physical measurement. Presumably we have the same ideas of feet and pounds and seconds. If not, the thing is hopeless. But in psychological terms, my notion of a foot goes back to some immediate image of visual so-long-ness or the movements which I make when I put my hands so far apart, or a relation between these two. Distances in general mean quite complex relationships between such visual images, muscle and contact-sensations, the feeling of fatigue, and so on. Weight goes back to muscle sensations, the "heft" of the thing. And our direct apprehension of time is that feeling of duration which is so familiar but so difficult to describe.

BFS: This is what Mach is *supposed* to have said, but the operational definition of these concepts, which does not require [any reference to] feelings and sensations, is more satisfactory and incidentally more behavioristic.

Lewis: The coincidence of two minds when they understand each other...

BFS: The coincidence of the behavior of two people when they are said to "understand each other." This little change makes it behavioristic (if meaning is defined objectively).

Lewis's argument against a copy theory is a great stroke for behaviorism since it greatly minimizes the significance of the content of consciousness.

Note that when conditioning is substituted for the If-then most of these problems disappear.

119 *subject matter of his science:*

In another section of my *Sketch for an Epistemology* I said that "behaviorism's most trenchant criticism has been directed at the uncritical practice of inferring the characteristics of subjective states from the verbal behavior of observers." An apparent way out was for the psychologist to be his own subject —observing his subject matter (i.e., sensations and so on) just as the physicist observed his scale readings.

But no science is possible, in any ordinary sense at least, if every scientist has his own private universe. . . . It is necessary to assume that similar events in two or more subjective universes may be shown to be identical on the basis of verbal communication, but this of course was the assumption in the old liaison between observer and experimenter, so that no essential change has really been effected.

It will suffice to note two differences between observing a dial and observing a sensation. . . . Two people may observe the same dial. It is therefore possible for the second person to describe the observing of the dial by the first. He can . . . show that the use of the word is correlated with an event on the dial face. . . . When he takes the word of the scientist about the dial he has independent justification that must always be lacking in the case of the sensation. . . . Putting the whole thing in terms of communication, we may define a referent in the case of the dial as something more than "the thing referred to" since we may investigate the use of the word in relation to certain classes of stimuli. It is not possible to do this in the case of a sensation. Or in still other terms—it is possible to define the meaning of the word dial but not of sensation.

The behaviorist may not be prepared at the present time to give any very convincing experimental treatment of all the behavior that turns up in a psychological experiment. All that [he] can claim at the moment is that [his] concepts are potentially capable of dealing with this material. . . .

119 *"chronaxies":*

Chronaxie was a measure of the responsiveness of a nerve to electrical stimulation. You found the weakest possible current (called the rheobase) that would stimulate a nerve; then you doubled it and stimulated the nerve again. The time it took the nerve to respond—usually a matter of a few thousandths of a second—was the chronaxie.

143 *The control they exerted was more subtle:*

Even as late as February 1935, I was still not clear about the role of the discriminative stimulus. I prepared an eight-page "Memorandum to Dr. Beebe-Center" entitled "The Special Status of the Stimulus among the Variables Affecting Response." In it I converted the equation in my thesis, $R = f(S,A)$, to $[S-R] = f(a, \beta, \gamma, \ldots)$, where $[S-R]$ represented "the strength of the reflex" and $a, \beta, \gamma, \ldots$ the various "states" of drive, conditioning, emotion, and so on. S differed from the other variables because it could be turned on and off instantly. It identified a particular response, whereas an operation like deprivation affected many responses. "For every R there is one S but not one δ" and "a response cannot be defined (except as an arbitrary part of behavior which has no experimental reality as a unit) without appeal to a correlation with a stimulus." I was also still unclear about rate as a measure of strength. "Latency, threshold, after discharge and especially the rate of responding (reducible to refractory phase?) have no meaning apart from a temporal or intensive measure of the stimulus."

148 my theory of extinction . . . in trouble:

Quite apart from disinhibition I thought it likely that a slight stimulus might bring the rat back to pressing the lever if it had fallen below its normal position on an extinction curve, and I considered introducing disturbing noises throughout the process, as one rocks a test tube back and forth to promote a chemical process.

154 newspapers were unkind:

An anonymous correspondent congratulated the *Scranton Times* on its editorial about my father's speech:

> *The facts you presented and the force with which you presented them should make Lawyer Skinner wish he never left Starrucca for the wicked city. I can imagine him as any other farm boy, fine and wholesome to start with, but like many other good boys from the sticks spoiled when they showed him the city through the eyes of the mining corporations, etc. It was an unheard of Lawyer Skinner until he became president of the Kiwanis Club, but from that time on it wasn't the farm boy from Starrucca but Skinner the attorney, special pleader for interests that are not expected to have anything in common with the sons of earth or the toilers of the mine.*

Even the *Scranton Republican* thought my father had gone too far! "He belongs to the old reactionary school whose theories of 'rugged individualism' and indiscriminate 'profit motive' stand like rocks of Gibraltar, it matters not how many or what kinds of economic hurricanes blow across the land." But the *Republican* published a letter agreeing with my father: "Mr. Skinner is an individualist, who believes that every man and every business should stand on its own feet. I agree with him. Now write another funny editorial and explain the last report of the Internal Revenue Department as to why incomes in the small brackets fell off, and the million dollar incomes went up by twelve."

167 *wholly mechanical "problem box":*

In that nonelectrical "problem box" the lever was a half-inch tube of light brass with rounded end plugs to discourage gnawing. The dispenser was a disk of black plastic turned by the fall of a lead weight. (The disk contained two rings of holes; when one ring had emptied, a small adjustment opened the other.) A delicate escapement allowed it to turn one step when the lever was pressed, but only when an arm was in a given position. The arm could be put in or out of position from outside the apparatus by pulling a silk thread. The movement of the lever stepped a ratchet which wound up a thread to a cumulative recorder. All this could be installed at one end of a soundproof box, with only the lever accessible to the rat and with two threads leading outside to the recorder and the reinforcement programmer.

169 *required weaker responses:*

Today it is easy to design an apparatus that selects for reinforcement only those responses emitted with a force above a given value, but if equipment of that sort was available at the time, I did not know about it. I used a small but heavy pendulum that was thrown forward as the lever moved. Its excursion depended upon how hard the lever was pressed, and an adjustable contact was closed when a given excursion was made. To record the force, I used a small lead flywheel on ball bearings, which spun when the lever was pressed. Through a train of gears it turned a shaft which wound up a thread going to the recorder. By dropping the lever with various weights attached, I determined the distance the recording point rose when the lever was pressed with a given force. The kymograph drum was turned by a ratchet and moved one step for each response. The slopes of the recorded curves could then be read as force per response.

174 *rhythmic patterns:*

My rhythm generator consisted of a small turntable with a strip of brass running from the center to the edge. Above it were half a dozen arms, like movable spokes, pivoting about the shaft of the motor. A pair of electrodes on each arm made a brief contact with the brass strip as the plate turned, and the contacts operated a telegraph receiver. By arranging the arms in various patterns I could generate a great variety of six-beat rhythms.

177 *the experimental book:*

When planning *The Behavior of Organisms* I made the following resolutions:

OMIT (from main body of text)

All arguments of the biological significance of any or all reflexes. Purpose, etc.

All arguments for or against accompanying subjective states.

All arguments reducible to objections to the mechanistic treatment of organisms.

All physiological hypotheses—synapse, etc.

All models, thermodynamic and otherwise, except reserve.
All theories of the origin or development of reflexes . . . (Aging)
All lists of *kinds* of behavior—instincts, ecology, etc. (No topology)
Rewrite arguments against reflex as unit to make it only an exposition.

181 *"Obey her":*

These results were reported in D. Shakow and S. Rosenzweig, "The Use of the Tautophone ["verbal summator"] as an Auditory Apperceptive Test for the Study of Personality," *Character and Personality*, 8 (1940): 216–26.

The verbal summator never came into serious use as a "device for snaring out complexes." My phonograph went from Worcester to Dwight Chapman at the Recorders Court in Detroit, where "an auditory inkblot" proved to be better than the Rorschach in screening psychopathic criminals because it could be administered as a test of their hearing, whereas the Rorschach looked like a child's game. The machine was eventually returned to me, and a graduate student, Mary Adah Trussell, made some new records with samples spoken by both a man and a woman. She compared a group of psychology laboratory students with thirty-two patients in a psychopathic ward of the University Hospital. The groups differed on such things as number of meaningless responses, lack of reference to external stimuli, number of references to special themes, and so on. W. K. Estes constructed a visual form in which subjects glimpsed meaningless phrases for a fraction of a second. For many years I supplied several kinds of phonographic disks to interested people.

181 *a much more elaborate one:*

In the other experiment on spontaneous recovery I had suggested:

breaking your group into two parts and let the schedule run something as follows:

Day 1: Extinguish for 1 and ½ hours. Both groups.
Day 2: Further extinction for Group A. Nothing for Group B.
Day 45—extinguish Group B further. You might extinguish Group A further too for the fun of it.

This would give you two groups for original extinction and one day of further extinction to show recovery with the difference that a month and a half elapses between the two processes in the one case and only twenty-four hours in the other.

As I reported in *The Behavior of Organisms* (p. 94), there was a somewhat bigger extinction curve after forty-five days, which seemed to answer a question I had raised about another experiment in which spontaneous recovery would be tested after either two or four months. "You ought to get a difference in the amount of spontaneous recovery from extinction as a function of time. . . . The question is: What do rats remember better—what they have learned or what they have unlearned?" I had predicted that they would remember what they had learned, and that now seemed to be the case.

183 *make you famous:*
Fred had done some experiments on "social eating." A rat that has stopped eating starts again if joined by a hungry rat, and rats eat more when they are with other rats. I thought there was a nonsocial explanation and I wrote to Fred:

> *Suppose you let a rat get pellets in runs of twenty only. After twenty responses take it out and give it no food for at least half an hour. Then in again for twenty responses. You could do this say three times each day. . . . After a while you will probably find the rat running to the lever as soon as you start to take him out, just as they now pick up food when you start to take it away. So far so good. Now begin to give some signal a few seconds before opening box to remove rat. Say, turn on the light. . . . Then you ought to get an increase in rate [of pressing] following this signal. If you get that . . . the social effect in your eating experiment will be explained. The second rat is not a little furry friend to the first, but merely a complex of stimuli which frequently accompanies the breaking of the chain, since the second rat frequently takes food away. Hence the strengthening of the eating reflexes and hence more food eaten. In other words you are analyzing out what aspect of the second rat is responsible for the increase in eating. It would be a fine example of method in analyzing social situations.*

Fred tried the experiment and reported slow progress. I suggested strengthening the stimulus and pointed out that my rats began to pick up food when I started to take them out of their feeding cages only after three or four weeks. Later I tried the experiment myself with negative results. I turned on a stimulus a few minutes before the end of a session in which a rat was being periodically reconditioned and continued to do so for weeks. I observed no increase in rate of responding when the stimulus came on.

183 *trying to get Pavlov to change:*
H. D. Kimmel, "Notes from 'Pavlov's Wednesdays': Pavlov's Law of Effect," *American Journal of Psychology*, 89 (1976): 553–56.

185 *very forceful responses:*
Konorski and Miller replied to my reply in a second article, which they sent to Murchison with a copy to me. I told Fred that I was not going to answer it because I thought *The Behavior of Organisms* would make my position clear enough. Murchison published their paper without giving the authors any help with their English. A phrase like "Type R as Skinner lastly calls it" in my typescript appeared unchanged in the published version.

192 *". . . two types of conditioned reflex":*
Another part of Delabarre's letter:

> *When you proposed the problem to me, you spoke of Konorski and Miller's having denied the possibility of the theoretical case given by you*

on page 67 of your article on the two types. . . . You say yourself that the "two kinds can apparently not be separated" although it is "a very special case" and "in no sense a reduction to a single type." . . . Although I can fit our thing into the general formulation of type R on page 66, I fail to see myself how it fits into that special case on page 67.

The question was whether salivation could be reinforced as an operant with food as the reinforcer; if it could, both would be salivation, and since both types of conditioning occur at the same time (the rat presumably salivates to the discriminative stimulus controlling the strength of pressing the lever), it would be hard to tease out the causal relations if salivation were treated as an operant. Something of the sort is likely to confuse any case of the operant reinforcement of autonomic behavior.

199 *predicted agreement:*
A graduate student at Minnesota named Schellenberg had collected other word-association data. Five hundred entering freshmen had responded to 200 words drawn from material in the field of emotion. I was able to get the tabulations from Schellenberg, and a graduate student, Stuart W. Cook, and I treated them in the same way. The line was straight again, but it had a different slope. There was less agreement on the more frequent responses and greater agreement on the less frequent. We felt that the difference could be explained by the fact that the students probably had a larger working vocabulary than the psychotics.

As a rough demonstration of the Zipf distribution to my class in Laboratory Psychology, I asked each student to write down the name of a city, a word for a color, an animal, a vegetable, and so on. There was clearly a most frequent word in each category (though Minneapolis and St. Paul caused trouble in the category of cities), the other words dropping off as expected. By averaging across categories I could get a reasonably straight line on logarithmic coordinates.

204 *having them bound:*
The bound volume of my reprints, lettered "Experiments in Learning. B. F. Skinner," was sent to me after Hull's death.

206 *discussed it with his students:*
Tolman's letter about my paper, dated November 6, 1931:

Dear Skinner,
Thanks a lot for the reprint. I have read it carefully and I hope amusedly or bemusedly or whatever—as you desire.
I do of course agree with the disposal of physiology which you suggest and of course do not agree with anything else, or mayhap I do.
Anyway, I learned a lot of history (which I have since forgotten) as a result of reading it.
No, really, I am awfully interested to see what you will do with the

concept in further articles. Of course my own bias and suspicion is that when you get in all the modifiers of the reflex (I have forgotten the technical term you suggested) that you will have everything in it which I call by a different and, no doubt, very mystical and reprehensible set of names, —to wit, sign-gestalts and demands—(see forcoming [sic] book.)

If your concepts cause you, as they do, to investigate first the simplest conceivable conditions where stimuli and response are very simple and very close together, all power to them. It is something that surely ought to be done. But, of course, I must still contend that the grosser situations also ought even at present likewise to be investigated—otherwise I should be out of a job. And I am staying optimistic and betting for the present that the necessary descriptive concepts found in your situations and those found in my type of situation will be found to fit nicely one into or one onto another.

In short, I will not admit now, and until you finally force me to, that my concepts are analagous to those of astrology.

I do think it is awfully decent of you to admit the whole organism and "behavior" as a subject for study—though I don't quite see why these also don't offend you as a bit too unanalysed and astrological.

> Yours towards bigger and better
> rats and fewer introspectors
> Edward C. Tolman

P.S. I am causing (perhaps I should say "purposing") my animal seminar to read the paper and when they have finished with it I shall know better what to think. There are some damn bright guys in it—almost up to the Harvard level.

> E. C. T.

212 dropped the experiment:

Murray Sidman would later make sense of the "avoidance of undesirable consequences."

219 Ph.D. candidates:

Not being able to work with graduate students would have been hard on Fred. At Colgate many of his students had been active researchers. One of them, Reinwald, had turned up a puzzling result. He had put a rat in a running wheel in a soundproof box. When it was not running, he had sounded a tone of medium intensity and noted that there was little effect. Then, in the absence of the tone, he shocked the rat through its feet. The tone then produced a great deal of running, and seventy presentations were needed to bring about "extinction." The shock had not been paired with the tone as in the Pavlovian situation. When Fred reported the experiment to me, I said the shock should be classed as an emotional variable:

> Because the operation inducing the emotion is the presentation of a sudden stimulus, there is a superficial resemblance to a CR, which of course is not actually the case. The only additional process that I can de-

tect as a possibility is some kind of induction—*the tone possesses one of the properties of the shock (e.g. it is presented suddenly against the same experimental background) and it is quite possible that through induction the rat comes to respond to the wheel-plus-tone in some measure the same as to the wheel-plus-shock. Hilgard and Marquis in their book on the* CR *(still in* MS*) call this sensitization.*

228 *fairly straight line:*

I put another student to work on a concordance of Joyce's *Ulysses*, which the compiler, Miles Hanley, had sent me. She was to look up the Kent-Rosanoff stimulus words and then tally ten words before and after each instance in the text. When I wrote to tell Hanley what I was doing, he sent me the cards bearing the full citations of the words I was interested in. We were then at war and I soon returned the cards with the job unfinished, but the first results had looked promising. "Chair" did seem to occur near "table" and "sweet" near "sour" more often than any other word, as the word-association experiment had suggested, but the frequencies were very low.

229 *verbal repertoire:*

Crozier once told me about a verbal process that threw a different light on storage. He and Gregory Pincus had asked people to give as quickly as possible all the words they could think of beginning with a given letter. Words poured out at first, but the flow dried up—along a parabolic curve. I wrote to Crozier for further details, but he replied that Pincus had the data and was spending the year in England.

231 *other reviewers:*

The four major reviews of *The Behavior of Organisms* were by I. Krechevsky (David Krech), Tolman's most promising student; Ernest R. Hilgard, who had received his doctorate at Yale a year after Hull had arrived there and who became perhaps the most important spokesman for the system that Hull later developed; John L. Finan, a student of Hull's; and Ernst Wolf, a student of Crozier's.

239 *a sort of puzzle-book:*

I was convinced that successive approximation could lead children into what my contemporaries would have called complex cognitive behavior, and it may be worthwhile listing some examples. My book would contain:

(1) A series of pictures showing the tracks left by a fox as it enters a snowy field and moves from one to another of half a dozen bushes. The child is to find the bush under which the fox is hiding—beginning with a single track to one bush and moving on to a complex maze of tracks. At one point the child is given a hint ("There is something odd about this") and eventually learns that the fox is always under the bush with an odd number of tracks going in and out.

(2) A series of progressively more complex maps to be colored with the smallest number of colors.

(3) A set of triangles, large or small and black or white, and a set of circles, large or small and black or white. The child is to draw the opposite of a given example—a small black circle, say, for a large white triangle.

(4) Descriptions of a wise man to be judged true or false—beginning with "He is a wise man," "He is an unwise man," "He is a not unwise man," and leading up to something like "It is not true that he is an unwise man."

(5) Permutations and combinations to be explored, starting with "How many different tunes of three notes each can be played on two keys of a piano?" and moving on slowly to more complex cases.

(6) Given a pair of letters (say, *ST* and *C*), the child is to find rhymes —for *stupid, cupid;* for *cage, stage;* for *stamp, camp;* and so on.

(7) Pictures to be labeled with rhymes. *Big wig* and *cook book* are given as samples and the child is to find similar labels for a *bent cent,* a *small wall,* a *fat cat,* moving on to more complicated examples such as a *crazy daisy* and a *candle handle.*

(8) Pictures to be labeled with spoonerisms of the labels given. For example, a picture of a cat catching a rat, labeled "The Rapture of a Cat," is to be given the alternative title "The Capture of a Rat." Unprogrammed material included optical illusions demonstrating that "things are not always what they seem" (e.g., in a perspective drawing Jack in the foreground proves when measured to be bigger than the giant in the distance), and illogicalities to be spotted (e.g., what is wrong with saying "I always wait in my seat until everyone else has left the hall to avoid being crushed in the crowd, and I can't understand why everyone else doesn't do the same thing"?).

241 *different effect on such behavior:*
Murray Sidman later discovered the effect we predicted.

255 *Norman Guttman:*
Norman Guttman, in a letter to me dated February 19, 1976, gives this account of his conversion to a science of behavior:

> *The day you hired me was the turning point of my life, so I will elaborate a bit. I was a senior undergraduate, and it had been arranged by Herbert Feigl that I would come to work for him in 1941–42 as an NYA student-assistant, to help with the translation of important articles by various Wiener Kreis people into some form of English. But the day I was to report for that job, on which I was absolutely dependent for finishing my B.A., was the holiest of days, Yom Kippur, and my mother would not allow me the transgression of taking the streetcar to campus. By the next morning the NYA job had evaporated, and I was desolate, desperate. For solace—for that alone, believe me—I went to your office to see my friend Professor Skinner. While we were chatting, about nothing really except the true and the good, in came Bill Estes and asked in his solemn, laconic way: "Fred, have you got anybody to fix the apparatus?" My ears perked*

up; I inquired what the requirements were, and inside of an hour you had taken me on, and I was saved; and from that moment on I was a psychologist and no longer a philosopher. (The conversion, of course, did not stick; when this letter is done I will revert for a good hour to Plato and the paradoxes of the Meno *with my history seminar.)*

257 De Florez:

De Florez evidently continued to take risks. He became an admiral during the war and was later Chairman of Research in the CIA. In January 1976 the *New York Times* reported that he had argued against disciplining the scientists responsible for the death of an unwitting subject in an experiment on LSD "in the interest of maintaining the spirit of initiative and enthusiasm so necessary to our work."

263 approximate specifications:

The first specifications were these: "The homing device output should be linear between 0 and 3° off course. The proportionality should be adjustable so that differential output is 8 milliamps at any predetermined point between 3° off course and the limit of proportionality. The output feeds into two 12,000-ohm coils."

264 reliable processing systems:

The similarity of our three-pigeon guidance systems to von Neumann's derivation of a reliable processing system from unreliable components is pointed out by J. G. Miller in his *Living Systems* (New York: 1978).

280 extinction curves were smaller:

I published one curve showing retention of the target behavior after four years. It contained about 700 responses, which I estimated, probably too generously, as from one-half to one-quarter of the responses that would have been emitted four years earlier. I ran two remaining pigeons after six years and got small extinction curves even then.

287 deserved further study:

I was not the first to do operant work with human infants. Fred had done some informal experiments with his daughter, Anne, and work had been done in an academic setting by Leslie Zieve and Kay Walker (Estes) at the Child Welfare Department at Minnesota and by Doris Mount at Mills College in California.

312 the following way:

The quotation about choice appeared in *Psychological Review*, 57 (1950): 193–216.

I planned but did not carry out an experiment with two keys either of which could be red or green. The pigeon would learn a series of "choices"— to peck either the right or the left key regardless of color or the red or green key regardless of side, or one side when both keys were the same color. I would run a long series and then average blocks of curves to see whether the pigeon relearned more and more quickly as it acquired this complex repertoire of discriminations.

320 superstitious behavior:

Adventitious contingencies producing superstitious behavior arise in many experiments. The presentation of an S^D, for example, may reinforce responding in S^Δ. I had shown this by making the presentation of light explicitly contingent on responding in the dark, but adventitious contingencies are to be expected. In my first experiment on discrimination my rats never quite stopped responding in S^Δ. An occasional response in the dark may have been accidentally reinforced by the appearance of the light.

344 a long way:

Bentley's letter ended:

Next comes Bühler getting me all excited over his use of Zeichen, but drifting then to Anzeichen in misty clouds, and then folding up altogether. Comes Brunswik with his work vom Gegenstand her, and hence the start of a distinction between distal and proximal. But in this country he seems to have fallen among evil companions, and come to distort his "achievement." I note his three references to you in his Encyclopedia of Psychology contribution fail to note any of what I regard as your main characteristics. (Incidentally Griffith's floods of words contain no hint either of what you or Kantor have stressed.) Among the latest attacks, Lewin's excites my greatest disgust, and Hull, I fancy, is most remote from anything I regard as worth while. This puts me in my place.

In other words, so far as my recent reading goes, I have not seen any trace of recognition of what you have done, let alone any influence from it. My reading has, however, been small. There must be some results somewhere. I do not want to go further without knowing of them.

348 John K. Jessup:

Not content with the *Life* editorial, Jessup reviewed *Walden Two* for *Fortune*. *Walden Two* was like "a peaceful kindergarten for adults in a well-run summer hotel." It was innocent in appearance but vicious in principle. A mad scientist ran the place and its "inmates" were "allegedly happy." The author was arrogant and dangerous. "If social scientists share Professor Skinner's values —and many of them do—they can change the nature of Western civilization more disastrously than the nuclear physicists and biochemists combined."

PAPERS CITED IN THE TEXT

PAGE

20 "The Progressive Increase in the Geotropic Response of the Ant *Aphaeno-gaster*," *Journal of General Psychology*, 4 (1930): 102–12 (with T. C. Barnes).

46 "On the Inheritance of Maze Behavior," *Journal of General Psychology*, 4 (1930): 342–46.

60 "On the Conditions of Elicitation of Certain Eating Reflexes," *Proceedings of the National Academy of Sciences*, 16 (1930): 433–38.

75 "The Concept of the Reflex in the Description of Behavior," *Journal of General Psychology*, 5 (1931): 427–58.

78 "The Measurement of 'Spontaneous Activity,'" *Journal of General Psychology*, 9 (1933): 3–23.

78 "Thirst as an Arbitrary Drive," *Journal of General Psychology*, 15 (1936): 205–10.

81 "Drive and Reflex Strength," *Journal of General Psychology*, 6 (1932): 22–37.

82 "Drive and Reflex Strength: II," *Journal of General Psychology*, 6 (1932): 38–48.

85 "A Paradoxical Color Effect," *Journal of General Psychology*, 7 (1932): 481–82.

92 "On the Rate of Formation of a Conditioned Reflex," *Journal of General Psychology*, 7 (1932): 274–86.

95 "On the Rate of Extinction of a Conditioned Reflex," *Journal of General Psychology*, 8 (1933): 114–29.

96 "'Resistance to Extinction' in the Process of Conditioning," *Journal of General Psychology*, 9 (1933): 420–29.

103 "The Rate of Establishment of a Discrimination," *Journal of General Psychology*, 9 (1933): 302–50.

103 "The Abolishment of a Discrimination," *Proceedings of the National Academy of Sciences*, 19 (1933): 825–28.

104 "A Discrimination Without Previous Conditioning," *Proceedings of the National Academy of Sciences*, 20 (1934): 532–36.

119 "Some Conditions Affecting Intensity and Duration Thresholds in Motor Nerve, with Reference to Chronaxie of Subordination," *American Journal of Physiology*, 106 (1933): 721–37 (with E. F. Lambert and A. Forbes).

136 "Has Gertrude Stein a Secret?" *Atlantic Monthly*, 153 (January 1934): 50–57.

139 "The Extinction of Chained Reflexes," *Proceedings of the National Academy of Sciences*, 20 (1934): 234–37.

142 "Two Types of Conditioned Reflex and a Pseudo Type," *Journal of General Psychology*, 12 (1935): 66–77.

146 "The Generic Nature of the Concepts of Stimulus and Response," *Journal of General Psychology*, 12 (1935): 40–65.

147 "Conditioning and Extinction and Their Relation to Drive," *Journal of General Psychology*, 14 (1936): 296–317.

148 "A Failure to Obtain 'Disinhibition,'" *Journal of General Psychology*, 14 (1936): 127–35.

157 "The Effect on the Amount of Conditioning of an Interval of Time Before Reinforcement," *Journal of General Psychology*, 14 (1936): 279–95.

157 "The Reinforcing Effect of a Differentiating Stimulus," *Journal of General Psychology*, 14 (1936): 263–78.

176 "The Verbal Summator and a Method for the Study of Latent Speech," *Journal of Psychology*, 2 (1936): 71–107.

184 "Two Types of Conditioned Reflex: A Reply to Konorski and Miller," *Journal of General Psychology*, 16 (1937): 272–79.

192 "Changes in Hunger During Starvation," *Psychological Record*, 1 (1937): 51–60 (with W. T. Heron).

198 "The Distribution of Associated Words," *Psychological Record*, 1 (1937): 71–76.

201 "Effects of Caffeine and Benzedrine upon Conditioning and Extinction," *Psychological Record*, 1 (1937): 340–46 (with W. T. Heron).

222 "An Apparatus for the Study of Animal Behavior," *Psychological Record*, 3 (1939): 166–76 (with W. T. Heron).

227 "The Rate of Extinction in Maze-Bright and Maze-Dull Rats," *Psychological Record*, 4 (1940): 11–18 (with W. T. Heron).

229 "The Alliteration in Shakespeare's Sonnets: A Study in Literary Behavior," *Psychological Record*, 3 (1939): 186–92.

237 "A Quantitative Estimate of Certain Types of Sound-Patterning in Poetry," *American Journal of Psychology*, 54 (1941): 64–79.

238 "A Method of Maintaining an Arbitrary Degree of Hunger," *Journal of Comparative Psychology*, 30 (1940): 139–45.

238 "The Psychology of Design." In *Art Education Today* (New York: Bureau Publications, Teachers College, Columbia University, 1941), pp. 1–6.

241 "Some Quantitative Properties of Anxiety," *Journal of Experimental Psychology*, 29 (1941): 390–400 (with W. K. Estes).

252 "The Processes Involved in the Repeated Guessing of Alternatives," *Journal of Experimental Psychology*, 30 (1942): 495–503.

294 "The Operational Analysis of Psychological Terms," *Psychological Review*, 52 (1945): 270–77; 291–94.

303 "Baby in a Box," *Ladies' Home Journal*, 62 (October 1945): 30–31; 135–36; 138.

313 "Are Theories of Learning Necessary?" *Psychological Review*, 57 (1950): 193–216.

320 " 'Superstition' in the Pigeon," *Journal of Experimental Psychology*, 38 (1948): 168–72.

321 "An Automatic Shocking-Grid Apparatus for Continuous Use," *Journal of Comparative and Physiological Psychology*, 40 (1947): 305–7 (with S. L. Campbell).

328 "Card-Guessing Experiments," *American Scientist*, 36 (1948): 456; 458.

343 "Experimental Psychology." In W. Dennis and others, *Current Trends in Psychology* (Pittsburgh: University of Pittsburgh Press, 1947), pp. 16–49.

ACKNOWLEDGMENTS

I thank the following for their help in the preparation of this book: Robert Epstein, Jean Kirwan Fargo, Norman Guttman, Suzanne Harmon, Ilona Lappo, Frank K. Lorenz, E. B. Newman, Eve Skinner, Eric Ward, Karin Wetmore, Alicia Caban Wheeler, M. J. Willard, and Maryanne Wolf-Ward.

Parts of letters from E. G. Boring are published with the permission of Mrs. E. G. Boring; parts of letters from Edwin C. Tolman with the permission of Professor Tolman's daughter, Deborah T. Whitney; and letters from Fred S. Keller and Cuthbert Daniel from the writers. I thank them for their kindness. The excerpt from the Preface of *Walden Two* is reprinted with permission of Macmillan Publishing Co., Inc. Copyright 1948, © 1976 by B. F. Skinner. An extract from "The Newest Utopia Is a Slander on Some Old Notions of the Good Life," from *Life*, June 28, 1948, is reprinted with permission of Time, Inc. Copyright 1948 Time, Inc.

A NOTE ON THE TYPE

The text of this book was set in Electra, a Linotype face designed
by W. A. Dwiggins (1880–1956), who was responsible for so
much that is good in contemporary book design. Although much
of his early work was in advertising and he was the author of the
standard volume *Layout in Advertising,* Mr. Dwiggins later devoted his prolific talents to book typography and type design and
worked with great distinction in both fields. In addition to his
designs for Electra, he created the Metro, Caledonia, and
Eldorado series of type faces, as well as a number of experimental cuttings that have never been issued commercially.

Electra cannot be classified as either modern or old-style.
It is not based on any historical model, nor does it echo a particular period or style. It avoids the extreme contrast between
thick and thin elements that marks most modern faces and
attempts to give a feeling of fluidity, power, and speed.

This book was composed by Maryland Linotype
Composition Company, Baltimore, Maryland.
It was printed and bound by American Book—
Stratford Press, Inc., Saddle Brook, New Jersey.
Typography and binding design
by Christine Aulicino